Frommer's®

Philadelphia & the Amish Country

15th Edition

by Lauren McCutcheon & Lenora Dannelke

Here's what the critics say about Frommer's:

"Amazingly easy to use. Very portable, very complete."
—BOOKLIST

"Detailed, accurate, and easy-to-read information for all price ranges."
—GLAMOUR MAGAZINE

"Hotel information is close to encyclopedic."
—DES MOINES SUNDAY REGISTER

"Frommer's Guides have a way of giving you a real feel for a place."
—KNIGHT RIDDER NEWSPAPERS

WILEY
Wiley Publishing, Inc.

Published by:

WILEY PUBLISHING, INC.

111 River St.
Hoboken, NJ 07030-5774

ISBN 978-0-470-43513-7

Editor: Stephen Bassman
Production Editor: Jonathan Scott
Cartographer: Andrew Dolan
Photo Editor: Richard Fox
Production by Wiley Indianapolis Composition Services

Front cover photo: JFK Plaza Love sculpture nicknamed "Love Park"
Back cover photo: Amish buggy and barn

For information on our other products and services or to obtain technical support, please contact our Customer Care Department within the U.S. at 877/762-2974, outside the U.S. at 317/572-3993 or fax 317/572-4002.

Wiley also publishes its books in a variety of electronic formats. Some content that appears in print may not be available in electronic formats.

Manufactured in the United States of America

5 4 3 2 1

CONTENTS

5 WHERE TO STAY 64

6 WHERE TO DINE 84

7 EXPLORING PHILADELPHIA 118

8 CITY STROLLS 159

9 SHOPPING 169

10 PHILADELPHIA AFTER DARK 187

11 SIDE TRIPS FROM PHILADELPHIA 213

12 LANCASTER COUNTY: THE AMISH COUNTRY 229

APPENDIX: FAST FACTS, TOLL-FREE NUMBERS & WEBSITES 254

INDEX 265

LIST OF MAPS

ABOUT THE AUTHORS

Lauren McCutcheon was born in, grew up outside of, and currently lives in Philadelphia. She loves it here. She is the author of *A Virgin's Guide to Everything* (Warner Books, 2005) and *The Right Way* (David & Charles, 2006). She's also an editor-at-large at *Philadelphia* magazine, former restaurant critic for *Philadelphia Weekly,* and former editor for the Philadelphia site of www.citysearch.com. She also scouts and styles homes for *Better Homes and Gardens* magazine, contributes to *Every Day with Rachael Ray,* volunteers for The Parkinson Council, and laments the prospect of casinos infecting her beloved city.

Lenora Dannelke was raised in the rural Pennsylvania Dutch community of Kutztown and has eaten her fair share of shoofly pie, funnel cakes, and scrapple. She currently lives with her husband, daughter, mother-in-law, and 20,000 books in the Historic District of Allentown. The family is owned by a 90-pound adopted boxer. As a food and travel writer, she's a regular contributor to *Backpacker, Women's Health, Chile Pepper, Visit Florida, Pennsylvania Wine-Spirits Quarterly,* and many other magazines.

ACKNOWLEDGMENTS

Thanks to the Greater Philadelphia Tourism Marketing Corporation (GPTMC), especially Donna Schorr, Caroline Bean, and Cathy McVey. Thanks, too, to all—Mickey, Nanny, Sisters, Knitters, and Sally—who put up with my deadline-strapped self (not a pretty or gentle person). Most of all, thanks to William Penn, who did a bang-up job of planning a city for brothers, sisters, and more to love.

—Lauren McCutcheon

Thanks to the helpful, hospitable staff of the Chester County Conference and Visitors Bureau in West Chester, especially Nina Kelly. At the Pennsylvania Dutch Convention and Visitors Bureau in Lancaster, I'd think to thank Joel Cliff in particular for his friendly, patient assistance and expert guidance.

—Lenora Dannelke

AN INVITATION TO THE READER

In researching this book, we discovered many wonderful places—hotels, restaurants, shops, and more. We're sure you'll find others. Please tell us about them, so we can share the information with your fellow travelers in upcoming editions. If you were disappointed with a recommendation, we'd love to know that, too. Please write to:

Frommer's Philadelphia & the Amish Country, 15th Edition
Wiley Publishing, Inc. • 111 River St. • Hoboken, NJ 07030-5774

AN ADDITIONAL NOTE

Please be advised that travel information is subject to change at any time—and this is especially true of prices. We therefore suggest that you write or call ahead for confirmation when making your travel plans. The authors, editors, and publisher cannot be held responsible for the experiences of readers while traveling. Your safety is important to us, however, so we encourage you to stay alert and be aware of your surroundings. Keep a close eye on cameras, purses, and wallets, all favorite targets of thieves and pickpockets.

FROMMER'S STAR RATINGS, ICONS & ABBREVIATIONS

Every hotel, restaurant, and attraction listing in this guide has been ranked for quality, value, service, amenities, and special features using a **star-rating system.** In country, state, and regional guides, we also rate towns and regions to help you narrow down your choices and budget your time accordingly. Hotels and restaurants are rated on a scale of zero (recommended) to three stars (exceptional). Attractions, shopping, nightlife, towns, and regions are rated according to the following scale: zero stars (recommended), one star (highly recommended), two stars (very highly recommended), and three stars (must-see).

In addition to the star-rating system, we also use seven feature icons that point you to the great deals, in-the-know advice, and unique experiences that separate travelers from tourists. Throughout the book, look for:

Finds	Special finds—those places only insiders know about
Fun Facts	Fun facts—details that make travelers more informed and their trips more fun
Kids	Best bets for kids, and advice for the whole family
Moments	Special moments—those experiences that memories are made of
Overrated	Places or experiences not worth your time or money
Tips	Insider tips—great ways to save time and money
Value	Great values—where to get the best deals

The following **abbreviations** are used for credit cards:

AE American Express	DISC Discover	**V** Visa
DC Diners Club	MC MasterCard	

FROMMERS.COM

Now that you have this guidebook to help you plan a great trip, visit our website at **www.frommers.com** for additional travel information on more than 4,000 destinations. We update features regularly to give you instant access to the most current trip-planning information available. At Frommers.com, you'll find scoops on the best airfares, lodging rates, and car rental bargains. You can even book your travel online through our reliable travel booking partners. Other popular features include:

- Online updates to our most popular guidebooks
- Vacation sweepstakes and contest giveaways
- Newsletter highlighting the hottest travel trends
- Podcasts, interactive maps, and up-to-the-minute events listings
- Opinionated blog entries by Arthur Frommer himself
- Online travel message boards with featured travel discussions

What's New in Philadelphia

Most visitors seek out Philadelphia's historic elements—the Liberty Bell, Independence Hall, Elfreth's Alley. But it's what's new in Philly that makes the city exciting and vibrant. Here's the latest:

PLANNING YOUR TRIP A few years ago, Philadelphia city councilperson Michael Nutter proposed a citywide **smoking ban** that was passed by the council. With few exceptions, hotels, restaurants, bars, and clubs are now 100% smoke-free. In 2008, Councilman Nutter became Mayor Nutter (laugh on, Brits). Positioned as a reformer, the mayor has nonetheless taken much flak for projected budget cuts, which include closing public libraries and pools.

ACCOMMODATIONS Hotels continue to offer great discounts in Philadelphia, especially on weekends and over holidays. Two new hotels on the scene are the *über*-modern, super-high-tech, 136-room **aloft** at the Philadelphia International Airport, 4301 Island Ave. (✆ **877/462-5638**), and the *über*-handsome, old boys'–clubby, 84-room **Inn at the League** at the Union League, 1450 Sansom St. (✆ **215/587-5570**). Another is the historically boutiquey **Independent,** 1234 Locust St. (✆ **215/772-1440**), whose 24 rooms reside atop a popular gay lounge.

The forthcoming expansion of the **Pennsylvania Convention Center** (p. 132) has inspired a new crop of hotels in that neighborhood. Just opened: a 90-room, eight-story **Four Points by Sheraton,** 1201 Race St. (✆ **215/496-2700**). Scheduled to open in August 2009 is a 204-room **Le Méridian** at 1421 Arch St. (✆ **215/575-6905**), in a 10-story Georgian Revival building that once was a YMCA. Mid-2009 will also see the debut of the **Hotel Palomar,** Philadelphia's first from the contemporary Kimpton chain, at 17th and Sansom streets (✆ **800/KIMPTON** [546-7866] or 800/546-7866). The second half of 2010 should see the opening of a 325-room **Vine Hotel** on Vine Street between 16th and 17th streets. The $320-million project plans to include condos, a spa, a 24-hour restaurant, a Whole Foods Market, and a Best Buy.

Outside the city, the **Marriott Lancaster,** adjoining the new **Lancaster County Convention Center,** 3 E. Vine St. (✆ **866/503-3786;** www.lancasterconventioncenter.com), brings 300 well-appointed rooms to a convenient location in the heart of historic downtown Lancaster. See p. 245.

DINING Philadelphia's dining scene continues to evolve at lightning speed, economy be damned. Some big-budget new restaurants include contemporary French steakhouse **Table 31** in the shiny Comcast Center, 1701 J.F.K. Blvd. (✆ **215/567-7111;** p. 99); glittery Paris-inspired breakfast-through-late-night Rittenhouse Square brasserie **Parc,** 227 S. 18th St. (✆ **215/545-2262;** p. 98); and super-clubby steakhouse **Butcher & Singer,** 1500 Walnut St. (✆ **215/732-4444;** p. 95). More-casual (but still somewhat pricey) spots include Chef Marc Vetri's refined and rustic **Osteria,** 640 N.

Broad St. (© **215/763-0920;** p. 97); pioneering Israeli culinary hot spot **Zahav,** 237 St. James Place (© **215/625-8800;** p. 89); the glamorous comfort foodery **10 Arts** by Eric Ripert in the Ritz-Carlton, 10 S. Broad St. (© **215/523-8273;** p. 99); University City's fun and funky Mexican **Distrito** from Chef Jose Garces, 40th and Chestnut (© **215/2222-1657;** p. 106); perfect, romantic, and French **Bistrot La Minette,** 623 S. 6th St. (© **215/925-8000;** p. 85); and gourmet Manayunk pizzeria **Cooper's,** 4356 Main St. (© **215/483-2750;** p. 112).

Even cheaper: a new **Du Jour Café & Market,** a gourmet breakfast-through-dinner diner for the Symphony House at Broad and Pine streets (© **215/735-8010**), and the locally owned quick-bite kiosks below ground at the **Market at Comcast Center** 1701 J.F.K. Blvd. (p. 117).

Two of my favorite dinner spots are relative newbies. **Bindi,** a cash-only BYOB at 105 S. 13th St. (© **215/922-6061;** p. 90), offers a sublime and approachable twist on Indian classics. Italian Market neighbor **James,** 824 S. 8th St. (© **215/629-4980;** p. 104), is a fantastic spot for refined Italian food in a dressy and chic setting.

Coming in 2009 is (yet another) grandly appointed steakhouse. **Union Trust** will occupy the old Quaker City Bank building at 719 Chestnut St. Nearby will be another project of Chef Jose Garces called **Chifa,** a Peruvian-Cantonese fusion spot at 707 Chestnut. Across town, look for edgy locavore fare at on the mini–Restaurant Row of 20th Sansom in **Nobel American Cookery,** due to open in early 2009, which will be neighbors with another project by Garces called **Village Whiskey.** Mid-2009, acclaimed chef Daniel Stern, owner of Gayle (p. 104), will revive his elegant America brasserie **Rae** on the 37th floor of skyscraping Liberty Two Place, between 16th and 17th streets and Chestnut and Market streets.

In the Brandywine Valley, two premiere restaurants recently opened excellent casual neighboring eateries: **Bistro on the Brandywine** (© **610/388-8090;** www.bistroonthebrandywine.com) joins **Brandywine Prime Seafood & Chops,** and **Blue Pear Bistro** (© **610/399-9812;** www.bluepearbistro.com), is next door to the **Dilworthtown Inn.** Serious foodies should head for **Talula's Table** (© **610/444-8255;** www.talulastable.com). Although the single farmhouse table at dinner is booked exactly 1 year in advance, this gourmet market has wonderful breads, pastries, and deli dishes that can be enjoyed on the premises at breakfast or lunch. See p. 228.

SIGHTSEEING Years of archaeological excavations on Independence Park have uncovered the foundations of the **President's House,** home to President George Washington from 1790 to 1797 and John Adams from 1797 to 1800. The house existed just across Market Street from the **Independence Visitor Center,** and a monument to the home's residents—including Washington's nine African slaves, which he kept despite the law—is being constructed behind the **Liberty Bell Center.**

If you haven't been to the **Philadelphia Museum of Art** (p. 128) in a while—or ever—take some extra time to visit the handsome new library and cafe, plus the design, textile, and costume exhibit halls of the **Perelman Building** across the parkway. You'll notice that the Perelman side of the art museum is undergoing some construction. An under-street tunnel—designed by celebrated modern architect Frank Gehry—is being built to connect the two buildings.

In 2008, the kid-centric **Please Touch Museum** (p. 143) moved to much more spacious—and way more spectacular—digs in Fairmount Park's Memorial Hall, site of the Centennial Exposition of 1876, aka the first World's Fair. Bigger, better, new, and familiar exhibits now include a vintage carousel—a big attraction for kids. And the facility now includes a spacious parking lot—a big attraction for parents.

The **National Museum of American Jewish History,** 55 N. 5th St. (✆ **215/923-8311;** p.142), plans to move across the street to 5th and Market by the fall of 2010.

Two big buildings are new: There's the **Comcast Center** at 17th St. and J.F.K. Blvd. (p. 130), the tallest building in town, and the, er, mauveish peach **Symphony House,** a Broad Street high-rise with the great, but still very 1980s-looking **Suzanne Roberts Theatre,** home to the **Philadelphia Theatre Company** (p. 190).

Exhibits at the **Hershey Story,** 111 W. Chocolate Ave., Hershey (✆ **717/534-3439**), depict the sweet tale of Milton Hershey's success. The interactive museum includes a cafe, gift shop, and a chocolate lab for hands-on experimentation. See p. 241.

SHOPPING Rittenhouse Row has gained a half-dozen or so stylish chain retailers, whereas Old City's North 3rd Street has upped the indie boutique quotient with another handful of women's clothing shops and artsy retailers. My absolute favorite housewares shop has moved to much larger digs, too. Fantastic **Foster's Homeware** is now at the corner of 4th and Market streets (✆ **800/734-8511;** p. 181), in the Colonial Penn building. Also new in town: adorable, essential **Bus Stop Boutique,** south of Fitzwater on 4th Street (✆ **215/627-2357**), a delightful shoe salon in a town desperately in need of fashionable footwear.

AFTER DARK The underground **G Lounge,** 111 S. 17th St. (✆ **215/564-1515**), is an attitudinous spot for sipping vodka and juice, shouting over the DJ, shaking those hips, and trying to sneak into the VIP room.

Bar patrons more interested in what's in the glass (rather than who's sipping from it) will be pleased to note that the **Tria** franchise is ever expanding, with a sophisticatedly fun wine and beer bar at 12th and Spruce streets (✆ **215/629-9200;** p. 208), and a third for the Graduate Hospital neighborhood on its way. More wine flows from **DiVino Wine Bar,** a former BYOB at 267 S. 19th St. (✆ **215/545-0441**), and Midtown Village's **Vintage Wine Bar,** 129 S. 13th St. (✆ **215/922-3015**), whose owners also run the newish **Time** at 13th and Sansom streets (✆ **215/985-4800**), a dimly lit spot for a whiskey, absinthe, and live (but not too loud) music. The corner bar is taken up a notch with a great beer list and an even better menu at the effortlessly perfect **Pub and Kitchen** at 20th and Lombard (✆ **215/545-0350**). Philly will be getting its first whiskey bar in Sansom Street's **Village Whiskey.** And, since the alcohol gods are apparently feeling generous, the 700 block of South Street will be the recipient of its very own serious beerery in **Brauhaus Schmitz,** where 100 bottled beers will supplement the 20 craft brews on tap, and the menu will doubtless include dishes ending in "schnitzel."

Fans of Northern Liberties' **Bar Ferdinand** (p. 205) are looking forward to its owner's second venture, **El Camino Real,** a Tex-Mex and barbecue smokehouse where the food will be great, but the nightlife will be greater, right across Liberties Walk at 1040 N. 2nd St.

1 The Best of Philadelphia

Cliché-sounding statement number one: Philadelphia is a lovely city. I live here, in a tiny fifth-floor walk-up studio on 8th Street, between Pine and Lombard. When I look out my back window, I can see the steeple of the old Pine Street church George Washington attended. Beyond the steeple are shiny-windowed high-rise apartments. Beyond them are blipping lights of planes coasting over the Delaware River into Philadelphia International Airport. The view from the front of my apartment is of 19th-century rooftops, rising skyscrapers—and a single roof deck with a pair of sunbathing poodles.

The nation's oldest hospital is a half a block from my home: I pass it every time I head out to shop in Old City, or to work in my office near Rittenhouse Square. Both are about a 15-minute walk, provided I don't stop in any of the dozen or so amazing little cafes along the way. About once a week, folks passing my apartment ask for directions to Pat's and Geno's, South Philly's famous cheesesteak stands.

These tiny details of my daily life make me hometown proud (cliché number two). To me, a reformed suburbanite, Philadelphia is the perfect American city. I love that it surrounds me with some of our country's most important historic monuments. I love that its buildings are a blend of the extremely old and the supernew. I love the mistakenly planted gingko trees, the Rocky footprints at the top of the art museum steps (although I'm not sure about the statue), the fresh mozzarella cheese at Claudio's in the Italian Market, New Year's Day's debauched Two Street party after the annual Mummer's Parade (which I also love). And I love that in 20 minutes I can walk anywhere in Center City; in less than an hour I can walk across town.

I haven't always gone weak in the knees for Philly, though. My crush came about gradually. When I moved back more than 10 years ago, I thought I was stopping over on my way to New York. But something strange happened: Philadelphia kept my attention. Every time I turned around, there was another great place to eat dinner, another incredible art opening, another amazing boutique, bar, band, exhibit, or event. As Philadelphia blossomed, so did my feelings for it.

And I'm not the only one who feels this way about Philadelphia. While other cities have seen small hardware stores and haberdasheries and independent coffee shops giving way to chains and big-box stores, here, people hung in, roasting their own coffee beans and defiantly creating their own art. The result: In 2005, *National Geographic Traveler* lauded Philadelphia as the "Next Great City." The *New York Times* called us the "Sixth Borough." And in the past few years, we've racked up "Best City for Singles," "Best City for New Graduates," and other accolades.

Of course, my City of Brotherly Love still has a long way to go. Not all Philadelphians live on a block as safe as mine. Beyond Center City, beyond University City and Chestnut Hill, are pockets—giant pockets—riddled with serious poverty and unspeakable violence. Massive, 24-hour casinos are starting to set up their depressing, addictive trade around town.

For better and for worse, Philadelphia is a living snapshot of life in urban America. Enjoy it, and enjoy its diversity. Take the family to ogle the spectacular art at the Barnes one day—and cheer on 2008 World Series Champs, the Fightin' Phils, the next. Explore the leafy paths of Fairmount Park in the morning—and mingle with Old City's high-heeled crowds after the sun sets.

If I had to choose one inspiring must do for visitors, I'd recommend a **Mural Arts Tour** (✆ **215/685-0754;** www.muralarts.org). (See the box, "Mural, Mural, on the Wall," in chapter 7.) Mural Arts guides take you into Philly's other neighborhoods, the ones that don't appear in guidebooks. You'll cruise by smooth walls blanketed in brilliant colors. You'll learn how beautifying communities, working with one paintbrush, one child at a time, can bring about positive transformation. The experience is moving, restorative, and educational. It reteaches you the classic lesson of the city, and America itself: One small step, one giant leap. Right here, on earth, in Philadelphia: a generally lovely place to be.

1 FROMMER'S FAVORITE PHILADELPHIA EXPERIENCES

- **Visiting the Barnes Foundation:** The Barnes Foundation Gallery in the quiet nearby western suburb of Merion houses the most important private collection of Impressionist and early French modern paintings in the world, displaying more Cézannes than all the museums of France put together. The building was designed by Paul Philippe Cret, and is amazing, not only for its lovely design, but also because founder Albert Barnes was meticulous about displaying the works, often juxtaposing them with objets d'art such as antique iron locks or African tribal masks. The museum plans to move to a brand-new home in Center City (along the Ben Franklin Parkway btw. the Rodin Museum and the Philadelphia Museum of Art) in 2012, so schedule your visit to the current location now: You may not get another chance to see these works as their collector originally arranged them. See p. 126.
- **Wandering Through Fairmount Park:** It would take dozens of outings to fully explore the 100 miles of trails in this 8,900-acre giant of an urban park—some of them are virtually unchanged since Revolutionary times. We'll settle for gazing at the hundreds of flame azaleas that bloom behind the Philadelphia Museum of Art in spring, warm-weather visits to the serene Shofuso Japanese teahouse, and autumn-through-winter strolls along the Wissahickon Creek. See p. 146.
- **Gallery Hopping on First Friday:** On the first Friday of every month, the galleries, stores, and studios of Old City—just north and slightly east of Independence National Historical Park—remain open with refreshments and artists on hand until 9pm. Wander along the cobblestone streets, popping in where you fancy, kicking off a night out in this very happening part of town. See p. 171.
- **Stepping Back in Time in Historic Philadelphia:** The reclamation of this country's Colonial capital has been nearly miraculous, from the Liberty Bell's gleaming glass–modern home to the renovation of hundreds of row houses with their distinctive brickwork and 18th-century formal gardens (and welcoming benches). But the costumed town criers with free maps and the Revolutionary War–era street theater really bring the experience to life. Just wander; they'll find you. See "Independence National Historical Park: America's Most Historic Square Mile," in chapter 7.

- **Eating *the* Sandwich:** We all love American history, international art, a great orchestral performance, and a swanky night on the town. But the craving for Philly's number-one fast food somehow surpasses all other desires. It's primal, an overwhelming urge that materializes the moment you enter city limits. The inimitable cheesesteak: one word (not two), "wid" or "widout" (onions), available with sharp provolone or gooey Cheez Whiz. See "The Ultimate Cheesesteak Taste Test," p. 114.
- **Strolling Around Rittenhouse Square at Night:** When the rest of Philadelphia's city squares grow quiet at night, the one between 18th and 19th, Walnut and Locust streets twinkles with activity. Patrons toast each other at bistro sidewalk tables. Couples cross the park, hand in hand. On a summer night, you're likely to come upon a free musical performance. In winter, you'll be dazzled by the park's bright balls of lights in the treetops.
- **Enjoying the Lights at Night:** The William Penn statue atop City Hall, the Ben Franklin Bridge, and seven Schuylkill River bridges are permanently lighted, joining the beautiful white pin lights that outline the boathouses along the Schuylkill River.
- **Breathing Deeply at the Philadelphia Flower Show:** In early March, the Philadelphia Flower Show—the largest and most prestigious indoor exhibition of its kind in the world—descends on the Pennsylvania Convention Center, with acres of orchids and traditional and exotic displays. See p. 33.
- **Exploring the Philadelphia Museum of Art:** It has a stupendous collection of masterpieces, period rooms, and crafts, and is becoming one of the hottest museums in the country for special exhibitions. Look for more blockbusters like the recent exhibits of Renoir (landscapes), Frida Kahlo (retrospective), Henri Matisse (along with other modern artists who worked on the French Riviera), and Cézanne (and beyond). Wednesday and Friday evenings have become convivial social scenes, with cocktails and live music. See p. 128.
- **Cheering the Regattas Along the Schuylkill:** On any spring weekend, stand along Boathouse Row just north of the Philadelphia Museum of Art, and get ready to cheer. Crews race each other every 5 minutes or so, with friends lining the riverbanks rooting for them. See p. 157.
- **Getting Lost in the Reading Terminal Market:** You'll never go completely missing, but you will definitely get caught up in the maze of stalls at this historic market. And when you stumble upon an Amish eatery, artisan bakery, local farm stand, artisan cheesemonger or Italian bakery, suddenly finding your way out doesn't seem so essential after all. See p. 101.
- **Exploring South Philly:** In the neighborhood South of South Street (generally btw. Front and Broad sts.), exuberant attitude punctuates every interchange you'll have, whether strolling (with ample tastings) through the Italian Market or seeking out the area's great pasta, cannoli, or famed cheesesteaks farther

Fun Facts **A Central City**

Thirty-eight percent of the nation's population lives within a $4\frac{1}{2}$-hour drive of Philadelphia.

south. See p. 62 for a description of the neighborhood and p. 104 for info on where to eat.

- **Drinking Local Beer:** One hundred years ago, Philadelphia was known as the greatest brewing city in the Western Hemisphere. Today, the city's attempting to regain that status with beer-centric pubs like **Standard Tap** (p. 204), **McGillin's** (p. 204), **Good Dog** (p. 203), **Royal Tavern** (p. 204), and, especially, **Monk's** (p. 204) all of which feature delicious craft brews, many of them by area brewers such as Philadelphia Brewing Company, Yards, Flying Fish, Dogfishhead, Victory, and Stout's.
- **Catching a Phillies Game at the Ballpark:** A summer night at the family-friendly Citizens Bank Park means great views from every seat in this old-fashioned-style stadium, with its amazing local foods such as Tony Luke's cheesesteaks and roast pork sandwiches, barbecue by former player Greg "The Bull" Luzinski, local microbrews, and, if you're lucky, a Hatfield hot dog shot from the Phanatic's on-field launcher. Sit on the third level, and you'll be treated to a perfectly framed view of the city skyline. When Ryan Howard or Jimmy Rollins or Chase Utley or Shane Victorino—or any of the "Fightins"—homers, watch the giant Liberty Bell come to life. See p. 156.
- **Watching the Mummer's Parade:** Grown men dancing in feathers, sequins, face paint, and gold sneakers mark the beloved New Year's Day tradition of the Mummer's Parade (www.mummers.com), in which thousands strut their way up Broad Street. The music is loud and antiquated, but the experience is festive and fun. Bundle up. See p. 33.
- **Letting the Kids Go Nuts at a Museum:** The 2008 relocation of the eminently kid-centric **Please Touch Museum** to Memorial Hall (on the edge of Fairmount Park) gives its pint-size guests oodles of space to perfect the art of play. They might be overwhelmed by the choices here: Be sure to explore the underground Alice in Wonderland maze, punch the time clock at the construction site, splash around in a flowing river, or take a ride on the historic carousel. Grown-ups won't want to miss the room-size model of the Centennial Exhibition, the first world's fair, which took place at this spot in 1876. See p. 143.

2 THE BEST HOTEL BETS

- **Best Airport Hotel:** Standing out from the virtually interchangeable low-rises that surround Philadelphia International is **aloft,** 4301 Island Ave. (✆ **267/298-1700**). Opened in 2008, Starwood's off-price version of their popular W brand is smart and hip, offering 135 spare, modern rooms; a sleek lobby; a cool bar and terrace; along with self-serve kiosks to print out boarding passes. Aloft almost makes flying seem cool and special again. See p. 81.
- **Best Historic Hotel:** It's only the "lite" version of what it used to be, when Thomas Edison designed the fixtures and the ballroom defined swank. But the top floor of the **Park Hyatt Philadelphia at the Bellevue,** Broad and Walnut streets, or 1415 Chancellor Court, between Walnut and Locust streets (✆ **800/223-1234**), with its nearly clandestine fireside lounge and elegant, pearl-bedecked Nineteen dining room, retains elegant traces of a century's worth of history. See p. 74.

- **Best for Business Travelers: Hotel Sofitel,** 120 S. 17th St. (✆ **800/SOFI-TEL** [763-4835]), has a convenient location and rooms that are large and elegant, with easy access to plugs and modem jacks at a handsome desk. The delicious French coffee doesn't hurt either. The service staff is efficient and courteous. See p. 73.
- **Best for Conventiongoers:** A trio of proudly service-oriented Marriotts (including a Courtyard and a Residence Inn) border the now-expanding center, making these vast spots along Market Street between 12th and Broad streets (✆ **800/228-9290**) the best bet for those meeting attendees who prefer easy room access and a few extra moments of sleeping. (My favorites are the Courtyard and Residence Inn's rooms facing City Hall.) See p. 69.
- **Best for a Romantic Getaway:** The affordable **Penn's View Hotel,** Front and Market streets (✆ **800/331-7634**), feels like an exquisite club, with views over the Delaware River, in-room whirlpool tubs (in some), and, downstairs, what the *New York Times* hailed as "the mother of all wine bars." See p. 69.
- **Best for a Good Night's Sleep:** The dream-worthy, five-pillow-topped "Heavenly" sleepers at the **Westin** on 17th Street between Chestnut and Market streets (✆ **800/228-3000**) still have a lock on this category. (Add in the spa-like showers, and you might find it difficult to take leave of your room.) See p. 75.
- **Best Boutique Hotel:** It's a far cry from a trendy Ian Schrager creation, but **Rittenhouse 1715,** between 17th and 18th streets on Rittenhouse Street (✆ **877/791-6500**) feels boutiquey in a more Parisian sense. It's located on a quiet side street, with small-to-large traditional rooms, simple croissant-and-coffee breakfasts, and luxe Frette bed linens. You could be quiet comfortable staying here a week, as many regular guests do. See p. 77.
- **Best Hotel Lobby:** For softly rubbing elbows with local movers and shakers, pro players from visiting (and sometimes home) teams, and whoever's in town to perform at a major concert, there's no place like the cool, plush, lobby-side Swann Lounge in the **Four Seasons Hotel,** 1 Logan Sq. (✆ **800/332-3442**). See p. 72.
- **Best for Families:** In Center City, **Loews Philadelphia Hotel,** 1200 Market St. (✆ **215/627-1200**), doesn't have the biggest rooms in town, but it's got a great game closet, allows pets, and trains concierges to please even the pickiest preteen guest. See p. 68. In West Philadelphia, the **Hilton Inn at Penn,** 3600 Sansom St. (✆ **800/445-8667**), is across town (about 30 blocks) from historical sights, but offers the whole family space to roam among spacious corridors, ever-present fruit to munch on, and tea to sip in a comfortable library lounge. The campus of U. Penn across the street is perfect for throwing a Frisbee or playing tag. See p. 79.
- **Best Inexpensive Hotel:** The **Alexander Inn,** 12th and Spruce streets (✆ **877/ALEX-INN** [253-9466]), is an independent, 48-room outfit whose strong suits are its location, simplicity, and value—usually less than $135 per night. Rooms are quite small—or cozy, depending on your outlook. Request one that faces the corner. See p. 71.
- **Best B&B:** The new-but-historic **Lippincott House,** 2023–2025 Locust St. (✆ **215/523-9251**), has a lot going for it: location (just 1 block from Rittenhouse Sq.), four quiet guest rooms, price (rates top out at $225), innkeepers who love to dine (which means homemade breakfasts plus great recommendations for neighborhood restaurants), Victorian decorative appointments (a fireplace in

each room; even the pool table is an antique), and free wireless Internet. See p. 78.

- **Best Service:** The staff at the **Ritz-Carlton Philadelphia,** 10 Avenue of the Arts (✆ **215/523-8000**), has recently amped up its hospitality factor. No pillow goes unfluffed. No child goes without picking a toy from the red wagon. No entrant has a door unheld. No cup of coffee gets unrefreshed at breakfast at **10 Arts.** See p. 75.
- **Best Hotel for Historic District Hopping:** If you're here to see Independence Park, why not wake up looking at it through the curtains at the **Omni Hotel at Independence Park,** 4th and Chestnut streets (✆ **800/843-6664**)? All 150 guest rooms have views of the Greek Revival Second Bank of the U.S. and a half-dozen of America's Georgian jewels. And the clip-clopping of horses with carriages below maintains the historical feel. See p. 65.
- **Best Hotel Health Club:** The **Sporting Club at the Bellevue,** on Broad Street between Walnut and Locust streets (✆ **215/985-9875**), counts Governor Rendell, Dr. J., and most of the city's movers and shakers among its members. Honorary membership is given to guests of the **Park Hyatt Philadelphia at the Bellevue.** The gym facilities are the best in town, and classes are top-notch. See p. 74.
- **Best Hotel Pool:** Splashing around the glassed-in pool of the **Hyatt Regency Philadelphia at Penn's Landing,** 201 S. Columbus Blvd. (✆ **215/928-1234**), is doubly fun, because just beyond the pool is the Delaware River. See p. 65.
- **Best Hotel Restaurants:** Locals show great loyalty to the kitchens, style, service, and menus at the **Fountain Restaurant** in the **Four Seasons,** 1 Logan Sq. (✆ **215/963-1500;** see p. 95), and **Lacroix** at the **Rittenhouse Hotel,** 210 W. Rittenhouse Sq. (✆ **215/546-9000;** see p. 95). Still, there's no denying everyone is impressed by the culinary cred (Eric Ripert) and seriously local French cuisine (Pennsylvania brook trout in brown butter sauce, wild boar prosciutto from the Italian Market) at the newer **10 Arts** at the **Ritz-Carlton Philadelphia,** 10 Avenue of the Arts (✆ **215/523-8000**). See p. 99.
- **Best Splurge Hotel:** There's a reason Madonna and Tom Hanks stay at the **Rittenhouse Hotel,** 210 W. Rittenhouse Sq. (✆ **215/546-9000**). The part-condo part–luxury hotel delivers an overwhelming dose of indulgence, with its massive-domed lobby, lavish furnishings, posh day spa, and clubby bars. Weekend rates start at $270 per night. See p. 74.
- **Best Hostel:** Centrally located near all the historical and nightlife attractions, **Apple Hostel** (formerly Bank Street Hostel) 32 S. Bank St. (✆ **800/392-4678** or 215/922-0222), is smack in the Old City/Society Hill nexus; it's perfect for budget or adventurous travelers—book online for cheaper rates. See p. 83.
- **Best Country Getaway:** Plush lodgings scattered throughout a picturesque hamlet, proximity to the gorgeous Brandywine Valley's fine attractions, plus an on-site spa and deliciously eclectic restaurant make the **Inn at Montchanin Village,** Route 100 and Kirk Road, Montchanin, DE (✆ **800/269-2473** or 302/888-2133; www.montchanin.com), an incomparable weekend retreat. See p. 227.
- **Best Place to Pop the Question:** At the plush and romantic **Inn at Bowman's Hill,** 58 Lurgan Rd., New Hope (✆ **215/862-8090;** www.theinnatbowmanshill.com), the elegant orchid conservatory is a popular setting for proposals. Let the friendly hosts know if you any need special arrangements for the occasion, from chilling champagne to lighting extra candles. See p. 219.

3 THE BEST RESTAURANT BETS

- **Best Overall:** In a city bursting with great Italian bistros, jewel-box **Vetri,** 1312 Spruce St. (✆ **215/732-3478**), has long stood out for its timeless approach and sophisticated but cozy setting. Get the spinach gnocchi with ricotta and brown butter, the prosciutto and mushroom-stuffed guinea hen breast, the chocolate polenta soufflé—or, if it's Saturday, whatever Chef Marc Vetri has whipped up for his tasting menu. See p. 96.
- **Best for Couples:** Tucked into bustling Old City is gently artful, effortlessly elegant, surprisingly serene **Fork,** 306 Market St. (✆ **215/625-9425**), a nouveau-American bistro with a just-gourmet-enough menu that's a far-and-away favorite for stylish, delicious celebrations for two. See p. 88.
- **Best Power Lunch:** In a city swollen with steakhouses, one new one is getting all the noontime players. **Butcher & Singer,** formerly Striped Bass, 1500 Walnut St. (✆ **215/732-4444**), is superclubby without being dim, and elegant without being fussy. The menu's prices seem built for bloated expense accounts—but it's worth it, if you want to close that deal before the cheesecake comes. See p. 95.
- **Best Casual Lunch:** On noon Monday through Friday, a vibrant bunch of office workers lines up outside funky **Devil's Alley** at 19th and Chestnut (✆ **215/751-0707**) for barbecue sliders, salmon burgers, mac and cheese and, if necessary, a midday pint of beer. See p. 93.
- **Best for a Fancy Meal:** Properly lavish, opulently mannerly, with classic French fare, atmosphere, service, and multiple utensils, Chef Georges Perrier's **Le Bec-Fin,** 1523 Walnut St. (✆ **215/567-1000**), has a four-star international reputation. Perrier's dessert cart alone is worth getting dressed up for. See p. 95.
- **Best for a Laid-Back Party:** No dress code—no reservations, even—at the vast, casual, beer-centric **Standard Tap** in Northern Liberties at Second and Poplar streets (✆ **215/238-0630**) make it a great spot to get together for chicken potpie, double burgers, and relaxed but festive atmosphere. See p. 111.
- **Best Decor:** Karim Rashid's spaceship-like design of **Morimoto** at 723 Chestnut St. (✆ **215/413-9070**), will take your breath away. So will the modern Japanese fusion, including absolutely divine sushi that's downright sculptural. See p. 84.
- **Best View:** Year-round, the Park Hyatt at the Bellevue's rooftop-level **Nineteen** (✆ **215/790-1919**) serves up three refined meals and sweeping views of the city skyline from classically arched windows. See p. 97.
- **Best Wine List:** The two locations of **Tria,** at 18th and Sansom streets and 12th and Spruce streets (✆ **215/972-TRIA** [8742] or **629-9200**) have become the most popular wine bars in town, thanks to their easy-to-navigate selection of boutique vintages, which seamlessly combine with a menu of gourmet snacks and, for brewphiles truly interesting microbrews. See p. 208.
- **Best Value, Lunch:** A mere $15 buys a delicious two-course "Bilbao Express" lunch of savory Spanish soup or salad, along with a rich *bocadillos,* sandwiches made of tuna and crème fraîche or Serrano ham and mustard, at trendy **Tinto,** 20th Street, between Chestnut and Sansom streets (✆ **215/665-9150**). See p. 99.
- **Best Value, Dinner:** No wonder little, cash-only, Italian, BYOB **La Viola,** 16th Street, between Spruce and Locust

streets (✆ **215/735-8630**) needed to annex a second dining room across the street: Straightforward entrees here top out around $15. (And $12 buys one of the city's best plates of homemade gnocchi.) See p. 102.

- **Best for Kids:** Just a block from the Liberty Bell and Independence Hall, hip, booth-filled, reservations-not-required **Jones** at 7th and Chestnut (✆ **215/223-5663**) prides itself on its informal decor, family-friendly service, and fresh, crowd-pleasing comfort food, including beef brisket, turkey burgers, chicken parm, big salads, french fries, and nachos. See p. 94.
- **Best Sushi:** Old City's itty-bitty BYOB **Zento,** 138 Chestnut St. (✆ **215/925-9998**), gets points for its perfect renditions of familiar to exotic rolls and sashimi. My favorite is the square-shaped signature roll, made with eel, avocado, plum paste, and tuna. See p. 92.
- **Best BYOB:** Bring-your-own-bottle restaurants abound. My favorite is **Bistro 7,** at 7 N. 3rd St. (✆ **215/931-1560**), which combines all-American ingredients from local farmers and classically French techniques for approachable seafood cassoulet, short ribs over risotto, and amazing *pot de crème* and rice pudding. See p. 108.
- **Best Casual Italian:** America's oldest Italian restaurant deserves its devoted following. At the northern edge of 9th Street's Italian Market, **Ralph's** (✆ **215/627-6011**) does basic but sublime renditions of spaghetti with marinara (old-timers call it "gravy"), garlicky broccoli rabe, and eggplant parmigiana. See p. 105.
- **Best Chinese Cuisine:** Nestled in bright and busy Chinatown, straightforward and note-perfect BYOB **Lee How Fook,** 219 N. 11th St. (✆ **215/925-7266**), provides a simple, handsome space, and does a beautiful job with everything they touch: hot pots, noodle soups, salt-baked seafood, and more. See p. 111.
- **Best French Cuisine:** Little **Bistrot La Minette,** at 623 S. 6th St. (✆ **215/925-8000**), is a spot-on rendition of a classy Parisian bistro, from its homemade pâtés and duck à l'orange to its pale yellow walls and gleaming cafe windows. See p. 85.
- **Best Steakhouse:** With a half-dozen great choices, including the Capital Grille, the Palm, Butcher & Singer, and Morton's, the top choice is the **Prime Rib,** 1701 Locust St. (✆ **215/772-1701**), offering tender porterhouse served with fresh shredded horseradish. The ambience is a timeless 1940s-style place—jazz combos and formally clad waiters included. See p. 98.
- **Best Burgers & Beer:** Discerning *Philadelphia Inquirer* restaurant critic Craig La Ban wrote a song about the blue cheese–stuffed burger at **Good Dog Bar and Restaurant,** 224 S. 15th St. (✆ **215/985-9600**), a youthful, boisterous Center City gastropub. There's a trick to it, though: You have to order it medium or rarer; otherwise, the cheese bakes out. See p. 203.
- **Best Pizza: Marra's,** 1734 E. Passyunk Ave., between Morris and Moore streets (✆ **215/463-9249**), in South Philadelphia, has pies with thin crusts and delicious, spicy toppings, baked in brick ovens; enjoy them in old wooden booths. Ask for the margherita with fresh mozzarella and basil. See p. 105.
- **Best Cheesesteak:** Late-night crowds line up for a cheesesteak fix at famed rivals Pat's and Geno's in South Philly—but our cheesesteak critic gives the crown to **Cosmi's Deli** just a few blocks southeast. Get there early; this family-owned business closes at 9pm (7pm on Sundays). See "The Ultimate Cheesesteak Taste Test" on p. 114.

- **Best Hoagies:** Using seeded Italian bread made a couple doors down, **Sarcone's Deli,** 9th and Fitzwater streets (✆ **215/922-1717**), comes up with the best Italian sandwiches in the city. (A bold statement, I know.) Choose from classic cold cuts, undressed tuna, and specialty sandwiches that combine roasted red peppers, sharp provolone, long hots, and whole cloves of garlic.
- **Best Desserts:** Cupcakes and beyond star on the sweet menus at a pair of cafes: At the always-packed **Naked Chocolate,** 1317 Walnut St. at Juniper St. (✆ **215/735-7310**), don't miss the petite, thick cocoa served in an espresso cup and a strawberry cupcake. At either location of **Brown Betty,** 1030 N. 2nd St. (✆ **215/629-0999**), and (for cupcakes only) 269 S. 20th St. (✆ **215/545-0444**), indulge in red velvet, carrot, or pineapple pound cupcakes.
- **Best Breakfasts:** At **Sam's Morning Glory Diner,** 10th and Fitzwater streets (✆ **215/413-3999**), the coffee comes in big, steely mugs; doughy biscuits are cut square; and the "glory" pancakes are the best you'll eat, anywhere, ever. But if you want to do a comparison, oodles of Philadelphians swear by and line up for seriously big breakfasts at both locations of **Sabrina's,** 910 Christian (✆ **215/574-1599**), and 1802 Callowhill (✆ **215/636-9061**). See p. 106.
- **Best Coffee:** *Food & Wine* and I agree: The best cafe in the States is **La Colombe,** 130 S. 19th St. (✆ **215/563-0860**), where the beans are proprietary, the clientele is quirkily glamorous, and a cup of the most delicious house blend comes in one size for $1.50. The Manayunk neighborhood has a just-as-good, less-sceney La Colombe at 4360 Main St. (✆ **215/483-4580**).
- **Best Brunch:** Nearly every restaurant offers Sunday brunch, ranging from standard bagels with spreads to a full breakfast menu. The **White Dog Café,** 3420 Sansom St. (✆ **215/386-9224**), in West Philadelphia, swings both ways, serving everything from simple breakfast dishes to elaborate late-morning feasts in a completely comfortable, unpretentious setting. See p. 108.
- **Best People-Watching:** Jockeying for primo sidewalk tables and coveted bar stools at Rittenhouse Square newcomer **Parc** (✆ **215/545-2262**) has become Center City's preferred see-and-be-seen blood sport. This big, bold brasserie is the place to ogle Philly's power set while nibbling a midday omelet or tucking into a steak frites. See p. 98.
- **Best for Pretheater Dinner: Ernesto's 1521 Café,** 1521 Spruce St. (✆ **215/546-1521**), is an affordable, modern Italian trattoria with handmade pasta—and a thorough understanding of how to feed you in time for you to see the curtain go up. See p. 102.
- **Best Outdoor Dining:** Hidden behind the Philadelphia Museum of Art, the **Water Works Restaurant and Lounge,** just off Kelly Drive (✆ **215/236-9000**), offers lovely tables by the river, the perfect spot to watch the sun set as the lights on Boathouse Row come up. See p. 100.
- **Best Late-Night Dining:** Follow the postbar crowd to **Pat's** and **Geno's,** the dueling cheesesteak vendors of South Philly, and you'll experience a culinary phenomenon: A greasy steak sandwich tastes much, much better at 3am. See p. 115.
- **Best Ice Cream:** Although **Franklin Fountain,** 116 Market St. (✆ **215/627-1899**), is a relatively new addition to Old City, it feels as though it's been here for about 50 years. Come here for sloppy sundaes, egg creams, ice-cream sodas, and other back-in-the-day treats. See p. 103.

- **Best Gelato:** Now with two locations (and another rumored to be on the way), divine **Capogiro,** in Midtown Village at 119 S. 13th St. (✆ **215/351-0900**), and in Rittenhouse at 117 S. 20th St. (✆ **215/636-9250**), serves up the best gelato and *sorbetto* this side of Firenze. My favorites are the out-there flavors—tahini, grapefruit and Campari, strawberry basil, heirloom apple—but *cioccolato,* hazelnut, or even extra plain *fior di latte* (milk) can't be beat.
- **Best Locavore Cuisine:** "Farm-to-table" is a short trip at Lancaster's **John J. Jeffries,** 300 Harrisburg Ave. (✆ **717/431-3307**). Chefs and co-owners Sean Cavanaugh and Michael Carson showcase their devotion to sustainable agriculture throughout their superb seasonal New American menus. Fresh produce is local and organic, and all meats are raised on nearby farms in confinement-free green pastures. See p. 252.

2

Philadelphia in Depth

Philadelphia is big, for a historic city. It has 1.4 million residents. Its immediate environs have 4.4 million more. All told, Philadelphia is the fifth-largest metropolitan area in the United States. So, Philadelphia is big. But here's the thing: Philadelphia feels small.

In the second half of the 17th century, city planner and religious freedom crusader William Penn envisioned the land between the Delaware and Schuylkill rivers as a "greene country town." Penn modeled plans for the area after rural England, laying out roads in neat grids comprised of spacious lots, intentionally leaving plenty of room for orchards and gardens. It wasn't long, however, until the enterprising owners of those lots realized the value of their real estate. Instead of planting their properties, they divided, and then subdivided, them. A few years hence, clusters of houses and businesses dominated Penn's grid. These neighborhoods were religiously diverse yet closely knit, and, all in all, they thrived. By the dawn of the 18th century, Philadelphia was officially a city.

As decades, then centuries, passed, Philadelphians continued to grow their city in this same manner. They built in rows, lived close together. They opened small businesses. They practiced their faiths. They absorbed new neighbors from far-away places. Even as shiny skyscrapers arose and gray highways cut in, Philadelphia, on the whole, remained a seamless series of urban villages.

Today, Philadelphia's easy-to-explore neighborhoods include Society Hill, Rittenhouse, Old City, Bella Vista, Northern Liberties, Powelton Village, Graduate Hospital, Passyunk Square, Queen Village, Chestnut Hill, and Manayunk. Still, beyond these friendly blocks lie vast residential stretches with far less visitor appeal. Philadelphia's rougher districts—neighborhoods not normally included on historical tours—have, in recent years, suffered record rates of crime and poverty. William Penn's vision of a verdant and free haven—a "City of Brotherly Love"—is yet to be realized.

Nonetheless, the promise of Philadelphia has come a long way. From his perch atop City Hall, the iconic statue of William Penn has witnessed the rise of industry, universities, bridges, museums, trains, stadiums, markets, suffrage, civil rights, and sports. He's seen his country town become a great American city—a city that, despite its large size, feels quite small indeed.

1 PHILADELPHIA TODAY

Growing up in the long shadows of New York City and Washington, D.C., has been a blessing and a curse for Philadelphia. On one hand, the city's in-between location offers guaranteed traffic, the best of both worlds. On the other, Philadelphia will never be New York. Nor will it ever be Washington. In fact, it's only recently that Philadelphia has come (back) into its own.

AMERICAN EVOLUTION

The decades following World War II were tough for many metropolises in the northeastern U.S., and Philadelphia was no exception. Urban flight, the planned relocation of residents—especially white residents—from cities to suburbs, left Philadelphia with vacant neighborhoods. For years—well into the '80s—even affluent sections (Rittenhouse, Society Hill) practically bled homeowners and businesses. It didn't help that City Hall stuck to a policy of increasingly hefty taxation for individuals and businesses, a policy that effectively encouraged companies and citizens to operate outside city limits. If you recall the dismal, grayish urban scenes from made-in-Philly movies *Rocky, Trading Places,* and even Jonathan Demme's *Philadelphia,* you get the picture. But, then again, just like Rocky, Philadelphia couldn't be kept down forever.

The election of 1991 wasn't much of a surprise. Since 1952, Philadelphia had voted for a Democratic mayor, and '91 was no exception. A New Yorker by birth, and a Philadelphian by way of the DA's office, Mayor Ed Rendell saw something bright beneath the gray and the grit. During his two terms in office, Rendell cut costs, balanced the budget, empowered neighborhoods—paying special attention to El Centro de Oro, North Philly's rapidly swelling Latino district—and inspired reinvestment (and became a close pal of the Clintons in the bargain).

As a result, slowly at first, then in a veritable deluge, restaurants, hotels, and shops opened and thrived. Soon, the suburbanites whose parents had fled the city were flocking back—if not to live, then at least for a night on the town. Even the typically New York–focused Ivy Leaguers attending the University of Pennsylvania—at one time the most transient of the city's dwellers—were spending their weekends (and their parents' credit) inside the watering holes and boutiques of Rittenhouse and Old City. Some Penn alumni even stuck around after graduation.

When such budding yuppies, early-onset empty nesters, former suburbanites, and even fed-up New Yorkers (who have, in more recent years, been known to refer to Philadelphia as their city's "sixth borough"), move to town, they have plenty of options for places to settle. Since the gorgeous old Georgian, Federal, and Victorian town houses of Center City are now restored and occupied, formerly lifeless warehouses and empty stretches of land have been transformed into loft apartments and luxury condos. Find such adapted and new construction along major avenues—such as the dusty rose Symphony House high-rise on South Broad, also home to the shiny Suzanne Roberts Theatre, and the towering Saint James on Washington Square, built to be the tallest building east of Broad. Find more new construction on the city's edges—gleaming Waterfront Square rising up along the Delaware, for example, or Northern Liberties' strikingly Mondrian-style complex on 2nd Street. More revived housing options include outlying Center City neighborhoods that were once considered undesirable and are now undergoing major gentrification, thanks to a swell of first-time homeowners looking for bargains and fixer-uppers.

Businesses have come back, too—at least, in part. The most salient examples of revived success in this area are the city's newest—and tallest—skyscraper, cable giant Comcast's glassy, high-tech headquarters at 17th Street and J.F.K. Boulevard (p. 130), and the rainbow-hued, law-firm-filled Cira Centre across from 30th Street Station. Farther south, the old Navy Yard is now the corporate home to burgeoning hipster retailer Urban Outfitters (which also operates Free People, Anthropologie, and Terrain brand stores), who live right next to two new stadiums for the beloved Eagles football and Phillies baseball franchises—with a third on its way for the ice hockey (Flyers) and basketball (76ers or "Sixers") team. Although the once-reliable presence of the pharmaceutical industry may be waning—in 2008,

Tips How to Speak Like a Philadelphian: Ten Terms

1. ***Philly:*** Use only if you're from here. Otherwise, it's "Philadelphia" to you.
2. ***Broad Street:*** The north-south boulevard bisecting Center City is really 14th Street. Broad runs north, becoming Old York Road and 611. Never call Broad Street "14th Street." Its new designation, the "Avenue of the Arts" is a little suspicious, too.
3. ***Second Street:*** Call it "Two Street," especially in South Philly.
4. ***Front Street:*** Really 1st Street. Call it "Front."
5. ***Schuylkill:*** Pronounced "Skoo-kill." The name of the river that flows by the Philadelphia Museum of Art between Martin Luther King Jr. and Kelly drives. Also the name of I-76, the interstate expressway running east-west through the city.
6. ***Blue Route:*** I-476, connects I-95, I-76, and I-276 (the Pennsylvania Tpk.).
7. ***Passyunk:*** Pronounced "Pass-yunk." This one-way avenue runs diagonally south to north from Broad to South Street, through South Philadelphia.
8. ***Sansom Street:*** Pronounced "San-som," not "Samp-son." Although if you're going to make a mistake, this is the one to make.
9. ***The Boulevard:*** This is Roosevelt Boulevard, Route 1 North, a high-speed thoroughfare running through Northeast Philadelphia, connecting the Schuylkill Expressway (I-76) to I-276 (the Pennsylvania Tpk., which leads to the New Jersey Tpk.).
10. ***Cheesesteak:*** One word. Not "cheese steak." Definitely not "Philly cheese steak."

SmithKline Beecham announced it would leave the city—Philadelphia's financial sector expects to remain strong.

THE DAYS AHEAD

Promises the city has yet to keep include a major expansion of the Pennsylvania Convention Center (p. 132), originally built in 1993 for $522 million. Although the current center has attracted hundreds of meetings, it has earned a reputation for frustration in the form of labor costs and difficulty in operations. Still, ground has been broken, with a plan to add 60% more meeting and exhibit space by 2011.

Another not-controversy-free prospect is Pennsylvania's plan to allow slots-only casinos within city limits. There are currently two such racing and gambling centers nearby: the Philadelphia Park Casino in Philadelphia's Northeast section, and a modest Harrah's, south of the airport across from a prison in Chester. (I would recommend visiting neither: If you want the full-on gaming experience, make the trip to Atlantic City, New Jersey, a seaside poker, blackjack, and steakhouse haven.) Attempts to open similar gaming operations in South Philadelphia near the residences in the well-established neighborhoods of South Philadelphia's Pennsport and north of Center City's Northern Liberties/Fishtown have met with enough grass-roots protest that, as of press time, the South Philadelphia project was being rerouted, with a proposal to locate it to Center City's Gallery shopping center, near the convention center and Chinatown (where neighbors have also launched similar protests). Stalling the Northern Liberties/Fishtown project is the discovery of significant archaeological ruins unearthed during initial construction.

In other slightly less but nonetheless somewhat contentious news: After years of debate and litigation, the famed Barnes Foundation, overseer of the largest collection of French Impressionist works outside of France, has begun work on a relocated museum along the Benjamin Franklin Parkway—alongside the Philadelphia Art Museum, the Franklin Institute, the Rodin Museum, and the Academy of Natural Sciences.

But these issues seem merely cosmetic compared to the city's human concerns. Philadelphia's population continues to decrease at an average rate of 4% annually. (The suburbs, however, continue to sustain their growth spurt.) When a new mayor—veteran city councilman Michael Nutter—took the job in 2008, he faced a 23% poverty rate, a spike in homicides, a setback-riddled public school system, and an increasingly onerous budget. Only time will tell if the upswing will reach into the neediest sections of the city.

But for now, Philadelphians and visitors alike can take great pride in the city's hard-won progress.

2 HISTORY 101

SETTLING IN

In the 1640s, a tiny group of Swedish settlers first established a foothold in the area that would become Philadelphia. (You can see two models of the ships that brought them over in Gloria Dei Church on p. 134.) Although justly credited with the creation of the city, William Penn was not the region's European discoverer. Instead, Penn owes his status to his father, an admiral and a courtier under Charles II of England. The king was in debt to Admiral Penn, and the younger Penn asked to collect the debt through a land grant on the west bank of the Delaware River, a grant that would eventually be named Pennsylvania, or "Penn's forest." Penn's Quaker religion, his anti-Anglicanism, and his contempt for authority had landed him in prison, and the chance for him to set up a Quaker utopia in the New World was too good to pass up. Since Swedish farmers owned most of the lower Delaware frontage, he settled upriver, where the Schuylkill meets the Delaware, and named the settlement Philadelphia—City of Brotherly Love.

A CITY IS BORN

Penn's original city plan still adequately describes Center City, down to the public parks, tree-lined streets, and the site for City Hall. Penn, who had learned the dangers of narrow streets and semidetached wooden buildings from London's terrible 1666 fire, laid out the city along broad avenues and city blocks arranged in a grid. As he intended to treat Native Americans—members of the Lenape tribe were among his friends—and fellow settlers equally, he planned no city walls or neighborhood borders. Front Street faced the Delaware, as it still does, and parallel streets were numbered up to 24th Street and the Schuylkill. Streets running east to west were named after trees and plants (although Sassafras became Race St., for the horse-and-buggy contests run along it). To attract prospective investors, Penn promised bonus land grants in the "Liberties" (outlying countryside) to anyone who bought a city lot; he took one of the largest for himself, now Pennsbury Manor (26 miles north of town). The Colonies were in the business of attracting settlers in those days, and Penn found that he had to wear a variety of hats—those of financier, politician, religious leader, salesman, and manufacturer.

Homes and public buildings filled in the map slowly. The Colonial row houses of Society Hill and Elfreth's Alley (continuously inhabited since the 1690s) near the Delaware docks were the earliest homes. Thomas Jefferson, when he wrote the Declaration of Independence almost a century later in 1776, could still say of his boardinghouse on 7th and Market that it was away from the city's noise and dirt!

BEN FRANKLIN, BUSYBODIES & THE BIRTH OF A NATION

One man who will always be linked with Philadelphia is the multitalented, insatiably curious Benjamin Franklin. Inventor, printer, statesman, scientist, and diplomat, Franklin was an all-around genius. It sometimes seems that his influence infiltrates every aspect of the city worth exploring. Colonial homes were protected by his fire-insurance company; the post office at 3rd and Market streets became his grandson's printing shop; and the Free Library of Philadelphia, the University of Pennsylvania, Pennsylvania Hospital at 8th and Spruce streets, the American Philosophical Society, and "busybodies," curious double-mirrored contraptions affixed to the fronts of row houses near upper-floor windows (which allow occupants to see who's at the door) all came into being thanks to Franklin's inspiration.

Like most important Philadelphians, Franklin considered himself a loyal British subject until well into the 1770s, though he and the other colonists were increasingly subject to what they considered capricious English policy. Colonists here weren't as radical as those in New England, but tremendous political debate erupted after Lexington and Concord and the meeting of the First and Second Continental Congresses. Moderates—wealthy citizens with friends and relatives in England—held out as long as they could. But with the April 1776 decision in Independence Hall to consider drafting a declaration of independence, revolutionary fervor gained a momentum that would become unstoppable.

"These are the times that try men's souls," wrote Thomas Paine, and they certainly were for Philadelphians, who had much to lose in a war with Britain. Thomas Jefferson and John Adams talked over the situation with George Washington, Robert Morris, and other delegates at City Tavern by night and at Carpenters' Hall and Independence Hall by day. On July 2, the general Congress passed their declaration; on July 8, it was read to a crowd of 8,000, who tumultuously approved.

Your visit to Independence National Historical Park will fill you in on the Revolution's effect on the City of Brotherly Love. Of the major Colonial cities, Philadelphia had the fewest defenses. The war came to the city itself because British troops occupied patriot homes during the harsh winter of 1777 to 1778. Woodford, a country mansion in what is now Fairmount Park, was hosting Tory balls while Washington's troops drilled and shivered at Valley Forge. Washington's attempt to crack the British line at Germantown ended in a confused retreat. The city later greatly benefited from the British departure and the Peace of Paris (1783), which ended the war.

Problems with the new federal government brought a Constitutional Convention to Philadelphia in 1787. This body crafted the Constitution that the United States still follows. In the years between the ratification of the Constitution and the Civil War, the city prospered. For 10 of these years, 1790 to 1800, the U.S.

government operated here while the District of Columbia was still marshland. George Washington lived in an executive mansion where the Liberty Bell is now; the Supreme Court met in Old City Hall; Congress met in Congress Hall; and everybody met at City Tavern for balls and festivals.

A GROWING GLOBAL CENTER

Around 1800, the city spread west to Broad Street. Philadelphia grew along the river—not west as Penn had planned. Southwark, to the south, and the Northern Liberties, to the north, housed the less affluent, including many sailors. These were Philadelphia's first slums—unpaved, without public services, filled with taverns set up in unofficial alleys, and populated by those without enough property or money to satisfy voting requirements.

Nonetheless, the quality of life was considered high. The resources of Franklin's Library Company became available to the public. Both men and women received "modern" educations, with more emphasis on accounting and less on classics. The 1834 Free School Act established a democratic public school system. Private academies, such as the William Penn Charter School, Episcopal Academy, Germantown Friends School, and Friends Select, are still going strong today.

Culture flourished: In 1805, painter and naturalist Charles Willson Peale and some contemporaries founded the Pennsylvania Academy of the Fine Arts (now housed in a glorious Frank Furness building at Broad and Cherry sts.), the first American museum, with exhibits that included a portrait gallery and the first lifelike arrangements of taxidermy animals. The Walnut Street Theater was founded in 1809 and is the oldest American theater in continuous use. The Musical Fund Hall at 808 Locust (now apartments) hosted operas, symphony orchestras, and chamber ensembles.

Manufacturing, financial services, excellent docking facilities, and fine Pennsylvania farm produce soon gave status to Philadelphia, the first city of the Colonies. It was the largest English-speaking city in the British Empire after London. Colonial Philadelphia was a thriving city in virtually every way, boasting public hospitals and streetlights, cultural institutions and newspapers, stately Georgian architecture, imported tea and cloth, and, above all, commerce. The "triangle trade" shipping route between England, the Caribbean, and Philadelphia yielded estimated profits of 700% on each leg.

After the capital moved to Washington, Philadelphia retained the federal charter to mint money, build ships, and produce weapons. The city's shipyards, ironworks, and locomotive works fueled the transportation revolution that made America's growth possible. Philadelphia vied with Baltimore and New York City for transport routes to agricultural production inland. New York eventually won out as a shipper, thanks to its natural harbor and the Erie Canal. Philadelphia, however, was the hands-down winner in becoming America's premier manufacturing city, and it ranked even with New York in finance. During the Civil War, Philadelphia's manufacturers weren't above supplying both Yankees and Confederates with guns and rail equipment. Fortunately for Philadelphians, the Southern offensive met with bloody defeat at Gettysburg before reaching the city. With the end of the Civil War in 1865, port activity rebounded, as Southern cotton was spun and shipped from city textile looms.

University City in West Philadelphia saw the establishment of campuses for Drexel University and the University of Pennsylvania, and public transport lines connected all the neighborhoods of the city.

Philadelphia became the natural site for the first world's fair held on American soil: the Centennial Exposition of 1876. It's

A Curse Broken, A Curse Uttered

In 1983, skyscraper developers broke a gentlemen's agreement to not build higher than City Hall's statue of William Penn. The resulting "curse of Billy Penn," is sports legend. For 25 years, the Sixers, Flyers, Eagles, and Phillies all went championshipless. So, when the Phils captured the World Series in 2008, and the city threw a massive parade, fans didn't fault second baseman Chase Utley for joyously dropping the f-bomb during his celebration speech.

hard to imagine the excitement that filled Fairmount Park, with 200 pavilions and displays. There's a scale model downstairs in Memorial Hall—now better known as the Please Touch Museum—one of the few surviving structures in the park; it gives a good idea of how seriously the United States took this show of power and prestige.

INTO THE 20TH CENTURY

A quick examination of the cornerstones of the massive buildings along Broad Street testifies to the city's turn-of-the-20th-century success in the banking industry. Still, for all its rising marble monuments to all things monetary, post-wartime Philadelphia became known for its public corruption and all-around acceptance of the way things were. Politics descended into an ugly business; Prohibition was flagrantly ignored; the mob rose to power, and, once the Depression hit, those banks closed in spades. It wasn't surprising that if you lived in the city around then, you were probably trying to move out.

Still, it wasn't all bad news. In the first half of the 20th century, the Philadelphia Art Museum opened, the Ben Franklin Bridge connected the city to New Jersey, subway lines first ran, and the skyline welcomed some of the world's most innovative skyscrapers, including the still-striking, International-style PSFS Building, now the Loews Philadelphia Hotel. Even the New Deal had some of its best dealings in the city; FDR's Works Progress Administration provided 40,000 jobs to Philadelphians.

World War II affected Philadelphia as it did much of America: Residents planted victory gardens, allowed their sons to enlist, met war bond quotas, and gave jobs to women and African Americans—many of whom lost those same jobs when the war ended.

Still, the city itself remained deeply mired in corruption until the 1950s, when a pair of reform-minded mayors, Joseph S. Clark and Richardson Dilworth, helped draft a new city charter that, at least temporarily, cleaned up the dirty dealings in and around City Hall. Today, you can still see the facade of Dilworth's simple Colonial house on the eastern edge of Washington Square Park, and the area in front of City Hall is known as Dilworth Plaza.

The tumult of the '60s and '70s manifested as marches and sit-ins in universities and colleges. The city became a hotbed of racial tension, playing host to riots in a prison as well as a neighborhood. In 1971, the city elected a hardscrabble former police chief as mayor, a controversial figure who came down with an iron fist on gang warfare, but divided the city with fiscal mismanagement and take-no-prisoners diplomacy. Later, under the nation's first African-American mayor, Philadelphia seemed beyond repair: In 1985, Mayor

Wilson Goode gave the go-ahead to bomb the home of MOVE, a radical black roots group. Eleven members of the group (including four children) died. Sixty-two neighboring houses were destroyed. And the city's infamy reached an all-time low.

Luckily, things seemed to turn around with the next mayor, an outsider who wiped away the deficit with investment, and glad-handed his way into the hearts of all manner of Philadelphians (see "Philadelphia Today," earlier in this chapter).

3 PUBLIC ART & ARCHITECTURE

Like the city itself, Philadelphia's architecture and art scene is a melting pot of schools and styles. Walk down most any Center City street, and you're likely to encounter Art Deco facades, Victorian town houses, Colonial brick, freshly painted murals—and, above it all, glass-and-steel skyscrapers. Look closer, and you'll notice art everywhere you turn—a giant clothespin across the street from City Hall, statues outside I. M. Pei's Society Hill towers, the bird mobile in Terminal A of Philadelphia International Airport—that's part of a promise to dedicate 1% of construction costs of any major new development to public art.

EARLY ARCHITECTURE

Philadelphia's very first buildings were simple log cabins, which have been all but lost to time. Philadelphia's second architectural wave was more enduring: Seventeenth-century settlers often built their houses of meeting and worship in brick, using a mix of architectural styles from their diverse backgrounds. One such brick edifice is the Old Swedes' Church (p. 134), built around 1700 and still active. It is a guild-built marriage of Gothic and medieval, with nods to the emerging Georgian aesthetic, featuring alternating Flemish Bond brick patterns.

More outstanding examples of Georgian architecture—typified by symmetry and simplicity, paned windows, and rectangular transoms—include plainly elegant Christ Church (p. 133), spiritual home to George Washington and 14 other signers of the Declaration of Independence; Carpenters' Hall, original meeting place of the First Continental Congress of the U.S. (p. 135); Powel House (p. 137); and Independence Hall itself. Although the style was an expression developed in England as a response to the ornate flourishes of the baroque period, Georgian architecture is now associated with the Colonial period.

About a half a century later came the next wave of building design, a marriage of classically Greek Palladian and Georgian, called Federal. This style dominated important buildings from pre-Revolutionary times until the mid-1800s, and can be found in four-pilastered Library Hall (p. 162) and the Pine Street side of Pennsylvania Hospital (p. 137), in addition to dozens of houses in Society Hill—look for a front door surrounded by glass panes and topped by an arched window. Another sure sign of a Federal building: the presence of a bald eagle.

ALL THE TRIMMINGS

The next several decades subtracted out the Georgian half of Federal, and revived the classically Greek. Not surprisingly, this early-19th-century architecture style is called Greek Revival—or, if you prefer, neoclassical. It was in Philadelphia, and with this architecture, that the first generation of American-born architects began to make names for themselves. See the work of civil engineer and artist-turned-architect William Strickland, who designed the heavily columned, dramatically domed Second Bank of the United States (p. 163),

Old City's round and imposing Merchants' Exchange at 2nd and Walnut streets, and the National Mechanic Bank, now a restaurant and bar at 22 S. 3rd Street in Old City.

Although architect William Haviland hailed from across the pond, he did some of his most important work on the creation of the Walnut Street Theatre (p. 190), the Atwater Kent Museum (p. 141), the University of the Arts building at Broad and Pine streets, and the now deliciously decrepit Eastern State Penitentiary (p. 141; visit during Halloween). Native Philadelphian Thomas U. Walter designed both the U.S. Capitol (in Washington, D.C.) and the obstinately classic Girard College on the edge of Philadelphia's Fairmount section.

Somewhat ironically, at the very time when buildings were becoming grandiose and distinctive, homes were becoming attached and identical. The "Philadelphia row" house was first introduced around 7th and Sansom streets at the beginning of the 19th century. Today, these houses form Jeweler's Row (p. 182), a retail and wholesale district with few residences. Contrast it with the houses along Elfreth's Alley (p. 136), built individually, in various heights and styles.

Frank Furness, another native son, designed buildings so distinctively ornamental, they are among the easiest to pick out. Polychromatic masonry, multicolored bricks laid in an icing-type fashion, was among the Victorian-Gothic trimmings of Furness's work. Although much of the grand oeuvre (once 600 buildings strong) has been demolished, you can still glimpse his genius in the elegant Pennsylvania Academy of the Fine Arts (p. 128) and Fischer Fine Arts Library at the University of Pennsylvania.

Another can't-miss style is that which bedecks City Hall, a Second Empire creation that remains the world's tallest all-masonry building—and the country's largest municipal building. Designed by Scotsman John McArthur, Jr., this wedding cake of a city block took 30 years to build—and nearly as many to, more recently, clean. A bronze statue of city planner William Penn by Alexander Milne Calder (also responsible for the 249 other sculptures on the building) tops City Hall. Penn's likeness is the tallest statue atop any building in the world. And Calder, for his part, gave more than his work to the city. His son Alexander Stirling Calder created Swann Memorial Fountain on Logan Square, and his grandson, Alexander Calder, made the modern, primary-color mobiles along the parkway leading up to the Philadelphia Art Museum, which, by the way, is another approximation of Greek Revival style, but from the early 20th century.

THE MODERN AGE

Philadelphia's earliest skyscrapers, glass-and-steel structures that included such modern inventions as elevators, wouldn't be considered skyscraping by today's standards. Still, the Ben Franklin House (ca. 1925) at 8th and Chestnut streets (stop in to see the amazing decorative ceiling), the 30th Street Station (built so that a plane could land on its roof), and the definitely Palladian Franklin Institute (p. 127) towered above most buildings of their day. By gentlemen's agreement, they weren't permitted to tower above the brim of William Penn's hat, however.

But the most modern of all was William Lescaze and George Howe's PSFS Building. The 1932 creation of this glass-and-steel monument to modernism is considered the first International Style building. Today, it houses the Loews Hotel (p. 68)—but has stayed true to its glamour with some of the loveliest examples of exotic wood paneling and spare, yet spectacular Cartier clocks throughout.

Louis I. Kahn was the next Philadelphia architect to make a world name for himself. Though much of his austerely modern work was built far from the city, his Richards

Public Displays of Art

"The most famous meeting place in Philadelphia is the statue of the eagle in Wanamaker's [now Macy's], and the most memorable outdoor object to whole generations growing up in Center City has been the goat in Rittenhouse Square."

—Michael Von Moschzisker, Philadelphia lawyer who established the city's One Percent for Art program.

Medical Library still functions as such at the University of Pennsylvania—and, as of press time, Esherick house, one of his few residential projects, was for sale in the Northwestern neighborhood of Chestnut Hill. Another modern marvel who has graced the city: I. M. Pei, whose Society Hill Towers still dominate the eastern skyline, and whose shining National Constitution Center (p. 126) more recently dominates Independence Park.

The 1980s, as they were wont to do, brought a new level of architectural, er, taste to the city with the chess piece–like Liberty One and Liberty Two buildings, which broke the gentlemen's agreement about not building above William Penn's statue. In 2008, the cable giant Comcast put its name on Philadelphia's tallest building, the tech-chocked Comcast Center at 17th and J.F.K. Boulevard (p. 130).

4 PHILADELPHIA IN POPULAR CULTURE

One way that Philadelphia feels small is in the city's dearth of celebrity life. Truth be told, Philly's biggest international stars passed through town more than 200 years ago. Not that Philadelphians shouldn't be proud of more recent hometown heroes Bill Cosby, Patti LaBelle, Grace Kelly, Hall & Oates, Will Smith, and Pink. It's just that referencing Philadelphia's role in pop culture more often elicits a bemused "oh really?" instead of an enthused "oh yeah!"

Still, there's no denying the fun of unexpectedly recognizing a street from a favorite book, or even making an effort to relive a scene from *It's Always Sunny in Philadelphia.*

MOVIE TIMES

One thing Philadelphia has been increasingly proud of is its presence in the filmmaking industry. Not too long ago, the city only exported movie stars. Today, while many box office celebs still move to Hollywood, others come back—to act. Much credit in this turn of events goes to native son M. Night Shyamalan, director-producer of widely successful set-in-Philly thrillers like *The Sixth Sense* and *Unbreakable.*

Still, it's the movies *about* Philadelphia that most tell the tale of the city. Here are a few of my favorites. You might want to rent or download a few before you visit.

First things first: The most famous movie character ever to come out of South—or any part of—Philadelphia is, was, and will always be Rocky Balboa. Sure, actor Sly Stallone first called New York and now sunny Southern California home. But his Academy Award–deserving (at least in the first rendition) portrayal of an underdog pugilist who worked out with frozen meat, fell in love with the girl from the pet store, and went from bobos to Cadillacs (but always lived in a row house) made him an instant honorary Philadelphian. Once you see the films (out of all six, the first two are the best), you absolutely must take a run up the steps of the Philadelphia Art Museum, and, when you reach the top, turn around and pump your fists in the air. Or, at the very least, fans will want to get their photos taken with the Rocky statue at the bottom of the museum steps. (For another great Philadelphia sports story—this one based on a *real* Philadelphia sports star—check out *Invincible,* the story of unlikely Eagles player Vince Papale, played by Mark Wahlberg.)

Another film classic—direct from the other side of the tracks—is 1940's *The Philadelphia Story.* This black-and-white movie adaptation of a play stars Katharine Hepburn, Cary Grant, and Jimmy Stewart, and lightheartedly depicts the genteel Main Line suburbs—Hepburn attended nearby Bryn Mawr College, so she knew the area well—taking a viewer back to the days of tiny waists and smashing parties and perfect manners and debonair men who swept petite socialites off their dainty feet.

More girlish fun can be had by watching a more recent adaptation, that of Philadelphia writer Jennifer Weiner's colorful novel *In Her Shoes.* The story is the tale of two sisters, a "dramedy" (half drama, half comedy), that's set, appropriately, half in Philadelphia and half in Florida. Toni Colette, Cameron Diaz, and Shirley MacLaine headline—and with a trio like this, you can expect several laughs and a few tears. To reenact the movie's sweetest scene (I swear, I'm not giving anything away), treat yourself to dinner at South Street's Jamaican Jerk Hut (p. 109).

Jonathan Demme's 1993 movie named after the city took home two Academy Awards: one for leading man Tom Hanks, and another for Bruce Springsteen's original song "The Streets of Philadelphia." *Philadelphia* tells the fictional story of a gay, HIV-positive lawyer who loses his job when his firm notices he displays the symptoms of AIDS. Denzel Washington costars as Hanks's unlikely legal counsel; Antonio Banderas plays Hanks's partner; Jason Robards plays Hanks's boss; and City Hall makes for a stunning backdrop.

For the sheer politically incorrect pleasure of it, *Trading Spaces* might be my favorite Philadelphia movie. Eddie Murphy "Billy Ray Valentine" and Dan Aykroyd "Louis Winthorpe III" star as a couple of opposites whose lives are switched. High jinks both in a downtrodden part of town and in swanky spots such as a Society Hill town house and the clubby Union League ensue. Jamie Lee Curtis also stars, as do the marvelously curmudgeonly dastardly duo of Ralph Bellamy and Don Ameche.

And, for the thrill of it all—and a real challenge identifying landmarks—check out *The Italian Job,* in which Mark Wahlberg, Charlize Theron, and Donald Sutherland whiz through the streets of Philadelphia (and the byways of LA, and the canals of Venice) in a cross, double-cross, gold heist that pits thieves against thieves against more thieves and delivers as many thrilling twists and turns as it does turns of fate.

REQUIRED READING

HISTORY For an encyclopedic, in-depth look into the city's history, invest in the 680-page *Philadelphia: A 300-Year History* (Norton, 1982), wherein the Barra Foundation provides a comprehensive portrait of the city and its people, including previously underreported stories of Philadelphia's first African Americans. Carl Bridenbaugh's *Rebels and Gentlemen* (Oxford University Press, 1965) is a good summary of events leading up to independence. For a specific—and wonderfully readable—portrait of the 1787 Constitutional Convention check out *Decision in Philadelphia* (Ballantine, 1987). For a more novelistic look into the city's roots—and the start of the country—read *1776*

(Simon & Schuster, 2006) and *John Adams* (Simon & Schuster, 2008) by two-time Pulitzer Prize–winning historian David McCullough, who brings Independence Hall, the City Tavern, and the streets of Philadelphia back to life.

ART & ARCHITECTURE *Philadelphia Architecture: A Guide to the City, Third Edition* (Paul Dry, 2009) expands upon housing expert–author John Andrew Gallery's grand tour of the city, documenting more than 400 buildings and delving into the lives of Louis I. Kahn, Frank Furness, and other Philadelphia architects. To glimpse the ghosts of buildings no more, pick up a copy of *Forgotten Philadelphia: Lost Architecture of the Quaker City* (Temple University Press, 2007), a lesson in the historic hows and why nots of architectural preservation.

A more redemptive city story is that of Philadelphia's renowned Mural Arts Program, as told through the once-bare walls of Philadelphia's neighborhoods, and inside two coffee-table-worthy volumes, *Philadelphia Murals and the Stories They Tell* (Temple University Press, 2002) and *More Philadelphia Murals and the Stories They Tell* (Temple University Press, 2006).

FOR THE KIDS While Frommer's guides are fine and well for grown-ups, younger readers might like making discoveries on their own via books such as author Susan Korman's *P Is for Philadelphia* (Temple University Press, 2005), Martha Zschock's *Journal Around Philadelphia from A to Z* (Commonwealth Editions, 2006), and Adam Gamble's perfect-for-bedtime *Good Night, Philadelphia* (Our World of Books, 2006). Only loosely affiliated with the city—but well deserving of credit—is *Philadelphia Chickens* (Workman, 2002), a CD and illustrated book singalong combo by Sandra Boynton and Michael Ford with help from Meryl Streep, Laura Linney, and Philadelphia's own Bacon Brothers.

CONTEMPORARY FICTION Popular novelist Jennifer Weiner is best known for her fun and readable tale of two sisters in *In Her Shoes* (Washington Square Press, 2002). If you liked it, you might also try *Little Earthquakes* (Washington Square Press, 2004), the tale of four diverse friends who bond over becoming mothers.

Prolific South Philadelphia author Lisa Scottoline started her career as a writer of legal thrillers with *Everywhere That Mary Went* (HarperTorch, 1993) and has since published more than a dozen page turners about the fantastical inner workings of Philadelphia lawyers, mobsters, and lovers. Any would be a great read for the trip over or back.

CONTEMPORARY NONFICTION For an insider's glimpse of how Philadelphia's most recent renaissance went down, delve into *A Prayer for the City* (Vintage, 1998) by Pulitzer Prize–winning journalist Buzz Bissinger, author of *Friday Night Lights* (Addison-Wesley, 1990). For this acclaimed work, Bissinger closely followed former mayor (and now Pennsylvania governor) Ed Rendell and Rendell's chief of staff, along with four more prominent Philadelphians through the mayor's first 4-year term. The result: Remarkable insight into inner workings of urban politics. Even though the book is just over a decade old, it's hard to imagine an up-and-coming politician allowing that kind of access today.

Another great, dramatic read belongs to longtime *Philadelphia Inquirer* crime reporter George Anastasia. *Blood and Honor: Inside the Scarfo Mob, Mafia's Most Violent Family* (Camino, 2003) is a chilling thriller and a great way for *Sopranos* fans to get their real-life fix. True story: When the South Philly, Atlantic City–based Scarfo clan took out a hit on Anastasia, they assured him "it's nothing personal."

A CENTURY (OR SO) OF MUSIC

Some of America's—and the world's—greatest musicians came from Philadelphia. In fact, the story of popular American music can be told through a series of Philadelphians who shaped their musical genres. Starting, perhaps, with a woman who was far from a pop star. Opera singer Marian Andersen (1897–1993) won over listeners with her once-in-a-lifetime contralto. As an African-American performer coming up in the 1920s and 1930s, Andersen faced extraordinary obstacles. Her most famous performance took place on Easter Sunday, 1939, when she stood on the steps of the Lincoln Memorial in Washington, D.C., and performed "My Country 'Tis of Thee" to a crowd of 75,000. One way she is remembered today is through the Marian Andersen Award, given annually to an artist who has excelled as a humanitarian.

Another local opera star: South Philadelphia's very own Mario Lanza (1921–59), who remains the voice you are most likely to hear belting out the Neapolitan classic "Funiculì Funiculà." His memory lives on today in a mural on South Broad Street, and inside a kitschy museum at 712 Montrose St. (✆ **215/238-9691;** www.mario-lanza-institute.org).

Philadelphia-born (and Baltimore-raised) Billie Holiday (1915–59) had an arrestingly textured, almost instrumental jazz quality about her voice. Although her performances—"God Bless the Child," "Lady Sings the Blues," "Strange Fruit," and "Lover Man"—have become essential to the American songbook, Lady Day's life story is a sad one. Today, find a marker commemorating her sometime home at 1409 Lombard St.

Unlike Holiday, jazz icon John Coltrane (1926–67) was a Philadelphian by choice. In 1943, he moved to the Strawberry Mansion section of the city (on an edge of Fairmount Park), where he studied jazz until he got the call from Miles Davis, and began a career in tenor saxophone that remains unmatched. Essential Coltrane: "Blue Train."

A number of Philadelphians made the big time as America's original radio pop stars in the '40s through the '60s. Among them, show businessman and marrier of starlets Eddie Fisher ("I'm Yours," "Sunrise, Sunset"); South Philadelphian Al Martino ("Daddy's Little Girl," "Volare"); *Beach Blanket Bingo* heartthrob Frankie Avalon ("Why"); thanks to the long Philadelphia-based *American Bandstand,* teen idol Fabian ("Turn Me Loose," "Tiger"); and the unstoppable Chubby Checker, creator of one of the most recognizable dance song of his era (the Twist).

Ardent supporter of all things Philadelphia, Patti LaBelle (1944–) was hitting the high notes decades before Mariah squeaked onto the scene. Petite yet powerful, the West Philly–born diva is best loved for such disco-meets-pop hits as "Lady Marmalade," "Danny Boy," "New Attitude," and "On Her Own."

Hit makers you may never have heard of—but whose songs you certainly know by heart—are Kenny Gamble (1943–) and Leon Huff (1942–) of Gamble & Huff, the soulful songwriting-producing team. The strong-in-the-70s duo—also known as the Sound of Philadelphia—worked with Aretha Franklin, Dusty Springfield, Harold Melvin and the Bluenotes, the O'Jays, Lou Rawls, Wilson Pickett, and Teddy Pendergrass (also a Philly native and resident, best known for "If You Don't Know Me By Now" and "Love T.K.O."). Together, they're responsible for 170 gold and platinum albums, and form the East Coast equivalent of Detroit's Motown.

Taking pages from rock and soul, Temple University students Daryl Hall (1946–) and John Oates (1949–) met up in the '70s, starting a relationship that resulted in six number-one hits on Billboard's Hot 100. The unlikely pair—Hall is tall, blonde, and skinny; Oates is small, dark, and hairy—killed it with such '80s classics as "Rich Girl," "Maneater," "Private Eyes," "Kiss on My List," and "I Can't Go for That (No Can Do)." In other words, they performed the soundtrack to my childhood.

The next decade of music saw the acceptance of hip-hop into the mainstream, led by two more West Philadelphians, Jeff Townes (1965–, aka DJ Jazzy Jeff) and Will Smith (1968–, aka the Fresh Prince). They spun and rapped, respectively, on highly relatable subjects such as girls being nothin' but trouble, parents just not understanding, and the joys of summertime. Although the pair parted ways—today, Will Smith fits better into the movie superstar category—they remain pals and, when they can, perform together.

More genre bending came with the millennial group, the Roots, who blended (and sometimes still blend) hip-hop, jazz, rock, and more to much serious acclaim. Born collaborators, the band won a 1999 Grammy for "You Got Me," featuring Erykah Badu and Eve, another Philadelphia rapper, one of the few women who've held their own at Def Jam records, famed for hits "Gotta Man" and "Let Me Blow Ya Mind" (with Gwen Stefani). The Roots member you're most likely to run into in town is drummer ?estlove (pronounced "Quest Love"), who shows up on special nights at Fluid (p. 198).

One last great performer got her start at poetry slams: North Philly girl Jill Scott (1972–). Scott smoothly blends jazz, hip-hop, R&B, and spoken word into heartfelt neosoul hits such as "Gettin' in the Way," "A Long Walk," and "Golden." Having won three Grammys, Scott's now making her move onto the screen, starring as Precious Ramotswe in HBO's *The No. 1 Ladies' Detective Agency.*

5 PHILADELPHIA EATS

Recent years have seen Philadelphia's gourmet credibility mushroom (or should I say, "morel"). In the culinary hub of Center City, celebrity chefs have become commonplace, and every eater's a critic. It's also become quite simple to go out to a dinner for two, and come home $200 poorer.

Still, for every eater relishing the artful comestibles of a Morimoto or a Ripert and for each bistro patron tucking into an esoterically embellished filet mignon or sitting down to an investment-worthy locavore tasting menu, there are dozens more Philadelphia diners with a wholly different culinary pursuit. Easily outnumbering the gourmets and the foodies, these single-minded culinary seekers are easy to spot. You don't even have to go inside a restaurant to find them. They consume their chosen meal while walking down the street. They sup seated, balanced on the curb. They dine *dans la voiture* (in the car). No flatware do they need. Just a free hand and an extra napkin.

Some enjoy their chosen repast at lunchtime. For others, it's dinner. Many savor it as sustaining, after-midnight snack. A few eat it as breakfast.

The meal is, of course, a sandwich. The sandwich is, obviously, a cheesesteak. This singular, workaday entree is not just the food most readily associated with Philadelphia. It is the edible symbol of the city.

For some, it is a reason to come to the city. I know. When I lived 10 blocks north of the famously dueling South Philly cheesesteak stands of Pat's and Geno's, I could hardly walk out my door and to the corner without an out-of-state-license-plated car pulling over to ask for directions to "those cheesesteak places."

Some other Philly foods locals love:

The Hoagie: Known elsewhere as a submarine, sub, or hero, this typically cold, cuts-stuffed sandwich is named locally for Hog Island, an Italian-American neighborhood in Southwest Philadelphia.

Scrapple: The mushier, milder, cornmeal-based cousin of the sausage patty is rumored to be America's very first pork product. Find it in diners and breakfast spots.

Tastykake: Baked in town since 1917, these prepackaged desserts star the Butterscotch Krimpet, Chocolate Junior, Kandy Kakes, and Tasty Pies. Find them at convenience stores.

Soft Pretzel: Philadelphians don't *exactly* deserve credit for this one. It's believed that the Germans—or Pennsylvania Dutch—brought these salty, doughy twists to town from Lancaster.

Goldenberg Peanut Chews: This old-fashioned candy bar has been pulling out dental fillings for more than 90 years. The company now belongs to Pennsylvania-based Just Born, manufacturer of marshmallow Peeps.

Philadelphia Cream Cheese: Just kidding. There's no local connection here. In 1882, food processor Kraft Foods wanted to class up their spread by adding "Philadelphia" to its name. Go figure.

3

Planning Your Trip to Philadelphia

This chapter tackles the hows of your trip. The aim here is to help you prepare for your visit, no matter if you're a frequent traveler, a first timer, a new resident, or a lifelong native of Philadelphia.

Standard U.S. rules apply for entry to the city. Read more about them in "Entry Requirements," below. Pack for the season: Light clothes for summer, layers for spring and fall, and a warm coat or jacket, plus hat, gloves, and muffler for winter. Philadelphians aren't the fashion plates that New Yorkers are, but they do tend to dress up for dinner and nightlife. If you're planning on exploring the city by foot, be sure to bring a pair or two of comfortable shoes.

Another important thing to bring: city smarts. Even Philadelphia's swankiest addresses are mere blocks from insecure neighborhoods. Be aware of your surroundings.

Although pockets of the city are bilingual, you'll find that most people you meet speak English, and don't have great experience interpreting other languages. Native Philadelphians tend to have interesting colloquialisms and accents, including pronouncing "water" as "wooder," greeting one another with "yo," and, in an unfortunate turn of grammar, employing the nonword "you's" as a plural form of "you."

For a list of on-the-ground resources in Philadelphia, please see the appendix.

1 VISITOR INFORMATION

TOURIST OFFICE The **Independence Visitor Center,** 1 N. Independence Mall W. (6th and Market sts.), Philadelphia, PA 19106 (© **800/537-7676,** 215/965-7676, or 636-1666; www.independencevisitorcenter.com) is a great first stop. Separating the Liberty Bell and Independence Hall from the National Constitution Center, this expansive center offers a concierge kiosk, regional publications, events calendars, city and regional maps, a book and gift shop, and a first-class exhibition on Philadelphia's place in history. Knowledgeable volunteers staff the phones and counters. Ask for the *Official Visitors Guide,* a seasonal compendium of exhibitions, events, and the like. The center also offers an increasing number of package tours, combining special museum exhibitions, concerts, or sporting events with discount hotel prices, free city transit passes, and Amtrak discounts. Many bus tours, historic trolley rides, and walking tours start from here.

International visitors who want special advice or would like to arrange meetings or home stays should reach out to the **International Visitors Council of Philadelphia,** 1515 Arch St., 12th floor (© **215/683-0999;** www.ivc.org).

WEBSITES Philly has umpteen sites to explore online. The best belong to the Independence Visitor Center (www.independencevisitorcenter.com), the Philadelphia Convention and Visitors Bureau

Philadelphia Predeparture Checklist

- Did you book in advance? If you're planning on going to a popular restaurant such as **Osteria** (p. 97), **Buddakan** (p. 85), or **Amada** (p. 85) or to a theatrical event at the **Kimmel Center for the Performing Arts** (p. 192), you'll need to reserve in advance. **Independence Hall** (among others in the historic district) has increased security and requires that you book a time slot, and museums such as the **Barnes Foundation** (p. 126) have limited hours and attendance, so call ahead.
- Did you confirm the hours of operation? Many scheduled tours, festivals, and special events change regularly, so call ahead for opening and closing hours.
- Did you bring your ID cards that could entitle you to discounts (AAA and AARP cards, student IDs, and such)?
- Did you bring emergency drug prescriptions and extra glasses and/or contact lenses?
- Do you have your credit card PINs?
- If you have an e-ticket, do you have documentation?
- Did you leave a copy of your itinerary with someone at home?

(www.philadelphiausa.travel), and my favorite, the Greater Philadelphia Tourism Marketing Corporation (www.gophila.com). Find updates to this guidebook at www.frommers.com. For news and information, along with restaurant reviews and arts and entertainment, visit www.philly.com, the site shared by the *Philadelphia Inquirer* and the *Philadelphia Daily News,* two daily newspapers, or www.phillymag.com, the online version of monthly glossy *Philadelphia* magazine.

2 ENTRY REQUIREMENTS

PASSPORTS

New regulations issued by the Department of Homeland Security now require virtually every air traveler entering the U.S. to show a passport. As of January 23, 2007, all persons, including U.S. citizens, traveling by air between the United States and Canada, Mexico, Central and South America, the Caribbean, and Bermuda are required to present a valid passport. As of January 31, 2008, U.S. and Canadian citizens entering the U.S. at land and sea ports of entry from within the Western Hemisphere will need to present government-issued proof of citizenship, such as a birth certificate, along with a government-issued photo ID, such as a driver's license. A passport is not required for U.S. or Canadian citizens entering by land or sea, but it is highly encouraged that you carry one.

For information on how to obtain a passport, see **"Passports"** in the appendix.

VISAS

The U.S. State Department has a **Visa Waiver Program (VWP)** allowing citizens of the following countries to enter the United States without a visa for stays of up to 90 days: Andorra, Australia, Austria, Belgium, Brunei, Denmark, Finland,

France, Germany, Iceland, Ireland, Italy, Japan, Liechtenstein, Luxembourg, Monaco, the Netherlands, New Zealand, Norway, Portugal, San Marino, Singapore, Slovenia, Spain, Sweden, Switzerland, and the United Kingdom. (***Note:*** This list was accurate at press time; for the most up-to-date list of countries in the VWP, consult www.travel.state.gov/visa.) Even though a visa isn't necessary, in an effort to help U.S. officials check travelers against terror watch lists before they arrive at U.S. borders, as of January 12, 2009, visitors from VWP countries must register online before boarding a plane or a boat to the U.S. Travelers will complete an electronic application, providing basic personal and travel eligibility information. The Department of Homeland Security recommends filling out the form at least 3 days before traveling. Authorizations will be valid for up to 2 years or until the traveler's passport expires, whichever comes first. Currently, there is no fee for the online application. Canadian citizens may enter the United States without visas; they will need to show passports (if traveling by air) and proof of residence, however. ***Note:*** Any passport issued on or after October 26, 2006, by a VWP country must be an **e-passport** for VWP travelers to be eligible to enter the U.S. without a visa. Citizens of these nations also need to present a round-trip air or cruise ticket upon arrival. E-passports contain computer chips capable of storing biometric information, such as the required digital photograph of the holder. (You can identify an e-passport by the symbol on the bottom center cover of your passport.) If your passport doesn't have this feature, you can still travel without a visa if it is a valid passport issued before October 26, 2005, and includes a machine-readable zone, or between October 26, 2005, and October 25, 2006, and includes a digital photograph. For more information, go to **www.travel.state.gov/visa**.

Citizens of all other countries must have (1) a valid passport that expires at least 6 months later than the scheduled end of their visit to the U.S., and (2) a tourist visa. To obtain a visa, applicants must schedule an appointment with a U.S. consulate or embassy, fill out the application forms (available from www.travel.state.gov/visa), and pay a $131 fee. Wait times can be lengthy, so it's best to initiate the process as soon as possible.

As of January 2004, many international visitors traveling on visas to the United States will be photographed and fingerprinted on arrival at Customs in airports and on cruise ships in a program created by the Department of Homeland Security called **US-VISIT.** Exempt from the extra scrutiny are visitors entering by land or those (mostly in Europe; see p. 258) that don't require a visa for short-term visits. For more information, go to the Homeland Security website at **www.dhs.gov/dhspublic**.

For specifics on how to get a visa, see **"Visas"** in the appendix.

MEDICAL REQUIREMENTS

Unless you're arriving from an area known to be suffering from an epidemic (particularly cholera or yellow fever), inoculations or vaccinations are not required for entry into the United States.

CUSTOMS

What You Can Bring Into the U.S.

Every visitor more than 21 years of age may bring in, free of duty, the following: (1) 1 liter of wine or hard liquor; (2) 200 cigarettes, 100 cigars (but not from Cuba), or 3 pounds of smoking tobacco; and (3) $100 worth of gifts. These exemptions are offered to travelers who spend at least 72 hours in the United States and who have not claimed them within the preceding 6 months. It is forbidden to bring into the country almost any meat products (including canned, fresh, and dried meat products such as bouillon, soup mixes, and so on). Generally, condiments including vinegars, oils, spices, coffee, tea, and some cheeses and baked goods are permitted. Avoid rice products, as rice can often harbor insects. Bringing fruits and vegetables is not advised, though not prohibited. Customs will allow produce depending on where you got it and where you're going after you arrive in the U.S. Foreign tourists may carry in or out up to $10,000 in U.S. or foreign currency with no formalities; larger sums must be declared to U.S. Customs on entering or leaving, which includes filing form CM 4790. For details regarding U.S. Customs and Border Protection, consult your nearest U.S. embassy or consulate, or **U.S. Customs** (www.cbp.gov).

What You Can Take Home from Philadelphia

U.S. Citizens: For specifics on what you can bring back and the corresponding fees, download the invaluable free pamphlet *Know Before You Go* from the U.S. Customs and Border Protection website, www.cbp.gov. (Click on "Travel," and then click on "Know Before You Go! Online Brochure.") Or contact the U.S. Customs and Border Protection, 1300 Pennsylvania Ave., NW, Washington, DC 20229 (✆ **877/287-8667**) and request the pamphlet.

Canadian Citizens: For a clear summary of Canadian rules, write for the booklet *I Declare,* issued by the Canada Border Services Agency (✆ **800/461-9999** in Canada or 204/983-3500; www.cbsa-asfc.gc.ca).

U.K. Citizens: For information, contact **HM Customs & Excise** at ✆ **0845/010-9000** or 020/8929-0152 from outside the U.K., or consult its website at **www.hmce.gov.uk**.

Australian Citizens: A helpful brochure available from Australian consulates or Customs offices is *Know Before You Go.* For more information, call the **Australian Customs Service** at ✆ **1300/363-263** or visit **www.customs.gov.au**.

New Zealand Citizens: Most questions are answered in a free pamphlet available at New Zealand consulates and Customs offices: *New Zealand Customs Guide for Travellers, Notice no. 4.* For more information, contact **New Zealand Customs,** The Customhouse, 17–21 Whitmore St., Box 2218, Wellington (✆ **04/473-6099** or 0800/428-786; **www.customs.govt.nz**).

3 WHEN TO GO

Philadelphia is great to visit any time, although given the city's seasonal popularity and the constant flow of conventions, you'll find the best deals in the fall and winter. Concert and museum seasons run from early October to early June, and July 4th draws a festive crowd to Independence Hall.

The city has four distinct seasons with temperatures ranging from the 90s (30s Celsius) in summer to the 20s (around 0°C) in winter. (Below-zero temperatures normally hit only one out of every four winters.) Summers, the height of tourist season, can get swelteringly humid. In the fall, the weather becomes drier. Spring temperatures are variable; count on comfortable breezes. I like late September and late May best.

Average Temperatures & Precipitation in Philadelphia

	Jan	Feb	Mar	Apr	May	June	July	Aug	Sept	Oct	Nov	Dec
High (°F)	40	41	50	62	73	81	85	83	77	66	54	43
High (°C)	4	5	10	17	23	27	29	28	25	19	12	6
Low (°F)	26	26	33	43	53	63	68	66	60	49	39	29
Low (°C)	–3	–3	1	6	12	17	20	19	16	9	4	–2
Precip. (in days)	11	9	11	11	11	10	9	9	8	8	10	10

PHILADELPHIA CALENDAR OF EVENTS

For more details and up-to-the-minute information, contact the **Independence Visitor Center,** 1 N. Independence Mall W., Philadelphia, PA 19106 (✆ **800/537-7676**), or see the calendar at www.gophila.com.

JANUARY

Mummer's Parade. New Year's Day wouldn't be the same without this wonderfully odd, century-old parade, which lasts from 8am through sunset. Mummers are 15,000 costumed members of performing troupes (referred to as "brigades" or "clubs"). Sometimes Mummers play a musical instrument. Sometimes they dance. Sometimes they carry a parasol in one hand and a can of Coors Light in the other. But they almost always wear a spangled, feathered, and/or sequined clownlike costume and face paint while strutting up Broad Street, from South Philly to City Hall. After the parade, head to the convention center at 11th and Arch to watch the fancy brigades ("fancies") compete onstage, or join tipsy revelers packed into Dirty Frank's, a neighborhood bar on the corner of 13th and Pine streets. Call the Mummers Museum at ✆ **215/336-3050** or visit www.mummers.com for details. January 1 (or the following Sat in case of bad weather).

FEBRUARY

Black History Month. The African American Museum at 7th and Arch streets offers a full complement of exhibitions, lectures, and music. Call ✆ **215/574-0380** or visit www.aampmuseum.org for details. Entire month of February.

Center City Restaurant Week. Nearly 100 restaurants participate in this biannual, citywide, bargain-priced dine around. The deal: Full-service restaurants such as **Fork** (p. 88), **Alma de Cuba** (p. 96), and **Table 31** (p. 99), and BYOB bistros like Mercato, La Bohème, Bistro 7, and **Audrey Claire** (p. 108) offer three-course dinners for $35. Reservations are almost universally required. Make them directly with the participating restaurants. For more information visit **www.centercityphila.org** or **www.opentable.com**. Early February. A second restaurant week takes place in mid-September.

Chinese New Year. Lucky dragons, Mongolian dancers, and fireworks festively fill the neighborhood around 11th and Arch streets, and traditional 10-course banquets are served at Chinese restaurants. You can also visit the Chinese Cultural Center at 125 N. 10th St. Call ✆ **215/923-6767** or visit www.chinesecc.com or www.phillychinatown.com for details on the festivities. Mid- to late February.

MARCH

Philadelphia Flower Show. Held in the ever-expanding Pennsylvania Convention Center, the world's largest indoor flower show offers acres of gardens, rustic to opulent settings—and more Red Hat Society members than you can count. With the citywide institution of Flower Show Week, the show and surrounding festivities are even bigger and better than before. Go early for the freshest displays. Tickets are usually available at the door. The Pennsylvania Horticultural Society at 100 N. 20th St. sells tickets in advance. Call ✆ **800/611-5960** or 215/988-8800, or visit www.theflowershow.com for more information. Early March.

St. Patrick's Day Parade. America's second-oldest St. Pat's Day parade—since 1771—starts at noon on 20th Street and the parkway, turns on 17th Street to Chestnut Street, then goes down Chestnut Street to Independence Mall. The parkway is the most spacious vantage point, and the Irish Pub at 2007 Walnut St. will be packed. Visit www.philadelphiastpatsparade.com or call the Independence Visitor Center (✆ **610/449-4320**) for details. Sunday before March 17.

April

Philadelphia Antiques Show. Founded in 1966, this antiques show is one of the finest in the nation, with 56 major English and American exhibitors. It's held in South Philadelphia at the Navy Yard, Philadelphia Cruise Terminal at Pier One, 5100 S. Broad St. Call ✆ **215/387-3500** or visit www.phila antiques.com for more information. First half of April.

Penn Relays. Established on April 21, 1895, this 5-day track-and-field meet—the largest and oldest of its kind—attracts more than 15,000 of the country's best college, high school, and track club runners and more than 100,000 spectators to the University of Pennsylvania's Franklin Field. Call ✆ **215/898-6145** or visit www.thepennrelays.com for more information. End of April.

May

Equality Forum. Formerly known as PrideFest Philadelphia, this weeklong, citywide conference aims to unite and to celebrate the gay, lesbian, bisexual, and transgender (GLBT) community with a diverse schedule of panels, programs, and parties. For more information, visit www.equalityforum.org or call ✆ **215/732-3378.** First week of May.

Philadelphia International Children's Festival. This week of multicultural, kid-centric, art-informed events features world-class performances, hands-on crafts making, and free outdoor events, taking place on Penn's campus, based at 3680 Walnut St. Call ✆ **215/898-3900** or visit www.pennpresents.org for programs and prices. First week of May.

Rittenhouse Row Spring Festival. Everybody in the neighborhood (50,000 people) turns out for this mega block party, featuring all manner of musical performers, fashion shows, and food from nearby restaurants. Visit www.rittenhouserow.org for more information. First Saturday in May.

Dad Vail Regatta. This collegiate rowing event is one of the largest in the country, drawing more than 100 colleges and universities to the waters and banks of the Schuylkill River. You can picnic on Martin Luther King Jr. Drive near Strawberry Mansion. Call ✆ **215/542-1443** or visit www.dadvail.org for details. Second Saturday of May (and the Fri before it).

Jam on the River. Each Memorial Day weekend, crowds pack into the Festival Pier at Penn's Landing to get down with local and national blues- and jazz-inspired bands. Recent performers have included the Dirty Dozen Brass Band and the Disco Biscuits. For more information, call ✆ **215/928-8801** or visit www.jamontheriverphilly.com. Last weekend in May.

Devon Horse Show, Route 30, Devon. This 10-day riding event takes place outside of Philadelphia on the edge of the Main Line suburbs. "Devon" encompasses jumping competitions, carriage races, riding classes, and a great country fair with plenty of food stalls—from burgers to watercress sandwiches—under cheerful awnings. Visit www.thedevon horseshow.org or call ✆ **610/688-2554** for details. Late May to early June.

June

Head House Farmers' Market. Twenty-some local farmers, food vendors, and craftspeople set up shop in the covered "shambles" market along South 2nd Street between Pine and Lombard streets on Sunday from 10am to 2pm. A smaller market is held on the same spot on Saturday 10am to 2pm, too. For more information, look for Head House Farmers' Market on www.thefoodtrust.org, or call ✆ **215/575-0444.** June through late November.

Independence Dragon Boat Regatta. This relative newcomer to the lineup celebrates the ancient Chinese with an all-day competition that's part athleticism, part jubilation, wherein teams paddle to the beat of an onboard drummer. For more information, visit www.independencedragonboat.com. Early June.

USPro Cycling Championships. The 156-mile course of this country's premier 1-day cycling event starts and finishes on the parkway, following the incredible climb up the hills of Manayunk. See www.procyclingtour.com or call ✆ **610/676-0390** for more information. First or second Saturday of June.

Rittenhouse Square Fine Arts Show. Philadelphia moves outdoors with this historic, biannual event, in which hundreds of professional and student works of art go on sale in the park. Call ✆ **877/689-4112** or visit www.rittenhousesquarefineartshow.org for details. First week of June, second weekend of September.

Flag Day. This day was invented here in 1891. Festivities are held at the Betsy Ross House at 12:30pm, usually with a National Guard band and a speech. Visit www.betsyrosshouse.org or call ✆ **215/686-1252** for details. June 14.

Bloomsday. The Rosenbach Museum and the Irish Pub at 2007 Walnut St. both celebrate the 24-hour time span of James Joyce's novel *Ulysses.* Visit www.rosenbach.org or call ✆ **215/732-1600** for details. June 16.

West Oak Lane Jazz and Arts Festival. This up-and-coming celebration has turned a neighborhood street festival into a concert- and art-chocked long weekend. Recent performers include spoken-word artists, tenor saxophonist Odean Pope, and WAR. Visit www.westoaklanefestival.com or call ✆ **877/WOL-JAZZ** (965-5299) for more details. Third or fourth weekend in June.

July

Welcome America! The whole town turns out for this weeklong festival to celebrate America's birthday with theater, free entertainment, and assorted pageantry. The Fourth of July brings special ceremonies to Independence Square, including a reading of the Declaration of Independence, a presentation of the prestigious Liberty Medal (past winners include Colin Powell), and an evening parade up the parkway. Principal locations are the terrace by the Philadelphia Museum of Art, City Hall (where the world's largest hoagie is assembled), and Penn's Landing. There are fireworks at Penn's Landing July 3 and on the Ben Franklin Parkway July 4. Call ✆ **215/683-2200** or visit www.americasbirthday.com for more information. The week leading up to July 4th and July 4th.

Mann Music Center Summer Concerts. This outdoor venue in Fairmount Park offers selected free concerts through August, and cheap lawn seats for performances by the Philadelphia Orchestra and Philly Pops, plus national funk, pop, folk, classical, rock, and dance acts. Bring a picnic and a bottle of wine and enjoy music under the stars. Visit www.manncenter.org or call ✆ **215/546-7900** for a schedule. June and August.

August

Pennsylvania Dutch Festival. Reading Terminal Market (p. 101) is the venue for this weeklong festival featuring quilts, music, food, crafts, and the like. Visit www.readingterminalmarket.org or call ✆ **215/922-2317** for more information. First week of August.

Philadelphia Folk Festival. Out at Poole Farm, in Schwenksville, this family-friendly festival (which feels a lot like a camping trip) celebrates bluegrass, Irish, Cajun, klezmer, and cowboy music, as well as dancing, juggling, puppetry, and crafts. Visit www.pfs.org or call ✆ **800/566-FOLK** (3655) or 215/242-0150 for details. Usually late August.

September

Philadelphia Live Arts Festival and Philly Fringe Festival. Inspired by the cutting-edge Scottish festival of the same name, this 2-week event offers offbeat performances, experimental films, and art installations to the nooks and crannies of the Old City. Visit www.pafringe.org or call ✆ **215/413-9006** for details. Throughout the first half of September.

Philadelphia Distance Run. One of the nation's premier races, this half marathon cuts through Center City and Fairmount Park. It is more popular than the November marathon, attracting 11,000 runners who jog to the beat of more than a dozen bands along the course. Visit www.runphilly.com or call ✆ **800/311-1255** for more information. Usually the second or third Sunday of September.

Restaurant Week. See "February," above. Mid-September.

Rittenhouse Square Fine Arts Show. See "June," above.

October

Philadelphia Open Studio Tours. For 2 weekends in October, painters, sculptors, and all manner of artists open their studios to the public. The first weekend is dedicated to studios west of Broad Street (Rittenhouse Sq., art museum area); the second features studios east of Broad (Old City, Bella Vista, Queen Village, Northern Liberties). Call ✆ **215/546-7775** or go to www.philaopenstudios.org for more information. First and second weekend in October.

Columbus Day Parade. Look for a parade along the parkway plus South Philadelphia fairs. Call ✆ **215/686-3412** for details. Second Monday of October.

November

Philadelphia Museum of Art Craft Show. This preeminent exhibition and retail sale of fine American and international contemporary crafts is held at the convention center and includes works in clay, glass, fiber, jewelry, metal, and wool. Tickets are $15. Visit www.philamuseum.org or call ✆ **215/684-7930** for more information. Usually the first weekend of November.

Philadelphia Marathon. The marathon starts and finishes at the Philadelphia Museum of Art, looping through historic districts of Center City and then Fairmount Park. Call ✆ **215/683-2122** or visit www.philadelphiamarathon.com for more information. Usually the Sunday before Thanksgiving.

Thanksgiving Day Parade. This parade starts from the Philadelphia Museum of Art and travels down the Ben Franklin Parkway. It features cartoon characters, bands, floats, and Santa Claus. For more information, visit www.6abc.com. Thanksgiving Day.

House Lights of South Philly. For a kitschy Christmas experience, visit the residential squares around the 2700 blocks of South Colorado and South Smedley streets, south of Oregon Avenue, between 16th and 18th streets. The sight of dozens of houses bathed in interconnected strands of holiday lights and the sound of streaming music is impressive indeed. The lights usually go up right after Thanksgiving. Late November through end of the year.

DECEMBER

Holiday Activities Around Town. Christmas sees many activities in Center City, beginning with tree lightings in the City Hall courtyard and in Rittenhouse Square. The festivities at the Gallery at Market East include organs and choirs, as does the famous, beloved light show at Macy's. Society Hill and Germantown Christmas walking tours are lovely. Chestnut Hill shops stay open late on Wednesday in December for "Stag and Doe" nights. For more information call the **Independence Visitor Center** (✆ **610/449-4320**) or visit www.phila.gov. Throughout December.

Army-Navy Game. This biggest of military sporting events—and rivalries—ends the college football season. For years, Philadelphia has hosted the Army-Navy game—and the thousands of fans it brings. The 2009 game will be played at Lincoln Financial Field. For the 2010 location, visit www.phillylovesarmynavy.com. For tickets, army fans call ✆ **877/TIX-ARMY** (849-2769); navy fans call ✆ **800/US-4-NAVY** (874-6289). Early December.

***Nutcracker* Ballet.** The Pennsylvania Ballet performs Tchaikovsky's classic at the stunning **Academy of Music** (p. 191) at Broad and Locust streets. Visit www.paballet.org or call ✆ **215/551-7000** for details. Performances offered throughout December.

Lucia Fest. It sounds Italian, but the Lucia Fest is a Swedish pageant held by candlelight at the **American Swedish Historical Museum** (p. 140), 1900 Pattison Ave. in South Philadelphia. Call ✆ **215/389-1776** or visit www.americanswedish.org for more information. First weekend of December.

Christmas Tours of Fairmount Park. The grand city park's colonial mansions sparkle with wreaths, holly, and fruit arrangements donated by local garden clubs. Visit www.fairmountpark.org for details. Last few weeks in December.

New Year's Eve. Fireworks are held at the Great Plaza of Penn's Landing. December 31.

For an exhaustive list of events beyond those listed here, check http://events.frommers.com, where you'll find a searchable, up-to-the-minute roster of what's happening in cities all over the world.

4 GETTING THERE & GETTING AROUND

GETTING TO PHILADELPHIA

By Plane

For a list of the major airlines flying to Philadelphia, please see "Toll-Free Numbers & Websites," in the appendix.

Most flights to and from Philadelphia use **Philadelphia International Airport**—airport code **PHL**—(✆ **215/937-6937;** www.phl.org), at the southwest corner of the city. For up-to-the-minute information on airline arrival and departure times and gate assignments, call © **800/PHL-GATE** (745-4283).

By air, Philadelphia is 2½ hours from Miami or Chicago, and 6 hours from the West Coast. Some 30 carriers fly from more than 100 cities in the U.S. and 16 destinations abroad. US Airways is the "hub" tenant, and avails itself of four of these terminals. B and C are the main terminals, the end Terminal F serves commuters, and ultramodern Terminal A West (gates A14–A26) services international travelers. Terminal B is the place to catch taxis, buses, and hotel limousines. There is a shopping corridor between terminals B and C, where you can buy gifts such as books, electronic gadgets, and jewelry and even browse at Gap.

Arriving at the Airport

IMMIGRATION & CUSTOMS CLEARANCE International visitors arriving by air, no matter what the port of entry, should cultivate patience and resignation before setting foot on U.S. soil. U.S. airports have considerably beefed up security clearances in the years since the terrorist attacks of September 11, 2001, and clearing Customs and Immigration can take as long as 2 hours.

Getting into Town from the Airport

Eight miles southwest of Center City, the Philadelphia International Airport is—best-case scenario—a 15-minute drive away. Usually, however, drivers can count on a good 30 minutes (more during rush hour) via either of the major thoroughfares, I-95 or I-76.

BY CAR At the airport exit, follow signs to I-95N and I-76. After ⅘ of a mile, take the right fork to I-76W/Valley Forge. This route takes you approximately 1 mile via Penrose Avenue and the George C. Platt Memorial until you arrive at a traffic light (26th St.). Turn left. After less than 1 mile, this road becomes I-76W. Continue on 1-76W for 2½ miles. Center City will be on your right. You may access the city via exits at South Street, Market Street, or 676W for Broad Street, 8th Street (for the Pennsylvania Convention Center), or 6th Street (for Independence Visitor Center, the Liberty Bell, and Independence Hall).

Alternate Route: At the airport exit, follow signs to I-95N. Continue on I-95 for 7 miles. Exit left for 676W. Exits for Broad Street or the Ben Franklin Parkway will appear in less than 1 mile on the right.

BY TRAIN Trains arrive at Penn Station (30th St.) in West Philadelphia, just on the other side of the Schuylkill River from Center City, and about 15 blocks from City Hall. Take a taxi or SEPTA (see below) from the station to your hotel.

Each baggage claim connects to taxi, limousine, and shuttle services. The Southeastern Pennsylvania Transportation Authority (SEPTA) provides train service from terminals A to E to Center City (30th St., Suburban, and Market East stations) via the R-1 regional rail line. A one-way ticket costs $7. The train runs every 30 minutes from early morning until late night. For more information, visit www.septa.org.

By Car

For a list of the major car-rental agencies in Philadelphia, please see "Toll-Free Numbers & Websites," in the appendix.

It's not surprising that two-thirds of all visitors arrive by car: Philadelphia is some 300 miles (6 hr. or so) from Boston; 100 miles (2 hr.) from New York City; 135 miles (3 hr.) from Washington, D.C.; and 450 miles (9 hr.) from Montreal.

Philadelphia's car rentals are easiest accessed at the airport. Center City and 30th Street Station also have rental offices, but not in such concentration. Shop around online before making a booking: Rates tend to vary considerably among companies. Airlines often partner with these agencies to offer package deals, too. Opting for an economy car will give you the least-expensive rate. You can almost always choose to upgrade your car's class on-site, although you might want to avoid an upgrade if it means having to pay to fuel up a gas-guzzling sport utility vehicle (SUV). One option you might consider: a GPS navigation system, to save yourself the otherwise inevitable hassle of getting lost during your trip. Nearly any car you rent in Philadelphia will be automatic, as opposed to manual shift. A number of agencies currently require that drivers be at least 25 years old. Some accept 21-year-old drivers, and will levy a surcharge for those 21 to 24 years old.

Philadelphia is easily accessible via a series of interstate highways that circle or pass through the city. I-95 (not to be confused with the New Jersey Tpk., which goes by the same name) runs along the city's eastern edge, running north and south. The six-lane I-276 (the original Pennsylvania Tpk.) comes in from the north/northeast, connecting to the New Jersey Turnpike. The oft-congested I-76 (aka the Schuylkill Expwy.) runs east and west, snaking along the Schuylkill River into town, connecting into the heart of Center City via I-676 (aka the Vine St. Expwy.) and reconnecting I-76 to Camden, New Jersey, via the Ben Franklin Bridge over the Delaware. (Confused yet?) Connecting all of the above is I-476, "the Blue Route," which edges along western suburbs, about 15 miles west of town, linking up I-276 and I-76 at its northern end with I-95 to the south.

A few things drivers ought to know about driving in the city of Philadelphia: Most Center City streets are one-way. The large majority are paved with asphalt, but a few—Dock Street, for example—remain cobblestone or brick. Pedestrians abound, and always have the right of way. Philadelphia parking laws are no joke: Allow a parking meter to expire or leave your car in a no-parking zone, and you just might find yourself on the next episode of *Parking Wars.*

By Train

Philadelphia is a major Amtrak stop (✆ **800/USA-RAIL** [872-7245]; www.amtrak.com). Amtrak terminal **30th Street Station,** 30th and Market streets (✆ **215/349-3196;** www.philadelphia.30thstreetstation.com), is on the Boston–Washington, D.C., northeast corridor, which has extensions south to Florida, west to Pittsburgh and Chicago, and east to Atlantic City. This station also connects via SEPTA regional rail and subway (www.septa.com) to Suburban Station (16th St. and J.F.K. Blvd.) and Market East Station (12th and Filbert sts.). Suburban and Market East are located near most Center City hotels, while 30th Street Station is closest to the hotels of University City.

From New York's Penn Station, Philadelphia is a 73- to 96-minute ride away. Regular rail service—called "Regional" or "Keystone"—is 7 to 23 minutes longer than Acela Express (73-min.) service, but the price is often worth the extra minutes. Fares for the Regional and Keystone trains run from $64 to $87 weekdays; Acela trains cost from $114 to $143. (Amtrak does not offer discounts for booking

Finds A Cool New Bus

Philadelphians are always looking for the cheapest, fastest way to get to New York City. Their most recent favorite means: The **Bolt Bus,** a clean, nearly sleek coach that operates by online reservations only, guarantees a seat for each reservation, charges $10 per person, offers wireless Internet during the trip, and arrives near Penn station in 2 hours. For more information visit www.boltbus.com.

round-trip travel.) Washington, D.C., is $1^1/_2$ to 2 hours away (fares run $44–$146). The ride to/from Boston is 5 to 7 hours ($80–$206); from Chicago, it's about an 18-hour ride, with fares from $83 to $106. Rates are as of press time.

GETTING AROUND

If it's sightseeing that you aim to do—and if your body is able—I recommend self-propulsion. From Center City, there are certain spots you'll want to hop into a vehicle to get to (the Barnes, for example, or the Philadelphia Zoo) but to explore the major areas of Old City, Rittenhouse, and Society Hill, all you'll need is natural-born mobility.

Still, you might want to get the lay of the land by taking a tour, which is why I say the best way to see Philadelphia's sights is:

By Trolley & Double-Decker Bus

Philadelphia Trolley Works (aka 76 Carriage Company; ✆ **215/389-TOUR** [8687]; www.phillytour.com) operates tour buses that resemble Victorian open-air trolleys and mammoth London-style double-decker buses. Both types of vehicles circle the city daily, offering excellent, orienting tours that cost $25 for adults and $8 for children, and include unlimited off-and-on privileges for 24 hours. Trolley tours originate at the Bourse Building at 5th Street between Market and Chestnut; Big Bus tours depart from 5th and Market streets (free shuttles are available from most hotels). Both rides are 90 minutes and include 20 stops in Old City, up to the art museum.

By Tour Bus

Purple trolley-style **PHLASH Buses** (✆ **215/636-1666;** www.phillyphlash.com), are custom-made for tourists, with wide windows and drivers accustomed to answering questions. Between 10am and 6pm from May 1 to October 31 the service links Independence Park sites, the Delaware waterfront, the convention center, Rittenhouse Square shopping, the cultural institutions around Logan Square, and the Philadelphia Museum of Art. The total city loop takes 50 minutes and makes about 20 stops. A one-time pass is available on board for $2, or get an all-day unlimited-ride pass for $5 per person or $10 per family. Children 4 and under and seniors 65 and over over ride free.

By Car

Even thouzgh the sights of Philadelphia are easiest seen by tour bus or on foot, most visitors come by car—and some even traverse the city that way. Drivers unaccustomed to enduring the often laborious pace of city traffic, and those unskilled at squeezing into parallel parking spots, might want to consider parking the car in a garage and leaving it there for the duration of your stay. Nonetheless, most visitors to Philadelphia do arrive by car, so if you're behind the wheel, you're certainly not alone.

Be forewarned that *most Center City streets are one-way.* Major exceptions include East Market Street, the Benjamin Franklin Parkway, Vine Street, and Broad Street. The Convention and Visitors Bureau at the foot of the parkway offers a Center City traffic map. Traffic around City Hall runs counterclockwise, a messy, but mostly meek, light-regulated traffic circle. Speed limits in town max out around 25 mph; expressways top out at 65 mph.

South Broad Street—just south of South Street—is home to a pair of fairly priced gas stations. There's also one at 10th Street and Washington Avenue, and another at 23rd and Walnut streets. Pumps are generally self-service—except if you fuel up across the bridge in New Jersey, where state law mandates full-service only.

RENTALS If you're visiting from abroad and plan to rent a car in the United States, keep in mind that foreign driver's licenses are usually recognized in the U.S., but you should get an international one if your home license is not in English.

Check out **Breezenet.com**, which offers domestic car-rental discounts with some of the most competitive rates around. Also worth visiting are Orbitz, Hotwire.com, Travelocity, and Priceline.com, all of which offer competitive online car-rental rates. For additional car-rental agencies, see "Toll-Free Numbers & Websites," in the appendix.

Philadelphia has no shortage of rental cars. Most major renters maintain offices at the airport. **Avis** (✆ 215/386-6426; www.avis.com), **Budget** (✆ 215/222-4262; www.budget.com), **Hertz** (✆ 215/492-2958; www.hertz.com), and **National** (✆ 215/387-9077; www.nationalcar.com) also have offices at the Amtrak 30th Street Station and elsewhere in Center City. Rates are competitive, averaging around $60 per day.

On top of the standard rental prices, other optional charges apply to most car rentals, including liability insurance (if you harm others in an accident), personal accident insurance (if you harm yourself or your passengers), and personal effects insurance (if your luggage is stolen from your car). If your own insurance or credit card company doesn't cover you for rentals, you should consider the additional coverages. But weigh the likelihood of getting into an accident or losing your luggage against the cost of these coverages (as much as $20 per day combined), which can significantly add to the price of your rental.

PARKING The streets of Philadelphia offer mostly metered, and very limited, free 1- or 2-hour parallel spots. Read parking signs carefully, as thoroughfares such as Walnut Street turn into tow-away zones during rush hour. Parking tickets start at $26, and are issued by the oft-harried employees of the **Philadelphia Parking Authority,** an agency accessible, for those so inclined, at ✆ **215/683-9600** or www.philapark.org. Garages are increasingly common (thanks to increasingly common demolitions of historic buildings). Their rates are fairly uniform: Outside of hotels, few places exceed $25 per day, with typical charges of $5 per hour and $12 for an evening out.

Few city blocks lack a parking garage or lot. The closest-possible parking for Independence Mall and Park is underneath the **Independence Visitor Center** between 5th and 6th streets and Market and Arch streets. The **convention center** area teems with garages. The closest parking facilities for **City Hall** are underneath Macy's (formerly John Wanamaker's), between Market and Chestnut streets at 13th Street.

CAR SHARING A newer way to drive around town or to take a day trip is by joining a car share program that allows members (who pay an annual fee) to check out cars that are already parked around the city. Zipcar is a national service with cars in Philadelphia (✆ **866/4-ZIPCAR** [494-7227]; www.zipcar.com). Philly Car Share (✆ **215/730-0988;** www.phillycarshare.org) is a locally based car share, with the most shareable cars in the city. Members of either service reserve the car they want for a determined amount of time online or by phone, then pay an hourly or daily fee, which includes gas and insurance.

BY TAXI

As of press time, taxi fares are $2.70 for the first 1/7 mile and 30¢ for each additional 1/7 mile or minute of the motor running, with a 50¢ fuel surcharge. Tips are expected, usually 20% of the fare. Count on spending a total of $10 for a crosstown trip. Although all city cabs are outfitted with credit card machines, drivers often try to discourage passengers from using them to pay. Even in cabs, cash is king.

If you need to call for a cab while in the city, two good operators are **Olde City Taxi** (✆ **215/338-0838**) and **Quaker City** (✆ **215/728-8000**).

Tips **Ride Cheap**

A $6 1-day Convenience Pass is valid for eight rides on any SEPTA bus, subway, or trolley (but not regional rail). A weekly TransPass, good from Monday through the next Sunday, is $21.

BY PUBLIC TRANSPORTATION

SEPTA (Southeastern Pennsylvania Transportation Authority) operates a complicated and extensive network of trolleys, buses, and subways. Ridership has increased since Center City has encouraged less auto traffic on historic streets, so it's crowded but safe. Center City's main stations are Market East (11th and Market sts.), Suburban Station (16th St. and J.F.K. Blvd.), and 30th Street (also the Amtrak station).

Fares for any SEPTA bus, trolley, or subway route are $2 cash or $1.45 with a token purchased before you ride (at stations, supermarkets, Rite Aid pharmacies, sidewalk newsstands, check-cashing centers, and machines in various city concourses). Transfers are 75¢, and exact change is required. Seniors pay only during rush hours, and passengers with disabilities pay half-fare during off-peak hours. Certain "Night Owl" buses and trolleys run 24 hours a day.

If you have questions about how to reach a specific destination, check SEPTA's website at www.septa.org. You can also call ✆ **215/580-7800** between 6am and midnight, but expect to wait.

BY SUBWAY & TROLLEY The two main rapid-transit subways are the Broad Street line and the Market-Frankford elevated line, the El. Both lines meet beneath City Hall, at 15th and Market streets. The Broad Street line (look for orange signs) runs north-south, down to and up from the sports stadiums of Pattison Avenue, with stops in Center City to Temple University and North Philadelphia's Fern Rock. The Market-Frankford El (look for blue signs) runs east-west, to and from Northeast Philadelphia's Frankford Transportation Center to Northern Liberties and Market Street in Old City, with stops at 2nd, 5th, 8th, 11th, 13th (convention center), 15th, and 30th Street stations, through University City to 69th Street Station. Local trolleys are a bit more difficult to navigate, but generally connect City Hall and 30th Street Station, with stops on Market Street at 19th and 22nd streets, and, after 30th Street Station, branching out, moving aboveground beyond the University of Pennsylvania to the north and south.

BY PATCO This Center City–to–South Jersey commuter rail line (✆ **215/922-4600** or 856/772-6900; www.ridepatco.org) begins at 15th and Locust streets with a few stops before crossing the Ben Franklin Bridge into Camden, Collingswood, and Lindenwold in New Jersey. To reach Camden's Adventure Aquarium or Tweeter Center, transfer at Broadway in Camden to the New Jersey Transit's Aqualink Shuttle. Transfer at Lindenwold to New Jersey Transit's rail line to Atlantic City. Operated by the port authority, these lines do not accept SEPTA tokens or tickets. Buy destination-based tickets ($1.25–$2.70) inside stations.

BY BUS SEPTA's buses crisscross the city in every direction. Boldly board one headed your way; just be sure to ask the driver if it's going in your direction before you drop your token into the machine. South Street offers an easy west-to-east route, while Walnut and Lombard streets are good bets for going east to west. Most numbered streets offer one-way routes north or south. All accept exact change or tokens and sell transfers.

BY REGIONAL RAIL (TRAIN) SEPTA's commuter-rail network is one of the best in America, with regional trains that often provide easier and quicker access to city and suburban destinations from early morning to late night. If you're planning on visiting the wealthy, walkable enclave of Chestnut Hill, take either of two regional rail lines (R7 or R8). Visitors to the affluent Main Line suburbs, home to noted colleges Bryn Mawr and Haverford and Villanova University; Devon's famed horse show and country fair in late spring; and, until it moves, the Barnes Foundation in Merion should take the R5. One-way fares for all destinations start at $3.50, and you can buy tickets at station counters or vending machines. Check www.septa.org for fare and schedule information.

5 MONEY & COSTS

Except for truly deluxe experiences (and for cab fares), you will find moderate prices in Philadelphia: less than those in New York and on a par with those in Boston or Washington, D.C.

Credit cards are widely accepted. Notable cash-only exceptions include mom-and-pop BYOB restaurants, famously casual cheesesteak stands, and, in many cases, taxis.

Automated teller machines or "ATMs" (or, in Philadelphia "MAC" machines) linked to national networks are strewn around the airport, tourist destinations, major streets, outside banks, and increasingly within hotels and bars. Fee-free machines can be found in Wawa convenience stores. Be sure you know your personal identification number (PIN) and daily withdrawal limit before you depart from home.

Note: Remember that many banks impose a fee every time you use a card at another bank's ATM, and that fee can be higher for international transactions (up to $5 or more) than for domestic ones (where they're rarely more than $2). In addition, the bank from which you withdraw cash may charge its own fee.

Credit cards are the most widely used form of payment in the United States: **Visa** (Barclaycard in Britain), **MasterCard** (Eurocard in Europe, Access in Britain, Chargex in Canada), **American Express, Diners Club,** and **Discover.** You can withdraw cash advances from your credit cards at banks or ATMs, provided you know your PIN.

Visitors from outside the U.S. should inquire whether their bank assesses a 1% to 3% fee on charges incurred abroad.

It's highly recommended that you travel with at least one major credit card. You must have one to rent a car, and hotels and airlines usually require a credit card imprint as a deposit against expenses.

Debit cards, major ATM cards with credit card backing, are widely accepted in stores and restaurants, and offer the added bonus of receiving "cash back" with a purchase. Both credit and debit cards provide a convenient record of all your expenses, and they generally offer relatively good exchange rates.

Traveler's checks are widely accepted in Philadelphia's larger hotels, restaurants, and shops. Still, foreign visitors should make sure that the checks are denominated in U.S. dollars; foreign-currency checks are difficult to exchange.

What Things Cost in Philadelphia	US$	UK£
A cup of coffee from La Colombe	1.50	0.87
Subway, bus, or trolley fare	2.00	1.11
A pint of Yards ale at Standard Tap	5.00	3.25
Cheesesteak "wid" or "widout" onions at Pat's	7.50	4.34
Admission to the Philadelphia Museum of Art	14.00	7.78
Taxi ride from airport to Center City	26.25	17.05
Train ride from airport to Center City	5.50	3.06
Dinner for two at Ralph's Italian Restaurant	59.00	38.31
Average hotel room rate, 1 night (before tax)	138.00	89.61

6 SAFETY

STAYING SAFE

Philadelphia's Center City (bordered by the Delaware and Schuylkill rivers from east to west, and from South St. to Spring Garden St. from south to north) is quite safe, especially in the high-traffic areas of Old City and along Walnut Street and Rittenhouse Square.

Still, it is a city: Be aware of others around you; keep handbags zipped and secured; don't leave laptops unattended; when in a cafe, bar, shop, or museum, do not leave your belongings on the ground or unattended. Pay attention to your surroundings, especially after dark on quiet streets, and in emerging neighborhoods such as Graduate Hospital, Northern Liberties, and the Italian Market area. If it's late, spring for a cab—or, at least, don't walk alone. Please, please don't walk by yourself at night talking on a cellphone or listening to an iPod.

Crime tends to increase in times of economic strife, and petty crimes increase at the year's end. On a (somewhat) more positive note: The city's whopping homicide rate is generally not because of the untimely departures of out-of-towners. (But you might want to hedge your bets by not wearing a Dallas Cowboys football jersey or a New York Mets baseball cap.)

The age to purchase and drink alcohol is 21, a law relatively strictly enforced throughout the city. Marijuana and all narcotics are illegal. The minimum age to buy and to smoke cigarettes is 18, a rule not as strictly enforced as the previous two.

7 SPECIALIZED TRAVEL RESOURCES

TRAVELERS WITH DISABILITIES

Most disabilities shouldn't stop anyone from traveling in the U.S. Thanks to provisions in the Americans with Disabilities Act, most public places are required to comply with disability-friendly regulations. Almost all public establishments (including hotels, restaurants, museums, and so on, but not including certain National Historic Landmarks), and at least some modes of public transportation provide accessible entrances and other facilities for those with disabilities.

For basic Philadelphia information, contact the **Mayor's Commission on People with Disabilities,** Municipal Services Building, Room 900, 1401 J.F.K. Blvd., Philadelphia, PA 19107 (✆ **215/686-2798**), or see the excellent website at www.phila.gov/mcpd. SEPTA (the local transit authority) arranges special transportation for people with disabilities through the Customized Community Transportation Program; offices are open weekdays until 4pm, at 1234 Market St., 4th floor, Philadelphia, PA 19107 (✆ **215/580-7145**). SEPTA buses are lift equipped. Market East and University City subway stations are wheelchair accessible, but many stations are not. Art-Reach maintains "Access the Arts: A Guide for People with Disabilities," online at **www.art-reach.org**, with listings for more than 140 area facilities; for more information, call ✆ **215/568-2115.** The Philadelphia airport's website, **www.phl.org**, also publishes a guide for travelers with disabilities—ADA services include 31 TDD telephones, elevators and escalators, Braille ATMs, curb cuts, and wheelchair-accessible shuttle buses. The airport hot line for travelers with disabilities is ✆ **215/937-6700** (TDD ✆ 215/937-6755).

Travelers with disabilities will find tourist areas accessible. All Center City curbs are cut at intersections. Nonetheless, some streets in Society Hill and around Independence National Historical Park have uneven brick sidewalks, and Dock Street is paved with rough cobblestones.

Parking can be tough, however, as handicapped parking spots—marked with blue meters—are in high demand. The Independence Visitor Center has a level entrance and publishes *Accessibilities,* a brochure detailing all parking sites.

Virtually all theaters and stadiums accommodate wheelchairs. Call ahead to plan routes. To aid people with hearing impairments, the Kimmel Center and Academy of Music provide free infrared headsets for concerts; the Annenberg Center rents them for $2.

The Free Library of Philadelphia runs a **Library for the Blind and Physically Handicapped,** very conveniently located at 919 Walnut St. (✆ **215/683-3213;** http://lbph.library.phila.gov); it's open Monday through Friday from 9am to 5pm. It adjoins the **Associated Services for the Blind,** which offers transcriptions into Braille for a fee.

The **America the Beautiful—National Park and Federal Recreational Lands Pass—Access Pass** (formerly the **Golden Access Passport**) gives visually impaired or permanently disabled persons (regardless of age) free lifetime entrance to federal recreation sites administered by the National Park Service, including the Fish and Wildlife Service, the Forest Service, the Bureau of Land Management, and the Bureau of Reclamation. This may include national parks, monuments, historic sites, recreation areas, and national wildlife refuges.

For more on organizations that offer resources to travelers with disabilities, go to www.frommers.com/planning.

GAY & LESBIAN TRAVELERS

Center City is welcoming to gay, lesbian, bisexual, and transgender (GLBT) residents and visitors, and even has a marketing campaign called "Get your History Straight and your Nightlife Gay" at www.gophila.com. The neighborhood known best for its GLBT residents is Washington West, also affectionately known as the "Gayborhood." Its borders are 9th and Juniper streets and Walnut and South streets. Go there for especially GLBT-friendly restaurants, bookstores, clubs, shops, and social services. See p. 208 for specific clubs and bars.

You can also check the weekly *Philadelphia Gay News* (www.epgn.com), which is widely available. The lesbian-oriented *Labyrinth* is available free at **Giovanni's Room,** a popular gay bookstore at 345 S.

12th St. (✆ **215/923-2960;** www.giovannis room.com), that also serves as a national resource for publications produced by and for gays and lesbians, as well as for feminist and progressive literature. The neighborhood's two great workout facilities are the no-nonsense **Twelfth Street Gym** at 204 S. 12th St. (✆ **215/985-4092;** www.12streetgym.com) and popular boutique cross-training class center **Fusion** at the corner of 12th and Sansom streets, mezzanine level (✆ **215/733-0633;** www.fusioncrosstraining.com).

Outside the city (see chapter 11), the village of New Hope is a popular destination for gay and lesbian travelers.

For meetings, gallery exhibitions, and social events, consult the **William Way Community Center,** 1315 Spruce St. (✆ **215/735-2220;** www.plgtf.org).

To report antigay violence or discrimination, call the **Philadelphia Lesbian and Gay Task Force Hot Line** (✆ **215/772-2000;** www.plgtf.org).

For more gay and lesbian travel resources visit www.frommers.com/planning.

SENIOR TRAVELERS

With its compact downtown and widely available senior discounts, Philadelphia is a popular city among seniors. Most museums, movies, and attractions offer discounts, as do some hotels. The Independence Visitor Center publishes "Seniors on the Go," which lists dozens of specific senior benefits and discounts around town. Seniors should bring photo ID.

Mention the fact that you're a senior when you make your travel reservations. Major U.S. airlines except America West have canceled their senior discount and coupon book programs, but many hotels still offer discounts for seniors. In Philadelphia, people over the age of 60 qualify for reduced admission to theaters, museums, and other attractions, as well as discounted fares on public transportation.

The U.S. National Park Service offers an **America the Beautiful—National Park and Federal Recreational Lands Pass—Senior Pass** (formerly the **Golden Age Passport**), which gives seniors 62 years or older lifetime entrance to all properties administered by the National Park Service (NPS)—national parks, monuments, historic sites, recreation areas, and national wildlife refuges—for a one-time processing fee of $10. The pass must be purchased in person at any NPS facility that charges an entrance fee. Besides free entry, the America the Beautiful Senior Pass also offers a 50% discount on some federal-use fees charged for such facilities as camping, swimming, parking, boat launching, and tours. For more information, go to www.nps.gov/fees_passes.htm or call the United States Geological Survey (USGS), which issues the passes, at ✆ **888/275-8747.**

For more information and resources on travel for seniors, see www.frommers.com/planning.

TRAVELING AS A FAMILY

Philadelphia is a wonderful destination for families, with its accessible layout and historical sites that are meaningful to all ages. From the kid-friendly **Please Touch Museum** (p. 143; recently relocated to a spectacular and huge new home) to **Sesame Place amusement park** (p. 214) to the "Once Upon a Nation" characters dressed in Colonial-era garb who, in summertime, perform throughout **Independence National Historical Park** (p. 118), there is a wealth of attractions for children. See "Especially for Kids," in chapter 7 or visit www.gophila.com/family for some excellent packages and ideas.

Children 11 and under (and in many cases, 17 and under) can stay free with parents in most Philadelphia hotels, and some hotels offer one-bedroom/pull-out-sofa suites geared toward families that can be more affordable than booking two rooms. Several hotels offer free breakfasts and even dinners to kids. A couple of our favorites: **Loews Philadelphia** (p. 68) and the **Four Seasons Hotel** (p. 72). (See "Family-Friendly Hotels," in chapter 5.) Be sure to reserve cribs, playpens, and cots in advance.

Many of Philadelphia's finest restaurants, such as **Fountain** at the Four Seasons (p. 95) and **Lacroix** (p. 95), are happy to accommodate children, and there are dozens of casual restaurants where kids and parents can all dine well. See "Family-Friendly Restaurants," in chapter 6.

A good resource for family travel in Philadelphia is *Metrokids,* a newspaper that lists cultural attractions geared toward families, along with special issues devoted to factory tours, Camden's **Adventure Aquarium** (p. 146), and the like. Visit www.metrokids.com for more information.

Children will love visiting **Sesame Place** (p. 214), **Washington Crossing Historic Park** (p. 216), **Hersheypark** (p. 241), and **Amish Country** (p. 229). These destinations are a wonderful mix of history and pure fun (and chocolate, of course, in Hershey) that conjure up a past or different way of life, and basic American themes such as freedom and independence.

To locate accommodations, restaurants, and attractions that are particularly kid friendly, refer to the "Kids" icon throughout this guide.

For a list of more family-friendly travel resources, visit www.frommers.com/planning.

STUDENT TRAVELERS

There are more colleges and universities in and around Philadelphia than in any other city in the country, so students will find a warm reception from area vendors and attractions. A valid student ID will get you reduced rates on cultural sites, accommodations, car rentals, and more. You'll also get a deep discount at **Apple Hostel** (formerly Bank Street Hostel), 32 S. Bank St. (✆ **877/275-1971**), right in the center of all of Old City nightlife and, oh yes, history.

When in Philadelphia, pick up a copy of student papers such as the *Daily Pennsylvanian* (www.dailypennsylvanian.com) at the Ivy League **University of Pennsylvania,** 34th and Walnut streets (✆ **215/898-5000;** www.upenn.edu); the *Temple News* (www.temple-news.com) at **Temple University,** North Broad Street (✆ **215/204-7000;** www.temple.edu); or the *Triangle* (www.thetriangle.org) at **Drexel University,** 32nd and Chestnut streets (✆ **215/895-2000;** www.drexel.edu).

Check out the **International Student Travel Confederation (ISTC;** www.istc.org) website for comprehensive travel services information and details on how to get an **International Student Identity Card (ISIC),** which qualifies students for substantial savings on rail passes, plane tickets, entrance fees, and more. It also provides students with basic health and life insurance and a 24-hour help line. The card is valid for a maximum of 18 months. You can apply for the card online or in person at **STA Travel** (✆ **800/781-4040** in North America or 132-782 in Australia, or 0871-2-300-040 in the U.K.; www.statravel.com), the biggest student travel agency in the world; check out the website to locate STA Travel offices worldwide. If you're no longer a student but are still under 26, you can get an **International Youth Travel Card (IYTC)** from the same people, which entitles you to some discounts. **Travel CUTS** (✆ **800/592-2887;** www.travelcuts.com) offers similar services for both Canadians and U.S. residents. Irish students may prefer to turn to **USIT** (✆ **01/602-1904;** www.usit.ie), an Ireland-based specialist in student, youth, and independent travel.

SINGLE TRAVELERS

Partner-free visitors to Philadelphia need not be lonely. Cafe culture abounds, and all manner of Philadelphians are more than willing to offer advice on where to go to meet the best people. For more solid planning, check out the Philly portion of www.singlesevents.com to find out where singles are horseback riding, networking, gallery hopping, and partying.

For more information on traveling single, go to www.frommers.com/planning.

8 SUSTAINABLE TOURISM

Sustainable tourism is conscientious travel. It means being careful with the environments you explore, and respecting the communities you visit. Two overlapping components of sustainable travel are **eco-tourism** and **ethical tourism.** The **International Ecotourism Society** (TIES) defines eco-tourism as responsible travel to natural areas that conserves the environment and improves the well-being of local people. TIES suggests that eco-tourists follow these principles:

- Minimize environmental impact.
- Build environmental and cultural awareness and respect.
- Provide positive experiences for both visitors and hosts.
- Provide direct financial benefits for conservation and for local people.
- Raise sensitivity to host countries' political, environmental, and social climates.
- Support international human rights and labor agreements.

You can find some eco-friendly travel tips and statistics, as well as touring companies and associations—listed by destination under "Travel Choice"—at the **TIES** website, www.ecotourism.org. Also check out **Ecotravel.com**, which lets you search for sustainable touring companies in several categories (water based, land based, spiritually oriented, and so on).

While much of the focus of eco-tourism is about reducing impacts on the natural environment, ethical tourism concentrates on ways to preserve and enhance local economies and communities, regardless of location. You can embrace ethical tourism by staying at a locally owned hotel or shopping at a store that employs local workers and sells locally produced goods.

Responsible Travel (www.responsibletravel.com) is a great source of sustainable travel ideas; the site is run by a spokesperson for ethical tourism in the travel industry. **Sustainable Travel International** (www.sustainabletravelinternational.org) promotes ethical tourism practices, and manages an extensive directory of sustainable properties and tour operators around the world.

In the U.K., **Tourism Concern** (www.tourismconcern.org.uk) works to reduce social and environmental problems connected to tourism. The **Association of Independent Tour Operators (AITO;** www.aito.co.uk) is a group of specialist operators leading the field in making holidays sustainable.

Volunteer travel has become increasingly popular among those who want to venture beyond the standard group-tour experience to learn languages, interact with locals, and make a positive difference while on vacation. Volunteer travel usually doesn't require special skills—just a willingness to work hard—and programs vary in length from a few days to a number of weeks. Some programs provide free housing and food, but many require volunteers to pay for travel expenses, which can add up quickly.

For general info on volunteer travel, visit **www.volunteerabroad.org** and **www.idealist.org**. Specific volunteer options in Philadelphia are listed under "Special-Interest Trips," below.

Before you commit to a volunteer program, it's important to make sure any money you're giving is truly going back to the local community, and that the work you'll be doing will be a good fit for you. **Volunteer International** (www.volunteerinternational.org) has a helpful list of questions to ask to determine the intentions and the nature of a volunteer program.

Animal-Rights Issues

For information on animal-friendly issues throughout the world, visit the **Tread Lightly** website at www.treadlightly.org.

9 SPECIAL-INTEREST TRIPS

ACADEMIC TRIPS & LANGUAGE CLASSES

For a truly inspiring look into how art can transform lives, join up with a tour of the world-renowned **Mural Arts Program ★★★**, 1727–29 Mt. Vernon St. (✆ **215/685-0750;** www.muralarts.org). Philadelphia has more public murals than any other U.S. city; each painted wall is part of a community-building, city-beautification program whose core belief is that people and neighborhoods can change for the better—one paintbrush, one child, one artist at a time. Trolley and bike tours are led by volunteers; mural artists lead special hands-on tours that allow participants to paint part of the artwork.

Every Saturday morning, rain or shine, quirky, prolific, delightful, tile-mosaic artist **Isaiah Zagar** leads a group of students in the blissful art of breaking tile, cutting mirror, gluing bits, and grouting in his weekend-long workshops that begin with a blank wall and end with a most unique art installation. All workshops meet at his one-of-a-kind, work-in-progress **Magic Garden ★**, 1020 South St. (✆ **215/733-0390;** www.phillymagicgardens.org).

The **Philadelphia Museum of Art (PMA;** p. 128) offers daylong workshops on artistic endeavors as diverse as preserving your own art collection to creating handmade books to the art of *Sunkaraku,* the Japanese tea ceremony; and, the PMA's exhibit-tailored lectures are not to be missed. Bella Vista find **Fleisher Art Memorial ★★**, 719 Catharine St. (✆ **215/922-3456;** www.fleisher.org) employs well-respected Philadelphia artists to teach tuition-free fine arts and art-history classes and (modest-tuition-bearing) workshops, such as digital photography, drawing composition, silk-screen, portrait painting, pottery, and more in a studio setting.

The **French Alliance of Philadelphia,** 1420 Walnut St., Ste. 700 (✆ 215/735-5283; www.afphila.com); the **America-Italia Society of Philadelphia,** 1420 Walnut St., Ste. 310 (✆ 215/735-3250; www.america-italysociety.com); **Spanish Language School,** 2004 Sansom St. (✆ 215/567-4446; www.tsls.net); and the **German Society of Pennsylvania,** 611 Spring Garden St. (✆ 215/627-5297; www.germansociety.org), all offer 1-day to longer-term language immersion courses to review the pronunciation, grammar, and vocabulary that you don't remember from high school.

ADVENTURE & WELLNESS TRIPS

The **Philadelphia Bicycle Coalition ★★** (www.bicyclecoalition.org) serves as a hub for all manner of cycling clubs and events. By joining up with the Philadelphia Mountain Biking Association, you will find built-in tour guides for a trek through Fairmount Park; connecting with, for example, the Central Bucks club might lead you to a covered bridges ride.

A relatively new option for discovering Center City is a guided tour by bike or moped—in season only. **Philadelphia Bike and Moped Tours** ★ (✆ 215/514-3124 or 334-0790; www.philadelphiabike-tour.com) start at the Atwater Kent Museum (p. 141), and smartly stop off at sites that are just a bit too out-of-the-way to walk to easily, such as the Eastern State Penitentiary (p. 141), the Edgar Allan Poe National Historic Site (p. 138), and the Independence Seaport Museum (p. 141). The service also offers half- and full-day bike and moped rentals, for DIY riders.

Those who prefer their touring high-tech ought to sign up for an **I Glide Tour** ★ of the art museum district (✆ 877-GLIDE-81 [454-3381] or 215/735-1700; www.iglidetours.com). Participants learn the basics of operating a Segway Human Transporter, pop on a wireless headset, and follow a guide along the edges of Eakins Oval and Fairmount Park. Daytime and evening tours are available.

Greater Philadelphia Gardens ★★ (www.greaterphiladelphiagardens.org) is a clearinghouse of sorts for wildflower walks, private garden tours, and horticultural workshops. Thirty of the area's most famous gardens, such as Bartram's Gardens (p. 149), Arboretum at the Barnes Foundation (p. 126), Shofuso Japanese House & Garden, and even the Philadelphia Zoo (p. 145) participate.

Spas to spend the day in include the serene and elegant **Rescue Rittenhouse Spa Lounge** ★★★, 255 S. 17th St., 2nd Floor (✆ 215/772-2766; www.rescuerit-tenhousespa.com), home to the best facials, waxing, and nail care in the city, and **Juju Spa & Organics** ★★, 728 S. 4th St. (✆ 215/922-3235; www.jujusalon.com), a jewel-box oasis for truly holistic massages and wraps and all-natural mani-pedis. For an overnight spa experience, tap the in-house retreats at the note-perfect **Four Seasons Hotel** (p. 72), where the products are absolutely top of the line, or the Rittenhouse Hotel's (p. 74) Aveda day spa **Adolf Biecker** for fabulous body treatments and sublime facials.

FOOD & WINE TRIPS

There are two great options for exploring the rough-hewn culinary delights of the Italian Market. One is Morello's **Italian Market Tour** ★ (✆ **215/334-6008;** www.italianmarkettour.com), a Friday morning group tour led by historian, criminologist, and author of *Italian Market Cookbook,* Celeste A. Morello. Morello's received major press for her vast knowledge of the food and culture of this area, and can easily talk and walk about and around the market for 5 hours. The other Italian Market tour is led by loveable chef Louise Cianfero Simpson, author of *Italian Food and Folklore.* Her **Philadelphia Food Tasting Tour of the Italian Market** ★ can be booked through Philly Tours at www.phillytours.com, or by calling ✆ **215/772-0739.** These tours are a bit more flexible: They require only four participants and take place, weather permitting, March through July and September through December.

Note: Rumor has it that these two tour guides have been at odds for years. At one point, the discord was enough to inspire butcher Sonny D'Angelo to cross out their names on the newspaper clippings displayed on his walls. Apparently, neither guide wanted to be displayed alongside the other.

Inspired by the "fermentation trio" of wine, cheese, and beer, popular Tria café (p. 208) founded **Tria Fermentation School** ★ at 1601 Walnut St. (the Medical Arts Building), Ste. 620 (✆ **215/972-7076;** www.triacafe.com), a great place to spend a few hours learning about at least one-third of the trio. Local brewers, international vintners, expert fromagers, and industry pros lead affordable classes on all manner of transformed grains, grapes, and milks.

Old City kitchen and shelter shop **Foster's Homeware** ★★, 399 Market St.

(✆ **215/925-0950;** www.shopfosters.com), has a state-of-the-art demonstration kitchen that looks straight out of the Food Network. Saturday afternoons there are free cooking demos with local and international chefs. Classes worth paying for include culinary basics such as knife skills, stocks and sauces, and baking, or advanced lessons in global fare such as Latin tapas, Asian fusion, and pasta making—all taught by well-regarded local chefs.

VOLUNTEER & WORKING TRIPS

Habitat for Humanity ★★, 1829 N. 19th St. (✆ **215/765-6000;** www.habitatphiladelphia.org), has developed a strong presence in the city—so much so that individual volunteers should sign up months ahead to build LEED-certified green homes or renovate traditional Philadelphia row homes. Habitat helpers must be at least 16 years of age. Groups of 3 to 10 are asked to raise $2,500 to cover the costs of a group build day.

Greater Philadelphia Cares ★ (✆ **215/564-4544;** www.philacares.org) is a wonderful citywide clearinghouse of all manner of volunteer opportunities. Go to their website and search by cause or date to find activities such as greening the city's parks and public spaces with the Pennsylvania Horticultural Society, tutoring with after-school programs, serving lunch at shelters, preparing a barn for an inner-city horseback riding program, and feeding people living with HIV/AIDS. There are experiences for all ages and abilities, with more than 100 jobs listed per month.

The **White Dog Café** ★, 3420 Sansom St. (✆ **215/386-9224;** www.whitedogcafe.com), is another center of community-minded efforts. Founded by a VISTA (Volunteers in Service to America) volunteer, the cafe is the local version of Alice Waters' Chez Panisse. The White Dog sponsors various service days that include learning about the city's newest murals, participating in a forum of community organizers, or helping out with a farm-to-city initiative. A modest fee for participation includes a locavore-inspired meal from the cafe.

10 STAYING CONNECTED

TELEPHONES

Phoning to a location within or around Philadelphia requires dialing (or, more likely pushing) 10 digits. The local area codes are 215, 267, and 610. To call a location outside these area codes but inside the U.S., you must first dial (or push) a 1, then the three-digit area code, then the seven-digit phone number. Calling internationally requires dialing (again, pushing) 011 + country code + city code + telephone number.

Coin- or credit card–operated pay phones are increasingly scarce. The best places to find them are train or bus stations, or outside convenience stores. To phone from a hotel room, follow the instructions affixed to the telephone—you'll likely be asked to dial/push a 9 first, and you'll likely see a somewhat immodest per-call surcharge tacked onto your bill.

Prepaid phone cards are readily available at convenience stores, Target stores, and phone stores.

CELLPHONES

AT&T, Sprint, Verizon, and T-Mobile are the largest cellphone network providers. Sign up with any of these companies, and you can count on decent reception throughout the city.

Philadelphia International Airport has three **Airport Wireless** stores (www.airportwireless.com) that sell mobile phones,

Palms, PDAs, laptops, and accessories. Find them in Terminal B (✆ 215/937-1065), C (✆ 215/937-9620), and A-West (✆ 215/365-2755). One of the nation's largest cellphone rental companies is based in Center City. **AllCell,** 1528 Walnut St. (✆ 877/724-CELL [2355] or 215/985-CELL [2355]; www.allcellrentals.com), rents standard cellphones, satellite phones, pagers, and two-way pagers by the day, week, or month.

If you're not from the U.S., you'll be appalled at the poor reach of the **GSM (Global System for Mobile Communications) wireless network,** which is used by much of the rest of the world. Your phone will probably work in most major U.S. cities; it definitely won't work in many rural areas. To see where GSM phones work in the U.S., check out www.t-mobile.com/coverage. And you may or may not be able to send SMS (text messaging) home.

VOICE-OVER INTERNET PROTOCOL (VOIP)

If you have Web access while traveling, consider a broadband-based telephone service (in technical terms, **Voice-over Internet Protocol,** or **VoIP**) such as Skype (www.skype.com) or Vonage (www.vonage.com), which allows you to make free international calls from your laptop or in a cybercafe. Neither service requires the people you're calling to also have that service (though there are fees if they do not). Check the websites for details.

INTERNET & E-MAIL

With Your Own Computer

It's hard to go anywhere in Center City and *not* be able to pick up a free Wi-Fi signal. Still, the surest places to find sanctioned wireless are independently owned coffee shops, which pretty much have to provide the service in order to stay in business. Starbucks offers free wireless Internet access to members of its frequent buyers' club—ask for a card to join.

Hotels are increasingly offering free Internet, although there are some holdouts that charge a daily or hourly fee for the service, via DSL or wireless.

At Philadelphia International Airport, Wi-Fi is free to everyone on weekends, and available for a fee of $7.95 for 24 hours, or $40 a month on weekdays. College students can obtain free wireless access anytime by presenting student ID to an airport information counter.

Without Your Own Computer

Most major airports have **Internet kiosks** that provide basic Web access for a per-minute fee that's usually higher than cybercafe prices. Check out copy shops like **FedEx Kinko's,** which offer computer stations with fully loaded software (as well as Wi-Fi). Branches of the **Free Library of Philadelphia** (✆ **215/686-5322;** www.freelibrary.org) also offer workstations with Internet access.

For help locating cybercafes and other establishments where you can go for Internet access, please see "Internet Access," in the appendix.

Suggested Philadelphia Itineraries

by Lauren McCutcheon

There are certain things you have to do in Philadelphia, regardless of how long you're staying. You have to visit Independence Hall and the Liberty Bell. Spins through Betsy Ross's and Ben Franklin's homes are also list toppers, as are whirls through the National Constitution Center, Franklin Institute, or Barnes Foundation (depending on what you're interested in).

But there's one activity you probably feel you must fit in, no matter what your age, gender, ethnicity, creed, or otherwise: You must eat a cheesesteak.

No worries: I've got you covered. Read on for tips on how to plan 1-, 2-, and 3-day visits. Remember: Philadelphia is a walking city. Wear comfy shoes, and take advantage of park benches for breaks. Oh, and bring your appetite.

Unless otherwise indicated, see chapter 7 for descriptions of the recommended attractions and activities.

1 THE BEST OF PHILADELPHIA IN 1 DAY

If you're the kind of person who can't get through the morning without a cup of joe, then stop by any one of the city's amazing coffee shops (p. 116) for your morning fuel. If, on the other hand, breakfast is your mainstay, stop by the **Reading Terminal Market** (p. 101) for a sit-down meal (and brief tour of one of Philadelphia's most vibrant landmarks). Once you're done, head to your jumping-off point. ***Start:*** *Independence Visitor Center, 6th and Market.*

1 Independence Visitor Center

Open from 8:30am, this is where you can park, pick up your tickets to Independence Hall, and get oriented for the day ahead. Need a map? A tricorn hat? A bathroom break? This is the place to take care of business before you head across the street to the Liberty Bell and Independence Hall. See p. 119.

2 Independence Hall ★★★

You're smart if you've come to this place first thing in the morning. (Smarter if you've reserved your tickets in advance.) As the day gets underway, the line for tours (held every 20 min.) can get quite long. Your visit to the original seat of the U.S. government will tell of the birth of the country's founding documents: the Declaration of Independence and the U.S. Constitution. Remember, if you remain within the fenced area around the hall, you won't have to go through another security screening when you go to your next stop. See p. 122.

3 The Liberty Bell ★★★

Depending on your interest level, you can either spend some quality time in the modern house of this historic symbol—or you could zip on through in 15 to 20 minutes. The Liberty Bell has always

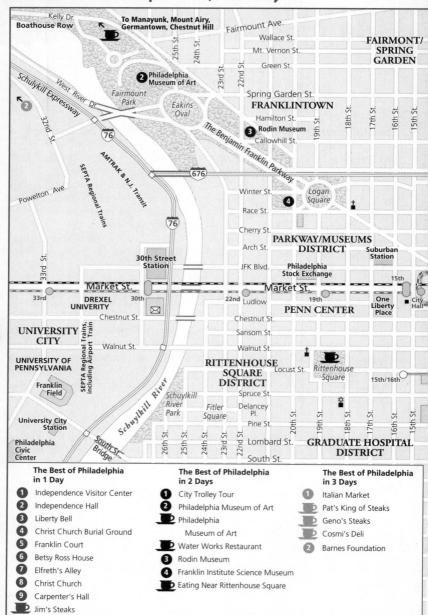

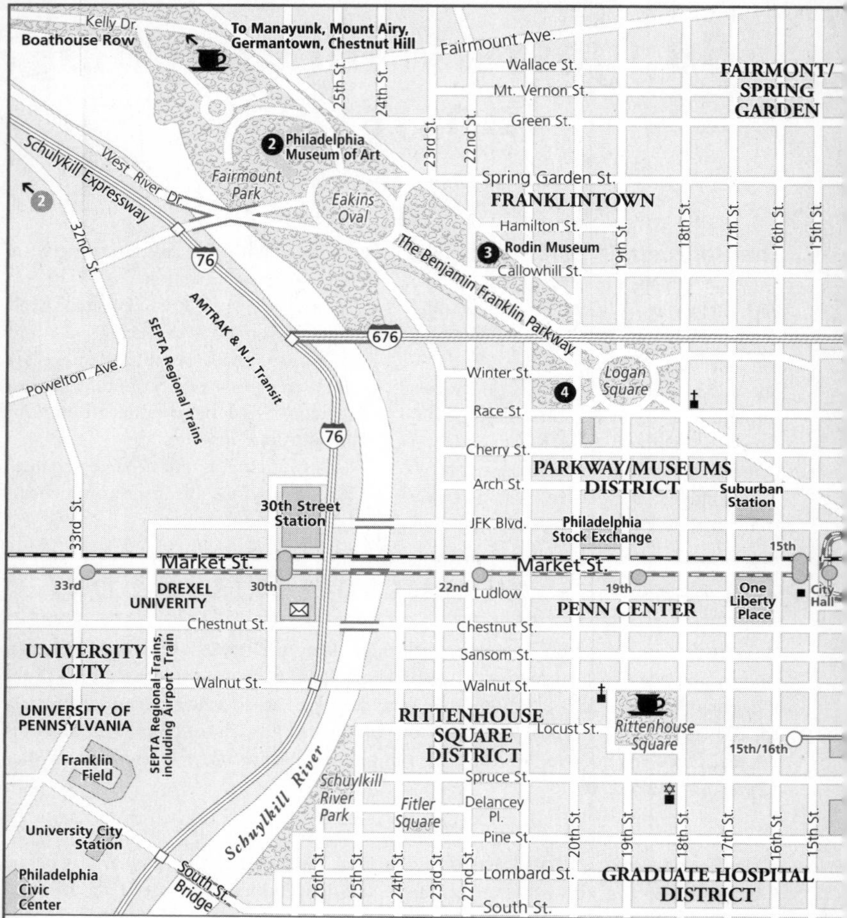

The Best of Philadelphia in 1 Day

1. Independence Visitor Center
2. Independence Hall
3. Liberty Bell
4. Christ Church Burial Ground
5. Franklin Court
6. Betsy Ross House
7. Elfreth's Alley
8. Christ Church
9. Carpenter's Hall

- Jim's Steaks

The Best of Philadelphia in 2 Days

1. City Trolley Tour
2. Philadelphia Museum of Art

- Philadelphia Museum of Art
- Water Works Restaurant

3. Rodin Museum
4. Franklin Institute Science Museum

- Eating Near Rittenhouse Square

The Best of Philadelphia in 3 Days

1. Italian Market

- Pat's King of Steaks
- Geno's Steaks
- Cosmi's Deli

2. Barnes Foundation

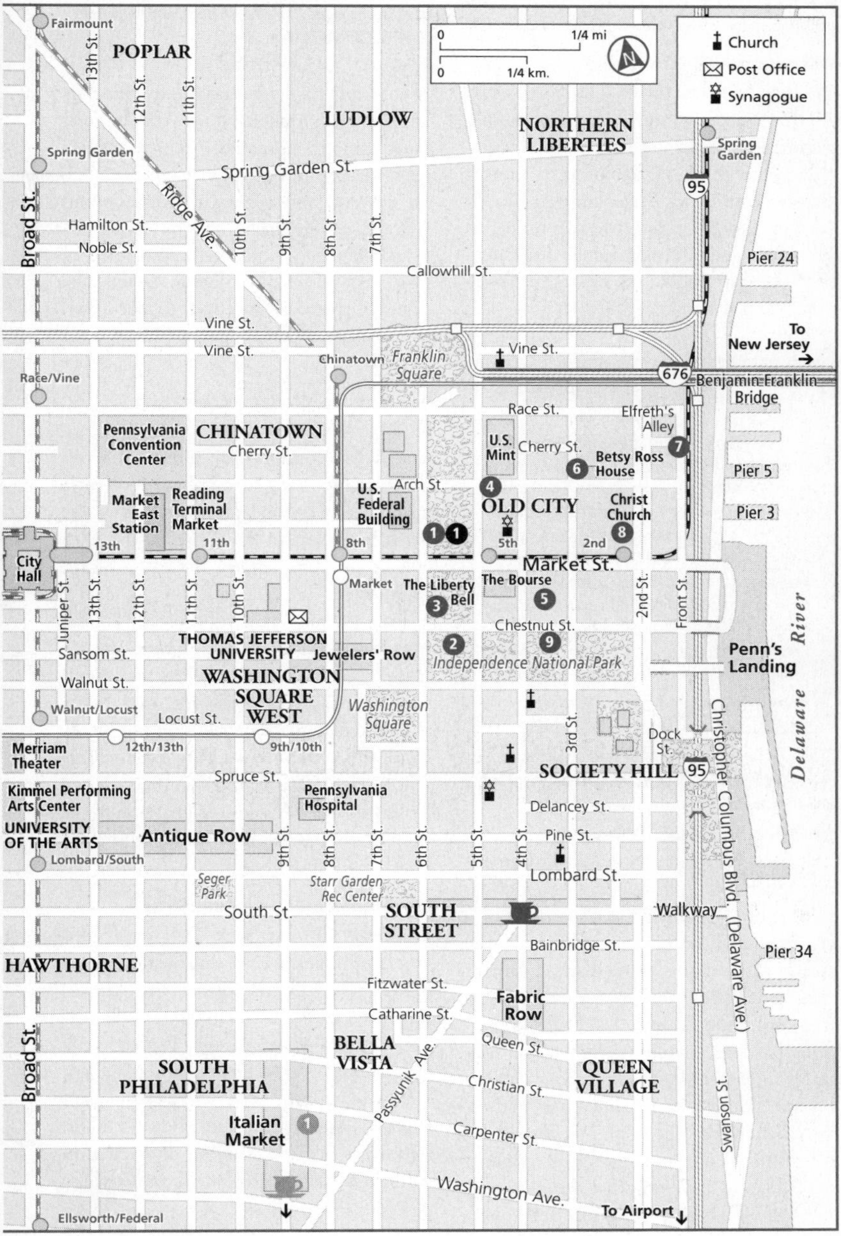
0
1/4 mi
0
1/4 km.
N
Church
Post Office
Synagogue
Fairmount
POPLAR
13th St.
12th St.
11th St.
LUDLOW
NORTHERN LIBERTIES
Spring Garden
Spring Garden
Spring Garden St.
95
Broad St.
Ridge Ave.
Hamilton St.
Noble St.
10th St.
9th St.
8th St.
7th St.
Pier 24
Callowhill St.
Vine St.
Vine St.
To New Jersey
Chinatown
Franklin Square
Vine St.
676
Benjamin Franklin Bridge
Race/Vine
Race St.
Elfreth's Alley
Pennsylvania Convention Center
CHINATOWN
Cherry St.
U.S. Mint
Cherry St.
Betsy Ross House
Pier 5
Arch St.
U.S. Federal Building
Market East Station
Reading Terminal Market
OLD CITY
Christ Church
Pier 3
City Hall
13th
11th
8th
5th
2nd
Market St.
Market
The Liberty Bell
The Bourse
Juniper St.
13th St.
12th St.
11th St.
10th St.
2nd St.
Front St.
Chestnut St.
THOMAS JEFFERSON UNIVERSITY
Jewelers' Row
Sansom St.
Independence National Park
Penn's Landing
Delaware River
Walnut St.
WASHINGTON SQUARE WEST
Washington Square
Walnut/Locust
Locust St.
3rd St.
Dock St.
Christopher Columbus Blvd. (Delaware Ave.)
Merriam Theater
12th/13th
9th/10th
Spruce St.
SOCIETY HILL
95
Kimmel Performing Arts Center
Pennsylvania Hospital
Delancey St.
UNIVERSITY OF THE ARTS
Antique Row
9th St.
8th St.
7th St.
6th St.
5th St.
4th St.
Pine St.
Lombard/South
Seger Park
Starr Garden Rec Center
Lombard St.
South St.
SOUTH STREET
Walkway
Bainbridge St.
Pier 34
HAWTHORNE
Fitzwater St.
Fabric Row
Catharine St.
Queen St.
BELLA VISTA
Passyunk Ave.
SOUTH PHILADELPHIA
Christian St.
QUEEN VILLAGE
Broad St.
Swanson St.
Italian Market
Carpenter St.
Washington Ave.
To Airport
Ellsworth/Federal

resonated most powerfully as a symbol. See it, get your photo taken with it, and you're pretty much done. See p. 125.

Walk north on 5th Street for 2 long blocks.

❹ Christ Church Burial Ground ★★

At this cemetery, you'll find the modest graves of Deborah and Benjamin Franklin, along with those of four other signers of the Declaration of Independence. Scour your pockets for a penny to toss onto Ben Franklin's grave, Philadelphia's equivalent of making a wish in Rome's Trevi Fountain. See p. 132.

> **LUNCH IN OLD CITY ★★★** A nice, sit-down lunch at an Old City restaurant is a great way to experience Philadelphia's rich dining scene—without spending all your own riches. Some places for fancier fare include **Fork** at 3rd and Market, **Buddakan** at 3rd and Chestnut, **Amada** at 2nd and Chestnut, and **Farmacia** on 3rd Street between Market and Chestnut. For a quick meal, grab a cheesesteak from **Sonny's** at 2nd and Market, or in the cafe section of **Fork** or **Farmacia.** For more information on these restaurants, see chapter 6.

Still in Old City, head to Market Street between 3rd and 4th streets.

❺ Franklin Court ★★

Alas, Ben and Deborah Franklin's home is not much more than excavated foundations and outdoor privy wells encased by a reconstructed frame that delineates the structure's original dimensions. What's most interesting here are the exhibits: a mirrored room dedicated to Franklin's far-flung passions, phones where you can hear international luminaries' opinions of Franklin, and a cleverly staged doll drama in three acts. Ben rented the adjoining houses for his printing company, newspaper publishing company, and post office. Employees at the post office will hand stamp your souvenir postcards. See p. 124.

Walk back to 3rd Street, cross Market Street, walk past shops and galleries (no one's looking, if you want to pop on in), cross Arch Street, and head right (east) 1½ blocks to the:

❻ Betsy Ross House ★

No one is certain whether this dwelling (p. 135) actually belonged to the nation's most famous seamstress, but the Betsy Ross House does do a great job of telling the story of the country's first Stars and Stripes. Touring the home is not a bad way to quickly get acquainted with the, er, snug joys of Colonial living, either. The front courtyard is a nice spot to take a rest, or to talk to a Once Upon a Nation actor (p. 122).

Walk north a half-block on 2nd Street to:

❼ Elfreth's Alley ★★

The oldest continuously inhabited street in America is easy to miss. Wedged on a narrow, cobblestone road off 2nd Street between Race and Arch streets, the alley will be on your left, to the east, toward Front Street.

Even if you don't head into no. 126, the **Mantua Maker's House** (*mantua* means "cape"), for a $2 visit ($1 for children), read the historical markers to learn more about this microcosmic melting-pot block. (And notice the house's busybody mirrors that let residents see who is at their doors.) A visit to the mini–visitor center and gift shop at no. 124 is free: Pick up a postcard or ask a question. See p. 136.

Double back on 2nd toward Market Street.

❽ Christ Church ★★

You can't miss the marvelous white steeple of this 1727 church. Light still streams through a grand Palladian window, illuminating the spot where Pennsylvania founder and Philadelphia planner William Penn was baptized, and where George and Martha Washington and Ben Franklin worshiped. The church's congregation still worships here, so plan accordingly. See p. 133.

Continue on 2nd to Chestnut Street, walk another block, and head either to one of Independence Park's many shaded benches, or, if you're feeling more ambitious, directly to your next stop.

9 Carpenters' Hall ★★

America's interior political disagreements aren't new: They date back at least to 1774, when this modest guildhall became the site of great debate over what to do about those pesky royals. Those handy with tools will also appreciate the exhibit of Colonial building methods. See p. 135.

> **CHEESESTEAK BREAK ★★** If you're in need of a break and a bite to eat, you might as well get your cheesesteak fix. The most popular place within reasonable walking distance is **Jim's Steaks** at 4th and South streets, although Old City's **Sonny's** (see above), does a pretty good version, too. See p. 115.

2 THE BEST OF PHILADELPHIA IN 2 DAYS

If you've already made your way through Day 1, you may be glad to hear that Day 2 involves a little less walking. You'll still want to fuel up, though, so head to a coffeehouse (p. 116), or the **Reading Terminal Market** (p. 101) for breakfast. ***Start:*** *Your hotel or the Independence Visitor Center.*

1 City Trolley Tour ★★

The green-and-burgundy Victorian-style trolleys roaming the city are the quickest and easiest way to get to and learn about a wealth of Philadelphia sights. The trolleys make regular pickups at most hotels, but you can also catch one at the Independence Visitor Center. Full tours are 90 minutes, and take in many of the sites described on Day 1 of the itinerary, plus harder-to-access spots like the **Eastern State Penitentiary** and the **Rodin Museum.** You can purchase a ticket on board, in advance at www.phillytour.com, or in person at the Independence Visitor Center. I recommend using the trolleys' on-and-off privileges (good for a whole day) for stopping at the following attractions.

Hop off the trolley at 26th and the Ben Franklin Parkway.

2 Philadelphia Museum of Art ★★★

Sure, Rocky trained by running up and down its steps, but what's truly great about Philadelphia's biggest art museum is its manageability. Spend a couple of quiet morning hours exploring the collections and you'll have ample time to take in masterpieces such as Cézanne's *Bathers,* Marcel Duchamp's *Nude Descending a Staircase,* and *Shad Fishing at Gloucester on the Delaware River* by Philadelphia's own Thomas Eakins. A few more minutes of exploring will lead you to rooms of Amish crafts and jousting gear, a sanctuary-like medieval cloister, and masterful, changing exhibits of modern artists. Sunday mornings are pay-what-you-wish admission. See p. 128.

> **LUNCH BREAK** If you're not ready to leave the museum, tucked beyond the gift shop is an above-average cafeteria and sit-down restaurant offering gourmet fare with an exhibit-influenced theme. Otherwise, you may choose to head to the **Water Works Restaurant** (p. 100) behind the museum. This fine-dining restaurant is housed in a historic building and has an amazing outdoor balcony overlooking the Schuylkill River.

Head a few blocks down the parkway on the north side.

❸ Rodin Museum ★★

This treasure is relatively unknown even to Philadelphians. The Rodin Museum houses the largest collection of Auguste Rodin's work outside of Paris's Musée Rodin. Bronze casts of *The Gates of Hell, The Thinker,* and *The Burghers of Calais* are among the extraordinary works housed in this cool building (ca. 1929). A self-guided tour will take less than an hour, not including the time you'll want to spend in the leafy confines of the museum's gardens. See p. 143.

❹ Franklin Institute Science Museum ★★★

Ben Franklin's scientific legacy lives on in this Logan Circle museum. Pay homage to the man—or rather a 20-foot-high marble statue of him—as you enter. Once in, you may want to head straight to the latest world-class exhibit, but do save time for Philadelphians' favorite hands-on exhibits.

These include walking through the 5,000-square-foot, thumping Giant Heart, riding three stories above the Bartol Atrium on a 1-inch cable while pedaling the SkyBike, and placing hands on Ben's Curiosity Show's static generator to make your hair stand on end. See p. 127.

From here, you're well positioned to head back to the ritzy, commercial fun of Rittenhouse Square, with its bars, restaurants, and shops.

> **EATING NEAR RITTENHOUSE SQUARE**
>
> You've got a wealth of choices here. **Continental Mid-Town** (p. 100), on the corner of 18th and Chestnut streets, is a fun, boisterous spot for a midday meal. A block away at 1907 Chestnut St., **Devil's Alley** (p. 93) serves great burgers, platters, and fries. If weather allows, **Di Bruno Brothers**, at 1703 Chestnut (✆ **215/665-9220**) is a great spot to buy a picnic and take it to grassy Rittenhouse Square, between 18th and 20th and Walnut and Spruce streets.

3 THE BEST OF PHILADELPHIA IN 3 DAYS

Your third day is all about getting into the real Philadelphia. Spend the morning experiencing the gritty, belly-busting, old-school charms of the Italian Market and the afternoon admiring the refined, world-renowned collections of the Barnes Foundation in Merion. Call ahead for reservations to the Barnes—and don't bother with your hotel's breakfast buffet. Your day is going to start out with serious sustenance, South Philly style. ***Start:*** *9th and Fitzwater streets.*

❶ Italian Market ★★

There are fancier places to buy produce, cheeses, meats, and fresh bread in town, but none is as authentic feeling as this stretch of 9th Street. I love to go here in the morning, when the vendors are just waking up, the fruit and vegetables seem freshest, and the crowds are thinnest. I recommend starting at Fitzwater and 9th streets to get to Sarcone's Bakery, where you'll pay less than $2 for a loaf of sesame-seed coated Italian bread.

Past Christian Street, market vendors, mostly on the east side of the street, hawk their broccoli rabe, strawberries, and oranges—just off the docks of South Philly—by shouting to passersby. The guys in the cheese shops (the west side of the street) dole out generous samples of sharp and dry Locatelli, soft French cheeses, and salty, shriveled cured olives. Locals like to start with a big breakfast at **Morning Glory** (p. 106) at 10th and Fitzwater streets or **Sabrina's** (p. 106) between 9th and 10th on Christian Street. But you could get by with a cappuccino from one of the cafes, and nibbling your way around.

> **ONE LAST CHEESESTEAK**
> From the market, it's a short walk south to Philly's most famous cheesesteak stands. **Pat's King of Steaks** and **Geno's Steaks** are farther down 9th Street, past Washington Avenue, at the intersection of 9th Street, Passyunk Avenue, and Wharton Street. We rate **Cosmi's Deli,** nearby on 8th and Dickinson, higher than both. See p. 114.

How you get to your last destination is up to you. If you've driven into town, take I-76 (Schuylkill Expwy.) west to City Line Avenue (Rte. 1), then south on City Line 1½ miles to Old Lancaster Road. Turn right onto Old Lancaster, continue 4 blocks, and turn left onto Latches Lane. If you're car free, take Paoli local train R5 to Merion Station, walk up Merion Road, and turn left onto Latches Lane; it's an easy, 10-minute walk. By bus, take no. 44 to Old Lancaster Road and Latches Lane.

❷ Barnes Foundation ★★★

Dr. Albert Barnes's amazing collection of Picassos, Renoirs, Cézannes, Matisses, and much, much more is famous not only for its impressive size and depth but also for its organization. America's greatest art collector apparently spent time each evening in the art-lined halls of his Merion mansion, arranging and rearranging his prizes. You'll be absolutely blown away by his displays of sculpture, paintings, African tribal masks, Amish chests, and antique doors. It's unlike anything else in the world. And, with the museum's plans to move to Benjamin Franklin Parkway in the coming years, you may never see anything like it again. See p. 126.

THE NEIGHBORHOODS IN BRIEF

Philadelphia is more of a collection of neighborhoods than a unified metropolis. Here are short descriptions of those that you're likely to find yourself in.

Bella Vista This is a vibrant section of South Philadelphia from South Street to Washington Avenue, 6th to 11th Street. The neighborhood includes the now-international Italian Market, many coffee shops, trattorias, and bakeries.

Center City In other places, this busiest section of town would be called "downtown." From east to west, the Schuylkill and Delaware rivers bind this easy-to-navigate main city section. South Street and Vine Street bind it to the south and north. Neighborhoods within this area include Old City, Society Hill, Rittenhouse Square, and Washington West.

Chestnut Hill This enclave of genteel city living is centered on cobblestone upper Germantown Avenue, and is the highest point within city limits. It's filled with art and antiques galleries, shops, tearooms, and comfortable restaurants. Visit it at www.chestnuthillpa.com.

Chinatown Nowadays it's largely commercial rather than residential. Most visitors come for its dozens of good restaurants, a growing number of hotels, and cheap parking only 5 minutes from the convention center. And it stays awake all night.

Fairmount Also known as the art museum area, this neighborhood stretches north from Benjamin Franklin Parkway to Girard Avenue. Although it's largely residential, Fairmount also includes the Free Library, the Rodin

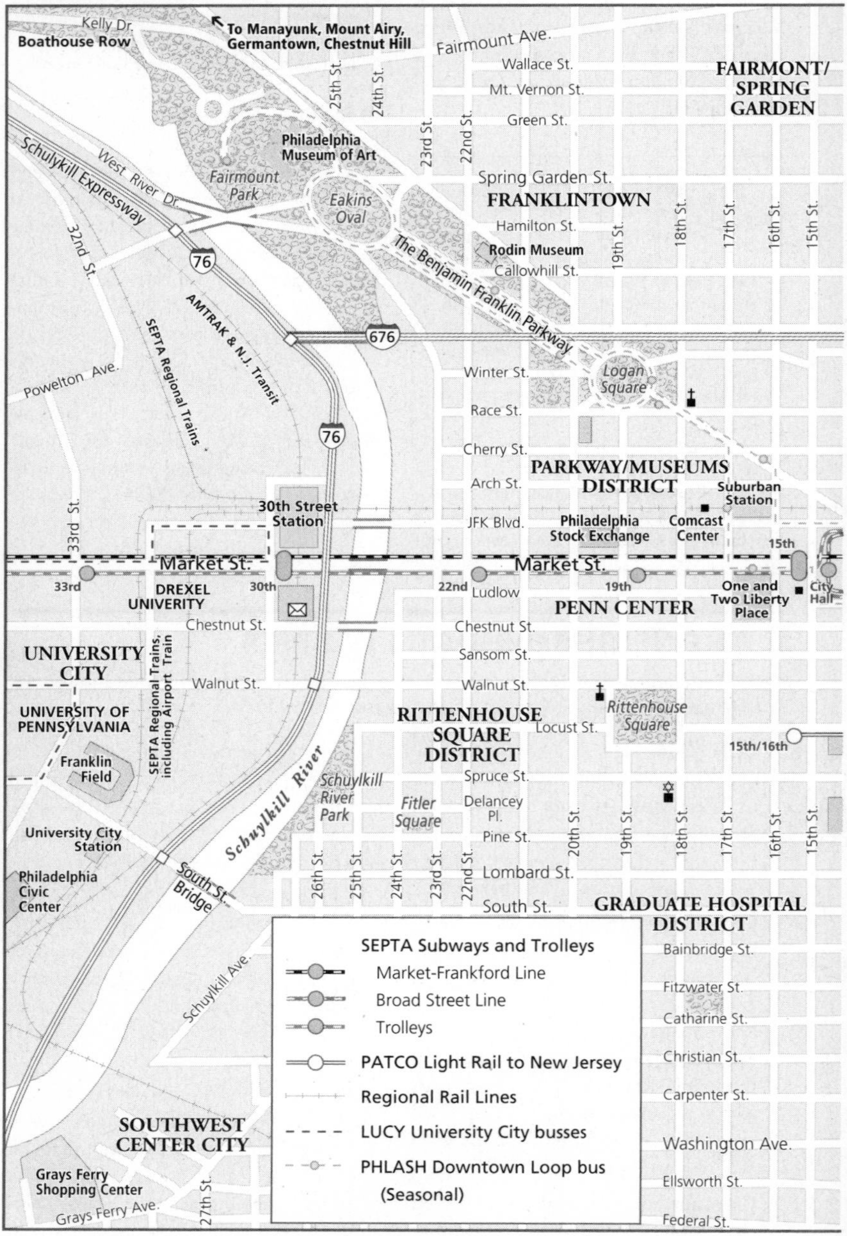

Kelly Dr.
Boathouse Row
To Manayunk, Mount Airy, Germantown, Chestnut Hill
Fairmount Ave.
Wallace St.
Mt. Vernon St.
Green St.
FAIRMONT/ SPRING GARDEN
Philadelphia Museum of Art
Fairmount Park
Eakins Oval
West River Dr.
Schuylkill Expressway
Spring Garden St.
FRANKLINTOWN
Hamilton St.
Rodin Museum
Callowhill St.
The Benjamin Franklin Parkway
25th St.
24th St.
23rd St.
22nd St.
19th St.
18th St.
17th St.
16th St.
15th St.
32nd St.
76
676
AMTRAK & N.J. Transit
SEPTA Regional Trains
Powelton Ave.
Winter St.
Logan Square
Race St.
Cherry St.
Arch St.
PARKWAY/MUSEUMS DISTRICT
Suburban Station
30th Street Station
JFK Blvd.
Philadelphia Stock Exchange
Comcast Center
15th
33rd St.
Market St.
33rd
DREXEL UNIVERSITY
30th
22nd
Ludlow
19th
One and Two Liberty Place
City Hall
PENN CENTER
Chestnut St.
UNIVERSITY CITY
Sansom St.
Walnut St.
SEPTA Regional Trains, including Airport Train
UNIVERSITY OF PENNSYLVANIA
RITTENHOUSE SQUARE DISTRICT
Locust St.
Rittenhouse Square
15th/16th
Franklin Field
Schuylkill River
Schuylkill River Park
Fitler Square
Spruce St.
Delancey Pl.
Pine St.
University City Station
20th St.
26th St.
Lombard St.
South St.
Philadelphia Civic Center
South St. Bridge
GRADUATE HOSPITAL DISTRICT
Bainbridge St.
Fitzwater St.
Catharine St.
Christian St.
Carpenter St.
Washington Ave.
Ellsworth St.
Federal St.
Schuylkill Ave.
SOUTHWEST CENTER CITY
Grays Ferry Shopping Center
Grays Ferry Ave.
27th St.
SEPTA Subways and Trolleys
Market-Frankford Line
Broad Street Line
Trolleys
PATCO Light Rail to New Jersey
Regional Rail Lines
LUCY University City busses
PHLASH Downtown Loop bus (Seasonal)

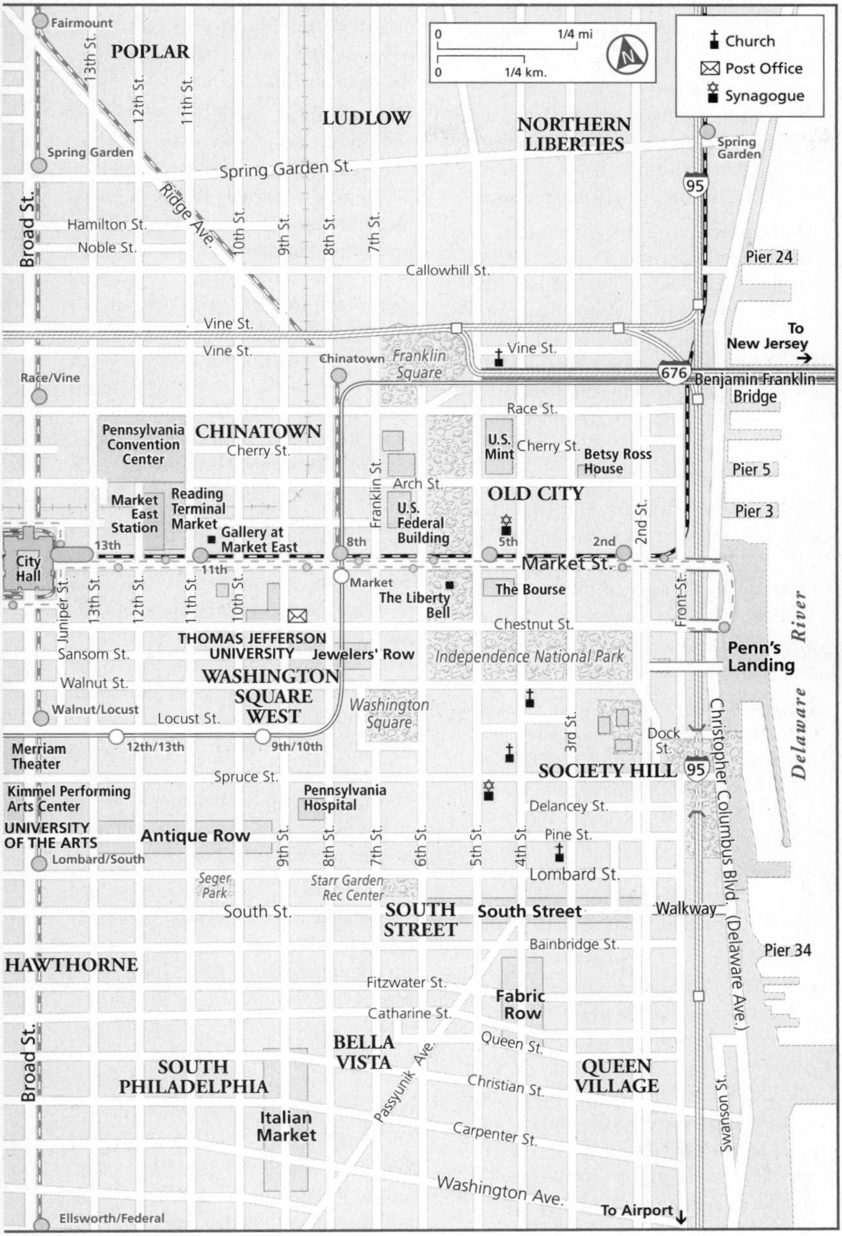
0
1/4 mi
0
1/4 km.
N
Church
Post Office
Synagogue
POPLAR
LUDLOW
NORTHERN LIBERTIES
CHINATOWN
OLD CITY
WASHINGTON SQUARE WEST
SOCIETY HILL
SOUTH STREET
HAWTHORNE
BELLA VISTA
SOUTH PHILADELPHIA
QUEEN VILLAGE
Fairmount
Spring Garden
Race/Vine
Chinatown
Walnut/Locust
12th/13th
9th/10th
Lombard/South
Ellsworth/Federal
13th
11th
8th
5th
2nd
Market
Broad St.
13th St.
12th St.
11th St.
10th St.
9th St.
8th St.
7th St.
6th St.
5th St.
4th St.
3rd St.
2nd St.
Front St.
Juniper St.
Franklin St.
Ridge Ave.
Spring Garden St.
Hamilton St.
Noble St.
Callowhill St.
Vine St.
Race St.
Cherry St.
Arch St.
Market St.
Chestnut St.
Sansom St.
Walnut St.
Locust St.
Spruce St.
Delancey St.
Pine St.
Lombard St.
South St.
Bainbridge St.
Fitzwater St.
Catharine St.
Queen St.
Christian St.
Carpenter St.
Washington Ave.
Passyunk Ave.
Dock St.
Swanson St.
Christopher Columbus Blvd. (Delaware Ave.)
95
676
Benjamin Franklin Bridge
To New Jersey
To Airport
Pier 24
Pier 5
Pier 3
Pier 34
Delaware River
Penn's Landing
Walkway
Franklin Square
Washington Square
Independence National Park
Seger Park
Starr Garden Rec Center
City Hall
Pennsylvania Convention Center
Market East Station
Reading Terminal Market
Gallery at Market East
U.S. Mint
Betsy Ross House
U.S. Federal Building
The Liberty Bell
The Bourse
THOMAS JEFFERSON UNIVERSITY
Jewelers' Row
Merriam Theater
Kimmel Performing Arts Center
UNIVERSITY OF THE ARTS
Pennsylvania Hospital
Antique Row
South Street
Fabric Row
Italian Market

Museum, Eastern State Penitentiary, and the Philadelphia Art Museum itself.

Germantown One of Philadelphia's oldest settlements, Germantown is northwest of Center City. This area was founded by German émigrés, attracted by Penn's religious tolerance. Outside of its wonderful historic mansions, however, it is not especially attractive now.

Manayunk This neighborhood, 4 miles up the Schuylkill River from Center City, has been gentrified over the last 20 years. Now boutiques, furniture and art galleries, and cafe/restaurants line Main Street, overlooking a 19th-century canal adjoining the river. It's a picturesque place for an afternoon stroll and an alfresco snack. Visit it virtually at www.manayunk.com.

Mount Airy Between Chestnut Hill and Germantown, this community is known for its pioneering diversity, beautifully mismatched houses, tree-lined streets, and independent shopping, dining, and entertainment. A great place for a Sunday drive.

Northern Liberties North of Old City, between the Delaware River and 6th Street, this developing area is home to both low-income housing and brand-new million-dollar lofts, and the artist-owned brownstones in between. Go here to see how hip bars and simple bistros are fueling the city's revival. For more information visit www.northernliberties.org.

Old City Think New York's SoHo or Chelsea, in the shadow of the Benjamin Franklin Bridge just north of Independence National Historical Park, with an eclectic blend of 18th-century row houses, 19th-century warehouses, and 20th-century rehabs. This is now the city's hottest neighborhood for the 20- and 30-something set, with chic restaurants, bars, and boutiques set in historic buildings and storefronts. The first Friday of every month is a pleasantly packed neighborhood-wide party, with galleries and stores open late. Visit www.oldcitydistrict.org.

Queen Village Between Society Hill and South Philly, this leafy neighborhood of old houses (once known as Wiccaco, then Pennsport) is bounded by South Street to the north, Washington Avenue to the south, the Delaware to the east, and 6th Street to the west. There are lots of small, reasonably priced cafes and bistros here, as well as Fabric Row, South 4th Street between Bainbridge and Catharine streets, where you'll find old-time fabric and notions shops along with newer galleries, salons, and clothing shops. For more information go to www.qvna.org.

Rittenhouse Square This beautifully landscaped park ringed by elegant condominiums built during the 1930s and historic mansions illustrates the elegance, wealth, and culture of Philadelphia. Now, sleek outdoor cafes and luxury hotels line the park also. From the Rittenhouse Hotel on a sunny day, walk through the square to Walnut Street, where the shopping rivals that of Boston and San Francisco for charm and sophistication. For more information go to www.rittenhouserow.org.

Society Hill This heart of reclaimed 18th-century Philadelphia is loosely defined by Walnut and Lombard streets and Front and 7th streets. Today, it's a fashionable section of the old city, just south of Independence National Historical Park, where you can stroll among restored Federal, Colonial, and Georgian homes—even the contemporary, architecturally modern is interesting and immaculately maintained.

South Philadelphia It's Rocky Balboa meets artist lofts and authentic tacquerias. Three hundred years of immigration have made South Philadelphia the city's most colorful and ethnically diverse neighborhood, although the overwhelming feel is distinctly Italian (think 1910s Calabria). Stroll the gritty, redolent Italian Market at 9th and Christian, heading south, snacking on cheeses, cured meats, pastries, and tamales, on your way to the famously flashy cheesesteak stands at Passyunk and 9th streets.

South Street The street that divides Society Hill and Queen Village was the city limit in William Penn's day. The 1960s saw bohemian artists reclaiming this street in the name of peace and love; an eclectic teen scene has replaced the previous hippies. Quiet by day and cruised by night, it's a colorful spot for casual dining, drinking, shopping, gallery hopping, and getting pierced (or tattooed). The neighborhood's website is www.southstreet.com.

University City West Philadelphia was farmland until the University of Pennsylvania moved here from 9th and Chestnut streets in the 1870s. Wander through Penn's campus for Ivy League architecture that includes an 1895 college green modeled on Oxford and Cambridge, but with Dutch gables. Also nearby are the bustling campuses of Drexel University, University of the Sciences, Lincoln University Urban Center, and the Restaurant School at Walnut Hill College.

Washington Square West "Wash West" extends from Washington Square Park at 6th and Walnut streets south to Lombard and west to Juniper Street. Still catching up to Rittenhouse or Society Hill, this quiet stretch includes Antique Row (Pine St.), the "Gayborhood," and a retail "Midtown Village" corridor along 13th Street.

5

Where to Stay

by Lauren McCutcheon

Philadelphia does not lack for places to spend the night. At press time, there were more than 10,000 rooms in Philadelphia, and over 30,000 in the surrounding region. Some of these rooms are extra-modern. Others are scrupulously traditional. A few thousand of those rooms are splurge-worthy. Others can be yours for a song.

Overall, room rates are rising. In 2006, rooms averaged $152. In 2007, the average was up to $169. Still, discounts and promotions, even at luxury hotels, abound.

Nonetheless, you'll pay above-average prices to snooze stylishly between high-thread-count sheets at the grand Park Hyatt at the Bellevue, the imposingly marble-columned Ritz-Carlton, the smoothly luxurious Four Seasons, or the impeccably boutiquey Rittenhouse Hotel. Visitors interested in more moderately priced, yet still memorable, digs can book the surprisingly upscale, historic locations of Marriott's Courtyard and Residence Inn, or the 20th-century marvel that houses the Loews (all near the convention center). Folks wanting to stay near Independence Hall and the Liberty Bell ought to look into the Omni or the Sheraton Society Hill. Those more interested in the swank Rittenhouse Square area of town might consider the Latham, Westin, or Embassy Suites. And, if you really want to save some dough, investigate rates at Old City's Comfort Inn, Best Western, and Holiday Inn.

Most hotels offer business amenities such as Internet access ports, wireless Internet, and functional desks.

The airport area is positively swollen with hotels, but unless you've got an early or late flight, it's much more pleasant to stay in Center City. (If I had to choose one, I'd definitely pick the new-in-2008, supermodern aloft hotel from the same people that do the fancy W Hotels.) Outside the city, you can find plenty of lovely, historic inns, such as Evermay on the Delaware in Bucks County, and upscale hotels, such as the Inns at Doneckers in Ephrata, Lancaster County—see chapters 11 and 12 for descriptions of inns in the surrounding areas.

The **Independence Visitor Center,** 1 N. Independence Mall W., Philadelphia, PA 19106 (✆ **800/537-7676;** www.independencevisitorcenter.com), can help with accommodations questions and reservations.

RATES Unless otherwise specified, all prices quoted are for double occupancy and all rooms have private bathrooms and phones. You can count on a state tax of 7%, plus a city surcharge of 6% and a county tax of 1% (total hotel tax is 14%). Remember that the prices listed here are "rack rates"—the room rate charged without any discount—and you can usually do better. Be sure to ask about parking and/or arrangements for children.

B&B AGENCIES One good agency to contact is **A Bed & Breakfast Connection/ Bed & Breakfast of Philadelphia,** Box 21, Devon, PA 19333 (✆ **800/448-3619** or 610/687-3565; www.bnbphiladelphia.com). This reservation service represents more than 80 personally inspected accommodations in Philadelphia, Valley Forge, the Brandywine Valley, and in Lancaster, Montgomery, and Bucks counties. The agency can select a compatible lodging for you or send you its free brochure. American Express, Visa, and MasterCard are accepted; phone reservations can be made Monday through Friday from 9am to 5pm. Be sure to ask if the property you are interested in accepts children.

Another website that lists 43 top bed-and-breakfasts and inns in Center City and in surrounding areas such as Chadds Ford and Bucks County, complete with photos, listings of amenities, and contact information, is **Bed and Breakfasts Online** (www.bbonline.com/pa/philadelphia.html).

Rates range from about $60 to about $250 for separate luxury cottages.

1 EAST OF BROAD STREET (OLD CITY & CONVENTION CENTER AREA)

VERY EXPENSIVE

Hyatt Regency Philadelphia at Penn's Landing ★ This efficiently run waterfront hotel may be close to historic, bustling Old City, but it feels somewhat isolated, making it popular with large groups wanting to stick together. Built in 2000, the Hyatt Regency towers between I-95 and the Delaware River; its solid, Art Deco–style angles and boxes are impossible to miss. Although walkways over the highway at Walnut and Dock streets allow for an easy, 5-block passage to historic sights, fast-paced Columbus Boulevard and the interstate separate the hotel from any particular neighborhood. My favorite part of the complex is the indoor pool, which overlooks the river and a dock full of old seafaring vessels. The Art Deco–themed rooms offer stupendous views of the riverfront or city, but I-95 noise does percolate up, so choose a river-view room if quiet is important to you. New beds were added in 2008, as were new flatscreen TVs. Self-parking can be tedious here, with long waits for the small garage elevator, so go with the valet for only $5 more (you can drive in and out as many times as you like without extra fees).

201 S. Columbus Blvd., Philadelphia, PA 19106. ✆ **800/233-1234** or 215/928-1234. Fax 215/521-6543. www.pennslanding.hyatt.com. 350 units. From $299 double. Children 21 and under stay free in parent's room. AE, DC, MC, V. Valet parking $27 per day; self-parking $21 per day. Bus: 21. **Amenities:** Restaurant; lounge; indoor lap pool; fitness center; sauna; concierge; meeting facilities; room service; laundry. *In room:* A/C, flatscreen TV w/pay movies, high-speed Internet, minibar, coffeemaker, hair dryer, iron/ironing board.

Omni Hotel at Independence Park ★ This small, polished corner hotel banks on its terrific Independence National Historical Park location, less than a block from Old City's trendy restaurant and gallery scene. Past the classic lobby with its huge vases of flowers and a clubby adjacent bar with a player piano, guest rooms, scheduled for renovation in 2009, are of modest size and cheerful and have park views, original pastels, live plants, and a sense of history—courtesy of the horse-drawn carriages clip-clopping past the valet parking drop-off and elegant glass-and-steel canopy. The staff here is noteworthy for its quality and its knowledge of the park. Another extra: The independent film–oriented Ritz Five movie theater is next door in the Bourse complex.

401 Chestnut St., Philadelphia, PA 19106. ✆ **800/843-6664** or 215/925-0000. Fax 215/931-1263. www.omnihotels.com. 150 units. From $189 double. Children stay free in parent's room, up to 4 people per room. AE, DC, DISC, MC, V. Valet parking $34; self-parking $27 (no in/out privileges). Bus: PHLASH, 21, or 42. The hotel is 3 blocks south of Ben Franklin Bridge; Chestnut St. runs one-way east, so approach from 6th St. **Amenities:** Restaurant; lounge; indoor lap pool; health club; Jacuzzi; sauna; concierge; free Wi-Fi in lobby; room service. *In room:* A/C, TV/VCR, Wi-Fi, minibar, coffeemaker, hair dryer, iron/ironing board.

Philadelphia Accommodations

Alexander Inn **23**
Apple Hostel **29**
Best Western Independence Park Inn **30**
Comfort Inn Downtown/Historic Area **27**
Courtyard by Marriott **7**
Crowne Plaza **6**
Doubletree Hotel Philadelphia **21**
Embassy Suites Center City **2**
Four Seasons Hotel **1**
Hampton Inn Convention Center **5**
Holiday Inn—Historic District **25**
Hyatt Regency Philadelphia at Penn's Landing **33**
The Independent **22**
Inn at the League **15**
The Latham **14**
Lippincott House B & B **17**
Loews Philadelphia Hotel **10**

- Marriott Philadelphia **9**
- Morris House Hotel **24**
- Omni Hotel at Independence Park **26**
- Park Hyatt Philadelphia at the Bellevue **16**
- Penn's View Hotel **28**
- Raddison-Warwick **19**
- Residence Inn **8**
- Rittenhouse Hotel **18**
- Rittenhouse 1715 **20**
- The Ritz-Carlton Philadelphia **12**
- Sheraton Philadelphia Center City **4**
- Sheraton Society Hill **32**
- Hotel Sofitel **13**
- Thomas Bond House **31**
- Westin Philadelphia **11**
- Windsor Suites **3**

EXPENSIVE

Doubletree Hotel Philadelphia ★ The Avenue of the Arts location of this hotel is good for culture seekers and families. The garage entrances ingeniously keep traffic flows separate for three floors of meeting facilities. The decor features rich paisleys and Degas-style murals alluding to the orchestral and ballet life at the Academy of Music across the street. Thanks to the saw-toothed design of the building, each of the guest rooms has two views of town. Obviously, the higher floors afford the better views, with outlooks toward the Delaware River (eastern corner) or City Hall (northeastern corner) being the most popular. The bathrooms are clean and bland, and the Doubletree signature is a box of great chocolate chip cookies delivered to your room upon arrival.

237 S. Broad St. (at Locust St.), Philadelphia, PA 19107. ✆ **800/222-8733** or 215/893-1600. Fax 215/893-1664. www.doubletreehotels.com. 427 units. From $152 Mon–Fri. Children 17 and under stay free in parent's room. AE, DC, DISC, MC, V. Valet parking $26; self-parking $22. SEPTA: Walnut-Locust. Bus: PHLASH, 21, or 42. **Amenities:** 2 restaurants; lounge; indoor lap pool; health club, rooftop jogging track; Jacuzzi; steam room; activities desk; laundry; dry cleaning. *In room:* A/C, TV w/pay movies, high-speed Internet, minibar, coffeemaker, hair dryer, iron/ironing board.

Holiday Inn Historic District This eight-floor Holiday Inn, with its line of international flags outside, is easy to find and offers lickety-split access to all your major historic sites. Renovated in 2006, the hotel is set back from the street, with rooms that are standard size and bright in decor. The rooftop bar is a bonus during summer months.

400 Arch St., Philadelphia, PA 19106. ✆ **800/315-2621** or 215/923-8660. Fax 215/923-4633. www.ichotelsgroup.com. 364 units. From $170 double. Extra person $10 (up to 5 people total). Children 17 and under stay free in parent's room. Children 11 and under eat free. AE, DC, DISC, MC, V. Parking $22 per day. Bus: PHLASH. **Amenities:** Restaurant; lounge; rooftop outdoor pool; children's programs in summer; game room; Wi-Fi in lobby; concierge and room service 6:30am–10pm; laundry room. *In room:* A/C, TV, high-speed Internet, coffeemaker, hair dryer, iron/ironing board.

Loews Philadelphia Hotel ★ Kids The Loews, opened in spring 2000 in the former PSFS Bank tower, is the fine product of the marriage of an Art Deco architectural landmark and a prestigious hotel chain. The tower, located across from the Reading Terminal and the convention center, was the nation's first skyscraper of modern design and construction, with gleaming polished stone and clocks by Cartier. Loews Hotels turned the 1932 granite-and-glass building into a first-class property. The three-story entrance hall has been preserved, and petite rooms feature 10-foot ceilings, modern Art Deco interiors, and miles of spectacular views. Business aids are extensive, but watch out for the surcharges levied on phone use. For convention travelers, the location is ideal, though this stretch of Market Street is a bit grittier than it is near Society Hill or Rittenhouse Square.

Kids get special treatment in the form of Fisher-Price welcome gifts and loaner Game Boys and DVDs. Pets are coddled, too: An animal-loving concierge can provide leashes, litter boxes, catnip, scratching posts, and, well, pooper scoopers.

Solefood is the hotel's seafood restaurant, and there is a pleasant lobby lounge off the restaurant; Channel 10, the local NBC affiliate, often uses the lobby as a set for interviews.

1200 Market St., Philadelphia, PA 19107. ✆ **800/235-6397** or 215/627-1200. www.loewshotels.com. 581 units. From $149 double. AE, DC, DISC, MC, V. Valet parking $34. SEPTA: 11th St. Station. Bus: PHLASH, 21, or 42. Pets $25. **Amenities:** Restaurant; bar; fitness facility w/lap pool ($10/day); concierge; laundry service; dry cleaning; library. *In room:* A/C, TV w/pay movies, fax, high-speed Internet, minibar, hair dryer, iron/ironing board.

Morris House Hotel ★ *Finds* This hidden historic city house turned comely boutique hotel feels like a Colonial bed-and-breakfast—but with more elbowroom. Built in 1787 by a pair of Revolutionary-era brothers and renovated as an expanded B&B in 2001 by a pair of area developers, the white-columned, ivy-covered brick structure faces away from the main street and toward the tallest building east of Broad Street, attracting little attention from passersby. Location alone—within shouting distance of Washington Square Park, Jeweler's Row, Independence Hall, and Pennsylvania Hospital—isn't all that sets the hotel apart. It has antique oil portraits, satin duvet covers, uneven original floorboards, loaded-up bookshelves, dining rooms with wood-burning fireplaces, a flowering bricked courtyard that hosts outdoor weddings, an adjacent restaurant and bar for seasonal, delicate American fare, and windows that actually open.

Standard rooms and bathrooms are of modest size with a Martha Washington–meets–Home Depot feel, while three more-recently annexed suites resemble spacious urban studios and lofts, some with Jacuzzis and kitchens, and are often booked for extended stays by families with relatives at nearby hospitals. A word of warning to light sleepers: Request a room facing the courtyard, where you'll avoid 8th Street's cacophony of rush-hour traffic.

225 S. 8th St. (btw. Walnut St. and Locust St., on St. James St.) Philadelphia, PA 19106. ✆ **215/922-2446.** Fax 215/922-2466. www.morrishousehotel.com. 15 units. From $179 double; from $199 suite; from $249 extended suite; $20 per additional person. Rates include continental breakfast and afternoon tea and cookies. Children 9 and under stay free in parent's room. AE, MC, V. Parking garage across street $22. SEPTA: Market East Station; 8th St. Station. **Amenities:** Restaurant. *In room:* A/C, TV/DVD, high-speed Internet, hair dryer, iron/ironing board.

Penn's View Hotel ★★ *Finds* Tucked behind the Market Street ramp to I-95 in a renovated 1856 hardware store, this small, exquisite inn exudes European flair; when you enter, you'll feel as though you're in a private club. It was developed by the Sena family, owners of La Famiglia restaurant 450 feet south (p. 89). The decor is floral and rich. The main concern is traffic noise, but the rooms are well insulated and contain large framed mirrors, armoires, and, in some cases, balconies. The ceilings have been dropped for modern heat and air-conditioning purposes, and you'll find marble Jacuzzi tubs and gas fireplaces in the 12 pricier rooms. A third bed can be wheeled into your room for $15. Popular Ristorante Panorama, adjacent to the lobby, offers excellent contemporary Italian cuisine at moderate prices. Also in the hotel is Il Bar, a world-class wine bar that pours 120 different wines by the glass.

Front and Market sts., Philadelphia, PA 19106. ✆ **800/331-7634** or 215/922-7600. Fax 215/922-7642. www.pennsviewhotel.com. 51 units. From $159 double. Packages available. Rates include European continental breakfast. Guarantee requested on reservation. AE, MC, V. Parking at adjacent lot $20. Bus: PHLASH or 21. **Amenities:** Restaurant; wine bar; free Wi-Fi. *In room:* A/C, TV, dataport, hair dryer, iron/ironing board.

Philadelphia Marriott, **Courtyard by Marriott**, and **Residence Inn** ★★ The largest hotel in the state, and then some, the thrice-incarnated Philadelphia Marriott is high volume—and surprisingly high service. Marriott opened the biggest hotel in Pennsylvania in January 1995, linked by an elevated covered walkway to the Reading Terminal Shed of the convention center—and it is scheduled for a $45-million renovation in 2009. In 1999, Marriott converted the historic 1926 City Hall Annex across 13th Street at Filbert into a 500-room Courtyard by Marriott, the largest in the Courtyard division, and, in 2004, Courtyard gained neighbor Residence Inn, which added 269 suites to the stew—plus a state-of-the-art fitness center. So all together, you have your choice of more than 2,100 rooms, three fitness centers, and 10 restaurants and lounges—all linked with one another and with the convention center. Guests at any of the locations would be smart to join Marriott's rewards program, which offers automatic discounts to members.

Marriott's major auto entrance is on Filbert Street (two-way btw. Market and Arch sts.), with a grand pedestrian entrance adjoining Champions Sports Bar and retail on Market Street. The main lobby is sliced up into a five-story atrium, enlivened by a 10,000-square-foot water sculpture, a lobby bar, and a Starbucks. Setbacks and terraces provide plenty of natural light and views from the rooms on floors 6 to 23. Rooms are tastefully outfitted with dark woods, maroon and green drapes and bedspreads, a TV armoire, a desk, a club chair and ottoman, and a round table, but, overall, are slightly less elegant than those at the top hotels. Comfortably sized bathrooms have heavy chrome fixtures and sinks and counters tucked in the corners for more dressing room space. Closets are spacious; there are large desks—and some amazing views of City Hall—in guest rooms of Residence Inn and Courtyard. Service throughout the megaplex is impeccable, thanks to the well-trained, knowledgeable staff.

Philadelphia Marriott: 12th and Market sts., Philadelphia, PA 19107. ✆ **800/228-9290** or 215/625-2900. Fax 215/625-6000. www.marriott.com. 1,409 units. From $259 double. AE, DC, MC, V. SEPTA: Direct internal connection to Market East Station and airport train. Bus: PHLASH, 21, or 42. **Amenities:** 2 restaurants; bar; 3 lounges; coffee bar; indoor lap pool; health club; Jacuzzi; saunas in concierge-level rooms. *In room:* A/C, TV w/pay movies, high-speed Internet, fridge, coffeemaker, hair dryer, iron/ironing board, down comforters.

Courtyard by Marriott: 21 Juniper St. (13th and Filbert sts.), Philadelphia, PA 19107. ✆ **800/321-2211** or 215/496-3200. Fax 215/496-3696. 498 units. Mon–Fri from $239 standard, from $329 suite. AE, DC, DISC, MC, V. Valet parking $42. **Amenities:** Restaurant; indoor pool; fitness center. *In room:* A/C, TV w/pay movies, high-speed Internet, kitchenette (in hospitality suite), coffeemaker, hair dryer, iron/ironing board.

Residence Inn by Marriott: 1 E. Penn Sq. (Juniper and Market sts.), Philadelphia, PA 19107. ✆ **215/557-0005.** Fax 215/557-1991. 269 units. Mon–Fri from $149 double. Rates include breakfast. Pets $100. AE, DC, MC, V. **Amenities:** Fitness center; coin-op washers and dryers. *In room:* A/C, TV w/pay movies, high-speed Internet, Wi-Fi, kitchen, fridge, coffeemaker, microwave, hair dryer, iron/ironing board.

Sheraton Society Hill (Kids) Three blocks from Head House Square, 4 from Independence Hall, this short, unassuming, hotel is popular among business travelers and families alike (kids are particularly fond of the splashy indoor pool). The Sheraton Society Hill sits on an unusually quiet stretch of a tree-lined cobblestone street, on a triangular 2½-acre site between Dock and South Front streets. The modern building was designed in keeping with the area's Georgian architecture and Flemish Bond brickwork, with a skylit, four-story atrium whose fountain and plants recall a lush, private courtyard in spring.

The guest rooms are on the long, low second, third, and fourth floors (the only Delaware River views are from the fourth floor). Rooms are a bit smaller than you'd expect (as are the bathrooms); half have one king-size bed and the others have two double beds. Rooms are furnished in serious, Drexel Heritage mahogany, with an upholstered love seat and chair, and glass-and-brass coffee tables. In each bathroom, dark marble tops the vanity, and bathrobes are provided.

1 Dock St. (at 2nd and Walnut sts.), Philadelphia, PA 19106. ✆ **800/325-3535** or 215/238-6000. Fax 215/238-6652. www.sheraton.com/societyhill. 365 units. From $109 double. Children 17 and under stay free in parent's room. AE, DC, MC, V. Valet parking $35. Bus: PHLASH, 21, or 42. Pets accepted. **Amenities:** 2 restaurants; lounge; courtyard bar; indoor pool; health club w/trainers; Jacuzzi; sauna; concierge; free shuttle to Center City Mon–Fri; meeting facilities; 24-hr. room service; laundry service. *In room:* A/C, TV, Wi-Fi, minibar, coffeemaker, hair dryer, iron/ironing board.

MODERATE

Alexander Inn ★★ Value The Alexander Inn bills itself as a four-star hotel at reasonable rates. The corner spot has all the comfort and friendliness of a bed-and-breakfast, with a classy 1930s Art Deco/cruise boat feel to the furnishings. Rooms feature DirecTV with eight all-movie channels and individual artwork, and bathrooms sparkle with cleanliness. Corner rooms are larger and brighter. The Alexander Inn is in the heart of the gay and lesbian district of Center City, and its clientele is both straight and gay. Another bonus: Tria, a popular wine bar and bistro, is just across the street.

12th and Spruce sts., Philadelphia, PA 19107. ✆ **877/253-9466** or 215/923-3535. Fax 215/923-1004. www.alexanderinn.com. 48 units. From $109 single; from $119 double; $12 per additional person. Rates include breakfast buffet. AE, DC, DISC, MC, V. Parking at nearby garage $10. SEPTA: Market East. **Amenities:** 24-hr. fitness center; business center; Wi-Fi. *In room:* A/C, TV w/pay movies, Wi-Fi, hair dryer, iron/ironing board.

Best Western Independence Park Hotel ★ This top choice for bed-and-breakfast-style lodging has a great location, 2 blocks from Independence Hall. Now a Best Western franchise, the inn is housed in a handsome 1856 former dry-goods store with renovated rooms and a renovated exterior.

The guest rooms, on eight floors, are normal size, but the ceilings are nice and high. The bathrooms have big beveled mirrors and dropped ceilings. Although all the windows are triple casement and double glazed, specify an interior room if you're sensitive to noise, since some rooms face the traffic on Chestnut Street. A third bed for a child can be wheeled into your room at no additional charge.

235 Chestnut St., Philadelphia, PA 19106. ✆ **800/624-2988** or 215/922-4443. Fax 215/922-4487. www.independenceparkhotel.com. 36 units. From $160 double. Rates include breakfast and afternoon tea. Children 12 and under stay free in parent's room. 15% AAA discount. AE, DC, DISC, MC, V. Parking at nearby garage $14. Bus: PHLASH, 21, or 42. Pets accepted. Dogs up to 20 lb. $50. **Amenities:** Health club nearby ($10 fee). *In room:* A/C, TV, dataport, hair dryer.

Comfort Inn Downtown/Historic Area Comfort Inn at Penn's Landing is a modestly priced, consistent waterfront hotel, located at a corner of Old City between I-95 and the Delaware River. It tends to attract a lot of student and senior groups. A courtesy shuttle van takes guests to Center City, and the crosstown subway line is 2 blocks away. Comfort Inn has been built to airport-area noise specifications, with insulated windows and other features to lessen the din of traffic. The eastern views of the river from the upper floors are stupendous.

100 N. Columbus Blvd., Philadelphia, PA 19106 (3 blocks from the northbound ramp off the expwy.). ✆ **800/228-5150** or 215/627-7900. Fax 215/238-0809. www.comfortinn.com. 185 units. From $139 double. Rates include continental breakfast. Children 18 and under stay free in parent's room. AAA discount available. AE, DC, DISC, MC, V. Parking in adjacent lot $22. SEPTA: 2nd St. Bus: PHLASH or 42. **Amenities:** Small health club; coin-op washers and dryers. *In room:* A/C, TV, high-speed Internet, coffeemaker, iron/ironing board.

Hampton Inn Philadelphia Convention Center Just a block from the current Pennsylvania Convention Center—and closer to the construction of the new center, this service-oriented lodging is known for its friendly staff. Rooms are on par with other Hampton Inns—not too big, not too small, nothing fancy. Bonuses include proximity to Chinatown and City Hall and an indoor pool.

1301 Race St. (at 13th St.), Philadelphia, PA 19107. ✆ **800/HAMPTON** (426-7866) or 215/665-9100. Fax 215/665-9200. www.hamptoninn.com. 250 units. From $149 double. Packages available. Rates include breakfast buffet. AE, DC, DISC, MC, V. Valet parking $23 per day; self-parking $20 per day. SEPTA: Market

East Station; 13th St. **Amenities:** Indoor pool; fitness center; whirlpool; concierge; business center; meeting space; room service; coin laundry. *In room:* A/C, TV, DSL, coffeemaker, hair dryer, iron/ironing board.

The Independent ★ This restored Georgian Revival–turned–boutique hotel sits in the heart of Midtown Village, Washington West, and the Gayborhood, atop a popular restaurant and bar. Reopened under new ownership in 2008, the spacious, contemporary-meets-traditional guest rooms here vary in shape and style: Choose one with exposed brick, or a fireplace, a cathedral ceiling, or a loft sleeping area. The lobby area stars a 30-foot-tall mural of Independence Hall by local artist Kim Senior. Other standouts: pillow-top mattresses and free wireless throughout.

1234 Locust St. (at 13th St.), Philadelphia, PA 19107. ✆ **215/772-1440.** www.theindependenthotel.com. 24 units. From $121 double. Packages available. AE, MC, V. Parking across the street $25 per day (no in/out privileges) or 1 block away $15. **Amenities:** Gym nearby; business center; Wi-Fi. *In room:* A/C, HDTV, fridge, microwave, hair dryer.

Thomas Bond House (Finds) This 1769 Georgian row house sits almost directly across from the back of Independence Park in busy Old City, and is owned by the federal government, which kept the shell and gutted the interior. The Colonial setting includes an entrance decorated with map illustrations and secretary desks, and a parlor with pink sofas and replica Chippendale furniture. Guest rooms—most with double beds, some with queen-size—are cheerful and comfortable, with period furnishings and basic, modern-day amenities. The inn serves a continental breakfast (with homemade muffins) on weekdays, and a full breakfast on weekends. Evening time calls for snacks: wine and cheese, and, later on, fresh-baked cookies. The hotel is named for its first occupant, the doctor who cofounded Pennsylvania Hospital with Benjamin Franklin.

129 S. 2nd St., Philadelphia, PA 19106. ✆ **800/845-2663** or 215/923-8523. Fax 215/923-8504. www.winston-salem-inn.com/philadelphia. 12 units. From $115 double; from $190 suite; $25 per additional person. Rates include breakfast and afternoon wine and cheese. AE, DISC, MC, V. Parking at adjacent lot $17. Bus: PHLASH, 21, or 42. Children 11 and over welcome. **Amenities:** Exercise room; limited business services; conference room. *In room:* A/C, TV, hair dryer.

2 WEST OF BROAD STREET

VERY EXPENSIVE

Four Seasons Hotel ★★★ (Kids) It was rated the best hotel in Philly in the 2007 Zagat guide, has earned five diamonds from AAA, and has been named one of the top 20 U.S. hotels in *Condé Nast Traveler:* The Four Seasons' luxury is refined and understated. Built in 1983, Logan Square's eight-story horseshoe offers views of the exquisite Swann Fountain and a lush interior courtyard. Enormous masses of flowers, intimate seating areas, and honey-colored woods adorn the lobby, lounge, and promenade. Guest rooms have a rich American elegance courtesy of overstuffed chairs, rich carpets, and top-notch in-room business and tech capabilities. The bathrooms have a wonderful marble dressing area and excellent lighting. All the rooms have windows boasting marvelous views of Logan Circle or the interior courtyard; those on the seventh floor enjoy private verandas. Request a room that looks down the parkway to the art museum and across to the Free Library, and you will be dazzled day and night.

The Four Seasons' restaurants collect major raves: Zagat rated the Fountain (p. 95) number one in Philadelphia and ranked it a top 10 in the country. Another great option is dining in the hotel's cafe room, which offers slightly more casual fare at about half the

Tips: The Four Seasons' Favorite Spots

We asked the Four Seasons' concierges to reveal a few of their favorite under-the-radar Philly spots. Here's what they said:

- **Shane Candies,** 110 Market St. (✆ **215/922-1048**). Try the rich, handmade chocolate butter creams at America's oldest candy store.
- **Japanese House and Garden (Shofuso),** Belmont and Montgomery drives (✆ **215/878-5097;** www.shofuso.com). Western Fairmount Park's beautifully preserved refuge is open May through October.
- **Dmitri's,** 3rd and Catharine streets (✆ **215/625-0556**). The original Queen Village BYOB always has long lines. See p. 108.
- **Christ Church,** 2nd and Church sts. The courtyard of Old City's prettiest Colonial church is the perfect spot for a picnic. See p. 133.
- **Eastern State Penitentiary,** 21st Street and Fairmount Avenue (✆ **215/236-5111**). Touring this decrepit, medieval-looking prison is a marvelous adventure. It is closed in winter. See p. 141.
- **Rosenbach Museum,** 20th Street and Delancey Place (✆ **215/732-1600**). Just off Rittenhouse Square, this paean to reading is a great place to rediscover James Joyce . . . and Maurice Sendak. See p. 139.
- **Mutter Museum,** 22nd and Market streets (✆ **215/563-3737**). Why do these four-star concierges like jars and jars of pickled organs? Maybe you should be nicer to them. See p. 142.
- **Wilma Theater,** Broad and Spruce streets (✆ **215/546-7824**). The Avenue of the Arts's premier venue for contemporary, original drama. See p. 191.

price of a Fountain dinner. The Swann Lounge has marble-top tables and a colorful, civilized look like something out of a Maurice Prendergast sketch. It's open for an extensive lunch, afternoon tea, and cocktails. Hidden in the hotel's day spa—right across from the pristine indoor pool—are amazing treatments with Philosophy, MD Skincare, and Naturopathica products.

1 Logan Sq., Philadelphia, PA 19103. ✆ **800/332-3442** or 215/963-1500. Fax 215/963-9506. www.fourseasons.com. 365 units. From $395 double. AE, DC, MC, V. Valet parking $36; self-parking $24. SEPTA: Suburban Station. Bus: PHLASH. Pets under 15 lb. accepted. **Amenities:** 2 restaurants; cafe; indoor heated pool; health club; spa; Jacuzzi; concierge; town-car service within Center City; salon; room service; babysitting; laundry service; dry cleaning. *In room:* A/C, TV w/pay movies, fax (upon request), high-speed Internet, minibar, fridge, iron/ironing board, safe, in-room exercise equipment (upon request).

Hotel Sofitel ★★ This stateside take on France's premier hotel chain is hospitable and chic, with its modern Art Deco vibe, classy bar off the marble lobby, and doormen that make a serious effort to greet you with an authentic "Bonjour." The location, half a block from the Walnut Street shopping corridor and between Rittenhouse Square and the Avenue of the Arts, is wonderful for business or pleasure visitors. Downstairs, the lobby is filled with inlaid marble, sleek wood, and flower arrangements; upstairs, guest rooms are upscale and Art Deco contemporary, with a glass coffee table, two armchairs, and an opulent bed with wall-mounted bedside lights on walls of handsome checkerboard cherrywood. The bathrooms are huge, with luxurious travertine marble throughout.

Chez Colette serves decadent French breakfasts (and complimentary coffee to guests), and remains quietly open for lunch and dinner. The lobby bar is a largely undiscovered gathering spot: a New York–style lounge, with tall windows overlooking Sansom Street, a long blue Brazilian granite bar, cozy seating areas, and varied wines by the glass.

120 S. 17th St., Philadelphia, PA 19103. ✆ **800/SOFITEL** (763-4835) or 215/569-8300. Fax 215/569-1492. www.sofitel.com. 306 units. From $160 double. AE, DC, DISC, MC, V. Valet parking in underground garage $30 per day. SEPTA: Suburban Station. Bus: PHLASH, 21, or 42. Pets accepted. **Amenities:** Brasserie; lounge; fully equipped fitness center; room service. *In room:* A/C, TV w/pay movies, high-speed Internet, Wi-Fi, hair dryer, iron/ironing board.

Park Hyatt Philadelphia at the Bellevue ★★ The "grande dame of Broad Street"—in 1904 the most opulent hotel in the country—remains a grand experience in a great location. Glitz- and glamourwise, the Park Hyatt ranks nearly among the Four Seasons, the Rittenhouse, and the Ritz-Carlton. The dazzling marble-mosaic ground floor houses high-end retailers Tiffany & Co., Williams-Sonoma, and Ralph Lauren. Below the hotel are Pierre & Carlo Spa Salon, Zanzibar Blue jazz bar and restaurant, and a gourmet food court. A separate elevator lifts you to the domed 19th-floor registration area and foyer for the hotel restaurants. The rooms, occupying floors 12 to 17, are large and all slightly different, with wall moldings reproduced from the 1904 designs. Each spacious, 831-square-foot room boasts extralarge goose-down duvets, a writing desk, a round table, and four upholstered chairs. The bathrooms are marble and have TVs and illuminated mirrors. In the morning, the hotel serves complimentary coffee; in the evening, it switches to bubbly.

The hotel's aptly named **Nineteen** restaurant (guess what floor it's on; p. 97) is worth a visit on its own. Adjacent to the hotel is the **Sporting Club,** 220–224 S. Broad St. (✆ **215/985-9875;** www.sportingclubbellevue.com), one of Philadelphia's top health clubs, a Michael Graves–designed facility with 93,000 square feet of health club space, including a half-mile jogging track; a four-lane, 25m junior Olympic pool; full basketball, squash, and racquetball courts; and some amazing yoga, Pilates, and boxing classes. (Nonguests who are members of partner health clubs in other cities may purchase day passes for $15 each. Call to find out if you qualify.)

1415 Chancellor Court (btw. Walnut and Locust sts.), Philadelphia, PA 19102. ✆ **800/223-1234** or 215/893-1234. Fax 215/732-8518. www.parkphiladelphia.hyatt.com. 172 units. $300 double; $340 suite. AE, DC, DISC, MC, V. Valet parking $25; self-parking $16. SEPTA: Walnut-Locust. Bus: PHLASH, 21, or 42. **Amenities:** Restaurant; lounge; indoor pool nearby; health club nearby; child care nearby; concierge; 24-hr. room service; laundry service; dry cleaning. *In room:* A/C, TV/VCR w/pay movies, high-speed Internet, Wi-Fi, minibar, hair dryer, iron/ironing board.

Rittenhouse Hotel ★★★ Kids Among Philadelphia's luxury hotels, the Rittenhouse has the fewest and largest rooms and the most satisfying views—which may be why Madonna stays here when she's in town. Built in 1989, it's a jagged concrete-and-glass high-rise off the western edge of Philadelphia's most distinguished public square. The lobby is tranquil and lovely, with inlaid marble floors, a series of frosted-glass chandeliers and sconces, and an amazing little gift shop. Next to the Four Seasons and the Ritz-Carlton, it's the only other AAA Five Diamond Award holder in the state.

Every guest room at the Rittenhouse is actually a suite with a full living room area, bay windows, reinforced walls between rooms, and solid-wood doors. All have great views: The park across the street is leafy and beautiful most of the year, and colorfully lit on wintry nights. The western view of the Schuylkill River and the parkway is dramatic. City scenes by local artists decorate the walls. Thirteen luxury suites include full European kitchens.

The in-house restaurant Lacroix is named after beloved founding chef Jean-Marie Lacroix, and is now helmed by maverick gastronome Matt Levin. The chic dining room overlooks the park, offering modern French cuisine. Smith & Wollensky, the New York steakhouse, has an outpost with a convivial bar off the main lobby, and the more casual Boathouse Row Bar & Grill has a late-night menu. The site was the original town house of painter Mary Cassatt's brother, and a charming trellised private garden features three of Cassatt's drypoints. Also on-site: A day spa and salon, connected to a sleek, spectacular health club and pool.

210 W. Rittenhouse Sq., Philadelphia, PA 19103. ✆ **800/635-1042** or 215/546-9000. Fax 215/732-3364. www.rittenhousehotel.com. 98 units. From $355 double. AE, DC, MC, V. Valet parking $24. Bus: 21 or 42. **Amenities:** 3 restaurants; bar; lounge; 5-lane indoor pool; Adolf Biecker fitness club; spa; sauna; steam room; concierge; business center; room service; massage; laundry service; dry cleaning. *In room:* A/C, TV/VCR w/pay movies, fax, high-speed Internet, minibar, hair dryer, iron/ironing board.

The Ritz-Carlton Philadelphia ★★★ Whereas its peers tend toward typical, Philadelphia understatement, the Ritz-Carlton puts on a grand show. Walk up the hotel's pale marble steps, between massive marble columns, and into the soaring, domed, Pantheon-like space that serves as lobby and cocktail lounge, and you'll instantly feel important. Designed in 1908 by McKim, Mead, and White as a bank, the Ritz's main building serves purely social functions (with a clubby "Vault" lounge, the handsome 10 Arts restaurant, and various ballrooms), while its adjacent 30-story former office houses the guest rooms.

Hotel rooms occupy floors 4 to 29, with a spectacular concierge/club area in a paneled former boardroom on the 30th floor. (Upgrading to this level is money well spent; the room is gorgeous, and the hors d'oeuvres, champagne, and lavish breakfast are the best club-floor spread we've ever seen.) The guest rooms are comfortable, not oversize, and the bathrooms are large and come with marble tub/shower alcoves. The furnishings are lovely, as are the old Philadelphia prints. Terry robes, Frette linens, a selection of pillows, a menu of bubble baths, and a chocolate on your pillow invite you to linger. Service doesn't get much better: Complimentary overnight shoeshine, subtle drop-ins from friendly housekeeping, even jolly valets can easily make a guest feel like getting used to this kind of treatment.

10 Arts ★★ is the hotel's boldly casual breakfast-through-dinner restaurant (p. 99). Conceptualized by celebrity chef Eric Ripert, the menu features local fare such as wild boar prosciutto from the Italian Market and Bucks County–grown vegetables, although you'd be just silly to turn down the banana pancakes at breakfast. Service here, too, is just impeccable.

10 Avenue of the Arts, Philadelphia, PA 19102. ✆ **800/241-3333** or 215/523-8000. Fax 215/568-0942. www.ritzcarlton.com. 299 units. From $359 double. Discounted holiday rates available. AE, DC, DISC, MC, V. Valet parking $34. SEPTA: 15th St./City Hall. Bus: PHLASH, 21, or 42. Some dogs accepted $25. **Amenities:** Restaurant; lounge; fitness center; spa; sauna; steam room; concierge; Wi-Fi; room service; massage; laundry service; dry cleaning. *In room:* A/C, TV w/pay movies, Wi-Fi, minibar, hair dryer, iron/ironing board, safe.

Westin Philadelphia ★★ (Kids) The best reason to stay at this Westin is to get an amazing night's rest in town. This hotel, attached to Liberty One, one of the city's tallest buildings, opened with great fanfare as a gorgeous, Parisian-proper Ritz-Carlton in 1990. While it's a bit higher priced than other Westins, it's a value compared to its luxury peers.

A small *porte-cochere* and a ground-floor entrance on 17th Street lead to elevators that lift you up to the main lobby, which is a series of living-room-like sitting rooms that serve wine and cheese nightly, plus a clubby bar and grill. The guest rooms are outfitted with bedside walnut tables, desks, and armoires, but the beds, with their spindle-top headboards, triple sheeting, and luxurious five pillows are the main attraction (baby guests will enjoy the bumper-protected, super-safe cribs, too). The modern bathrooms include an oversize, dual-head shower, magnifying mirrors, and Brazilian cotton towels. The hotel also caters to the health conscious, with a state-of-the-art fitness center and a concierge who offers maps and advice on nearby jogging routes.

99 S. 17th St. (at Liberty Place, btw. Chestnut and Market sts.), Philadelphia, PA 19103. ✆ **800/228-3000** or 215/563-1600. Fax 215/564-9559. www.westin.com. 290 units. From $229 double. AE, DISC, MC, V. Valet parking $36; self-parking $28. SEPTA: Suburban Station. Bus: PHLASH, 21, or 42. **Amenities:** Restaurant; lounge; small exercise facility; sauna; 24-hr. concierge; airport transportation ($8); business center; meeting rooms; internal access to Liberty Place; 24-hr. room service; laundry service; dry cleaning. *In room:* A/C, TV w/pay movies, fax, high-speed Internet, coffeemaker, hair dryer, iron/ironing board, safe.

EXPENSIVE

Embassy Suites Center City ★ Value This big 28-story cylinder of marble and glass on the parkway at 18th Street started out as a luxury apartment building in the 1960s. The all-suite structure coupled with the location and the price makes this a good choice for families, and guest rooms were renovated and new fitness and business centers opened in early 2008.

The kitchenette includes a microwave, an under-the-counter refrigerator, and a coffeemaker (no oven or dishwasher); dishes and silverware are provided upon request. A table with four chairs overlooks the small balcony. Bedrooms can offer one or two beds, and there is a pull-out couch in the living room.

TGI Friday's, connected on two levels, is open until 1am daily; full complimentary breakfast is served in the atrium. A manager's reception happy hour is included in your room rate.

1776 Benjamin Franklin Pkwy. (at Logan Sq.), Philadelphia, PA 19103. ✆ **800/362-2779** or 215/561-1776. Fax 215/963-0122. www.embassysuites.com. 288 units. $255 suite. Rates include full breakfast and happy hour. Children 17 and under stay free in parent's room. AE, DC, DISC, MC, V. Valet parking $24. SEPTA: Suburban Station. Bus: PHLASH, 21, 33, or 42. **Amenities:** Restaurant; fitness center; sauna; laundry service; dry cleaning. *In room:* A/C, 2 TVs w/pay movies, Internet, minibar, coffeemaker, microwave, hair dryer, iron/ironing board.

Inn at the League ★ Finds In 1862, a cadre of Philadelphia gentleman founded a society to support the policies of President Abraham Lincoln. Almost 150 years later, the Union League, a stoic French Renaissance–style brownstone building that cuts quite a profile at the heart of Broad Street, opened select floors for overnight stays by nonmembers. Although the vibe here is undoubtedly old boys' club, and there are some seemingly quirky rules about where guests may roam—and what they may wear—this inn nonetheless provides a certainly memorable lodging, what with its leather trimmings, gentlemanly wood paneling, polished marble floors, 28,000-book library, and impressive art collection—including quite an imposing portrait of President Ronald Reagan.

Guest rooms are traditionally furnished and modest in size. Reservations are by phone only. Breakfast is included, but don't dare show up late, for such behavior wouldn't be prudent for a place as proper as this.

1450 Sansom St., Philadelphia, PA 19102. ✆ **215/587-5570.** www.unionleague.org/the-inn-at-the-league. 84 units. $232 double. Rate includes breakfast. AE, DC, MC, V. Garage parking across the street $21. SEPTA: Walnut-Locust. Bus: PHLASH, 21, or 42. **Amenities:** 5 restaurants; lounge; fitness center; 24-hour business center; concierge; room service; laundry service; dry cleaning. *In room:* A/C, TV, DSL, minibar, hair dryer, iron/ironing board, bathrobes, newspaper.

The Latham ★ Value A landmark apartment house from 1915 to 1970, the Latham's charm, congeniality, and attention to small details bring to mind a small, superbly run Swiss hostelry. On weekday mornings, the lobby—a high-ceilinged salon with terrazzo highlights—is filled with refreshed executives, though the hotel does little convention business. The reception staff is quick and professional. The guest rooms, redone in Victorian motif, are not huge or lavish but perfectly proportioned and decorated with cheerful striped silk.

135 S. 17th St. (at Walnut St.), Philadelphia, PA 19103. ✆ **877/528-4261** or 215/563-7474. Fax 215/568-0110. www.lathamhotel.com. 139 units. From $107 double. Up to 2 children stay free in parent's room. AE, DC, DISC, MC, V. Valet parking $20. SEPTA: Walnut-Locust. Bus: PHLASH, 21, or 42. **Amenities:** Restaurant; lounge; small fitness center; concierge; laundry service; dry cleaning. *In room:* A/C, TV, Wi-Fi, minibar, coffeemaker, hair dryer, iron/ironing board.

Rittenhouse 1715 ★★ Finds Steps from chic Rittenhouse Square, the pristine park ringed by million-dollar apartments and historic mansions, this find does a marvelous impression of a small, European-style luxury hotel. The inn is at the heart of Center City, a 10-minute walk to the convention center, the Franklin Institute, and City Hall, but feels secluded on its tiny, leafy street a block from Walnut Street's shopping corridor. Set in a large mansion built around 1911, the lobby exudes haute-British style, and wine is served at 5pm. Upstairs, burrow under Frette linens and revel in cream-colored Berber carpets, antiques, and reproductions of Louis XIV and Chippendale furniture in 1 of 10 surprisingly large guest rooms and suites. All guest rooms have new marble bathrooms, and pastries and fruit are served in the morning from the city's best bakery, Metropolitan, to round out the sophisticated experience.

1715 Rittenhouse Sq., Philadelphia, PA 19103. ✆ **877/791-6500** or 215/546-6500. Fax 215/546-8787. www.rittenhouse1715.com. 10 units. $239–$699 double. $50 surcharge for Sat-only stay. AE, DC, MC, V. Parking in nearby lot $15. SEPTA: Suburban Station. Bus: PHLASH, 21, or 42. No children 11 and under. **Amenities:** 24-hr. concierge; small meeting rooms; high-speed Internet. *In room:* A/C, plasma TV, hair dryer, iron/ironing board, CD player, iPod hookup.

Sheraton Philadelphia Center City Value The city's biggest Sheraton (formerly the Wyndham at Franklin Plaza) feels like a cross between a business convention and a cruise ship. The hotel, which has been functioning as a meeting center since 1980, dominates a city block and is dominated by conventioneers. Lobby, lounge, and steakhouse reside beneath an impressive 70-foot glass roof. Request a westward-facing room above the 19th floor and you'll have an unobstructed view down the parkway, but be forewarned that the cathedral bells below ring at 7am, noon, and 6pm daily. Unfortunately, the hotel is in need of updating; it might want to begin by offering free Internet.

17th and Race sts., Philadelphia, PA 19103. ✆ **215/448-2000.** Fax 215/448-2864. www.sheraton.com. 759 units. From $159 double. Children 18 and under stay free in parent's room. AE, DC, MC, V. Valet parking $32; self-parking $25. SEPTA: Race-Vine. Bus: PHLASH. Pets up to 50 lb. accepted. **Amenities:** Restaurant; indoor pool; health club; Jacuzzi; sauna; racquetball courts; squash courts; handball courts; Wi-Fi in lobby; limited room service. *In room:* A/C, TV w/pay movies, high-speed Internet, fridge, coffeemaker, hair dryer, iron/ironing board.

MODERATE

Crowne Plaza Philadelphia Center City Value The Crowne Plaza offers solid, generic, well-located, business-traveler-oriented accommodations. It's popular with conventioneers and relocating executives, and prices are competitive in an effort to maintain occupancy. The lobby, which dispenses coffee and apples all day, has entrances from both 18th Street and the garage, and is just a hop and skip from the restaurants, bars, and

Best-Kept Secret of a B&B

In 2008, the **Lippincott House** (✆ **215/523-9251;** www.lippincotthouse.com) finished restoration of a pair of buildings (ca. 1897), and opened for business. Though the B&B takes up two adjacent addresses—2023 and 2025 Locust St.—it offers a mere four guest rooms, each one spacious and quiet. The look here is Victorian. There's a Brazilian rosewood lounge, a grand piano from 1887, an antique pool table, claw-foot tubs, and fireplaces throughout. Still, the facilities are anything but old school. Each room has a satellite TV, and the whole place is wired for Wi-Fi. The location, 1 block from Rittenhouse Square, is ideal, and so are the prices, which start at $175 a night.

shops around Rittenhouse Square. A parking garage and meeting halls occupy the next six floors, and rooms and several suites fill the next 17 floors. By Philadelphia standards, the rooms are large, although the bathrooms are on the smaller side. Two floors are devoted to executive-level suites, offering upgraded decor and complimentary breakfast. There is an espresso bar and a forgettable pub on the lobby level.

1800 Market St., Philadelphia, PA 19103. ✆ **800/980-6429** or 215/561-7500. Fax 215/561-4484. www.cpphiladelphia.com. 445 units. From $150 double Mon–Fri. Children 19 and under stay free in parent's room. Children 12 and under eat free with parent. AE, DC, MC, V. Valet or self-parking $31. SEPTA: 19th St. Bus: 21, 33, or 42. **Amenities:** Restaurant; outdoor pool; 24-hr. fitness room; Jacuzzi. *In room:* A/C, TV w/ pay movies, dataport, coffeemaker, hair dryer, iron/ironing board.

Radisson Plaza—Warwick Hotel Philadelphia ★★ Value Beloved by Philadelphians since 1926, the Warwick (which locals pronounce as "War-ick") has witnessed its fair share of banquets and balls. Today, the building is divided among guest rooms and swank condos. Both have windows that—get this—actually open. Guests pull up alongside the valet. Pets are welcome at a dedicated pet-friendly floor. The Prime Rib, the in-house steakhouse, is known for being the best and most formal in town. And the 2,000-square-foot fitness center is state-of-the-art. Rittenhouse Square is a block away, as are the shops and restaurants of Walnut Street. The Warwick—sorry, Radisson—also offers package deals that involve treatments at Rescue Rittenhouse Spa (p. 179), a blissful oasis of pampering across the street.

1701 Locust St. (entrance on 17th St. btw. Walnut and Locust), Philadelphia, PA 19103. ✆ **888/201-1718** or 215/735-6000. Fax 215/789-6105. www.radisson.com. 301 units. From $119 double. AE, DC, DISC, MC, V. Valet parking $30. SEPTA: Suburban Station. Bus: PHLASH, 21, 33, or 42. Pets accepted. **Amenities:** 2 restaurants; lounge; piano bar; fitness center; meeting space; salon; laundry service; coin laundry. *In room:* A/C, TV, free high-speed Internet, coffeemaker, hair dryer, iron/ironing board, newspaper.

Windsor Suites Philadelphia Kids Value This half-hotel, half-apartment building is popular with families planning extended stays in the city. It's very close to the Franklin Institute, the Academy of Natural Sciences, the Philadelphia Museum of Art, City Hall, and shopping. The lobby is pleasant enough. Most rooms have balconies. Living rooms and bedrooms are spacious and bland, with large, efficiency-style kitchens, including pots, pans, dishware, and utensils. All suites were renovated in 2003 and have marble bathrooms; the one-bedroom suites have a king-size bed and a pull-out sofa in the living room. Another bonus: the rooftop pool with a view of the city.

1700 Benjamin Franklin Pkwy., Philadelphia, PA 19103. ✆ **877/784-8379** or 215/981-5600. Fax 215/981-5608. www.windsorhotel.com. 110 units. From $94 double. Children 17 and under stay free in parent's room. AE, DC, DISC, MC, V. Valet parking $22. SEPTA: Suburban Station. Bus: PHLASH, 21, 33, or 42. **Amenities:** Restaurant; rooftop pool; 24-hr. fitness center; laundry service. *In room:* TV, high-speed Internet, kitchen, coffeemaker, hair dryer, iron/ironing board.

3 UNIVERSITY CITY (WEST PHILADELPHIA)

EXPENSIVE

The Hilton Inn at Penn ★★ (Kids) The handsome and elegantly appointed Inn at Penn feels well suited to the Ivy League campus it calls home. Hilton Hotels manages the facility, the six-story keystone of the block-long Sansom Commons (also home to collegiate restaurants and shops). While pedestrians may access the inn via Walnut Street, drivers enter through a *porte-cochere* off the north side of Sansom Street. Expansive stairways and corridors connect entrances to registration and to the Living Room, a fully stocked library where complimentary tea and coffee are dispensed until 4pm, and wine and spirits are sold thereafter. Artwork and bas-reliefs of U. Penn's athletic triumphs from decades past adorn the mission-style walls. The rooms are cozy, with top-quality furnishings and firm beds.

3600 Sansom St., Philadelphia, PA 19104. ✆ **800/445-8667** or 215/222-0200. Fax 215/222-4600. www.theinnatpenn.com. 238 units. From $143 double. Children 18 and under stay free in parent's room. AE, DC, DISC, MC, V. Valet parking $25. SEPTA: 34th St. Station. Bus: 21. **Amenities:** 2 restaurants; library lounge; 24-hr. exercise room; concierge. *In room:* A/C, WebTV w/pay movies, high-speed Internet, Wi-Fi, coffeemaker, hair dryer, iron/ironing board.

Penn Tower Hotel There's a reason the U. Penn website no longer makes mention of this smallish hotel: The accommodations are modest, at best. Still, the facility serves an important purpose for folks with friends or family at the adjacent University of Pennsylvania Hospital and Children's Hospital of Philadelphia: It's right across the street. The hotel portion of the tower comprises floors 17 and 18, although the university seems to take over more floors every year for medical offices. You'll have to get used to spirited displays of red and blue, Penn's colors, and a long lobby corridor of rough-textured concrete that leads to the reception desk. A coffee cart serves pastries and sandwiches in the lobby starting at 6am.

399 S. 34th St. (at Civic Center Blvd.), Philadelphia, PA 19104. ✆ **215/387-8333.** Fax 215/386-8306. 50 units. $175 double. Discounts for relatives of patients in U. Penn and Children's hospitals. Packages available. AE, DC, MC, V. Parking $9. Bus: 42. *In room:* A/C, TV, high-speed Internet, Wi-Fi, coffeemaker, hair dryer, iron/ironing board.

MODERATE

Sheraton University City This concrete block of a Sheraton, midway between Drexel University and the University of Pennsylvania, has long served parents of nearby students. Although it's not a spot you'd want to while away the hours, luxuriating in a tub, ordering up bottles of champagne, it does have comfortable beds and oversize business desks with ergonomic chairs (better to serve visitors who go across the street to take medical boards). One block from the subway, and 4 from the Amtrak station and three University City hospitals, it's all about convenience. On the Chestnut Street side of the building are a heated outdoor pool and sun deck. Skip the restaurant, Pallet: There are plenty of better places to dine in the neighborhood.

3549 Chestnut St., Philadelphia, PA 19104. ✆ **877/459-1156** or 215/387-8000. Fax 215/387-7920. www.philadelphiasheraton.com. 316 units. From $169 double. Packages available. Rates include continental breakfast. Children 18 and under stay free in parent's room. AE, DC, MC, V. Self-parking $15. SEPTA: 34th St. Station. Bus: 42. Pets up to 70 lb. accepted. **Amenities:** Restaurant; lounge; heated outdoor pool; fitness center; Enterprise car rental adjacent to the hotel; Wi-Fi in lobby; dry cleaning. *In room:* A/C, WebTV w/pay movies, high-speed Internet, coffeemaker, hair dryer, iron/ironing board.

INEXPENSIVE

Gables (Value) This lovely 1889 Victorian, once one of West Philadelphia's first and finest mansions, now serves as a charmingly eclectic bed-and-breakfast. About 8 blocks west of the University of Pennsylvania's main campus, it's right at the SEPTA trolley line stop in Center City, 5 minutes from 30th Street Station, and 15 minutes from the airport. If you want to get to Center City, you'll have to catch some kind of ride. It's an excellent choice for visiting academics, parents of students, prospective applicants, and relaxed tourists.

Eight formal areas are filled with antiques. There are sitting rooms, a breakfast room, and a wraparound porch; six bedrooms with private bathrooms and four bedrooms with adjacent bathrooms are on the top two floors. All rooms have gorgeous inlaid wood floors, and three have charming corner turrets. Some have gas fireplaces. Closets, armoires, lamps, and desks fit in with the grandmotherly Victorian decor. There is a lovely yard and garden. Breakfasts consist of home-baked peach crumble, quiches, fresh fruit, and muffins.

4520 Chester Ave. (at S. 46th St.), Philadelphia, PA 19143. ✆ **215/662-1918.** Fax 215/662-1918. www.gablesbb.com. 10 units, 8 with bathroom. $115–$185 double. Rates include full breakfast. AE, DISC, MC, V. Free off-street parking. SEPTA: #13 Green Line trolley stop. *In room:* A/C, TV, fax, dial-up Internet, Wi-Fi, fridge, microwave, hair dryer, iron (upon request), private phone w/answering machine.

4 NEAR THE AIRPORT

If you want to be close to the city—and expect great dining—don't stay near the airport. If, however, necessity calls for you to stay far outside of town, you'll find a bevy of chain options at the moderate-to-inexpensive level. Your more run-of-the-mill choices include **Hampton Inn Philadelphia International Airport,** 8600 Bartram Ave., Philadelphia, PA 19153 (✆ **800/426-7866** or 215/966-1300), with rates starting around $185; **Holiday Inn Philadelphia Stadium,** 10th Street and Packer Avenue, Philadelphia, PA 19148 (✆ **877/211-3289** or 215/755-9500), which averages $192 for a double; **Four Points by Sheraton,** 4101 Island Ave., Philadelphia, PA 19153 (✆ **800/325-3535** or 215/492-0400), a slimmed-down version of the Sheraton Suites across the way, whose average rate is $167 (and books far in advance); **Airport Ramada Inn,** 76 Industrial Hwy., Essington, PA 19029 (✆ **800/277-3900** or 610/521-9600), with a rate of $121 for a double; **Comfort Inn Airport,** 53 Industrial Hwy., Essington, PA 19029 (✆ **800/228-5150** or 610/521-9800), with a rate of $130 for a double; and **Holiday Inn Airport,** 45 Industrial Hwy., Essington, PA 19029 (✆ **800/843-7663** or 610/521-5090), offering $90 for a double.

EXPENSIVE

Philadelphia Airport Marriott Hotel ★ Value Opened in 1995 and renovated throughout in 2004, this is the only hotel linked by skywalk (via Terminal B) to Philadelphia International Airport, and the best of the airport options. The facility caters to business travelers but it's also decent for families, with concierge-level rooms that sleep up to five people. The soundproof rooms are mostly angled away from the runways, and it's convenient to I-95. When you throw in the complete fitness center and pool, the pleasant restaurant, the easy train or bus shuttle into Center City, and frequent weekend packages, it's well worth considering.

1 Arrivals Rd., Philadelphia, PA 19153. ✆ **800/628-4087** or 215/492-9000. Fax 215/492-6799. www.marriott.com. 419 units. From $284 double; $279 concierge-level (up to 5 people). AE, DC, DISC, MC, V. Parking $20. SEPTA: R1 Airport. **Amenities:** Restaurant; lounge; indoor pool; exercise room; Jacuzzi; Wi-Fi in public spaces; laundry service; dry cleaning. *In room:* A/C, TV w/pay movies, high-speed Internet, fridge, coffeemaker, hair dryer, iron/ironing board.

Renaissance Philadelphia Airport Jutting up from preserved marshlands, this shiny silver hotel has a great, glassed-in pool and a reputation for above-and-beyond service. The Renaissance is the only airport-area hotel to receive four diamonds from AAA. The sunny atrium is a popular meeting-up space. From clean, standard rooms, you can see planes taking off and landing. Weekend guests have complained about too much hustle and bustle. The facility is much quieter weekdays, when it's full of business travelers.

500 Stevens Dr., Philadelphia, PA 19113. ✆ **800/HOTELS-1** (468-3571) or 610/521-5900. Fax 610/531-4362. www.marriott.com. 349 units. $230 double. AE, DC, DISC, MC, V. Free parking. SEPTA: Airport shuttle and courtesy bus. **Amenities:** Restaurant; lounge; indoor pool; fitness center; Jacuzzi; courtesy airport transportation; limited room service. *In room:* A/C, TV w/pay movies, high-speed Internet, fridge, hair dryer, iron/ironing board.

Sheraton Suites Philadelphia Hotel Value Pony up a few more bucks than you would at the Four Points across the street and get a suite with a beautifully furnished bedroom and living room that encircle a dramatic eight-story atrium. The outer room contains a business desk and chair, convertible sofa bed, and armoire with TV. The bedroom, with the choice of a king-size or two cushy twin beds, has another TV and phone, and bathrooms are similarly handsome. Airport noise is minimal.

4101b Island Ave., Philadelphia, PA 19153. ✆ **800/325-3535** or 215/365-6600. Fax 215/492-9858. www.sheraton.com. 251 units. From $129 suite. Children 18 and under stay free in parent's room. AE, DC, DISC, MC, V. Parking $5. SEPTA: Airport shuttle and courtesy bus. **Amenities:** Restaurant/lounge; indoor pool; exercise room; sauna; steam room; Jacuzzi; car-rental desk; complimentary airport shuttle; same-day laundry service and dry cleaning. *In room:* A/C, 2 TVs w/pay movies, high-speed Internet, fridge, coffeemaker, hair dryer, iron/ironing board, multiport speakerphone.

MODERATE

aloft Philadelphia Airport ★★ Finds A glimpse of the future of overnighting can be had from this lower-priced branch of Starwood's upscale W Hotels chain. Opened in 2008, aloft brings a younger, higher-tech vibe to the neighborhood via airport check-in kiosks, a lounge à la George Jetson, a 24/7 self-serve snack bar, Bliss Spa bath amenities, clear and present (and free) wireless Internet throughout, a car wash, and, spare, well, loftlike rooms with iPod docking stations, ergonomic workspaces, walk-in showers, and a novel concept: platform beds that face the windows.

4301 Island Ave., Philadelphia, PA 19153. ✆ **877/GO-ALOFT** (462-5638) or 267/298-1700. Fax 267/298-1705. www.starwoodhotels.com/alofthotels. 136 units. $149 double. Packages available. AE, DC, MC, V.

Self-parking $5. Pets up to 70 lb. accepted. **Amenities:** Restaurant; lounge; indoor pool; fitness center; free Wi-Fi throughout; car wash. *In room:* A/C, TV w/free games and pay movies, iPod docking station, Wi-Fi, fridge, coffeemaker, hair dryer, iron/ironing board.

Embassy Suites Hotel Philadelphia Airport Travelers who need to catch an early-morning flight—or who missed one the night before—avail themselves of the basic, comfortable beds and spacious two-room suites in this roadside hotel. They can also make use of a larger-than-average workout space and indoor pool, which is often splashing with kiddies. Each morning, a complimentary, cooked-to-order breakfast is served in the atrium. Rooms are large, comfortable, and clean—pull-out couches in doubles are great for families traveling with kids.

9000 Bartram Ave., Philadelphia, PA 19153. ✆ **215/365-4500.** Fax 215/365-4803. www.embassysuites.com. From $169 double. Rates include breakfast. AE, DC, MC, V. Free parking. **Amenities:** Restaurant; indoor pool; health club w/basketball court; limited room service; coin-op washers and dryers. *In room:* A/C, 2 TVs w/pay movies, high-speed Internet, fridge, coffeemaker, microwave, hair dryer, iron/ironing board.

Philadelphia Airport Hilton The Philadelphia Airport Hilton is out of the way of flight patterns and features a just-renovated lobby and cocktail lounge built around a lushly planted indoor pool. Like all airport hotels, business travelers predominate during the week, and reservations are recommended. Renovated in 2005, the guest rooms, with whirlpool-equipped bathrooms, are classically American—spacious and comfortable.

4509 Island Ave., Philadelphia, PA 19153. ✆ **800/HILTONS** (445-8667) or 215/365-4150. Fax 215/937-6382. www.hilton.com. 331 units. $179 double. Children 18 and under stay free in parent's room. AE, DC, DISC, MC, V. Free parking. SEPTA: Airport shuttle and courtesy bus. **Amenities:** Restaurant; lounge; indoor pool; health club; Jacuzzi; sauna; courtesy airport transportation; 24-hr. room service; laundry service; dry cleaning. *In room:* A/C, TV w/pay movies, high-speed Internet, minibar, coffeemaker, hair dryer, iron/ironing board.

5 CITY LINE & NORTHEAST

City Line Avenue (U.S. 1), just off the Schuylkill Expressway, is a good jumping-off point for the western suburbs, Lancaster County, or even the Philadelphia Zoo, Fairmount Park, and the river drives. It's also near Northeast Philadelphia, home to the discount shopping at Franklin Mills Mall, and near to both Bucks County and the entrance to the fabulous New Jersey Turnpike.

Thoroughly comfortable national chains dot this area. These include **Homewood Suites Philadelphia,** 4200 City Line Ave., Philadelphia, PA 19131 (✆ **800/362-2779** or 215/966-3000); **Holiday Inn City Line,** 4100 Presidential Blvd. (City Line Ave. at I-76), Philadelphia, PA 19131 (✆ **800/465-4329** or 215/477-0200); the newly renovated **Hilton City Line,** 4200 City Line Ave., Philadelphia, PA 19131 (✆ **800/445-8667** or 215/879-4000); and the **Best Western Philadelphia Northeast,** 11580 Roosevelt Blvd., Philadelphia, PA 19116 (✆ **800/528-1234** or 215/464-9500).

6 HOSTELS

A $28 annual membership (free to those 17 and under; $18 for seniors 55 and over) with **Hostelling International USA,** 8401 Colesville Rd., Ste. 600, Silver Spring, MD 20910 (✆ **301/495-1240;** www.hiusa.org), will give you discounts on already-low hostel rates.

Apple Hostel (formerly Bank Street Hostel) ★ Value This 140-year-old former factory and its two neighbors, located in the heart of Old City, offer basic, dependable accommodations for travelers on a budget. The dormitory-style rooms are spread over four floors of the complex. Extras include free coffee and tea, a billiards table, a lounge with a large-screen TV—and no curfew. Kitchen facilities, washers, and dryers are available to use for free. Clean, dorm-style bathrooms are shared. Discounts on food and other items at area merchants are available. The hostel sponsors a neighborhood pub-crawl on Thursday nights.

32 S. Bank St. (btw. 2nd and 3rd sts. and Market and Chestnut sts.), Philadelphia, PA 19106. ✆ **800/392-4678** or 215/922-0222. Fax 215/922-4082. www.bankstreethostel.com. 70 beds, shared bathrooms. Hostelling International members $29 Mon–Fri, $32 Sat–Sun; nonmembers $32 Mon–Fri, $35 Sat–Sun. MC, V. Parking at nearby garages from $18. SEPTA: 2nd St. Station. Bus: PHLASH, 21, or 42.

Chamounix Hostel Mansion ★ Finds This renovated 1802 Quaker farmhouse isn't just the cheapest overnight in town, it's also the most bucolic. Chamounix Mansion is a Federal-style edifice constructed as a country retreat at what is now the upper end of Fairmount Park. It has six air-conditioned dormitory rooms for 44 people, with limited family arrangements, and another 37 spots in a fully renovated adjoining carriage house. Guests have use of the renovated self-serve kitchen, the TV/VCR lounge, videos, and bicycles. Write or call ahead for reservations, since the hostel is often 90% booked in summer by groups of boat crews or foreign students. You can check in from 8 to 11am and 4:30pm to midnight (curfew) daily. Lockout is from 11am to 4:30pm each day. Checkout is from 8 to 11am. Call **American Youth Hostels** at ✆ **215/925-6004** for information on hostel trips in the area.

3250 Chamounix Dr. (W. Fairmount Park), Philadelphia, PA 19131. ✆ **800/379-0017** or 215/878-3676. Fax 215/871-4313. www.philahostel.org. 81 beds. Hostelling International & ISIC members $20; nonmembers $23; children 16 and under $8. MC, V. Closed Dec 15–Jan 15. Bus: Take SEPTA route 38 from J.F.K. Blvd. near City Hall to Ford and Cranston sts. (a 30-min. ride), then walk under the overpass and left onto Chamounix Dr. to the end. By car: Take I-76 (Schuylkill Expwy.) to exit 33, City Line Ave., turn right (south) on City Line Ave. to Belmont Ave., left on Belmont to first traffic light at Ford Rd., left on Ford, through stone tunnel to stop sign, then a left onto Chamounix Dr. and follow to the end. **Amenities:** Bikes; game room w/Ping-Pong and piano; TV/VCR lounge; Internet kiosk; kitchen; coin-op washer and dryer. *In room:* A/C.

6

Where to Dine

by Lauren McCutcheon

Dining out in Philly requires some serious decision making. Among your choices: gourmet glamour along Walnut Street, culinary crowding at a BYOB, cocktail-infused supping in Old City, Italian-American feasting in South Philly, or cheesesteak sinking-into at a sidewalk picnic table.

Some dining rooms are made for special occasions, such as Vetri, Le Bec-Fin, the Fountain, Lacroix, and Morimoto. Some casual standouts—Standard Tap, Famous Fourth Street, Monk's, Tacconelli's—are so good, diners travel from miles around just to eat at them.

This chapter, unfortunately, does not have enough space to include many renowned suburban restaurants. If you're heading out that way, consult with your hotel concierge or volunteers at the desk at the **Independence Visitor Center,** 1 N. Independence Mall W. (6th and Market sts.), Philadelphia, Philadelphia, PA 19106 (✆ **215/965-7676;** www.independencevisitorcenter.com), or go online to the restaurant pages of **www.philly.com**, **www.phillymag.com**, **www.foobooz.com**, or **www.menupages.com** for downloadable menus and reader reviews. Most restaurants have their own sites; many schedule reservations through www.opentable.com.

This chapter categorizes **very expensive** restaurants as those charging $55 or more per person for dinner without wine; **expensive** as $40 to $55 per person; **moderate** as $20 to $40; and **inexpensive** as under $20. Meal tax is 7%, and standard tipping is 18% to 20% (tips are rarely included on the tab).

The service of wine and liquor is fraught with politics. Some restaurants are BYOB due to high fees to get a license, and restaurants with licenses may charge as much as 300% what they paid for a bottle of wine. The state Liquor Control Board does allow restaurants with licenses to permit customers to bring their own bottles, but don't look for quick acceptance of this policy.

Lunch is a fantastic way to experience the city's high-end restaurants at a less daunting price. See p. 93 for some ideas.

1 CENTER CITY: EAST OF BROAD

VERY EXPENSIVE

Morimoto ★★★ FUSION/JAPANESE Morimoto may serve the priciest oh-toro tuna in town, but when you're eating in the eponymous modern showplace of Japan's *Iron Chef,* you're paying for a meal and a show. First, the show: Beyond neon yellow glass doors, the narrow space stretches back along an undulating bamboo ceiling. Filling it are boxy booths that subtly change colors every few minutes.

Next, the meal: Whitefish carpaccio melts in your mouth. Barbecued eel is a revelation. Caviar and white wasabi adorn the best tuna tartare you'll ever nibble. Kobe beef is cooked tableside in a hot stone bowl. Tofu is mixed to order. If you're feeling especially flush, go for the *omakase* (chef's choice) multicourse menu of edgy dishes (prices start at

$80). If you're feeling especially star-struck, chef-owner Masahuru Morimoto, provided he's in town, will sign your menu.

Solo diners may want to request a seat at the sushi bar. If you're in the mood for drinks, head upstairs to the mezzanine bar for a sake-infused martini. Lunch is a relative bargain—$13 to $26 for three courses—but is more subdued.

723 Chestnut St. ✆ **215/413-9070.** www.morimotorestaurant.com. Reservations recommended. Main courses $23–$49; sushi $3–$8 per piece (higher for market-price items). AE, DC, MC, V. Sun–Wed 11:30am–2pm and 5–10pm; Thurs 11:30am–2pm and 5–11pm; Fri 11:30am–2pm and 5pm–midnight; Sat 5pm–midnight.

EXPENSIVE

Amada ★★★ **Moments** CONTEMPORARY TAPAS Since 2005, chef Jose Garces's sprawling destination restaurant has been the sleekest see-and-be-seen spot in Old City. On any given night, a young, professional crowd squeezes four-deep into the bar to sip thoroughly modern white pear sangria in the presence of antique sangria casks, a Spanish meat slicer, and a mini-groceria. That Amada serves stunningly authentic, meant-for-sharing tapas is merely delicious icing on the cake (or, in this case, the truffled lavender honey on the Manchego).

Standouts include Spain's best-loved cheeses, tissue-thin slices of cured pork, grilled octopus, and warm fava bean salad. Bigger plates like overflowing bowls of paella and order-ahead roasted suckling pig are also terrific. Still, it would be a mistake to miss out on Garces's impeccable fusion. Try his signature green plantain empanadas, duck flatbreads, and his chocolate hazelnut or garlic dulce de leche spread for cheeses. Many patrons call months ahead for reservations. The busiest times—although it's rarely quiet—are around 8pm on Wednesday and Saturday nights, an hour before flamenco dancers perform on an elevated platform in the restaurant's center, their stomping feet and whisking skirts turning diners into a frenzied, clapping audience.

217–219 Chestnut St. ✆ **215/625-2450.** www.amadarestaurant.com. Reservations strongly recommended. Tapas dishes $5–$32. AE, DC, DISC, MC, V. Mon–Thurs 11:30am–11pm; Fri 11:30am–1am; Sat 5pm–1am; Sun 4–11pm.

Bistrot La Minette ★★ **Finds** FRENCH New in 2008, this tucked-away bistro has the patina of a much older establishment. As authentically Gallic as Philadelphia gets, this chef-run spot does a smashing job of sticking to culinary tradition. The country pâté is homemade, the rabbit is braised in mustard, and the simple *salade verte* is sublimely straightforward. Among the entrees, my favorite is the brown-buttery trout meunière. On a list of authentic desserts, the cheese plate, raspberry mille feuille and tarte tatin are meal-ending perfection. The wine pours aren't huge, so you might want to consider ordering a bottle instead. Another money-saving option for groups of 4 to 20: Call 24 hours in advance, and order a family dinner for $45, $55, or $65. Dress here is casual—but French casual, so no sweat pants, please.

623 S. 6th St. (btw. South and Bainbridge sts.). ✆ 215/925-8000. www.bistrotlaminette.com. Reservations recommended. Main courses $17–$29. AE, DISC, MC, V. Mon–Thurs 5:30–10:30pm; Fri–Sat 5:30–11:30pm.

Buddakan ★★ **Moments** ASIAN FUSION Named for the giant, gilded Buddha who lords over a communal dining table, this ever-trendsetting establishment remains, since 1998, one of the toughest reservations in town. No wonder. The space—an old post office—is stunning. The white-clad servers are top-notch. And the menu, which is family style and stars wok-seared lobsters, sesame-encrusted tuna steak, lobster mashed

Philadelphia Dining

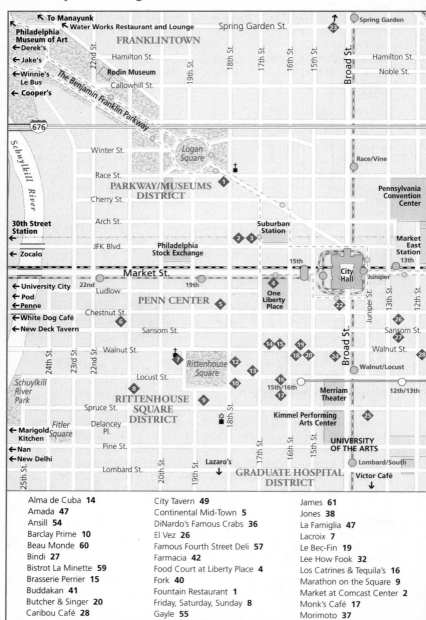

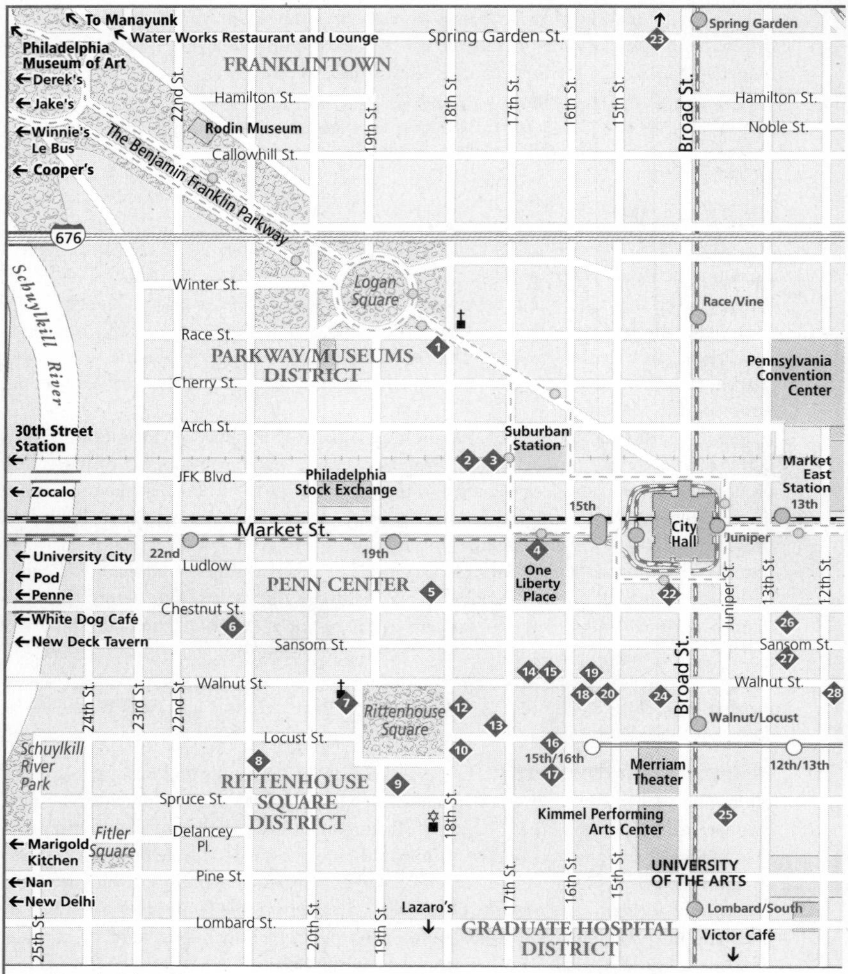

Alma de Cuba **14**
Amada **47**
Ansill **54**
Barclay Prime **10**
Beau Monde **60**
Bindi **27**
Bistrot La Minette **59**
Brasserie Perrier **15**
Buddakan **41**
Butcher & Singer **20**
Caribou Café **28**
City Tavern **49**
Continental Mid-Town **5**
DiNardo's Famous Crabs **36**
El Vez **26**
Famous Fourth Street Deli **57**
Farmacia **42**
Food Court at Liberty Place **4**
Fork **40**
Fountain Restaurant **1**
Friday, Saturday, Sunday **8**
Gayle **55**
James **61**
Jones **38**
La Famiglia **47**
Lacroix **7**
Le Bec-Fin **19**
Lee How Fook **32**
Los Catrines & Tequila's **16**
Marathon on the Square **9**
Market at Comcast Center **2**
Monk's Café **17**
Morimoto **37**

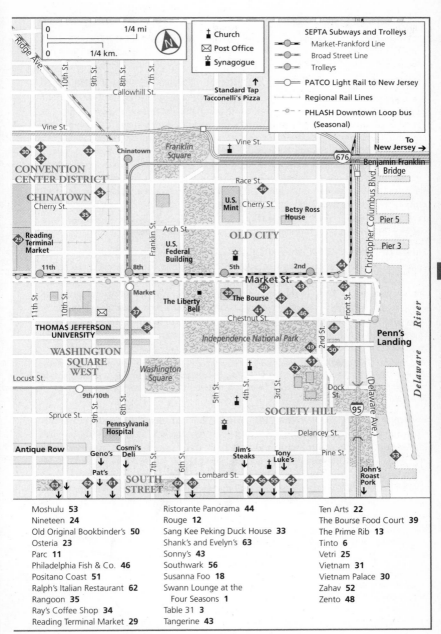

Moshulu **53**
Nineteen **24**
Old Original Bookbinder's **50**
Osteria **23**
Parc **11**
Philadelphia Fish & Co. **46**
Positano Coast **51**
Ralph's Italian Restaurant **62**
Rangoon **35**
Ray's Coffee Shop **34**
Reading Terminal Market **29**
Ristorante Panorama **44**
Rouge **12**
Sang Kee Peking Duck House **33**
Shank's and Evelyn's **63**
Sonny's **43**
Southwark **56**
Susanna Foo **18**
Swann Lounge at the Four Seasons **1**
Table 31 **3**
Tangerine **43**
Ten Arts **22**
The Bourse Food Court **39**
The Prime Rib **13**
Tinto **6**
Vetri **25**
Vietnam **31**
Vietnam Palace **30**
Zahav **52**
Zento **48**

potatoes, and edamame ravioli, is so good, you won't want to share, family or not. The sculptural desserts are splurge-worthy: Go for the sugar-spired banana tower or the gravity-defying chocolate pagoda.

325 Chestnut St. ✆ **215/574-9440.** www.buddakan.com. Reservations required. Main courses $12–$18 lunch, $18–$32 dinner. AE, DC, MC, V. Sun–Thurs 11:30am–2:30pm and 4–10pm; Fri 11:30am–2:30pm and 5pm–midnight; Sat 5pm–midnight.

City Tavern ★ TRADITIONAL AMERICAN Though the original building was demolished in 1854, this replica is a fun place to get a taste of the past. Paul Revere, John Adams, and George Washington all downed mead and vittles at the City Tavern. The design is Colonial, the servers wear historically correct costumes, and the menu offers respectable versions of pepperpot soup, Martha Washington's turkey potpie, and prime rib rubbed with 18th-century herbs and served with a right proper Yorkshire pancake. Another bonus: local beer, made according to Jefferson's and Washington's specifications. German-born chef-owner Walter Staib specializes in Black Forest fare, so expect excellent specials involving spaetzle and schnitzel. The restaurant stays open on holidays, and feels especially festive on Thanksgiving and Christmas.

138 S. 2nd St. (at Walnut St.). ✆ **215/413-1443.** www.citytavern.com. Reservations recommended. Main courses $10–$20 lunch, $18–$33 dinner. AE, DISC, MC, V. Daily 11:30am–9pm.

Farmacia ★★ AMERICAN MODERN A quiet, contemporary, casually upscale restaurant and bar along an otherwise bustling Old City strip, Farmacia makes the best of locally produced ingredients. A baker and a chef co-own and operate the joint, which itself doubles as a bakery. Early in the morning, shoppers pop in for loaves of multigrain and chocolate croissants. At lunchtime, it's a nice, sunny spot for a better-than-average burger or trout salad. Homey dinners include honey-garlic grilled Niman Ranch pork chops and savory eggplant cannelloni (one of a handful of vegetarian/vegan options). Don't miss dessert or the cocktail "tonics" that combine fresh herbs and fruit purées with champagne and the like.

15 S. 3rd St. ✆ **215/627-6274.** www.farmiciarestaurant.com. Reservations accepted. Main courses $13–$26. AE, MC, V. Restaurant Tues–Thurs 11:30am–2:30pm and 5:30–10pm; Fri 11:30am–3pm and 5:30–11pm; Sat 10:30am–3pm and 5:30–11pm; Sun 10:30am–3pm and 5–9pm. Bakery/cafe Tues–Fri 8am–4pm; Sat–Sun 8:30am–4pm.

Fork ★★★ Finds CONTINENTAL Fork, with its tall green banquettes, beautifully shaded light fixtures, oval-shaped bar, and open rear kitchen, is an affordable, stylish bistro—and a local favorite. Set in a historic brick former warehouse, it is intimate and convivial, with 68 impeccable seats, and sought-after bar stools where regulars like to perch for classic sidecars and heirloom tomato salads. Most of the ingredients come from organic farms and Amish purveyors, and the menu changes daily. Signature dishes include mustard seed–crusted scallops over butternut squash risotto, and chimichurri-laced hanger steak with matchstick-thin yucca frites. Sunday brunch is excellent, featuring brioche French toast and creamy cheddar grits.

Next door at 308 is **Fork, Etc.,** an all-day cafe selling eat-in or takeout gourmet sandwiches, salads, soups, baked goods, beverages, artisan breads, and wonderful, food-centric hostess gifts—antique corkscrews, pottery bowls, vintage cordial glasses. On Wednesday nights, this space hosts a first-come, first-served four-course dinner around a tall, shared table. The $40 price tag includes wine.

306 Market St. ✆ **215/625-9425.** www.forkrestaurant.com. Reservations recommended. Main courses $10–$14 lunch, $19–$33 dinner. AE, DC, DISC, MC, V. Mon–Thurs 11:30am–10:30pm; Fri 11:30am–11:30pm; Sat 5–11:30pm; Sun 11am–3pm and 5–10:30pm. Bar menu Thurs until midnight; Fri–Sat until 1am.

La Famiglia ★★ Finds ITALIAN Several generations of the Sena family are involved in this successful restaurant, which has spawned Penn's View Inn and Ristorante Panorama (see below). The restaurant seats 60 in a warm, old-world setting of hand-hammered Venetian chandeliers and majolica tiles. Most pasta is homemade. Try the *pappardelle ai funghi,* served in appetizer or entree portions, or save room for an excellent veal chop with fresh garlic-basil sauce. For dessert, I love *mille foglie,* the Italian version of the napoleon, or the profiteroles in chocolate sauce, accompanied by one of the grappas (kept over the fireplace). People often linger long after closing.

8 S. Front St. ✆ **215/922-2803.** www.la-famiglia.com. Reservations required. Main courses $24–$40; lunch fixed-price menu $26. AE, DISC, MC, V. Mon 5:30–9:30pm; Tues–Thurs noon–2:30pm and 5:30–9:30pm; Fri noon–2:30pm and 5:30–10pm; Sat 5:30–10pm; Sun 5–9:30pm.

Old Original Bookbinder's Overrated AMERICAN SEAFOOD Celebrating a special occasion with a meal at "Bookie's" is a Philadelphia tradition as immutable as eating cheesesteaks at 3am or running up the art museum steps, à la Rocky. This historic restaurant—open from 1865, with a few years' break in the early aughts—is the place many Philadelphia kids experience their first $50 lobster. It's the place grandmothers remember fondly, and that concierges always seem to suggest. A millennial renovation offered a much-needed interior design refresher, handsomely blending old-school tradition—see the black-and-white celebrity photos on the way to the restroom or the wall of oyster platters—and contemporary spaciousness.

The menu does best with old-fashioned classics: big crab cakes, cheese-topped seafood specials, and those big, broiled lobsters plucked from the tank. The kitchen is less successful, however, with modern fare. (Avoid anything with wasabi, ginger, or avocado.)

125 Walnut St. ✆ **215/925-7027.** www.bookbinders.biz. Reservations recommended. Main courses $14–$24 lunch, $28–$62 dinner. AE, MC, V. Mon–Thurs 11:30am–9pm; Fri 11:30am–10pm; Sat 1:30–10pm; Sun 4–9pm.

Tangerine ★★ MEDITERRANEAN Modern Moroccan decor and edgy Mediterranean dinners meet in this dimly lit, spacious lair of rose-infused cocktails, grand lamb and honey tagines—and expense accounts. Tangerine is smack-dab in the middle of one of Old City's busiest nightlife blocks, and has dedicated its storefront to a low-slung lounge that feels like a hookah joint as imagined by architect David Rockwell. Beyond the lounge, past a wall of shimmering votives, are dining chambers divided by sheers and lit by pin-dotted chandeliers.

Tangerine's cuisine gives an exotic edge to upscale basics. Whole bronzino, grilled pork chops, and filet mignon are amped up with spicy couscous, pomegranate marinades, tahini, preserved lemon, and other vaguely exotic trimmings. Sharing-size portions and big tables make this an ideal choice for large groups out to have some fun.

232 Market St. ✆ **215/627-5116.** www.tangerinerestaurant.com. Reservations recommended. Main courses (meant for sharing) $18–$31. AE, DC, MC, V. Mon–Thurs 5–11pm; Fri–Sat 5pm–midnight; Sun 5–10pm.

Zahav ★★★ ISRAELI Tucked into a quiet corner of Old City, in the shadow of Society Hill towers, this rustic but edgy Israeli restaurant opened in 2008 to rave reviews. Food here is savory and comforting: Tahini-rich hummus (try the buttery Turkish variety) served with soft *laffa* flatbread, baked sheep's milk cheese with dates and pine nuts, cauliflower fried with garlic and shrimp, coal-fired house-made merguez redolent with cumin and served with couscous. I highly recommend the kabobs, and, if you're not in the mood to make choices, the $48 tasting menu. Oh yes, and spiked Israeli lemonade, made with lemon verbena, bourbon, and mint.

The space itself is surprisingly countrylike, with terra-cotta tiles and cafe tables. Servers wear T-shirts, and so can you. Zahav also has a great bar for snacking and sipping cocktails made with rye infused with pumpernickel and caraway, or a gin and tonic that's healthed up with tomato water, and a large private dining room for extralarge groups.

237 St. James Place. ✆ **215/625-8800.** www.zahavrestaurant.com. Reservations recommended. Small dishes $6–$10; larger plates $14–$8; tasting menu $48. AE, DISC, MC, V. Mon 11:30am–2pm; Tues–Wed 11:30am–2pm and 5–10pm; Thurs–Fri 11:30am–2pm and 5–11pm; Sat 5–11pm; Sun 5–10pm.

MODERATE

Bindi ★★ MODERN INDIAN Tiny, stylish, romantic BYOB Bindi consistently surprises Indian food aficionados with its authentic, innovative fusion fare. Chef Marcie Turney puts a seasonal, nouveau spin on traditional samosas, tikkas, vindaloos, and biryani—even the homemade nan gets stuffed with goat cheese, coconut, and dates. Both carnivore and vegetarian friendly, this spot accepts reservations for weeknights only: on Friday and Saturday nights, it's first-come, first-served. Another highlight: Every night the kitchen mixes up batches of fresh fruit juices (think: mango cardamom) to use as mixers for the BYO rum.

105 S. 13th St. (btw. Chestnut and Sansom sts.). ✆ **215/922-6061.** www.bindibyob.com. Reservations accepted Mon–Fri. Main courses $18–$24. No credit cards. Tues–Thurs 5–10pm; Fri–Sat 5–11pm; Sun 5–10pm.

Caribou Cafe ★ FRENCH This classic French brasserie is one of those lunch and dinner spots you can count on, meal after meal. Chef-owner Olivier Desaintmartin has a way with cafe standards. His steak frites is impeccable; his onion soup, idyllic; and his cassoulet, *magnifique.* The place itself is classy and casual, with booth and cafe table seats downstairs and on the mezzanine level. It's perfect for chilling out over a goat cheese salad after a long morning at the nearby convention center, or to indulge in escargots in puff pastry before a fancy night on the town. Caribou's bar is especially nice, with its mirrored wall and modestly perfect selection of wines by the glass. Brunch, with croque-monsieurs, waffles with ice cream, and smoked salmon eggs Benedict, is a nice option, too. Desaintmartin also runs tiny **Zinc Bar** ★ at 246 S. 11th St. (✆ **215/351-9901**), serving up tweaked French fare such as salmon over ratatouille, grilled steak frites, clever salads, and marvelous wines.

1126 Walnut St. ✆ **215/625-9535.** www.cariboucafe.com. Reservations recommended. Main courses $8–$18 lunch, $16–$25 dinner. AE, MC, V. Mon–Thurs 11:30am–10:30pm; Fri–Sat 11:30am–11:30pm; Sun 11:30am–10pm.

Continental ★★ CONTINENTAL The jampacked Continental has comfy booths lit by overhead lights that resemble olives. It serves burgers, pad Thai, lobster mashed potatoes, and salads bigger than most beehives, plus 15 (most of them sugary) cocktails served in martini glasses (some, like the sugar-rimmed "champagne-a-rama," and the Tang-y "Buzz Aldrin," seem custom-made for drinkers in training). It's a perfectly nice place for lunch—and even an early dinner with the family. But this place really gets going after dark, when the volume goes up and drinks go down.

138 Market St. ✆ **215/923-6069.** www.continentalmartinibar.com. Main courses $12–$24. AE, DC, MC, V. Mon–Wed 11:30am–11pm; Thurs–Fri 11:30am–midnight; Sat–Sun 10am–midnight.

DiNardo's Famous Crabs ★ Value SEAFOOD This 30-year-old seafood house is one of the few Old City spots that doesn't stand on stylishness alone. The building was an inn for Tory soldiers in 1776, served as a stop along the underground railroad, and became a brothel during Prohibition. Today, it's modestly decorated with fishing lures and Mummers costumes.

Wear a bib while you dig into the trays of secretly spiced hard-shell crabs. Less work are the straightforward crab cakes, steamed clams, raw oysters, and captain's-style fried or broiled seafood platters, served with baked potatoes and pitchers of beer. Service is especially patient with families with small kids. Monday is all-you-can-eat crab night, $32 per person.

312 Race St. ✆ **215/925-5115.** www.dinardos.com. Reservations required for 5 or more. Main courses $8–$20 lunch, $18–$35 dinner; crabs $3–$5 each. AE, DC, MC, V. Mon–Thurs 11am–10pm; Fri–Sat 11am–11pm; Sun 3–9pm.

El Vez ★ MEXICAN Flashy, fun, and just a block from Broad Street, this colorful corner eatery is an excellent spot to wash down just-made guac and chips with fruity margaritas. El Vez is the kind of restaurant you'd want in your neighborhood. Its big, circular bar with its centerpiece low-rise bike always seems to have a couple of empty stools. Its giant, golden booths are comfy and chic. It's got plenty of tables, a menu that suits most budgets, and, best of all, an arcade-style photo booth. Highlights include straight-shooting tortilla soup, wee spicy tuna tostadas, and just gussied-up-enough takes on traditional tacos, enchiladas, guacamole, and carne asada. Dessert's fine, but those tequila drinks—made with freshly squeezed lime, blood orange, pomegranate juice, and guava—are the bomb.

121 S. 13th St. (at Sansom St.). ✆ **215/928-9800.** www.elvezrestaurant.com. Reservations recommended. Main courses $15–$26; tacos and enchiladas $9–$19. AE, DISC, MC, V. Mon–Thurs 11:30am–3pm and 5–11pm; Fri 11:30am–3pm and 5pm–midnight; Sat noon–midnight; Sun 11am–3pm and 5–10pm.

Moshulu (Moments) AMERICAN SEAFOOD Penn's Landing's venerable, century-old, four-masted tall ship offers a combined 600 seats of below-deck supping, bar chilling, and, weather permitting, deck dancing. Service is known to be spotty, but the view can't be beat. The food is trendy: Look for sesame crusts, wasabi trimmings, and ginger soy glazes and the like—sometimes without the expertise to back it up, sometimes with.

To my mind—and for the money—the best part of this ship is its open-air deck, which, in summer, serves much of the dining room's menu, plus burgers.

401 S. Columbus Blvd. (on Delaware River btw. South and Pine sts.). ✆ **215/923-2500.** www.moshulu.com. Reservations recommended. Main courses $15–$20 lunch, $27–$55 dinner; $16–$28 in the bar. AE, DC, DISC, MC, V. Mon–Sat 11:30am–3pm and 5:30–10:30pm; Sun 10:30am–2:30pm and 5:30–10:30pm. Bar and Deck Mon–Fri 5:30–10:30pm; Sat 11am–9:30pm; Sun 11:30am–8pm.

Philadelphia Fish & Company ★ (Value) SEAFOOD/AMERICAN This tried-and-true restaurant is easy to miss, but that would be a mistake for any choosy diner on a budget. Without much fuss or frill, owner Kevin Meeker delivers a reasonable, high-quality selection of fresh fish. The main courses run from basic crab cakes with coleslaw to innovative dishes like surf and turf with scallops and lamb dolmas. The dinner special ($9–$12) at the bar—maybe grilled bluefish, maybe fish tacos, maybe lobster mac and cheese—is another bargain (as is the delicious lobster roll for $17). The wine list, skewed toward whites, is of a good quality and very reasonable for Philadelphia. There's outdoor dining in season.

207 Chestnut St. ✆ **215/625-8605.** www.philadelphiafish.com. Reservations recommended. Main courses $8–$17 lunch, $21–$28 dinner. AE, DC, MC, V. Mon–Thurs 11:30am–4pm and 4:30–10:30pm; Fri 11:30am–4pm and 5pm–midnight; Sat noon–3pm and 4:30pm–midnight; Sun 4–10:30pm.

Positano Coast ★ SOUTHERN ITALIAN Inspired by its young chef's vacations to the Almafi coast, this sunny, glassed-in restaurant specializes in "crudo," or raw fish. The spot wraps around the second floor of an office building, stretching from a sunny bar past photomurals of homes stretching down to the sea. Despite the decorative flip-flops tacked to walls, the menu is quite serious. Favorite dishes: rich and springy artichoke and lemon soup floating with ricotta croutons, raw tuna tonnato topped with fried caper dressing and chopped egg, and even some more typically Italian American dishes like eggplant parm and chopped salad. The star here: The fresh crudos, the Boot's version of seviche. It's across the street from one of the Ritz Cinemas, making it perfect for dinner and a movie.

212 Walnut St. (upstairs). ✆ **215/238-0499.** www.lambertis.com. Reservations accepted. Main courses $7–$16 lunch, $14–$36 dinner. AE, DC, DISC, MC, V. Mon–Thurs 11am–10pm; Fri 11:30am–11pm; Sat noon–midnight; Sun 12:30–10:30pm.

Ristorante Panorama ★★ ITALIAN Well known for its 150-by-the-glass wine bar, the Sena family's intimate trattoria specializes in handmade pastas. Patrons sit in the shadow of a mural of an Italian countryside while dipping bread into pesto and pondering different wine flights. Pastas are available in appetizer or entree portions. Favorites include ricotta agnolotti with fresh spinach sauce, pappardelle with duck ragout, or pillowy gnocchi with prosciutto and peas. Veal is another house specialty. Chef Luca Sena even does chicken right, layering it with roasted peppers, prosciutto, and mozzarella. The tiramisu, with its triple-cream mascarpone cheese drizzled with chocolate, is especially good with espresso or a dessert wine.

14 N. Front St. (at Market St. in Penn's View Hotel). ✆ **215/922-7800.** www.pennsviewhotel.com. Reservations recommended. Main courses $18–$28. AE, DC, MC, V. Mon–Thurs noon–10pm; Fri noon–11pm; Sat 5–11pm; Sun 5–9pm.

Zento ★★ JAPANESE This tiny box of a BYOB is clean lined, modern touched, always friendly—and absolutely perfect for a quick, unpretentious meal in Old City. I come here for the white tuna sashimi, signature square zento rolls (dressed with sweet plum paste, and totally splurge worthy at $15 per roll), but even nonsushi eaters like it for the tempura and simple chicken teriyaki dishes. Servers are superaccommodating, glad to store your BYO beer in the fridge in the back, and always happy to see a new (or old) face.

138 Chestnut St. (btw. Front and 2nd sts.). ✆ **215/925-9998.** www.zentocontemporary.com. Reservations recommended. Main courses $18–$30. AE, MC, V. Mon–Thurs 11:30am–3pm and 5–10pm; Fri 11:30am–3pm and 5–11pm; Sat noon–11pm; Sun 5–10pm.

INEXPENSIVE

Beau Monde ★★ Value FRENCH This pretty, Parisian-looking (but noisy) 65-seat restaurant specializes in crepes, and is usually filled with Gen Xers or lively groups, thanks to its affordable prices. The restaurant prepares two types of crepes: savory, made with buckwheat flour and filled with anything from andouille sausage to mushrooms, goat cheese, and chicken; and a sweet wheat-flour dessert crepe, filled with fruit or layered with Nutella. Great salads are served, too—try the spinach with hazelnuts and goat cheese. Upstairs from the bistro is **L'Etage,** an elegant, cozy bar with a casually chic crowd, where DJs spin and cabaret acts perform.

624 S. 6th St. (at the corner of Bainbridge, 1 block south of South St.). ✆ **215/592-0656.** www.creperie-beaumonde.com. Reservations accepted for 6 or more. Crepe main courses $6.50–$19 ($1–$12 for each filling). AE, DC, DISC, MC, V. Tues–Fri noon–11pm; Sat 10am–11pm; Sun 10am–10pm.

Business Lunch: Meet & Eat or Grab & Go

FOR A SIT-DOWN MEAL

Fork ★★ Take a client here, and you'll score points. While other polished Old City restaurants serve lunch, this elegant, unmarked spot does it quietly and seamlessly. See p. 88.

Le Castagne ★ The Sena family brings classy Italian west of Broad with this spare bistro. Order the gnocchi. 1920 Chestnut St. ✆ **215/751-9913.**

The Palm Part of a national chain of upper-crust steakhouses, the Palm has become synonymous with the power lunch. Politicos and other status seekers angle for noontime tables, hoping to get their caricatures up on the walls, next to those of former mayors, newscasters, and such. Bellevue, 200 S. Broad St. ✆ **215/546-7256.**

Twenty21 ★ Finds Tucked below the offices of 1 Commerce Square, this handsome restaurant serves an appealing mix of American-Continental fare. Tables and booths are oversize, better to accommodate briefcases and PowerPoint presentations. 2005 Market St. ✆ **215/851-6262.**

FOR A CASUAL MEAL

Devil's Alley ★ This laid-back spot gets crowds at noon for its comfort food. Pizzas, burgers, and, if it's been that kind of day, a beer are best bets. 1907 Chestnut St. ✆ **215/751-0707.**

Good Dog ★ The blue cheese–stuffed burgers are famous at this always-packed, two-floor gastropub. The calamari salads and grilled cheeses are good, too. 224 S. 15th St. (btw. Walnut and Locust sts.). ✆ **215/985-9600.**

EAT IN OR TAKEOUT

Di Bruno Bros. Pronto ★ This outpost of a South Philly cheese shop has an upstairs counter for ordering quick and delicious lasagna Bolognese, balsamic chicken, and eggplant Parmesan, plus soups, salads, and panini. 1730 Chestnut St. ✆ **215/564-9339.**

El Fuego ★ On the edge of Washington Square and a few blocks from Rittenhouse, this stylish little build-your-own burrito (or taco, or quesadilla) joint does Mexi-Cali right, with fresh basics and fast counter service. 723 Walnut St. ✆ **215/592-1901** and 2104 Chestnut St. ✆ **215/751-1435.**

Picnic ★★ Finds Just across the Walnut Street Bridge, on the edge of Drexel and Penn, this cheerful spot serves some of the city's best takeout fare: Gorgonzola salads with spiced pecans, savory dips, yummy sandwiches, lemon bars, and chocolate *pots de crème.* What's more, they'll assemble a complete picnic for you, using one of their vintage picnic baskets. 3131 Walnut St. ✆ **215/222-1608.**

Famous Fourth Street Delicatessen ★★ (Kids JEWISH DELI Pastrami sandwiches thicker than phone books, matzo balls as big as baseballs, homemade éclairs the size of bedroom slippers: This gleaming white corner deli doesn't just make authentic, comforting, spot-on comfort fare. It makes it huge. When Famous—which honestly is famous, especially among politicians—changed owners a couple of years ago, it changed for the much, much better. Now locals file in loyally, lining up along the cases of corned beef, macaroni salad, and checkerboard cake to wait for a sidewalk-side table. This is the best place in town to get your fix of stuffed cabbage, potato knishes, kosher hot dogs, matzo brei, and scrambled eggs with lox.

Don't be taken aback by the prices. They seem steep, for just a sandwich. But when you see the sandwich, you'll realize you're paying for size—and quality. Meals here start with a dish of dill pickles and end with a little dish of the deli's signature homemade chocolate chip cookies.

700 S. 4th St. (at Bainbridge St.). ✆ **215/922-3274.** Reservations not accepted. Sandwiches $6–$20. AE, MC, V. Daily 8am–9pm.

Jones ★ (Kids AMERICAN COMFORT This busy spot is one of the few places near Independence Hall where you can have a reasonably priced, sit-down (and late-night) meal with the kids and feel slightly hip in the process. The spacious one-room Jones bears a slight resemblance to the Brady Bunch's living room. It's sunken, with a gas fireplace and youthful servers. Weekday lunches are especially popular. Since reservations are not accepted, expect to wait for a table. What to eat: chicken nachos, brisket with gravy, meatloaf with mashed potatoes and peas, fried calamari salad, and grilled cheese and tomato soup. With plenty of booths and a menu that appeals to all ages, this is a great place to take the family. It does, however, get louder as the hour gets later.

700 Chestnut St. (at 7th St.). ✆ **215/223-5663.** www.jones-restaurant.com. Reservations not accepted. AE, DC, MC, V. Snacks and entrees $8–$26. Mon–Thurs 11:30am–midnight; Fri 11:30am–1am; Sat 10am–1am; Sun 10:30am–11pm.

2 CENTER CITY: WEST OF BROAD

VERY EXPENSIVE

Barclay Prime ★★★ STEAKS When this glamorous Rittenhouse Square steakhouse opened in 2004, it instantly became the toniest restaurant in the city. Credit for this achievement goes, in part, to the chic-boutique decor. Mod cutout bookshelves are gracefully backlit; modular white, yellow, and Kelly green leather couches and chairs fill the loungey dining room; and black-and-white checkerboard tiles floor the lounge.

More credit, however, goes to the flawless meat-and-potatoes menu. New York's Gachot & Gachot (the Prada of beef) supplies the beautifully marbled steaks (sauce is $3 extra). Sides include a creamed spinach as rich as many of the deep-pocketed patrons themselves. There are predictably impeccable oysters, caviar, and seafood cocktails; fun-to-nibble Kobe beef sliders; palate-cleansing salads; and decadent lobster bisque. The menu's most extravagant dish, however, is the Kobe beef "cheesesteak," which, as its $100 price tag suggests, is not topped with Cheez Whiz. When the bill's already this big, there's no reason to resist rounding out the meal with delicate takes on banana cream pie or toasted peanut butter s'mores.

237 S. 18t St. (btw. Locust and Spruce sts.). ✆ **215/732-7560.** www.barclayprime.com. Reservations required. Main courses $29–$56; Kobe steak $80–$90; Kobe cheesesteak $100. AE, DC, MC, V. Sun–Thurs 5–10pm; Fri–Sat 5–11pm.

Butcher & Singer ★★ STEAK What was once the much-lauded Striped Bass is now a thoroughly grand steakhouse inspired by supper clubs—and expense accounts—of yore. This truly marvelous (although, again, pricey) alternative to nearby Morton's of Chicago, the Palm, and Capitol Grille outclasses its neighbors by a mile. The setting: A former brokerage house that bore the same name, beneath vaulted ceilings, a substantial chandelier, and a mighty bull's head, where, somehow, digging into massive hash browns, everything-but-the-kitchen-sink chopped salads, $65 surf and turfs, and baked Alaska roughly the size of, well, Alaska, doesn't seem one bit over-the-top. Lunch is a tad less humongous, with daintier portions that include a delightful lobster BLT, steak salad, and a just-right steak sandwich. After a meal, the horseshoe-shaped bar seems the perfect spot for a spot of bourbon.

1500 Walnut St. ✆ **215/732-4444.** www.butcherandsinger.com. Reservations strongly recommended. Main courses $14–$30 lunch, $26–$65 dinner. AE, DC, MC, V. Mon–Thurs 11:30am–2:30pm and 5–10pm; Fri 11:30am–2:30pm and 5–11pm; Sat 5–11pm; Sun 5–10pm.

Fountain Restaurant ★★★ **Moments** INTERNATIONAL The Fountain is Philadelphia's most acclaimed restaurant (it was rated number one in Zagat's survey). Located in the Four Seasons, it serves breakfast, lunch, and dinner daily—three impeccable meals to similarly impeccable diners, many of them the city's top attorneys, bankers, and socialites.

Food here is both understated and sophisticated. Prix-fixe *mange tout* menus merit their price tags ($85 for four courses, $110 for six). The menu changes seasonally. Lobster and steak star, but edgier choices include such seasonal delights as red snapper with snow pea tempura and truffled Caesar salad. One not-to-miss meal is the lavish Sunday brunch ($65 per person). Service and surroundings straddle the line between formal and down-to-earth, never even hinting at pretension.

1 Logan Sq. (btw. 18th St. and Benjamin Franklin Pkwy. in the Four Seasons Hotel). ✆ **215/963-1500.** www.fourseasons.com/philadelphia. Reservations required. Main courses $29–$34 lunch, $42–$60 dinner; buffet brunch $68; fixed-price 6-course dinner menu $115 ($190 with wine). AE, DC, MC, V. Mon–Fri 6:30–11am, 11:30am–2pm, and 5:45–10pm; Sat 7–11am, 11:30am–2pm, and 5:45–10pm; Sun 7am–2pm (brunch at 11am) and 5:45–10pm.

Lacroix ★★★ **Moments** FRENCH Another top-notch hotel restaurant, Lacroix offers an amazing treetop view over Rittenhouse Square—and an even more amazing menu that borders on daring. Founding namesake chef Jean-Marie Lacroix ceded his post to ambitious Matthew Levin, who, in turn, concocts halibut with egg yolk sauce, muscovy duck breast with parsnip coconut and pestoed lobster—and still manages to please meat-and-potatoes clientele with rib-eyes and veal chops. More experimental diners can sample small plates from his tasting menu: three plates for $69, four plates for $78, five for $85. Dishes here include arctic char with white chocolate, artichokes, udon noodles, and passion fruit, and rabbit saddle with barbecue lentils and grapefruit. For just-as-clever pre- or postdinner libations, try the restaurant's petite **Bar 210.**

210 W. Rittenhouse Sq. ✆ **215/546-9000.** www.lacroixrestaurant.com Reservations strongly recommended. A la carte main courses $14–$26 lunch, $30–$45 dinner; dinner tasting menu $69–$85. AE, DC, DISC, MC, V. Mon–Sat 6:30am–2:30pm and 5:30–10pm; Sun 6:30am–10:30pm.

Le Bec-Fin ★★★ **Moments** FRENCH With its jewel-box atmosphere and multicourse, formal meals, Le Bec-Fin is a destination dining spot that has been ruled for almost 4 decades by owner-chef Georges Perrier. The chef, who is a celebrity in Philadelphia, hails from Lyon, France's gastronomic capital, and is a favorite of critics such as *Esquire's* John Mariani. Perrier is frequently seen in the dining room, which resembles an elegant turn-of-the-20th-century Parisian salon.

All dishes are exquisite and change seasonally, with recent offerings including a first course of *cassolette d'escargots,* with champagne-hazelnut-garlic sauce; the signature *galette de crabe;* and beef tenderloin au poivre. The dessert cart is a grand vehicle for more than a dozen beautiful options, including opera cake topped with 24-karat gold leaf.

Le Bec's $55 lunch tasting menu is a wonderful way to experience the restaurant (and dessert cart), or you can visit the tiny, lower-level **Le Bar Lyonnais,** with more affordable but very rich dishes from the same kitchen, and where you can expect to spend about $18 a nibble and $12 for a glass of house wine. The later it gets, the more likely dishes from upstairs are to arrive—and M. Perrier himself, for that matter.

1523 Walnut St. ✆ **215/567-1000.** www.lebecfin.com. Lunch tasting menu $55; 6-course dinner $155; 10-course degustation $185. AE, DC, MC, V. Mon–Fri 11:30am–2pm and 5:30–10:30pm; Sat 5:30–10:30pm. Bar Mon–Fri 11:30am–midnight; Sat 6pm–1am.

Vetri ★★★ (Finds ITALIAN The best Italian restaurant in America? That's what the critics say. Chef-owner Marc Vetri's showplace offers 35 seats on the first floor of a walk-up brownstone. Diners sit elbow to elbow, anticipating each bite of ethereal spinach gnocchi in brown butter, watching as warm olive oil melts a chocolate disc suspended over a scoop of lavender gelato. Vetri takes extra pride in his milk-fed baby goat with soft polenta, his sweetbread dumplings in broth, his tissue-thin antipasto meats—which he makes a display of slicing on an antique meat slicer at the center of the dining room. It is very hard to get a reservation here, so call ahead. And, for goodness sakes, dress up. And order wine. Sommelier Jeff Benjamin is justly proud of the exceptional wine list.

1312 Spruce St. ✆ **215/732-3478.** www.vetriristorante.com. Main courses $30–$40; 8-course tasting menu $115 Mon–Thurs, $135 Fri–Sat. AE, MC, V. Mon–Fri 6–9pm; Sat 7–9pm. Closed Sat in summer.

EXPENSIVE

Alma de Cuba ★★ MODERN CUBAN Three stylish—but not necessarily Cuban-looking—floors form this flashy restaurant, known for its marvelously fresh and refreshing mojitos, glorious black-bean soup, and slow-roasted pork shank. The decor encompasses glass walls shimmering with tobacco leaf images; an all-white downstairs lounge with mod seating; black-and-white photos projected onto the walls; loud, Buena Vista–style music; and dim lighting.

1623 Walnut St. ✆ **215/988-1799.** www.almadecubarestaurant.com. Reservations recommended. Main courses $21–$32. AE, DC, DISC, MC, V. Mon–Thurs 5–11pm; Fri–Sat 5pm–midnight; Sun 5–10pm.

Friday Saturday Sunday AMERICAN/CONTINENTAL A romantic survivor of Philadelphia's 1970s "restaurant renaissance," Friday Saturday Sunday has adapted to the times through an appealing informality, a renovated bar upstairs, and approachable cuisine. Every bottle on the wine list is marked up a mere $10, making it the best value in town. Decor is pretty but casual: The cutlery and china don't match, flowers are rare, and the menu is a wall-mounted slate board. Dress is everything from jeans to suits, and the service is vigilant but hands-off.

The restaurant is famous for its rich mushroom soup, made from local Kennett Square mushrooms, chicken broth, cognac, and cream. Have anything from the specials board, or pear and fennel salad, wild mushroom ravioli, and grilled filet mignon. The wine card lists about 30 vintages. The desserts change often.

261 S. 21st St. (btw. Locust and Spruce sts.). ✆ **215/546-4232.** www.frisatsun.com. Reservations accepted. Main courses $18–$29. AE, DC, MC, V. Mon–Sat 5:30–10:30pm; Sun 5–10pm.

Los Catrines & Tequila's ★★ MEXICAN If you, like me, fantasize about chasing the world's best nachos with a can of Tecate in an elegant old mansion whose walls are covered in bright Mexican murals, then I'll see you at Tequila's. The menu describes every dish in fluid, historic detail, offering tidbits such as: The Caesar salad was invented in—who knew?—Mexico. Chipotle-spiked filet mignon, flavor-layered mole poblano chicken, whole red snapper bursting with *chiles de árbol,* and lime butter are some of my favorites. The dining room is lovely for a big-deal dinner, while the bar is perfect for an early-evening nosh. I recommend the *queso fundido* (melted Chihuahua cheese served with tortillas) and the jar of margaritas. According to local legend, owner David Suro never forgets a customer. On his list of 75 tequilas, three are his. The house brand is Siembra Azul.

1602 Locust St. ✆ **215/546-0181.** www.tequilasphilly.com. Reservations recommended. Main courses $10–$22 lunch, $16–$22 dinner. AE, DC, MC, V. Mon–Thurs 11:30am–2pm and 5–10pm; Fri 11:30am–2pm and 5–11pm; Sat 5–11pm; Sun 5–10pm.

Nineteen Restaurant, Café and Bar ★★ **Moments** CONTEMPORARY AMERICAN Three separate, elegant entities make up the grand 19th floor of the Park Hyatt at the Bellevue. Nineteen's dining room is its showpiece. Draped in light fabrics, and, beneath a second rotunda, strands of giant pearls, it's the perfect spot for an anniversary dinner. The menu is approachably modern. Definitely order something from the raw bar menu, but don't stop there. Fried orange wedges adorn a fall beet salad. A delicate hard-boiled quail egg tops tuna tartare. Wild mushrooms and summer corn hides inside house-made pirogi. Desserts are elegant, sweet tastes.

The less formal cafe is a round, handsome space set beneath a rotunda, offering marvelous rooftop views of the city. This is the site of breakfast and proper afternoon tea, and wonderful, reasonably priced lunches and dinners. The menu includes steamed lake trout with Swiss chard and herbed potatoes (at a modest $10), lobster club sandwiches, four-star burgers, and fish and chips. Beyond the cafe, a snug lounge has walls of glassed-in wine bottles, and a roaring fireplace.

200 S. Broad St. (at Walnut St. in the Park Hyatt at the Bellevue, 19th floor). ✆ **215/790-1919.** www.nineteenrestaurant.com. Reservations recommended. Main courses $16–$38 dining room, $14–$20 cafe. AE, DC, DISC, MC, V. Mon–Fri 6:30am–11pm; Sat–Sun 7am–11pm. Bar until past midnight.

Osteria ★★★ **Finds** ITALIAN Chef Marc Vetri's smashing sequel to his eponymous bistro (see Vetri, above) takes a good thing—refined rustic Italian fare—and adds lots more space and a casual vibe. A few blocks north of City Hall (so it's not *officially* in Center City, even if the crowd clearly is), this industrial loft–meets–wine cave trattoria specializes in black-crusted pizzas topped with egg and cotechino sausage, with octopus and red chilies, with apples and black walnuts, or with new potatoes and smoked ricotta. Antipasta plates include rabbit terrine, or porchetta with parmigiana salad; pasta standouts include wild boar Bolognese with candele noodles, or chicken livers with house-made rigatoni, plus perhaps more familiar fare in their classic margherita pizza, or ribs with black pepper sausage. The much-praised wine list is 100% Italian, and ranges from a simple Sicilian Syrah for $42 to delicious Umbrian, Tuscan, and more varietals into the $200s. Tastes available from $3; glasses, $7 to $16.

Tips Vegetarian Philly

Philly's vegetarian and vegan dining scene is up-and-coming. The best spot for an upscale vegan dinner is **Horizons Café ★★**, 611 S. 7th St. (✆ **215/923-6117;** www.horizonsphiladelphia.com). This restaurant and bar does wonders with tempeh and tofu. My favorites are edamame hummus, wild mushroom enchiladas, and mock chicken wings. My favorite spot for a Kosher veggie lunch is **Mama's Vegetarian,** 18 S. 20th St. (✆ **215/751-0477**), where the falafel, fried eggplant, hummus, and pita are homemade and inexpensive.

Reservations can require weeks to obtain. Singles and couples that haven't booked might want to try their luck at the first-come, first-served bar. Or, stop by on a Thursday or Friday for a quiet, comfortable lunch.

640 N. Broad St. (at Wallace St.). ✆ **215/763-0920.** www.osteriaphilly.com. Reservations strongly recommended. Main courses $24–$35; pizzas $15–$22; pastas $16. AE, DC, MC, V. Sun–Wed 5–10pm; Thurs–Fri 11:30am–2pm and 5–11pm; Sat 5–11pm.

Parc ★★ FRENCH In 2008, this 250-plus-seat Paris-inspired brasserie officially (Okay, unofficially) overtook neighbor Rouge (see below) as *the* see-and-be-seen spot on Rittenhouse Square. Parc, a sparkly creation of prolific restaurateur Stephen Starr (Morimoto, Buddakan, Tangerine, Butcher & Singer, Barclay Prime, Pod, both Continentals), has faux smoke-stained ceilings and mirrors, purposefully fading signage, and lovely not-quite-vintage tile floors, not to mention a thoroughly fun pair of restrooms. It also has quite the traditional French menu.

Pâté de campagne (country pâté), hazelnut-buttered escargots, classic onion soup, coq au vin, steak au poivre, croque madame sandwiches, and omelets all day absolutely channel typical French cafe cuisine. Even the house-baked baguettes and straightforward desserts will take you back to Paris—even as the boisterous cocktail crowd is doubtlessly all-American. If you manage score a spot at the zinc, order a classic kir royale. The quietest time here is weekday breakfasts, where, appropriately, both pain au chocolat and eggs en cocotte are served.

227 S. 18th St. (at Locust St.). ✆ **215/545-2262.** www.parc-restaurant.com. Reservations strongly recommended. Main courses $11–$24 lunch, $13–$36 dinner. AE, DC, MC, V. Mon–Thurs 7:30am–11pm; Fri 7:30am–midnight; Sat 10:30am–midnight; Sun 10:30am–10pm.

The Prime Rib ★★★ STEAK Philly swarms with jumbo-chain steakhouses, but this one rules them all. Sure, there are Prime Ribs in D.C. and Baltimore, but do they have a sunken dining room with black lacquered walls? Leopard-print carpeting and a showpiece piano bar? Okay, so the Prime Rib may not be unique, but it is old school—in the best possible way—with indulgent creamed spinach, an oversize shrimp cocktail, and six preparations of potato. Fellas: Wear a jacket. And a tie.

1701 Locust St. (in the Radisson Plaza-Warwick Hotel). ✆ **215/772-1701.** www.theprimerib.com. Reservations recommended. Jackets required for men. Main courses $22–$42. AE, DC, MC, V. Sun–Mon 4:30–9pm; Tues–Thurs 4:30–10pm; Fri–Sat 4:30–11pm.

Rouge ★★ AMERICAN-FRENCH This tiny bistro with a circular white bar and velvet curtains serves amazing food. Subtly spiced mussels, a peerless roasted chicken, chiffon-thin carpaccio of beef on pristine arugula: This effortlessly elegant spot excels at

French classics with a twist. They also do a lavish $15 hamburger with amazing frites; a two hander with caramelized onions and bleu cheese is considered by burger-meisters to be the best in the city and has won numerous awards. A stylish crowd gathers at the cafe tables along the sidewalk from April through October to sip and flirt. P.S. Please don't come here without your most expensive shoes and bag.

205 S. 18th St. ✆ **215/732-6622.** Reservations accepted depending on the season. Main courses $15–$34. AE, DISC, MC, V. Mon–Fri 11:30am–2am; Sat–Sun 10am–2am; closing may be later, depends on when the crowd departs.

Table 31 ★★ STEAK Beneath the Comcast Center, Philadelphia's newest, tallest skyscraper, this posh steakhouse serves up serious cuts of meat to a power-dining crowd. The spot is the brainchild of chefs Chris Scarduzio and Georges Perrier, who named it after the best table in the house at one of their other restaurants, Brasserie Perrier (now closed). The main dining room is two tiered, with a long banquette that's practically built for elbow rubbing—and a wall of windows built for peering in. All offerings are refined all-American. Dinnertime standouts include rich wagyu sliders on brioche; olive-oil and garlic-marinated filet; hefty, marbled prime rib; peppered Peking duck; and sides of lobster mashed potatoes and macaroni gratin (read: fancy mac and cheese) and a splurge-packed wine list. Lunch is still pretty upscale, but also includes finger foods like a juicy French dip, bacon-topped smoked salmon sandwich, and a burger. The number-one dessert here: a seriously huge slice of chocolate cake.

During warm and nonrainy weather, Table 31 operates the **Plaza Café,** a picnic-inspired alfresco spot where patrons nosh salads, pizza, and sushi beneath bright orange umbrellas. Happy hours here, and inside at the bar, get extremely crowded, so get here early if you want to get a seat for a "smoking" Manhattan or a blackberry-and-sage bourbon cocktail.

1701 J.F.K. Blvd. (Comcast Center). ✆ **215/567-7111.** www.table-31.com. Reservations recommended. Main courses $12–$18 lunch, $24–$58 dinner. AE, DC, MC, V. Mon–Thurs 11:30am–2:30pm and 5:30–10:30pm; Fri 11:30am–2:30pm and 5:30–11pm; Sat 5:30–11pm. Plaza Café (weather permitting) Mon–Thurs 11am–11pm; Fri 11:30am–midnight; Sat 5pm–midnight.

10 Arts ★★ AMERICAN Celebrity chef Eric Ripert (award-winning chef of New York's Le Bernardin) brings a cleverly casual sort of fare—a combo of regionally raised ingredients, French comfort food, signature seafood, and such esteemed Philadelphia culinary traditions as the soft pretzels, alphabet soup, and Tastykakes to the Ritz-Carlton's loungey dining room. The result is a gentle high-low fusion that shines brightest with just-this-side-of-daring dishes, nonsweet pork and beans, hazelnut buttered Pennsylvania brook trout, slider-style fish burgers, and sea-salted corn chowder. This is also the place to try a classic rabbit paillard, or bacon-touched, pearl onion–studded striped bass *grand-mère.* Another standout: Breakfast, for banana pancakes and eggs any way. All in all, it's a delightful spot that seems perfect for hotel dining: The food is serious, the service is top-notch, but the dress is casual.

10 S. Broad St. (inside the Ritz-Carlton Philadelphia). ✆ **215/523-8273** or 523-8221. www.10arts.com. Entrees $18–$34 lunch and dinner. AE, DC, MC, V. Mon 6:30am–10pm; Tues–Fri 6:30am–10pm; Sat 7–10pm; Sun 7am–noon.

Tinto ★★ SPANISH-BASQUE The small, stylish, dimly-lit and clandestine-feeling cousin of *über* popular Amada (p. 85) serves petite, Basque-inspired plates out of two narrow side-by-side storefronts. Small portions called "pintxos" are the order of the evening, and chef-owner Jose Garces turns out perfectly snackworthy Serrano ham–wrapped figs, Iberian ham, baby artichokes, lamb-and-eggplant brochettes, cockle-studded sea bass, grilled beef and lobster with aioli and peanuts, and absolutely sublime charcuterie and cheese plates.

Snack-size servings make Tinto a great spot for aperitifs and noshes, unless, that is, you go all the way with the $55 tasting menu ($30 more with wine), which includes delightfully tiny desserts such as goat's milk mousse with huckleberry preserves or olive oil cake with grapefruit curd. A 50-bottle wine list offers a variety of tasteworthy Basque vintages; but the sangria here makes for a marvelous first drink of the night, too. I like to come here for lunch, where the Bilbao Express offers soup or salad—crab and seafood chowder, truffled chestnut and duck soup—and a *bocadillo* sandwich—over-easy egg with *queso de cabra* and grilled veggies; hanger steak with asparagus and celery root aioli; cured salmon with caviar and crispy shallots on a croissant—for $15.

116 S. 20th St. ✆ **215/665-9150.** www.tintorestaurant.com. Reservations recommended for dinner. Prix-fixe lunch $15; a la carte lunch entrees $7–$18; dinner plates $4–$18 (order more than 2); chef's tasting menu $55 ($85 with wine). AE, DC, MC, V. Mon–Thurs 11:30am–11pm; Fri 11:30am–midnight; Sat 5pm–midnight; Sun 5–11pm.

Water Works Restaurant and Lounge ★ AMERICAN-INTERNATIONAL The spectacular renovated site of Philadelphia's historic former water system is now a worldly minded standout. Here, location is everything. To its one side: the imposing Philadelphia Museum of Art. To the other: the twinkling lights of Boathouse Row and the Schuylkill River. Around happy hour, the elegant bar crowds with a mature clientele. During warm weather, everyone wants to sit on the outdoor terrace. The dining room is large, with beautiful wood paneling.

The menu subtly tends toward Greek cuisines: tuna over grape leaves, grilled octopus, grilled haloumi cheese, and rack of lamb with goat cheese "pillows," plus a tried-and-true selection of traditional upscale fare such as filet mignon with truffle mashed potatoes and herb-crusted salmon. Regulars swear by the Sunday brunch.

640 Waterworks Dr. (behind Philadelphia Museum of Art, at Benjamin Franklin Pkwy. and Kelly Dr.). ✆ **215/236-9000.** www.thewaterworksrestaurant.com. Reservations recommended. Main courses $12–$22 lunch, $19–$37 dinner. AE, DC, DISC, MC, V. Tues–Fri 11:30am–2:30pm and 5–10pm; Sat 5–11pm; Sun 11am–2pm and 5–9pm.

MODERATE

Continental Mid-Town ★ MODERN INTERNATIONAL Like its older, Old City sister (p. 90), this colorful corner martini bar and restaurant is all about good looks, good times, and surprisingly good food. Stylish servers resembling extras on *That '70s Show* deliver sweet signature cocktails and oversize salads to diners sitting in baby-blue-vinyl car seat booths, a sunken center dining room, swinging chairs on the tile-walled mezzanine, and a popular rooftop deck. This is not the place for a quiet meal, although the noise level diminishes in the back of the second floor.

What to eat here? Most everything on the rainbow-decorated menu is pretty yummy. I especially like the piled-high fried calamari salad, Szechuan shoestring fries, BLT with avocado, rich lobster mac and cheese, beer-battered shrimp and calamari, and juicy lamb chops with ratatouille, hummus, and raita. A word to the hungry: Many plates are small, meant to taste, not to sate. Included in this small-world category are the irresistible, flashback, bite-size desserts: fruit-flavored cotton candy and peanut butter and jam cake.

1801 Chestnut St. (corner of 18th St.). ✆ **215/567-1800.** www.continentalmidtown.com. Reservations not accepted. Main courses $7.50–$28. AE, DC, MC, V. Mon–Wed 11:30am–3:30pm and 5–11pm; Thurs–Fri 11:30am–3:30pm and 5pm–midnight; Sat 10am–4pm and 5pm–midnight; Sun 10am–4pm and 5–11pm.

A Taste of Ethnic Philly: Reading Terminal Market

The **Reading Terminal Market,** at 12th and Arch streets (© **215/922-2317;** www.readingterminalmarket.org), has been a greengrocer, snack shop, butcher, fish market, and sundries store for Philadelphians since the late 1800s. The original idea was to use the space underneath the terminal's tracks for food vendors so that commuters could stock up easily and cheaply. Today, it's lively, charming, redolent, and noisy, and overall a great place to have lunch or breakfast, or pick up a picnic. Half the fun of shopping among the market's grid of indoor stalls is getting lost. Don't miss a single aisle. Scrapple, mangoes, clam chowder, pretzels, and cheese worth its weight in gold—if it's fresh, it's here.

Prices vary by vendor, and about half accept cash only. Public restrooms are on the nonstreet side of the market, behind the Beer Garden. Market hours are Monday through Saturday 8am to 6pm; in December only, many vendors open Sunday 9am to 4pm. Pennsylvania Dutch vendors have market days Wednesday 8am to 3pm and Thursday through Saturday 8am to 5pm. If you're lucky enough to be marketing then, pick up hot cross buns at **Beiler's Bakery,** soft pretzels made before your eyes at **Fisher's,** and individual egg custards ($1) and chicken potpies ($6) at the counter of the **Dutch Eating Place.**

On Saturday, local, organic-minded farm collectives **(Fair Food Farmstand, Livengood's Produce)** set up shop. Strawberries, just-clipped watercress, butternut squash, and ripe tomatoes are offered seasonally. Also look for locally produced raw-milk cheese from **Fair Food Farmstand** (Wed–Sat), and grass-fed, hormone-free meat, poultry, and homemade sausage at **Guinta's Prime.**

Gourmets won't be able to resist asking for samples of the incredible variety at **Downtown Cheese Shop.** Caffeine addicts can get their fix at **Old City Coffee.** Sweet tooths can get their cannoli at **Termini Brothers Bakery,** their vanilla rooibos cake and green tea pound cake at **Flying Monkey Patisserie,** and their daisy mints and boxes of dark chocolate ears at **Chocolate by Mueller.** Carbaholics will gobble up the baguettes, bagels, coffeecakes, and croissants at **Le Bus** and **Metropolitan** bakeries.

For more protein, **Pearl's Oyster Bar** practically gives away six Top Neck clams for $4.95, and a shrimp platter with french fries, bread, and coleslaw goes for $8.95. Or try **Coastal Cave Trading Co.,** which has great clam chowder, oyster crackers, and smoked fish. Across the market, **DiNic's Roast Pork** gets lines for their namesake sandwich—oft considered the cheesesteak's superior cousin. **12th Street Cantina** sells not only tasty enchiladas and burritos, but also authentic ingredients, like blue cornmeal. Those off the meat wagon aren't ignored, either. The **Basic Four Vegetarian Snack Bar** makes delicious, meatless chicken salad and fishless tuna sandwiches, and veggie burgers.

Wash it all down with a pint of Yuengling Lager—just call it "lager"—at the odd and less-than-comely **Beer Garden.** Or better yet, treat yourself to a scoop of genuine, egg-included French vanilla at the outpost of Philly-based **Bassett's** ★ America's oldest ice-cream company. A cone will set you back $2.25.

Susanna Foo ★★★ Finds CANTONESE/SHANGHAI Worldly Susanna Foo has been touted in *Gourmet, Bon Appétit,* and *Esquire* for her skill in blending Asian cuisine and French techniques: Her elegant, eponymous bistro reflects her talents. The two dining rooms of this Restaurant Row restaurant are beautifully dressed in stone, glass, and silks, plus a collection of Chinese art and textiles.

The cuisine is the main thing, but be forewarned: If you're the type that finds exquisite but small portions at high prices off-putting, you may find these dishes too rarefied. Dim sum features such delicacies as shrimp dumplings with apples, edamame, and sun-dried tomato sauce. Noodle dishes, salads, and main courses combine East and West: tofu and Napa cabbage, crispy duck and peach salad, Mongolian lamb and jalapeño, honey walnut chicken with mango, and roasted salmon and coconut polenta. The wine list, designed to complement these dishes, specializes in French and California white wines. Desserts are delightfully French: banana chocolate tartlets and crème brûlée samplers. The service is rather formal. Lunchtime is fixed-price menu only, in two or three courses.

1512 Walnut St. ✆ **215/545-2666.** www.susannafoo.com. Reservations recommended for dinner. Dinner main courses $16–$31; 2-course lunch $19; 3-course lunch $23. AE, MC, V. Mon–Thurs 11:30am–2:30pm and 5–10pm; Fri 11:30am–2:30pm and 5–10pm; Sat 5–10pm; Sun 5–9pm.

INEXPENSIVE

Marathon Grill ★ Kids AMERICAN Throughout Center City are six modern, comfortable Marathon Grills, each with a gigantic menu boasting an enormous selection of comfort foods. Think of them as high-maintenance diners. On the menu are seven versions of grilled chicken-breast sandwiches, matzo ball soup, and a "control freak" selection of choose-it-yourself omelets, sandwiches, and salads. The Marathons mostly service on-the-go business clientele. Lunch is by far the busiest meal, with lines for tables at the more popular outposts. Still, casual weekend brunches are available at the 16th and Sansom, 19th and Spruce (Marathon on the Square), 13th and Chestnut, and 40th and

Tips Simple Pretheater Choices

Not every performance on the Avenue of the Arts requires a pretheater extravaganza. Since the December 2001 opening of the Kimmel Center, simple restaurants serving mostly no-frills Italian pastas and quick main courses have sprung up in the neighborhood, to get you in and out before your show. Chic bistro **Bliss,** 220 S. Broad St. (✆ **215/731-1100**), a block from the Kimmel Center, has a winning, eclectic menu with pasta, Asian, and grilled dishes. Right across from the Academy of Music, **Estia,** 1407 Locust St. (✆ **215/735-7700**), specializes in Greek preparations of fish, with excellent octopus and plenty of bar seating, but a hefty price tag. My favorites for early-evening Italian fare are cozy **La Viola,** 253 S. 16t St. (✆ **215/735-8630**), with its spinach gnocchi in pomodoro sauce and BYOB policy; and the affordable wines, squash-stuffed ravioli, and grilled salmon with basil at **Ernesto's 1521 Café,** 1521 Spruce St. (✆ **215/546-1521**). Also nearby (although 19 floors up) is the Bellevue's elegant **Nineteen** (p. 97), which offers both formal dining and a more casual cafe for a quick meal.

Kids Family-Friendly Restaurants

Ben's Bistro In the Franklin Institute at Logan Circle (p. 127), Ben's is well set up for kids, serving cafeteria food, hamburgers, and hot dogs. You can enter without museum admission. (Never mind that Ben himself contracted gout from his own poor eating habits.)

Famous Fourth Street Delicatessen (p. 94) This classic Jewish deli serves everything up in portions big enough to share: stuffed cabbage, pastrami dogs, matzo ball soup, kosher bologna sandwiches, and potato knishes. Meals end with free chocolate chip cookies.

Franklin Fountain ★★ This old-fashioned ice cream "saloon" is for *after* the kids clean their plates. Open daily (until late) in the heart of Old City, the polished parlor offers throwback sundaes, banana splits, egg creams, and, for the picky eater, plain ol' scoops. 116 Market St. ✆ **215/627-1899.** www.franklinfountain.com.

Jones (p. 94) Close to the Liberty Bell and Independence Hall, this stylish lunch, dinner, and brunch eatery serves an all-encompassing menu that includes burgers, salads, and meat-and-potatoes platters.

Marathon Grill (p. 102) You can dine on wonderful grilled salmon and have a nice glass of sauvignon blanc at this modern former diner just off Rittenhouse Square, while the kids choose from chicken fingers, pastas, and burgers. If they're noisy, no problem—the atmosphere is very casual. Weekend brunch is incredibly popular here, too.

Winnie's Le Bus (p. 112) This Manayunk eatery offers kids toys and crayons, plus more healthful—but no less delicious—versions of the grilled cheeses and burgers they would no doubt eat elsewhere.

Walnut (West Philly) locations. The West Philly and Rittenhouse Square locations also have liquor licenses. This last one, at 19th and Spruce, seats 60, and is perfect for a casual dinner with the kids, or for a posttheater meal. All branches allow takeout.

121 S. 16th St. ✆ **215/569-3278;** 1818 Market St. ✆ **215/561-1818;** 1339 Chestnut St. ✆ **215/561-4460;** 1839 Spruce St. ✆ **215/731-0800;** 2 Commerce Sq., 2001 Market St. ✆ **215/568-7766;** 40th and Walnut sts. ✆ **215/222-0100.** www.marathongrill.com. Reservations not accepted. Main courses $8–$20. AE, DC, MC, V. Daily. Hours vary by location.

Monk's Café ★ BELGIAN This Belgian pub has two claims to fame: The beer—20 artisan-made brews on tap, plus dozens more by the bottle—and the mussels—generous bowls of dark-shelled mollusks dressed in five sauces, from spicy Thai to classic white wine and garlic. Popular with beerperts and the Wharton students who imitate them, this narrow, no-nonsense spot also serves satisfying burgers, fries with bourbon mayonnaise, and hearty salads. The kitchen is open until 1am. A word to the sports addicted: Monk's has no TVs.

264 S. 16th St. (btw. Locust and Spruce sts.). ✆ **215/545-7005.** www.monkscafe.com. Reservations not accepted. Main courses $11–$24. AE, DC, DISC, MC, V. Mon–Sat 11:30am–2am; Sun 11am–2am.

EXPENSIVE

Ansill ★★ Finds MODERN FRENCH If the sound of lamb's tongue over chickpeas and mint, or bone marrow over parsley salad makes your tummy grumble, then this corner bistro is the place for you. Portions here are small—small!—and meant to be ordered in large numbers. And not everything comes from an unusual body part. There are eggs (from ducks, granted) scrambled with truffles and cream. There are miniburgers and garlicky tomato bread. You could eat a full meal of regular-style ingredients. But, if you've ever wanted to try sweetbreads or pigs' trotters, this is the place to do it. Tables are cafe style. Many diners opt to eat at the wooden bar, and to enjoy yummy wines by the glass or carafe. A bonus for night-owl gourmands: The kitchen serves a late-night menu Monday through Saturday 10pm to 1am.

627 S. 3rd St. (at Bainbridge St.). ✆ **215/627-2485.** www.ansillfoodandwine.com. Reservations recommended. Starters $5–$14; large plates $9–$15. AE, MC, V. Mon–Sat 5:30pm–1am; Sun 5:30–9pm.

Gayle ★★★ Finds MODERN AMERICAN Just beyond South Street, the fare at chef Daniel Stern's cozy, 35-seat bistro is cleverly postmodern. Dishes—most of which are small—bear somewhat mysterious names such as "Gayle Chowder, Casino Pizza." Another option might consist of skate, liver, and onions (trust me: it's delicious). "Risotto fingers" could possibly come with sabayon dip containing soy and truffles. "Breakfast" is the name of a French-toastish dessert. This type of eating isn't for everyone, but for the adventuresome gourmet, it's sheer, stylish delight. Wines can be meticulously paired with each dish. By the way: I'm *so* not telling what's in the "chicken, purple and green."

617 S. 3rd St. (btw. South and Bainbridge sts.). ✆ **215/922-3850.** www.gaylephiladelphia.com. Reservations recommended. Main courses $24–$34; 5-course tasting menu $75; 8-course tasting menu $95. AE, DISC, MC, V. Tues–Sat 5:30–10pm.

James ★★★ ITALIAN This elegantly modern trattoria, just a block from the Italian Market, has earned kudos from local foodies and *Food & Wine* alike. (Chef-owner Jim Burke earned the magazine's coveted "Best New Chef" honor in 2008.) His innovation: Contemporizing Italian classics, combining rabbit agnolotti and walnut sauce, langostinos and warm ricotta, and duck pappardelle and shaved chocolate. The atmosphere here is warm but chic, with crystal chandeliers, two-toned murals, and a cozy fireplace. Effusive servers gladly explain the origins of the very non-Italian-American oyster risotto, and do an expert job of matching wines to dishes. Portions here are far from belly busting, which just makes the contents of each plate seem all the more precious. For a quick bite and a sip, have a herb-infused cocktail and some olives at the bar.

834 S. 8th St. (btw. Catharine and Christian sts.). ✆ **215/629-4980.** www.jameson8th.com. Reservations recommended. Entrees $15–$37 lunch and dinner. AE, DC, MC, V. Mon–Thurs 5–10pm; Fri–Sat 5–11pm.

Paradiso ★ MODERN ITALIAN Deep in South Philly, this contemporary Italian brasserie stands out among its smaller, older neighborhood predecessors. The menu here ranges from classic to edgy; the wine list is big into California, if you can believe it. Chef-owner Lynne Marie Rinaldi bedecks hanger steak with white bean purée and horseradish gremolata. She wraps scallops in speck and endives, and dresses them with saffron vinaigrette. Come wintertime, there's rabbit cacciatore. In the summer, it's sushi-grade tuna with blood oranges and Gaeta olives. There's track lighting, jazz bands on weekends, and tall windows that open out to the sidewalk during warm weather. Lunch offers scaled-down Italian sandwiches and basic linguine with clams. Those of us who know South Philly know this spot is new school. But we like it anyway.

1627 E. Passyunk Ave. (btw. Tasker and Morris sts.). ✆ **215/271-2066.** www.paradisophilly.com. Reservations recommended Fri–Sun. Main courses $21–$25. AE, MC, V. Tues–Thurs 11:30am–3pm and 5–10pm; Fri 11:30am–3pm and 5–11pm; Sat 11am–2:30pm and 5–11pm; Sun 11am–2:30pm and 4–9pm.

Southwark ★★ Finds CONTINENTAL Foodies flock to the handsome, Chi-town-feeling bar for terrific Manhattans—and even better seasonal fare. Southwark's menu changes regularly. Past favorite dishes have included a poached Bosc pear with a melted core of fontina cheese and duck confit; homemade capellini with poached egg and mushrooms; and dark, buttery, roasted-to-order half chicken with herb stuffing and maple butter. Owners Sheri and Kip Waide are the chef and barkeep, respectively. Don't skip the herb Parmesan bread served with compound butter: It's one of Sheri's specialties. Small-maker wines are reasonably priced and uniformly delicious. Sunday brunch is gaining a following.

701 S. 4th St. (4th and Bainbridge sts.). ✆ **215/238-1888.** www.southwarkrestaurant.com. Reservations required. Main courses $20–$30. AE, MC, V. Tues–Thurs 5:30–10:30pm; Fri–Sat 5:30–11:30pm; Sun 11am–5pm.

MODERATE

Victor Cafe ★ Finds ITALIAN Victor's is a South Philly shrine to opera, with servers who deliver arias along with hearty Italian classics—redefining the expression "sing for your supper." Opened in the 1930s by John DiStefano, who covered the walls with photos of Toscanini, local Mario Lanza, and the like, the restaurant still has more than 45,000 classical recordings from which to choose and hires the best voices it can find. The menu changes frequently, with such choices as meat lasagna, two fresh fish offered daily, three types of veal (including a hefty veal chop), and a filet. Pastas are homemade.

1303 Dickinson St. ✆ **215/468-3040.** www.victorcafe.com. Reservations recommended. Main courses $17–$28; 3-course menu $30. AE, MC, V. Mon–Thurs 5–10pm; Fri 5—11pm; Sat 4:30–11pm; Sun 4:30–9:30pm. SEPTA: Board and Tasker sts.; 1 block north of Tasker; make a right onto Dickinson. By car: Follow Broad St. 15 blocks south of City Hall, then 2 blocks east on Dickinson.

INEXPENSIVE

Marra's ★★ Value ITALIAN Marra's, in the heart of South Philadelphia (supposedly the oldest surviving restaurant here), has thin-crust pizzas; classic escarole soup; big, inexpensive carafes of chianti; old black-and-white photos in the window; and, coincidentally, my heart. To me, there's nothing better than scoring a tall-backed, red-vinyl-cushioned wooden booth in the first (and best) of the three dining rooms. There's something revelatory about Marra's simple garden salad, with its straightforward vinaigrette and oil-cured olives, and about their pizza, which is best served plain, just homemade sauce and cheese. I've never been let down by a meal here, and I've had pretty much everything on the menu. By the way: Wait for a downstairs booth. It's worth it.

1734 E. Passyunk Ave. (btw. Morris and Moore sts.). ✆ **215/463-9249.** Reservations accepted for large parties. Main courses $7–$16; basic pizza $9 small, $11 large. DISC, MC, V. Tues–Sat 11:30am–11pm; Sun 2–10pm.

Ralph's Italian Restaurant ★ ITALIAN Garlic lovers alert: This two-story restaurant a few blocks north of the Italian Market is the epitome of the "red gravy" Italian style: unpretentious, comfortable, reasonable, and owned by the same family for decades.

Finds Breakfast All Day

The top spots for casual but creative, first-come, first-served breakfast? **Sam's Morning Glory** at 10th and Fitzwater, near the Italian Market, serves coffee in cool metal cups, yummily topped frittatas, focaccia egg sandwiches, deservedly famous pancakes, and roasted potatoes with homemade ketchup. Up in Northern Liberties at the corner of 4th and Brown, **Honey's Sit 'N' Eat** is another comfortably cozy spot for potato pancakes, huevos rancheros, free-range omelets, homemade veggie burgers, and limeade. In both in Bella Vista and Fairmount, eaters gladly wait hours for the cream-and-fruit-stuffed French toast, Greek salad, and mega portions at both locations of **Sabrina's.** Then again, if it's even the quirkiest fare and atmosphere you're after, you absolutely must squeeze into South Philly's **Carman's Country Kitchen,** a wee corner luncheonette that charms with a capricious little menu that could include conch fritters, cheddar pancakes, lima bean omelets, and more oddly delicious combinations dreamed up by Carman, the oddly delicious chef-proprietress.

The baked lasagna, spaghetti with sausage, and chicken Sorrento have fans all over the city. The extensive menu is long on veal and chicken dishes. It's always busy, especially before and after sporting events.

760 S. 9th St. (btw. Fitzwater and Catharine sts.). ✆ **215/627-6011.** www.ralphsrestaurant.com. Reservations recommended. Main courses $11–$23. No credit cards. Sun–Thurs noon–9:45pm; Fri–Sat noon–10:45pm.

4 UNIVERSITY CITY (WEST PHILADELPHIA)

EXPENSIVE

Distrito ★★ MEXICAN You almost can't help but have fun at this kitsch-filled, neon-lit version of Mexico City. Distrito's walls are bubble-gum pink. One has dozens of *luchador* (Mexican wrestling) masks hanging from it. There's an old VW Beetle where you can do shots of 70 kinds of tequila, dining arrangements that involve swings, a widescreen TV that regularly screens *Nacho Libre,* bar stools with glittery rubber seats, and a hidden, striped room for private karaoke parties.

And that's not even getting to the menu. Chef-owner Jose Garces (of Amada and Tinto) may have a sense of humor, but he also has a marvelous sense of creative balance. Order three to four small plates per person: atun seviche with Serrano-coconut sauce, plantains and queso fresca, pineapple-salsa pork carnitas, queso fundido over duck stew, mushroom huarache flatbread, and hamachi tacos with lime and avocado. Add a couple of fresh-fruit juice margaritas, and your mouth will have as much fun as your eyes and ears are having. At lunch, go for the $15 meal of two courses and an iced tea or soda.

3945 Chestnut St. (entrance on 40th St.). ✆ **215/2222-1657.** www.distritorestaurant.com. Reservations recommended. Main courses $12–$18 lunch, $24–$58 dinner; 2-course lunch $15. AE, DISC, MC, V. Mon–Thurs 11am–11pm; Fri 11am–midnight; Sat 5pm–midnight.

Pod ★★ (Finds) MODERN ASIAN Pod has a fun, futuristic decor (molded rubber, sculpted plastic, and video displays punctuated by a glass exterior curtain wall), generous portions, and a great selection of sushi. The young waitstaff is clad in what looks like *Star Trek* outfits, and the bathrooms resemble airplane loos. You can self-select the color of your "pod" (a curved semiprivate seating area) from nine different pastels, depending on your mood. Another gimmick is the conveyor belt that carries sushi or small, delectable Japanese dishes like crab spring rolls, vegetable pot stickers, and gingery pork dumplings around an oval seating area with stools that light up when you sit down. (Dishes revolve unclaimed only 20 min. before they're whisked away.)

3636 Sansom St. ✆ **215/387-1803.** www.podrestaurant.com. Reservations recommended. Entrees $9–$29 lunch, $18–$29 dinner; sides $3–$14. AE, DC, MC, V. Mon–Thurs 11:30am–11pm; Fri 11:30am–midnight; Sat 5pm–midnight; Sun 5–10pm.

MODERATE

Marigold Kitchen ★★ (Finds) CONTEMPORARY AMERICAN/SOUTHERN West Philly professors, artists, and foodies take refuge in this charming and chic BYOB, where comfort fare takes a modern twist. So, if you like butternut squash soup, you might love it with vanilla-poached figs. Ditto for fritters, here, made with parsnips and collard greens, or beet, onion, and cabbage-stuffed ravioli. The restaurant is housed on the first two floors of a rambling Victorian boardinghouse. It stores its wineglasses in an old iron oven, but has modern blue tables and some spalike touches. It's fun to discover—and even more fun to dine in.

501 S. 45th St. (at Larchwood Ave.). ✆ **215/222-3699.** www.marigoldkitchenbyob.com. Reservations recommended. Main courses $17–$25; 5-course tasting menu $50. AE, DISC, MC, V. Tues–Sun 5:30–10pm (closing can vary, call ahead); Sun brunch 10am–2pm.

Nan ★ THAI-FRENCH FUSION Nan is one of those modest-looking places that you forget about, rediscover, and then wonder how you got along so long without such note-perfect renditions of chicken and shrimp curry, escargots in puff pastry, and tamarind and plum-glazed roast duck. Chef-owner Kamol Phutlek was making these, along with reliable pad Thai and chicken-lemon-grass soup, long before the rest of the world discovered the joys of ginger and goat cheese. His clean, white-tableclothed BYOB bistro lacks the bells and whistles of newer places, but it's a truly nice place for a meal.

4000 Walnut St. ✆ **215/382-0818.** www.nanrestaurant.com. Reservations accepted. Main courses $17–$29. MC, V. Tues–Thurs noon–2:30pm and 5–10pm; Fri noon–2:30pm and 5–11pm; Sat 5–11pm.

Penne ★ ITALIAN Don't be fooled by this eatery's hotel-like appearance: Penne has real personality—and some delicious pasta, too. It's a convenient stop after a performance at Penn's Annenberg Theatre or a stroll around campus. Chef Roberta Adamo calls her

> **(Value) Good to Go**
>
> Dozens of vendors have permits to operate on the streets around the University of Pennsylvania campus. I like **Magic Carpet** for vegetarian meatball subs at 36th and Walnut streets, the plantain burritos at **Mexicali** at 37th and Walnut, and the Greek salad and zucchini feta balls at **Aladdin** at 34th and Spruce near University Museum.

Bring Your Own . . .

Philadelphia boasts more bring-your-own-bottle restaurants per capita than any other American city, mainly because the region's post-Prohibition laws limit the city's number of liquor licenses. BYOBs, or BYOs as most locals call them, generally fit into the bistro category. They're often small and most serve only dinner. Many are cash only. Some accept reservations; some are first-come, first-served. Below are some of my favorites, but you'll find others elsewhere in this chapter, including **La Viola** (p. 102), **Lee How Fook** (p. 111), **Marigold Kitchen** (p. 107), **Nan** (p. 107), and **Tacconelli's** (p. 112).

Audrey Claire ★ This stylish spot serves flatbreads topped with pears, Gorgonzola, and walnuts; grilled Romaine salads; and roast chicken with pomegranate molasses. In summer, the sidewalk tables are idyllic. 20th and Spruce streets. ✆ **215/731-1222.** www.audreyclaire.com.

Bistro 7 ★★ **Finds** This is a breath of fresh air among the crowded bars of Old City. Chef and co-owner Michael O'Hallaran works wonders with gnocchi, Spanish seafood stews, and, for dessert, Asian puddings. The atmosphere is friendly and neighborhoody. Reservations are accepted, as are credit cards. 7 N. 3rd St. ✆ **215/931-1560.**

Chloe ★★ Try for a last-minute table at this lovely little Old City spot. The owners are both chefs who love to give comfort food an elegant twist. Cash only. No reservations. 232 Arch St. ✆ **215/629-2337.**

Dmitri's ★★ **Finds** This place in Queen Village is the mack daddy of this genre. Greek, seafood oriented, and tiny, it has amazing hummus, grilled octopus, fresh bluefish, and rice pudding. Reservations and cash are not accepted. Expect long waits during the dinner rush. Hostesses often find waiting patrons hanging out at the bar across the street. 3rd and Catharine streets. ✆ **215/625-0556.**

kitchen a lab, and has her pasta down to a science. My recommendation: Go for the plainest noodle dish possible, and finally understand the meaning of al dente. Nice Italian wines are available, by the bottle, glass, or flight.

3611 Walnut St. (in the Hilton Inn at Penn). ✆ **215/823-6222.** www.pennerestaurant.com. Reservations accepted. Main courses $10–$18 lunch, $18–$28 dinner. AE, DISC, MC, V. Mon–Thurs 11:30am–10pm; Fri 11:30am–11pm; Sat 5–11pm; Sun 5–10pm.

White Dog Café ★★ **Finds** AMERICAN To understand this very tweedy, yet very socially left yet very, very Penn restaurant and bar, you must understand its owner, Judy Wicks. Wicks is not a chef. She is, however, one of Philadelphia's great citizens. She gives generously to charities, holds thought-provoking dinners with authors and international academics, and always buys from and promotes small local farmers. Inside the two row houses that contain her day-through-night restaurant are cozy living spaces converted into dining rooms. Checkered tablecloths, antique furniture, lights, and white dogs accessorize the look.

Jamaican Jerk Hut ★ Finds The most casual of this bunch, the Jamaican Jerk Hut serves authentic island fare right off Broad Street. I love the salt cod and accras. Large-party reservations are accepted, but not credit cards. Try to go in the summer, when you can sit at a table on the large back porch. 1436 South St. ✆ **215/545-8644.**

Lolita ★★ One of my favorite restaurants in the city, BYOB or otherwise, Lolita serves contemporary Mexican that adds flavorful touches like *huitlacoche* (a fungus) to its inspired dishes. Reservations are accepted; credit cards are, too. Bring a bottle of tequila, and they'll mix up a pitcher of margaritas for the table using seasonal fruit juice. 13th Street, between Sansom and Chestnut streets. ✆ **215/456-7100.**

Matyson ★★ The owners here use only the freshest ingredients, and open for lunch. Steak frites, trout over risotto, and desserts are house specialties. Reservations and credit cards are accepted. The business district location is convenient. 19th Street, between Market and Chestnut streets. ✆ **215/564-2925.** www.matyson.com.

Melograno ★★ This Roman-inspired, no-reservations corner spot specializes in homemade pastas and seasonal meats. Although unfussy, it's undeniably chic. Go early to get a table. 2012 Sansom St. ✆ **215/875-8116.**

Mercato ★★ Just a block from Broad Street, Mercato doesn't accept cash or reservations. Specialties include scallops over spring pea risotto, pumpkin-stuffed ravioli, and short ribs. Another bonus is the olive-oil tasting menu. 1216 Spruce St. ✆ **215/985-2962.**

Pumpkin ★ At this tiny, casually pretty spot with an open kitchen, you can watch chef Ian Moroney plate up a Mediterranean fish stew rich in saffron, or the whole fish of the day. Cash only. Reservations recommended. 1713 South St. ✆ **215/545-4448.**

I like to hang out at the bar here, drinking warm (spiked) apple cider in the winter, or chatting with the affable bartenders over a glass of house chardonnay. The servers deliver small to major platefuls of seasonal fare. I like the veggie plates, rosemary-grilled strip steak, and, during lunch, the Cuban Reuben.

3420 Sansom St. ✆ **215/386-9224.** www.whitedogcafe.com. Reservations recommended. Main courses $12–$25 lunch, $16–$26 dinner. AE, DC, DISC, MC, V. Mon–Thurs 11:30am–2:30pm and 5:30–10pm; Fri–Sat 11:30am–2:30pm and 5:30–11pm; Sun 10:30am–2:30pm and 5–10pm.

INEXPENSIVE

New Deck Tavern IRISH/AMERICAN The New Deck Tavern is less restaurant than a relaxed watering hole, with Irish beer and bartenders, and a 37-foot solid cherrywood bar. The tavern specializes in crab cakes, homemade soups, and fare such as shepherd's pie. Specials abound during the 5-to-7pm happy hour.

3408 Sansom St. ✆ **215/386-4600.** Main courses $7–$14. AE, DC, MC, V. Daily 11am–2am.

New Delhi INDIAN New Delhi is a fairly good Indian restaurant near the U. Penn campus, with a 26-item all-you-can-eat buffet, including desserts like pistachio ice cream and sweet rice pudding. It boasts quality ingredients, a tandoor clay oven, and friendly service. Given these prices, it's often crowded with students and teachers from the university. Look for discount coupons in student newspapers.

4004 Chestnut St. ✆ **215/386-1941.** Reservations not required. Main courses $8.95–$11; all-you-can-eat lunch buffet $6.95; dinner buffet $9.95. AE, DISC, MC, V. Mon–Thurs noon–3pm and 4:30–10pm; Fri noon–3pm and 4:30–11pm; Sat noon–11pm; Sun noon–10pm.

Zocalo ★ MEXICAN This restaurant, 4 blocks from the U. Penn campus, offers contemporary Mexican cuisine from all the provinces. It sprawls through four or five separate dining areas, so it is quiet and civilized. You'll find everything from traditional dishes like mole chicken to modern classics like fresh shrimp in chili sauce. There's lively Latin music on most nights, with a pleasant deck in back for use in summer. Tasty margaritas, too.

36th St. and Lancaster Ave. (1 long block north of Market St.). ✆ **215/895-0139.** www.zocalophilly.com. Reservations recommended. Main courses $19–$23. AE, DC, MC, V. Mon–Thurs 11:30am–3pm and 5–10pm; Fri 11:30am–3pm and 5–11pm; Sat 5:30–11pm.

5 CHINATOWN

MODERATE

Rangoon Burmese Restaurant ★ BURMESE I'm grateful to the Burmese women who run this modest Chinatown eatery for introducing me to the joys of tealeaf salad, coconut rice, and crispy lentil fritters. Try the extrahot curries or spicy basil tofu. Although Rangoon does fine with familiar stir-fries, it does best with more summery fare, like beef and mint kabobs and lemon-grass soup.

112 N. 9th St. ✆ **215/829-8939.** Reservations accepted for 5 or more. Main courses $8.50–$20. MC, V. Sun–Thurs 11:30am–9pm; Fri–Sat 11:30am–10pm.

Sang Kee Peking Duck House ★ CHINESE A stalwart since 1980, Sang Kee still churns out Chinatown's best Peking duck (crispy on the outside, juicy on the inside, and delectable in a wrap with scallions and hoisin sauce), Szechuan duck, and barbecued pork. Other menu highlights are the spareribs, fried dumplings, the wonton noodle soup, and just about every fish dish. Its fans are many, fervent, and varied, and service is quick and bilingual. The dining rooms are basically devoid of atmosphere, but the large groups and multigenerational Asian families kick up the fun level.

238 N. 9th St. ✆ **215/925-7532.** Reservations recommended. Main courses $10–$25. No credit cards. Sun–Thurs 11am–10:45pm; Fri–Sat 11am–11:45pm.

Finds Dim Sum for Everyone

Taking the family out for China's traditional meal of "tiny plates" is a fun way to spend a weekend afternoon. **Ocean Harbor** at 1023 Race St. and **Imperial Inn** at 142–146 N. 10th St. both offer plenty of shrimp dumplings, steamed pork buns, and radish cakes from rolling silver carts.

INEXPENSIVE

Lee How Fook ★★ CHINESE/CANTONESE Spare and cozy, this 38-seat BYOB serves terrific salt-baked squid, gingery oyster hot pots, and chow fun noodles. This family-run restaurant is comfortable and sharp, with wood paneling and matching tables. Menuwise, there's no going wrong, not with the duck noodle soup, with its tangles of pasta and golden broth, nor with the snow peas bearing up egg and crab sauce. One hint though: This food tastes especially good during a cold snap.

219 N. 11th St. (next door to Vietnam restaurant). ✆ **215/925-7266.** www.leehowfook.com. Main courses $6.50–$25. MC, V. Tues–Sun 11:30am–10pm.

Ray's Coffee Shop ★ CHINESE/COFFEE BAR This unlikely precursor to the city's penchant for coffee bars, with 30 seats in a pleasant room located near the convention center, features an unusual combination of subtle Taiwanese cuisine (the dumplings are especially recommended) and dozens of exotic coffees, each smartly priced and brewed to order in lovely little glass siphons. The iced coffee and house special noodle soup here are great.

141 N. 9th St. ✆ **215/922-5122.** Main courses $9–$19; coffee $4–$8. AE, MC, V. Mon–Tues and Thurs 8:30am–8pm; Wed and Fri 8:30am–6pm; Sat 11:30am–9pm.

Vietnam VIETNAMESE This attractive spot with glossy wood tables and black-and-white photos serves sweet, oversize cocktails and wonderful, affordable dishes such as charbroiled pork, crispy spring rolls, lime-glazed chicken, and flavorful noodle soups. Love those cocktail names—especially the Virgin's Downfall.

221 N. 11th St. ✆ **215/592-1163.** Main courses $7–$15. AE, MC, V. Sun–Thurs 11am–9pm; Fri–Sat 11am–10pm.

Vietnam Palace ★ VIETNAMESE Right across the street from better-known Vietnam is its bigger, friendlier, and, I might argue, more authentic sister. You'll find many of the same menu items as across the street. Here, though, I like the garlicky beef in grape leaves, any of the broken rice platters, and the refreshingly stuffed summer rolls. For dessert: rice pudding with taro. No contest there.

222 N. 11th St. ✆ **215/592-9596.** Main courses $7–$14. AE, MC, V. Daily noon–10:30pm.

6 NORTHERN LIBERTIES

MODERATE

Standard Tap ★★ Value AMERICAN With excellent local beers and marvelously hearty fare to match, this casual restaurant and pub has anchored Northern Liberties since opening a few years back. The Tap, as regulars call it, pretty much embodies this part of town. On any given night of the week, you'll find indie rockers, artists, and off-duty servers hanging out at the downstairs jukebox. That same night, you might head up the staircase and out to the open deck, and come upon a boisterous party of eight eating and drinking off the day's marketing meetings. Go early, and it's families with their kids.

The menu is printed on wall-mounted chalkboards throughout. Meals—the kitchen takes pains to use locally grown ingredients—include double burgers, fried smelts, chicken potpie, seasonal beet salad, and great, great fries. Although the bar serves mixed drinks and wine, it specializes in regional ales from area brewers like Victory, Yards, Dogfishhead, and Stout's. It would be a shame to come here and not order one. The Tap is open nightly and serves an a la carte brunch on weekends.

Corner of 2nd and Poplar sts. ✆ **215/238-0630.** www.standardtap.com. Main courses $8–$20. AE, MC, V. Mon–Fri 4–11pm; Sat–Sun 11am–3:30pm (brunch) and 4–11pm.

INEXPENSIVE

Tacconelli's ★★ Finds ITALIAN A real insider recommendation for pizza is Tacconelli's—not, as you'd think, in South Philly (and not exactly in Northern Liberties) but way up past No Libs in Port Richmond. This local legend is open until the thin, crispy crusts run out (about 9pm). It's imperative to call ahead to reserve the type of pizza you want, which is prepared in a brick oven. The white pizza with garlic oil and the spinach and tomato pies are heavenly.

2604 E. Somerset St. (at Aramingo Ave.). ✆ **215/425-4983.** Reservations required; place pizza orders in advance. Pizzas $13–$21. No credit cards. BYO wine. Wed–Sat 4:30–9pm; Sun 4–7pm. SEPTA: Frankfort subway line from Market St. to Somerset St., then walk 8 blocks east. By car: from Society Hill, take Front St. north, make a right onto Kensington Ave., then another right onto Somerset.

7 MANAYUNK

EXPENSIVE

Jake's ★★★ CONTEMPORARY AMERICAN Decked out in shades of amber, gold, and light-brown leather, with richly textured fabrics on the cozy booths, this 20-year-old fine-dining spot is Manayunk's upscale destination for dinner or brunch. Owner Bruce Cooper is famous for his crab cakes and wonderful spring roll and tuna tartare appetizers. Meats and dishes are inventive and perfectly prepared. Jake's Sunday brunch omelet is a voluptuous beauty, with asparagus and home fries. In 2008, the restaurant annexed the spot next door and opened **Cooper's Brick Oven Wine Bar** (✆ **215/483-2750**), serving lunch, dinner, and a late-night menu of gourmet—pear, hazelnut, and Roquefort; Benton's ham and egg; margherita—thin-crust pizzas, salads, small plates, and vino.

4365 Main St. ✆ **215/483-0444.** www.jakesrestaurant.com. Main courses $24–$39. AE, DC, MC, V. Mon–Thurs 5:30–9:30pm; Fri 5:30–10:30pm; Sat 5–11pm; Sun 10:30am–2:30pm (brunch) and 5:30–9pm.

MODERATE

Derek's ★ CONTEMPORARY AMERICAN Opened as Sonoma in 1992, this spot was Manayunk's original new-deal restaurant. Today, chef-owner Derek Davis, has made it a nice spot to have a business dinner or to nibble a salad and have a glass of wine, especially at the sidewalk cafe. Menu specialties include tomato mozzarella and chopped salads, spicy or grilled chicken pizza, and double burgers.

4411 Main St. ✆ **215/483-9400.** www.dereksrestaurant.com. Reservations accepted. Main courses $8–$34. AE, DC, DISC, MC, V. Daily 10am–2am (Sun brunch 11am–3pm).

Winnie's Le Bus Kids AMERICAN/ECLECTIC Bring the babies, the toddlers, and the grandparents: Le Bus got its name dishing out funky homespun food from a van on the U. Penn campus, and still dishes out fresh, affordable, home-style cuisine based on American classics. Homemade breads and pastries are baked fresh daily, and breakfast features omelets, frittatas, and blueberry pancakes. Lunch and dinner include veggie chili, grilled pizzas, meatloaf, and simple pastas. The wholesomeness of the place makes it especially attractive to families. There's outdoor seating, weather permitting. Watch out for lines at peak hours.

4266 Main St. ✆ **215/487-2663.** www.lebusmanayunk.com. Reservations accepted. Main courses $5–$9 lunch, $10–$18 dinner. AE, MC, V. Sun–Thurs 9am–10pm; Fri–Sat 9am–11pm.

8 LOCAL FAVORITES: CHEESESTEAKS, ROAST PORK & HOAGIES

CHEESESTEAKS

Philadelphia cheesesteaks are nationally known. Preparing a cheesesteak is an art here—ribbons of thinly sliced steak are cooked quickly on a steel diner grill with onions (unless you order otherwise) and then slapped onto a roll on top of overlapping slices of provolone or a thick smear of Cheez Whiz. The perfect cheesesteak achieves a flavorful but not soggy balance between the cheese, onion, meat, and roll. Hoagie is the local name for the sandwich known variously throughout the Northeast as a submarine, grinder, or torpedo. Remember, if you dislike onions, you have to specify "Widout!" or they come chopped into the meat.

Some directions to South Philly might be in order from Center City. *On foot:* Walk South on 9th Street through the Italian Market, crossing Christian Street, Washington Avenue, Federal Street, the intersection of 9th Street and Passyunk Avenue. *By subway:* Broad Street line south (toward Pattison Ave. and stadiums) to Ellsworth and Federal, exit east to Federal Street; walk 5 blocks to 9th Street. *By car:* South on Broad Street; Left on Wharton Street, 5 blocks to Passyunk Avenue/9th Street. (Or, if you want to get tricky, south on 10th St., left on Wharton, or south on 8th and right on Federal St.)

Philly's Italian Market

While touring South Street or South Philadelphia, make an effort to head a few blocks south to the **Italian Market** ★★, located along 9th Street, from Fitzwater to Wharton. This gritty outdoor market—part of Rocky's famous run—has stands hawking fresh produce, pasta, seafood, and other culinary delights. With the atmosphere of a street fair, it's a tad rough-and-tumble, what with the merchants yelling and the trash fires burning (in winter) and the chickens squawking (at the butcher south of the main area). Some of the more famous vendors include **Sonny D'Angelo's** butcher shop; **Di Bruno Bros. House of Cheese,** a cramped space for the ultimate in dairy; and **Giordano's** produce stand at the corner of 9th and Washington. Before you reach the market, be sure to pick up a loaf of sesame seed–coated Italian bread "seeded" at **Sarcone's Bakery,** between Fitzwater and Catharine streets. Here's a fun tidbit for you: The big mural across from Di Bruno Bros. Pronto is of controversial former mayor Frank Rizzo. According to the Mural Arts Commission, it's the most defaced mural in the city. The market is open daily from dawn to dusk but many vendors close early on Sunday. Bus: 47 or 64.

The Ultimate Cheesesteak Taste Test

Cheesesteak taste test? you think. *Aren't they all basically the same?* Don't say that aloud in this city. We Philadelphians take our cheesesteaks very seriously, though we know finding the perfect cheesesteak requires patience and a hearty stomach. So hats off to Richard Rys at *Philadelphia* magazine, who wolfed down 50 cheesesteaks in 34 days in a quest to crown a Cheesesteak King. Richard ordered steaks with American cheese and no extras, also known as an "American, without": "This leaves only the three essential elements to any good steak—meat (judged on taste and quality), cheese (amount and thorough distribution throughout the sandwich), and roll (freshness, consistency, proper meat-to-bread ratio). A great steak shouldn't hide behind onions or condiments."

Here's a sample of his top picks closest to Center City, rated on a scale of 1 to 5 Clogged Arteries (clogged arteries are a good thing in the world of cheesesteaks).

Cosmi's Deli, 1501 S. 8th St. (✆ **215/468-6093**), is just around the corner from famous rivals Pat's and Geno's, but Richard swears Cosmi's is the real king of steaks. "Fresh roll, meat chopped with a samurai's precision, and melted cheese embracing each piece like Mama giving Raj a bear hug on *What's Happening*." Richard's rating: 5.

Swann Lounge at the Four Seasons (p. 72) serves an $18 plate of four dainty cheesesteak spring rolls. "It's the culinary equivalent of flipping cheesesteak purists everywhere the bird. But you know, this is good. Meat, cheese distribution—perfect." Rating: 4.5.

Tony Luke's, 39 E. Oregon Ave. (✆ **215/551-5725**), is in South Philly, near the Walt Whitman Bridge. "Strips of meat stuffed into a hearty, rugged roll that was built for handling a serious payload. My only complaint is that for all its mass, it's a little light on cheese." Rating: 4.5.

Chubby's, 5826 Henry Ave. (✆ **215/487-2575**), is a favorite in Manayunk. "That wet-hot dairy goodness is mixed in well. Perfectly sized roll filled well with meat that's tasty and gristle-free." Rating: 4.

D'alessandro's, 600 Wendover Ave. (✆ **215/482-5407**), also in Manayunk, has an ongoing rivalry with Chubby's. "They give up the crown this year. Not a bad sandwich, but it has its flaws. The roll is way overstuffed, leaving as much meat in my lap as in my mouth, and the meat is dry." Rating: 3.5.

FOOD COURTS

The Bourse Food Court This location has 10 snack/restaurant operations, all moderately priced and designed for takeout to be eaten at the tables that fill this cool and stunning restoration of the 1895 merchant exchange. The entire operation was recently upgraded, and stalls include **Bain's Delicatessen** for turkey sandwiches and **Flamers** for burgers.

Jim's Steaks, 400 South St. (✆ **215/928-1911**), is just south of Society Hill. "The roll looks like it just wandered in off the set of a Sally Struther's infomercial, the meat is only moderately chopped, and the cheese is barely melted. Yet the damn thing is inexplicably good." Rating: 3.5.

John's Roast Pork, Weccacoe and Synder avenues (✆ **215/463-1951**), is close to Tony Luke's (above), near the Walt Whitman. "I was thrown off by the sesame seed–speckled roll, which wasn't nearly as crusty as it appeared—thin, but strong enough to handle the healthy portion of tasty meat stuffed inside it. Perfect amount of cheese." Rating: 3.5.

Lazaro's, 1743 South St. (✆ **215/545-2775**), claims to have the biggest steaks in town, at 18 inches. Richard ordered a half. "Soft roll, though maybe a bit too much so. Steak diced nicely, but I detected a subtle, unidentifiable spice that I didn't enjoy. There also could have been a little more meat on this puppy." Rating: 3.

Sonny's, 228 Market St. (✆ **215/629-5760**), gets a lot of traffic in Old City. "Good cheese distribution and loads of meat, but although it's well diced, is a bit stringy at times. The roll is too thin for the load." Rating: 3.

Geno's Steaks, 1219 S. 9th St.(✆ **215/389-0659**), is a Philly landmark, but Richard gives it modest praise. "Decent amount of cheese. Good roll. The meat is another story. It's riddled with pockets and veins of fat and contains a rainbow of colors from brown to gray. Oddly enough, the taste isn't bad." Rating: 2.5.

Pat's King of Steaks, 1237 Passyunk Ave. (✆ **215/468-1546**), around the corner from Geno's, gets no special treatment, either. "The cheese distribution on my sandwich makes me think Stevie Wonder is working dairy duty on the grill line. It's spotty, leaving some regions bare. Like Geno's, a good roll, but a frightening amount of fat in the meat." Rating: 2.

So how much weight did Richard gain from his cheesesteak binge? He tells us that he was stunned to find that his cholesterol actually went down and his weight stayed the same, though he admits that he worked out four times a week during the taste-test period. "Either I have a superhuman metabolism, or I should get to work on a Cheesesteak Diet book. That South Beach thing was overrated, anyway."

—courtesy of Richard Rys and Philadelphia *magazine (www.phillymag.com)*

111 S. Independence Mall E. (just east of the Liberty Bell). Mon–Sat 10am–6pm; Sun 11am–5pm. Closed in winter.

Downstairs at the Bellevue Upscale, and very quiet, with bright tiles, great lighting, and public restrooms, this is a great spot for a quick lunch when shopping on Walnut Street. Center tables surround better-than-average food-court vendors such as **Full of Soup, Asahi Japanese,** and **12th Street Cantina.**

Indie Coffee Shops

Going to a Starbucks in Philly is sort of like going to a Pizza Hut in Sicily. Sure, you'll get a reliable, familiar product. But you'll be missing out on something truly exceptional. Here are some of the best coffee shops in town. Most offer free wireless Internet.

CENTER CITY (WEST OF BROAD)

The city's top restaurateurs, artists, hairstylists, and aesthetes love **La Colombe,** both as a supplier of beans for New York's best, such as Daniel, and as its own very French-style shop at 130 S. 19th St. The roaster's second cafe is located in Manayunk at 4360 Main St., where it serves the same buttery croissants and perfectly foamy cappuccino in pretty Fima Deruta pottery as the first location, and also offers tasty panini.

America's very first outpost for Trieste's popular **Hausbrandt** coffee can be found at 207 S. 15th St., just south of Walnut Street. Practice your Italian on the baristas while you sip your espresso.

A few of blocks south of the busy business district, **Ants Pants,** 2212 South St., is a sunny spot for lingering over a cup of joe and an open-face bacon stack breakfast sandwich.

CENTER CITY (EAST OF BROAD)

Tucked between 2nd and 3rd streets on tiny, cobblestone Church Street (down from Christ Church) **Old City Coffee** roasts and brews its own, yummy beans. The cafe sells pastries and light lunches, and offers a pretty spot for hanging out. There's also an Old City Coffee in the Reading Terminal Market.

SOUTH STREET & BELLA VISTA

Popular **Chapterhouse,** 620 S. 9th St., is a spare, modern space with monthly art shows; plenty of elbowroom; excellent, fair-trade coffees and teas; and homemade sodas and smoothies.

Families and students have made **Philadelphia Java Co.,** 518 S. 4th St., a regular hangout: They serve La Colombe roast and yummy open-faced sandwiches smeared with thick yogurt cheese, green olives, and herbs.

If you're looking for a latte to wash down your cheesesteak—or, if you're the one person out of your group who would prefer a brie panini—walk 1 block east of Pat's and Geno's to the corner of 8th and Wharton streets to **Benna's Café.** Owner Nancy Trachenberg is the consummate hostess. (I should know: Much of this book was written from Nancy's second cafe, **B2,** at the corner of 10th and Dickinson.) Thanks, Nancy!

Below-ground level of the Park Hyatt at the Bellevue Hotel (S. Broad and Walnut sts.). Mon–Fri 10am–6pm; Sat 10am–5pm.

The Food Court at Liberty Place Kids At this court, on the second floor of a gleaming urban mall in the heart of Center City, are quick-grab favorites like **Sarku Japan, Café Spice,** and **Original Turkey,** along with **Subway, Saladworks,** and **Chick-Fil-A.** It's spotless, large, and reasonably priced, with full lunches from $3.75. You'll find it easy to keep your eyes on the kids as they wander.

2nd level (accessible by escalator or elevator) of Liberty Place (btw. Chestnut and Market sts. and 16th and 17th sts.). Mon–Sat 9:30am–7pm; Sun noon–6pm.

The Market at Comcast Center Beneath Philadelphia's tallest skyscraper is one of its best boutique food courts. **Di Bruno Bros.** has a gourmet-to-go spot here, alongside **Frank's,** a stand offering roast pork, chicken cutlet, and cheesesteak. I like the juice bar, and am hoping the proposed dumpling stand by **Susanna Foo** opens as promised.

1701 J.F.K. Blvd. (underground level of Comcast Center). Mon–Fri 8am–7pm; Sat 10am–5pm.

The Reading Terminal Market In the space underneath the train terminal, this market has served Philadelphians since the turn of the 20th century. For a full description, see "A Taste of Ethnic Philly: Reading Terminal Market," earlier in this chapter.

12th and Arch sts. ✆ **215/922-2317.** www.readingterminalmarket.org. Mon–Sat 8am–6pm.

7 Exploring Philadelphia

by Lauren McCutcheon

Consider Philadelphia's sightseeing possibilities—the most historic square mile in America; more than 90 museums; innumerable Colonial churches, row houses, and mansions; an Ivy League campus; more Impressionist art than you'll find in any place outside of Paris; and leafy, distinguished parks, including the largest one within city limits in the United States.

Most of what you'll want to see within the city falls inside a rectangle on a map between the Delaware and Schuylkill rivers in width, and between South and Vine streets in height (although you'll want to get out of the grid to visit the art museum and Fairmount Park). It's easy to organize your days into walking tours of various parts of the city—see chapter 8 for suggestions. Nothing is that far away. A stroll from City Hall to the Philadelphia Museum of Art takes about 25 minutes. A walk along Walnut Street to Independence National Historical Park and Society Hill should take a little less time. If you'd rather ride, the spiffy PHLASH buses loop past most major attractions every 12 minutes, and the fare is $2 each time you board, or $5 for an all-day individual pass ($10 for an all-day family pass for two adults and two children 6–17). SEPTA also has an all-day $6 fare for unlimited city rides on buses, trolleys, subways, and the El. The two systems do *not* accept each other's passes.

The city wraps up six attractions in one via the **Philadelphia Citypass,** which offers admission to the Franklin Institute, National Constitution Center, Philadelphia Zoo, Adventure Aquarium, the Academy of Natural Sciences (*or* Eastern State Penitentiary)—and a Philadelphia Trolley Works tour. Prices are $54 for adults and $37 for children 3 to 12, and they may be purchased in advance at www.citypass.com (click on "Philadelphia") or at any one of the attractions. Tickets are good up to 9 days from first use, and they represent about a 50% discount from full admissions to all of the attractions.

1 INDEPENDENCE NATIONAL HISTORICAL PARK: AMERICA'S MOST HISTORIC SQUARE MILE ★★

In the annals of Philadelphia tourism, the best-known and most-visited sites are, hands down, the Liberty Bell and Independence Hall. These historic attractions stand across from one another on the very spot where the United States was conceived in 1776, and, in 1787, the future of the young nation was assured by the Constitutional Convention. A few steps from that, the Founders of the nation lived and dined. Philadelphia was the nation's capital during Washington's second term, so the U.S. Congress and Supreme Court met here for 10 years while awaiting the construction of the new capital in Washington, D.C. From the first penny to the First Amendment, Philadelphia led the nation.

Independence National Historical Park ★ comprises 40 buildings (half are open to the public) on 45 acres of Center City real estate (see the "Walking Tour: Historic Highlights & Society Hill" map, in chapter 8). The entire park spans 2nd to 6th streets, from Walnut Street to Market Street. Independence Hall and the Liberty Bell lie between 5th and 6th streets at Chestnut Street, and the park has been overhauled, with some $300 million poured into new attractions, renovations, and landscaping. The Independence Visitor Center 1 block north is well equipped to illustrate the early history of this country, and the new National Constitution Center explores the U.S.'s core document.

This neighborhood is a superb example of successful revitalization. Fifty years ago, this area had become glutted with warehouses, office buildings, and rooming houses. The National Park Service stepped in, soon followed by the Washington Square East urban renewal project now known as Society Hill, after the historic neighborhood it's in. To the east, gardens replaced buildings as far as the Dock Street food market, which was replaced by Society Hill Towers in 1959. Graff House, City Tavern, Pemberton House, and Library Hall were reconstructed on their original sites. Franklin Court is a contemporary structure erected for the Bicentennial of the Declaration of Independence celebrations. The Liberty Bell Center (ca. 2003) is even more modern.

The terrorist attacks on September 11, 2001, had an inevitable impact on the spontaneous excitement of stepping into the birthplace of American independence: You must pass through a security-screening center on Market Street before visiting the Liberty Bell and Independence Hall, but most days the process moves fairly quickly.

From March and through December, everyone in your group—including infants!—will need a **ticket** to visit Independence Hall. Tickets themselves are free. But for guaranteed reservations, you can call ✆ **800/967-2283** or visit www.recreation.gov up to a year in advance. Reserving ahead incurs a $1.50 per ticket handling charge, but many visitors find the convenience worth the fee. Families may request up to 10 tickets at a time, and everyone absolutely must pick up the tickets at will call at least 45 minutes before your scheduled tour, as unclaimed tickets are resold, and there are no refunds. If you don't book in advance, go early to the visitor center (open from 8:30am) to avoid lines. While you're there, you may also pick up tickets for the frequent, 10-visitors-at-a-time interior tours of the Bishop White House and the Todd House. There is no tour required for the Second Bank of the United States: It's open to the public Wednesday through Saturday from 11am to 5pm. See p. 122 for more information.

The place to get tickets—and most everything else you need to get started—is the **Independence Visitor Center,** 1 N. Independence Mall W. (at 6th and Market sts.), Philadelphia, PA 19106 (✆ **800/537-7676** or 215/965-7676; www.independencevisitorcenter.com). The visitor center should be your first stop in the park, since it's the official visitors' service for the park, and also provides general tourism services and trip-planning information. There's a cafe and a gift shop selling mementos and park publications, and every 30 minutes the center shows a John Huston feature, *Independence,* free of charge.

To get to Independence Park, you can take the SEPTA Market-Frankford Line to 5th and Market streets. By bus, take the PHLASH or any Chestnut Street bus from Center City.

If you're driving, from I-76, take I-676 east to 6th Street (last exit before the Ben Franklin Bridge), then turn south (right) along Independence Mall. From the Ben Franklin Bridge, make a left onto 6th Street and it's right there after the National Constitution Center. From I-95 southbound, take the Center City exit to 2nd Street. From I-95

Philadelphia Attractions

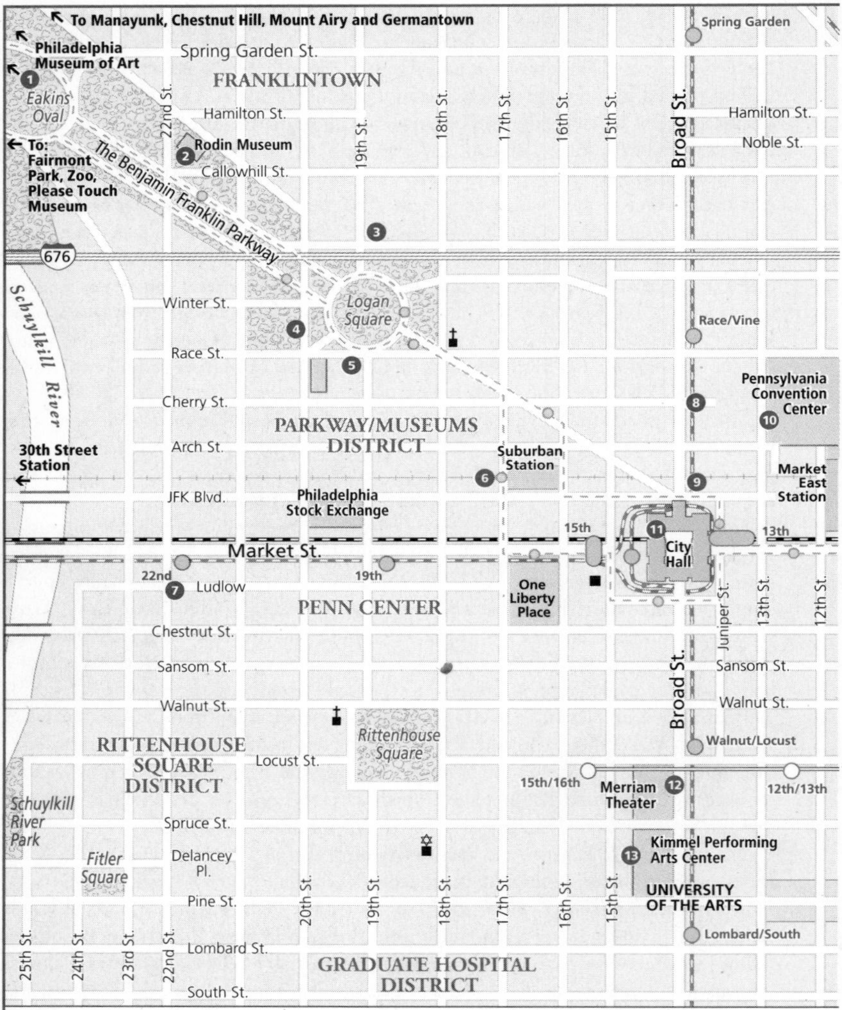

Academy of Music **12**
Academy of Natural Sciences **5**
The African-American Museum in Philadelphia **15**
Arch Street Meeting House **22**
Athenaeum of Philadelphia **34**
Atwater Kent Museum **28**
Benjamin Franklin Bridge **14**
Betsy Ross House **19**
Carpenters' Hall **29**
Christ Church **21**
Christ Church Burial Ground **20**
City Hall **11**
Comcast Center **6**
Declaration House (Graff House) **23**
Eakins Oval **1**
Edgar Allen Poe National Historic Site **41**
Elfreth's Alley **18**
Franklin Court **27**
Franklin Institute Science Museum **4**
Free Library of Philadelphia **3**
Independence Hall **31**
Independence Seaport Museum **28**
Independence Visitor Center **25**
Kimmel Performing Arts Center **13**
The Liberty Bell **24**

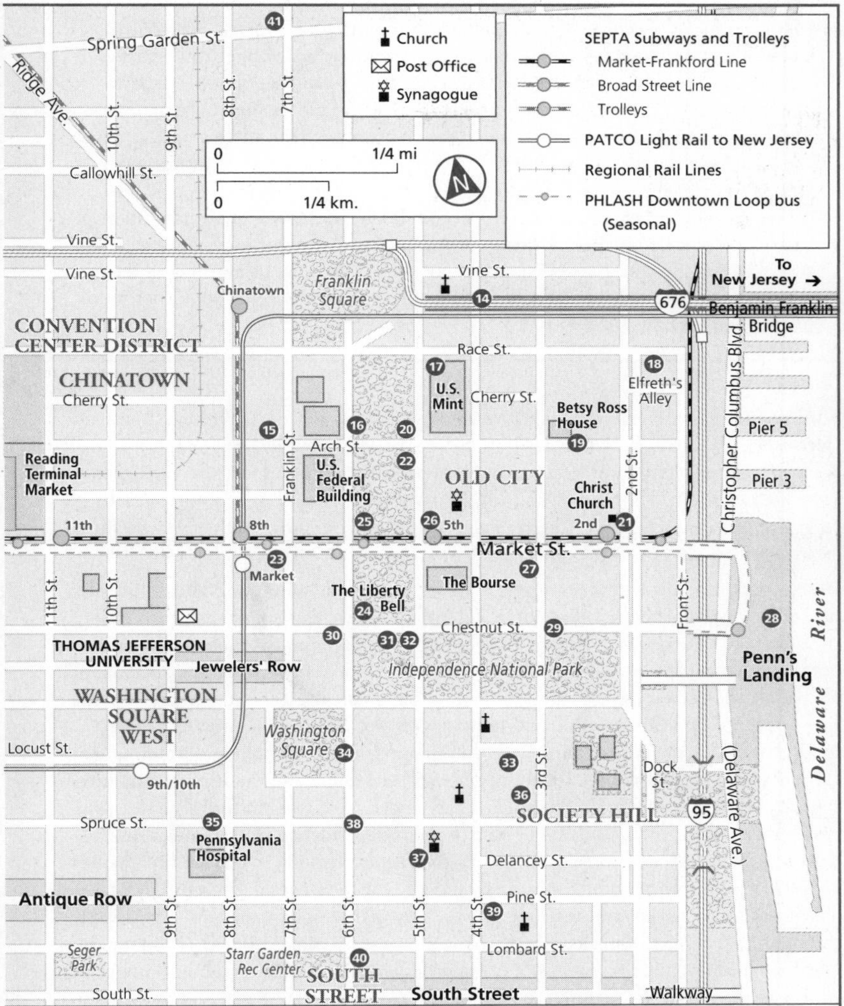

Lights of Liberty **29**
Masonic Temple **9**
Mikveh Israel Cemetery **35**
Mother Bethel African Methodist Episcopal Church **40**
Mutter Museum **7**
National Constitution Center **16**
National Museum of American Jewish History **26**
Old City Hall **32**
Old St. Joseph's Church **33**
Penn's Landing **28**
Pennsylvania Academy of the Fine Arts **8**
Pennsylvania Convention Center **10**
Pennsylvania Hospital **38**
Philadelphia Museum of Art **1**
Physick House **37**
Powel House **36**
Rodin Museum **2**
Rosenbach Museum & Library **10**
St. Peter's Episcopal **39**
U.S. Mint **17**

(Finds) Old City's Crazy Colonials

Every summer, they come back to town. You're enjoying an oversize bowl of miso soup in Buddakan, and you see a man in white knickers walking by. You're taking a shortcut behind the Second Bank of the U.S., and you get caught up in a bayonet charge. On Elfreth's Alley, in Carpenters' Hall, in the blocks that make up Old City, actors clad in Colonial garb roam. These performers' jobs are to wander about, answer questions about the historic personages they're portraying, and to stop at scheduled times to tell a story, proclaim, lead a military muster, play the glass Armonica, and take visitors on special tours around town. The organization they work for is **Once Upon a Nation** ★★★. Find out more about them and their performances at www.onceuponanation.org. And don't be surprised if they appear befuddled when you ask directions to the closest Wi-Fi hot spot: They're just staying in character.

northbound, use the exit marked HISTORIC AREA. Turn left on Columbus Boulevard (formerly Delaware Ave.) and follow it to the exit for Market Street (on the right). There's metered parking along most streets, as well as parking facilities under the visitor center (which charges $4.25 for a half-hour; $17 for all day), as well as at 2nd and Sansom streets, at 125 S. 2nd St. (btw. Chestnut and Walnut sts.), and just south of Market Street at 36 and 21 S. 2nd St.

Independence Hall ★★★ (Moments) Even if you knew nothing about Independence Hall, you could guess that noble and important events took place here. Although these buildings are best known for their national role, they also functioned as the seat of government for the city of Philadelphia and the state of Pennsylvania both before and after Philadelphia was the capital of the U.S. From an architectural standpoint, the edifice is graceful and functional; from the standpoint of history and American myth, it's unforgettable. Independence Square sets you thinking about the bold idea of forming an entirely sovereign state from a set of disparate colonies and about the strength and intelligence of the representatives who gathered here to do it. For some historical context, visit www.ushistory.org, the wonderful website of the **Independence Hall Association.**

When the French and Indian War (1754–63) required troops, which required money, King George III believed the colonists should pay for their own defense through taxes. The colonists disagreed, and the idea that the king harbored tyrannical thoughts swept through the Colonies. Philadelphia, as the wealthiest and most cultured of the seacoast cities, was leery of radical proposals of independence. Even Ben Franklin himself, an American agent in London at the time, was wary of this scheme. But the news that British troops had fired on citizens defending their own property in Concord pushed even the most moderate citizens to reconsider what they owed to England and what they deserved as free people endowed with natural rights.

The Second Continental Congress convened in May 1775, in the Pennsylvania Assembly Room, to the left of the entrance to Independence Hall. Each colony had its own green baize-covered table (the original of which was used as firewood when British troops occupied the city in Dec 1777). The Congress acted quickly, appointing a tall Virginia delegate named George Washington as commander of the Continental army. After the failure of a last "olive branch" petition, the Congress, through John Adams, instructed each colony's government to reorganize itself as a state. Thomas Jefferson worked on a summary of why the colonists felt that independence was necessary. The resulting Declaration of Independence, wrote noted historian Richard Morris, "lifted the struggle from self-interested arguments over taxation to the exalted plane of human rights." Most of the signatories of the Declaration of Independence used Philip Syng's silver inkstand, which is still in the room. The country first heard the news of the Declaration on July 8 in Independence Square.

Before and after the British occupied the city, Independence Hall was the seat of the U.S. national government. Here, the Congress approved ambassadors, pored over budgets, and adopted the Articles of Confederation, a loose and problematic structure for a country composed of states. Congress moved to New York after the war's end, and it grudgingly allowed delegates to recommend changes to the Articles.

The delegates who met in the Assembly Room in Philadelphia in 1787 created a new Constitution that has guided the country for more than 200 years. Jefferson's cane rests here, as does a book belonging to Franklin. Washington, as president of the convention, kept order from his famous "Rising Sun Chair." Delegates were mature, urbane, and trained to reason, and many had experience drafting state constitutions and laws. They decided on approaches to governance that are familiar today: a bicameral Congress, a single executive, an independent judiciary, and a philosophical belief in government by the people and for the people. No wonder John Adams called the convention "the greatest single effort of national deliberation that the world has ever seen."

Across the entrance hall from the Assembly Room, the courtroom served as Pennsylvania's Supreme Court chamber. Like the court at Williamsburg, Virginia, this room exemplifies pre–Bill of Rights justice. For example, your ranger guide will probably point out the tipstaff, a wooden pole with a brass tip that was used to keep onlookers subdued. Other period details include little coal-burning boxes to keep feet warm on chilly days. This was one of the first courtrooms in America to hear the argument that disagreement with a political leader isn't sedition, one of the great concepts in modern Anglo-American law.

The stairwell of Independence Hall held the Liberty Bell until 1976. The ranger will conduct you upstairs to the Long Gallery. Now it's set up as a banquet hall with a harpsichord (some of the guides even play) and a rare set of maps of the individual 13 colonies. Its view of Independence Mall is superb.

Two smaller rooms adjoin the Long Gallery. To the southwest, the royal governors of Pennsylvania met in council in a setting of opulent blue curtains, silver candlesticks, and a grandfather clock. Beneath a portrait of William Penn, governors met with foreign and Native American delegations, and conducted their everyday business. On the southeast side, the Committee Room fit the whole Pennsylvania Assembly while the Second

"Self-Evident" Not So Self-Evident

In the Declaration of Independence, Thomas Jefferson boldly declares, "We hold these truths to be self-evident"—but not in the rough draft. Jefferson originally found those truths to be "sacred and undeniable" before changing his mind. You can read his first handwritten copy along with documents like Ben Franklin's will and William Penn's 1701 Charter of Privileges, at **Library Hall,** 105 S. 5th St. between Chestnut and Walnut streets.

Continental Congress was meeting downstairs. When it wasn't being used to house the assembly, it stored the assembly's reference library or arms for the city militia.

As you descend the stairs, look at leafy, calm **Independence Square,** with its statue of Commodore John Barry. The clerk of the Second Congress, John Nixon, first read the Declaration of Independence here, to a mostly radical and plebeian crowd. (Philadelphia merchants didn't much like the news at first, since it meant a disruption of trade, to say the least.)

Chestnut St. (btw. 5th and 6th sts., flanked by Old City Hall to the left and Congress Hall to the right). ✆ **215/965-2305.** www.nps.gov/inde. Free admission. Daily 9am–5pm, later in summer. Free tours by park rangers every 15 min. 9am–4:45pm. You must take a tour in order to see the interior of the building. Guaranteed reservations ✆ 800/967-2283 or www.recreation.gov; $1.50 per ticket handling fee. Bus: PHLASH, 9, 21, or 42.

Franklin Court ★★ Kids Franklin Court is an imaginative, informative, and downright fun (and free) museum run by the National Park Service. Designed by noted Philadelphia architect Robert Venturi, it was very much a sleeper when it opened in April 1976, because Market and Chestnut streets' arched passages give little hint of the court and exhibit within.

Franklin Court is the site on which the home of Benjamin Franklin once stood. Franklin resided with his family in smaller row houses in the neighborhood prior to living here. Like Jefferson at Monticello, Franklin planned much of the interior design of the house, though he spent the actual building period first as Colonial emissary to England, and then to France. His wife, Deborah, oversaw the construction, as the flagstones engraved with some of her correspondence show, while Ben sent back continental goods and a constant stream of advice. Sadly, they were reunited in the family plot at Christ Church Burial Ground, since Deborah died weeks before the end of Ben's 10-year absence. Under the stewardship of Ben's daughter Sarah and her husband, Richard Bache, Franklin Court provided a comfortable home for Ben until his death in 1790.

Since archaeologists have no exact plans of the original house, a simple frame in girders indicates its dimensions and those of the smaller print shop. Excavations have uncovered wall foundations, bits of walls, and outdoor privy wells, and these have been left as protected cutaway pits. It is all very interesting, but enter the exhibition for the really fun part. After a portrait and furniture gallery, a mirrored room reveals Franklin's far-ranging interests as a scientist, an inventor, a statesman, a printer, and so on. At the Franklin Exchange, dial various American and European luminaries to hear what they thought of Franklin.

The middle part of the same hall has a 15-minute series of climactic scenes in Franklin's career as a diplomat. On a sunken stage, costumed doll figures brief you, and each other, on the English Parliament in 1765, the Stamp Act, the Court at Versailles (when its members were wondering whether to aid America in its bid for independence), and the debates of the Constitution's framers in 1787, which occurred right around the corner at Independence Hall. Needless to say, Ben's pithy sagacity wins every time.

On your way in or out on the Market Street side, stop in the 1786 houses that Ben rented out. One is the Printing Office and Bindery, where you can see Colonial methods of printing and bookmaking in action. The house at 322 Market St. is the restored office of the *Aurora and General Advertiser,* the newspaper published by Franklin's grandson. Next door, get a letter postmarked at the Benjamin Franklin Post Office (remember, Ben was postmaster general, too!). Employees still stamp the marks by hand. Upstairs, a postal museum is open in summer.

314–322 Market St. (another entrance is on Chestnut St. btw. 3rd and 4th sts.). ✆ **215/965-2305.** Free admission. Fragments of Franklin Court Wed–Sun 10am–5pm; Franklin Court Museum Shop Wed–Sun 10am–4:30pm; Printing Office and Underground Museum daily 11am–5pm; U.S. Post Office Mon–Sat 9am–5pm. SEPTA: Market-Frankford El, 2nd St. Station. Bus: PHLASH, 9, 21, or 42.

The Liberty Bell ★★★ You almost can't leave Philadelphia without seeing the Liberty Bell. The bell resides in a 13,000-square-foot, $12.9-million modern glass gazebo, 235 feet long and 50 feet wide, angled so you can see it against the backdrop of Independence Hall.

The Liberty Bell, America's symbol of freedom and independence, was commissioned in 1751 for the Pennsylvania State House to mark the 50th anniversary of a notable event: William Penn, who governed Pennsylvania alone under Crown charter terms, decided that free colonists had a right to govern themselves, so he established the Philadelphia Assembly under a new Charter of Privileges. The 2,000-pound bell, cast in England, cracked while it was being tested, and the Philadelphia firm of Pass and Stow recast it by 1753. It hung in Independence Hall to "proclaim liberty throughout the land" as the Declaration of Independence was read aloud to the citizens. In 1777, it survived a trip to an Allentown church so the British wouldn't find it and melt it down for ammunition. In the 1840s, the term *Liberty Bell* was coined by the abolitionist movement, which recognized the relevance of its inscription, "Proclaim Liberty throughout all the land unto all the inhabitants thereof," in the fight against slavery. The last time it tolled was to celebrate Washington's birthday in 1846.

The new building offers excellent information and interactive exhibits, including an X-ray of the bell's crack and a film produced by the History Channel about how the bell became an international icon of freedom. Language options for the narrative videos range from Russian to Chinese to German.

Chestnut St. (btw. 5th and 6th sts., enter on 6th St. btw. Market and Chestnut sts.). ✆ **215/965-2305.** Free admission. Tickets not required. Daily 9am–5pm; visitors must clear security by 4:45pm. You can see the bell at all times from 6th and Chestnut sts. Bus: PHLASH, 9, 21, or 42.

Lights of Liberty Overrated Kids Since the summer of 1999, Independence Park's most important sights have been the backdrop for hour-long, interactive sound-and-light walking tours. The tour's purpose: Provide visitors with a high-tech, smoke-and-light-filled, and definitely unsubtle immersion into the drama of the American Revolution. From April through October, you'll walk as night falls over the Old City past trendy bars and restaurants (wearing, ahem, huge wireless headphones, something you wouldn't be caught dead wearing *inside* any of those bars), as you enter today's version of the Philadelphia of 2 centuries ago. Five-story projections on historic buildings and wireless headsets equipped with movie-style "surround" sound make the tour a "virtual" and, arguably cheesy Colonial experience.

The ground floor of the PECO Energy Center, next to Independence and Congress Halls on Chestnut Street, is the *Lights of Liberty*'s group ticketing and holding area. Tours are first-come, first-served, so arrive early if you're worried about the wait. You'll pick up headsets automatically tuned to a script read by such actors as Ossie Davis and Charlton Heston, and which are triggered automatically as your group arrives at the planned park destinations. Younger children might prefer the alternative kids' headsets.

Led by a guide, you'll walk across cobblestone streets to park sites, where the Revolutionary story is compressed into five acts. Rifles crackle, cannons boom, the Founders of America argue, images project, the Philadelphia Orchestra plays in the background, and colored smoke rises, making you wonder when the disco ball is going to drop. The finale of 1776 takes place right in back of Independence Hall. Afterward, you'll either be elated—or you'll need a drink from one of those trendy bars.

1-hr. tours depart from PECO Energy Center, 6th and Chestnut sts. ✆ **877/462-1776** or 215/LIBERTY (542-3789). www.lightsofliberty.org. Admission $20 adults, $17 seniors and students with ID, $17 children 12 and under. 10% AAA discount. Up to 6 shows per hour Apr–Oct Tues–Sat dusk–11:15pm. Shows available in English, German, Italian, Japanese, and Spanish. Print versions available in Hebrew and Russian. SEPTA: Market East. Bus: PHLASH, 21, or 42.

National Constitution Center ★★★ Kids Opened July 4, 2003, on Philadelphia's redesigned Independence Mall, the stunning, modern National Constitution Center is the first museum in the world devoted to the U.S. Constitution—its history and its relevance in the daily lives of Americans. The 160,000-square-foot, state-of-the-art facility, designed by Pei Cobb Freed & Partners, in angular glass, steel, and limestone, has departments of history, education, and outreach, all using a blend of the most exciting and attention-grabbing technological tools to offer something for everyone, from scholars to casual visitors. While same-day tickets are usually available, it's a good idea to buy tickets in advance, and arrive 20 minutes early for the timed theater shows that welcome visitors twice each hour.

As you stroll north from Independence Visitor Center, you'll cross Arch Street and a broad walkway to the gleaming white stone entrance to the Constitution Center, emblazoned with those three magic words, "We the People" A 15- to 17-minute multimedia show with an inspiring live actor and 360-degree movie screen explains the Constitution's early history. From there, visitors learn how the Constitution affects the functioning of government—you can take your own Presidential Oath of Office, explore a national family tree, try on a Supreme Court robe, and check out the Bill of Rights. Signers Hall has bronze life-size figures of the 39 men who signed the Constitution, and the three who dissented. Especially good are exhibits featuring a voting machine from Palm Beach, Florida, from the contested 2000 presidential election, and one featuring tools used by G. Gordon Liddy in the Watergate burglary. There are plenty of daily events, lectures, and programs, as well as a 225-seat, glass-enclosed restaurant and store.

525 Arch St. ✆ **215/409-6600** or 409-6700 for advance ticket sales. www.constitutioncenter.org. Admission $12 adults, $11 seniors, $8 children 4–12, free for children 3 and under and active military. Mon–Fri 9:30am–5pm; Sat 9:30am–6pm; Sun noon–5pm. Bus: PHLASH, 9, 21, 42, 38, 44, 48, or 121.

2 THE TOP MUSEUMS

Barnes Foundation ★★★ The magnificent Barnes Foundation, just outside the city limits in suburban Merion, will enchant you with its thoroughly unique display of one of the world's most important art collections. Albert Barnes crammed his French Provincial mansion (ca. 1925) with more than 1,000 works of genius—181 Renoirs, 69 Cézannes, 46 Picassos, innumerable Impressionists and post-Impressionists, early moderns and a generous sampling of European art from the Italian primitives onward. Each wall is filled with recognizable masterpieces, hung, literally, from floor to ceiling. The Barnes reopened in November 1995 after a world tour of more than 80 masterworks from the collection and a $12-million renovation of the galleries.

Barnes believed that art has a quality that can be explained objectively—for example, one curve will be beautiful and hence art, and another that's slightly different will not be art. That's why the galleries display antique door latches, keyholes, keys, and household tools with strong geometric lines right next to the paintings. Connections beg to be drawn between neighboring objects—an unusual van Gogh nude, an Amish chest, New Mexican rural icons. Virtually every first-rank European artist is included: Degas, Seurat, Bosch, Tintoretto, Lorrain, Chardin, Daumier, Delacroix, Corot, and more. Not a bad use of a fortune made from patent medicine!

In 2004, a federal judge ruled that the Barnes may move its collection to Philadelphia. The planned spot is along the Benjamin Franklin Parkway, replacing a boys' prison. Ground broke in October 2008 for the new facility. Opening date is to be announced.

300 N. Latches Lane, Merion Station. ✆ **610/667-0290.** Fax 610/667-8315. www.barnesfoundation.org. reserve@barnesfoundation.org. Admission $12 per person. Sept–June Fri–Sun 9:30am–5pm; July–Aug Wed–Fri 9:30am–5pm. Make reservations 45–60 days in advance for Apr, May, Oct, or Nov visits; 35–45 days in advance for Mar, June, Sept, or Dec; 2 weeks in advance for Jan, Feb, July, or Aug. SEPTA: Take Paoli local train R5 to Merion Station, walk up Merion Rd., and turn left onto Latches Lane. Bus: 44 to Old Lancaster Rd. and Latches Lane. Car: I-76 (Schuylkill Expwy.) west to City Line Ave. (Rte. 1), then south on City Line 1½ miles to Old Lancaster Rd. Turn right onto Old Lancaster, continue 4 blocks, and turn left onto Latches Lane.

Franklin Institute Science Museum ★★★ Kids The Franklin Institute Science Museum isn't just kid stuff. All ages love this thoroughly imaginative trip through the world of science. The complex has four parts. The first is the home of the Franklin National Memorial, with a 30-ton statue of its namesake and a collection of authentic Franklin artifacts and possessions.

The second part is a collection of science- and technology-oriented exhibition areas, with innovative hands-on displays such as a gigantic walk-through heart (beloved by Philadelphians, and restored after years of climbing and exploration by curious children) and the Train Factory, an interactive setting where you can play engineer for a 350-ton locomotive. For a hair-raising experience, plug into a Van de Graaff generator at the lightning gallery. On the third floor, an energy hall bursts with Rube Goldberg contraptions, noisemakers, and light shows. The nearby Discovery Theater holds afternoon shows featuring liquid air and other oddities. The fourth floor specializes in astronomy and mathematical puzzles. The basement **Fels Planetarium,** just renovated and accompanied by the new "space station" on the first floor, rounds out the offerings here.

The third part of the Franklin Institute is the **Mandell Futures Center.** Just past the Franklin National Memorial on the second floor, you'll enter an atrium with cafes, ticket counters, and ramps and stairs leading to the exhibits. Just beyond is a separate-admission IMAX arena, showing films ranging from undersea explorations to the Rolling Stones in spectacular 70mm format. Eight permanent interactive exhibits, including space, earth, computers, chemistry, and health, take you into the 21st century with Disney World–style pizazz. My personal favorites are the Sports Challenge, a full-body exploration of the science behind popular sports like surfing and rock climbing, and the See Yourself Age computer program in Future and You. The texts throughout are witty and disarming. Quite thrilling is the **Skybike,** which you can ride along a 1-inch cable three stories above the Bartol Atrium floor and its huge new sci-store.

The fourth section is the 1995 **CoreStates Science Park,** a collaboration with the Please Touch Museum (which has since relocated to Memorial Hall; p. 148). It uses the 38,000-square-foot lawn between the two museums—it's free with admission to the museum. The imaginative urban garden is filled with high-tech play structures, including a high-wire tandem bicycle, 12-foot tire, step-on organ, maze, and optical illusions.

20th St. and Benjamin Franklin Pkwy. (Logan Circle). ✆ **215/448-1200.** www.fi.edu. Admission to exhibitions, planetarium, science park, and Discovery Theater $14 adults, $13 seniors, $12 children 4–11; additional $5–$6 per person for IMAX Theater. Exhibitions, planetarium, and Discovery Theater daily 9:30am–5pm; IMAX Sun–Thurs 10am–6pm and Fri–Sat 10am–9pm; science park May–Oct daily 10am–4pm. Bus: PHLASH or 33.

Pennsylvania Academy of the Fine Arts ★★ Two blocks north of City Hall is the Pennsylvania Academy of the Fine Arts (PAFA), a wonderful museum and teaching facility that was the first art school in the country (1805) and at one time the unquestioned leader of American Beaux Arts. After a major renovation in late 1994, the academy, housed in a stunning Frank Furness building, unveiled a major reinstallation of 300 works from the past 200 years. Another 2004–05 restoration effort brightened the jewel tones of the gorgeous, hand-painted decorative ceilings and the overall look of the landmark museum and school.

The ground floor houses an excellent bookstore, a cafe, and the academy's offices. A splendid staircase, designed by Furness, shines with red, gold, and blue. Each May, the annual academy school exhibition takes over the museum. The school itself moved to 1301 Cherry St. years ago, but has renovated the factory building to its north to recentralize operations.

As is evident from the PAFA galleries, such Early American painters as Gilbert Stuart, the Peale family, Washington Allston, and Benjamin West (America's first fine painter) congregated in Philadelphia, America's capital and wealthiest city. The main galleries feature works from the museum's collection of more than 6,000 canvases. The rotunda has been the scene of cultural events ever since Walt Whitman listened to concerts here. The adjoining rooms display works from the illustrious mid-19th-century years, when PAFA enjoyed its most innovative period.

118 N. Broad St. (at Cherry St.) ✆ **215/972-7600.** www.pafa.org. Admission $10 adults, $8 seniors and students with ID, $6 children 5–18. Admission to special exhibitions $15 adults, $12 seniors and students with ID, $10 children 5–18. Free admission to gallery exhibitions and Landmark Bldg. ground floor. Tues–Sat 10am–5pm; Sun 11am–5pm. Free tours Mon–Fri 11:30am–1:15pm, Sat–Sun 2:45pm. SEPTA: Market-Frankford El, 15th St. Station. Broad St. subway, Race/Vine Station. Bus: 48.

Philadelphia Museum of Art ★★★ Even on a hazy day you can see America's third-largest art museum from City Hall—a resplendent, huge, beautifully proportioned Greco-Roman temple on a hill. Because the museum, established in the 1870s, has relied on donors of great wealth and idiosyncratic taste, the collection does not aim to present a comprehensive picture of Western or Eastern art. Its strengths, however, are dazzling: It houses undoubtedly one of the finest groupings of art objects in America, and no visit to Philadelphia would be complete without at least a walk-through; allow 2 hours minimum. Late hours on Friday have become a city favorite, and there is a new bar open in summer in the elegant front courtyard overlooking the city skyline.

The museum is designed simply, with L-shaped wings off the central court on two stories. Paintings, sculptures, and decorative arts are grouped within set periods. The front entrance (facing City Hall) admits you to the first floor. Special exhibition galleries and American art are to the left; the collection emphasizes that Americans came from diverse cultures, which combined to create a new and distinct aesthetic. French- and English-inspired domestic objects, such as silver, predominate in the Colonial and Federal galleries, but don't neglect the fine rooms of Amish and sturdy Shaker crafts. The 19th-century gallery has many works by Philadelphia's Thomas Eakins, which evoke the spirit of the city in watercolors and oils.

The once controversial 19th- and 20th-century European and contemporary art galleries highlight Cézanne's monumental *Bathers* and Marcel Duchamp's *Nude Descending a Staircase.* The recent gift of the McIlhenny $300-million collection of paintings is one of the great donations of this type and adds strength in the French Impressionist area.

Upstairs, spread over 83 galleries, is a chronological sweep of European arts from medieval times through about 1850. The John G. Johnson Collection, a Renaissance treasure-trove, has been added to the museum's holdings. Roger van der Weyden's diptych *Virgin and Saint John* and *Christ on the Cross,* one of the Johnson Collection, is renowned for its exquisite sorrow and beauty. Another, van Eyck's *Saint Francis Receiving the Stigmata,* is unbelievably precise (borrow the guard's magnifying glass). Other masterpieces include Poussin's frothy *Birth of Venus* (the USSR sold this and numerous other canvases in the early 1930s, and many were snapped up by American collectors) and Rubens's sprawling *Prometheus Bound.* The remainder of the floor takes you far away—to medieval Europe, 17th-century battlefields, Enlightenment salons, and Eastern temples.

The museum also owns and operates a massive, gorgeous Art Deco gallery across the Fairmount and Pennsylvania avenues. The Perelman Building showcases some of the museum's most comprehensive, colorful, and cutting-edge collections in elegant new design and textiles galleries. Among its other welcoming spaces is a library open to the public with a changing display of rare books, precious documents, and graphic arts. There are also a 100-seat cafe overlooking a landscaped terrace, a new bookstore, and a skylit walkway. Coming (hopefully) soon: A new tunnel designed by Frank Gehry that will connect the main building and this one.

The museum has excellent dining facilities. Art After 5 is the museum's unique blend of entertainment from 5 to 8:45pm on Friday in the Great Stair Hall. On the first Friday of each month, there's an eclectic mix of international music, with both renowned and emerging jazz artists performing all other Fridays.

26th St. and Benjamin Franklin Pkwy. ✆ **215/763-8100** or 684-7500 for 24-hr. information. www.philamuseum.org. Main bldg. and Perelman Bldg. admission (does not include special exhibits) $14 adults, $12 seniors 65 and over, $10 students with ID and children 13–18, free for children 12 and under; Perelman Bldg. admission $7 adults, $6 seniors 65 and over, $5 students with ID and children 13–18, free for children 12 and under. Pay what you wish on Sun. Tues–Sun 10am–5pm (main bldg. until 8:45pm Fri). Bus: PHLASH, 7, 32, 38, 43, or 48. A shuttle btw. the main bldg. and the Perelman Bldg. operates every 10 min. 10am–5pm. Car: From the parkway headed west (away from City Hall), follow signs to Kelly Dr. and turn left at the first light at 25th St. to the lots at the rear entrance.

3 MORE ATTRACTIONS

Reading Terminal Market (p. 117) is an attraction in itself, as is the **Italian Market** (p. 113) if you're exploring South Philadelphia.

ARCHITECTURAL HIGHLIGHTS

Benjamin Franklin Bridge ★ Great cities have signature bridges, and this is Philadelphia's. The Benjamin Franklin Bridge, designed by Paul Cret (one of the architects of the parkway across town) was the largest single-span suspension bridge in the world ($1^3/_4$ miles) when it was finished in 1926. The bridge carries cars and commuter trains and also has a foot/bicycle path along its south side, more reachable than ever since Independence Mall has been expanded to the edge of the bridge. For the bicentennial of the U.S. Constitution, a Philadelphia team including Steven Izenour, a leading American architect and planner, created a computer-driven system for illuminating each and every cable. At night, Philadelphians are treated to the largest lighting effects show since Ben Franklin's kite. Walkers and bikers are welcome to cross during daylight hours. Those of us who are slightly lazier can opt to pay $2.05 to see it from the bridge-crossing PATCO train. (See www.ridepatco.org for stations and schedules.)

Entrance to free bicycle/pedestrian walkway on 5th btw. Vine and Race sts. Daily 6am–dusk. Bus: 5.

City Hall ★ When construction of City Hall began in 1871, it was to be the tallest structure in the world. But plans were scaled back, other buildings surpassed it, and the elaborate 1901 wedding cake by John McArthur, Jr., with an inner courtyard straight out of a French château, quickly became outdated. The charming building is still in use as the mayor's office and is home to offices from the Register of Wills to city courtrooms to city council's quarters. Philadelphians love the crowning 37-foot statue of William Penn by A. M. Calder. For years, the structure appeared rather rusty and grimy, but now, with repainting, new cast iron work, and cleaning, City Hall has reclaimed its pride.

You may wish to wander inside the vast floors, which range from the breathtaking to the bureaucratically forlorn. Both inside and out, City Hall boasts rich sculptural decoration. The Mayor's Reception Room (no. 202) and the City Council Chamber (no. 400) are especially ornate. A tour of the building itself (not the tower) lasts up to 2 hours.

A rare highlight of your tour is heading up to the observation deck. This attraction being run by, well, functionaries, you're not guaranteed to get up there. Best bet: Call ✆ **215/686-2840** the morning of for a timed reservation. Admission is $5, but there's no extra charge for reserving over the phone. Tickets can be picked up in room 121.

The elevator up to Penn statue's recently cleaned shoestrings, at 548 feet, can hold only four people, and the outdoor cupola cannot hold many more. On the way, notice how thick the walls are—City Hall is the tallest building ever constructed without a skeleton of steel girders, so its white stone is 6 feet thick at the top and 22 feet thick at ground level. The view from the top encompasses not only the city but also the upper and lower Delaware Valley and port, western New Jersey, and suburban Philadelphia. It's windy up there, though. If you look straight down, you can see more of the hundreds of sculptures designed by Calder, the works of whose descendants—Alexander Stirling Calder (1870–1945) and Alexander Calder (1898–1976)—beautify Logan Circle and the Philadelphia Museum of Art. You could spend hours, although 45 minutes should do it for the highlights.

Broad and Market sts. ✆ **215/686-2840.** www.phila.gov/property/virtualcityhall. Observation deck admission $5 per person. Interior tour including observation deck $10 per person. Mon–Fri 9:30am–4:15pm. Tours daily 12:30pm. Reservations recommended. Bus/Subway: Most lines converge beside or underneath the bldg.

Comcast Center The newness—and tallness—of this skyscraper is reason enough to enter its glassy, three-story atrium lobby. Well, those reasons, plus the weirdly lifelike sculpture of people "walking" on beams overhead the atrium. And the 83-foot-wide, 10-million-pixels-rich, high-definition video screen, whose pictures couldn't be more real looking if they were in 3-D. Cable giant Comcast put its name on this 975-foot-tall tower in 2008 when it became the company's headquarters. Soon thereafter, the *Philadelphia Inquirer* referred to the building as a giant USB memory stick. The public is welcome in the lobby to ogle the screen any time. In December, the center puts on festive, 10-minute shows (every hour on the hour); it's a smooth, high-tech version of the beloved light show at Macy's in the John Wanamaker Building.

Finds Mural, Mural, on the Wall

The **Mural Arts Program (MAP)** was established in 1984 as a component of the Anti-Graffiti Network. Today, Philadelphia has more than 2,800 murals, more than any other city. The MAP says it works "to help beautify the city; help create a sense of community; and turn graffiti-scarred walls into scenic views, portraits of community heroes, and abstract creations."

The paintings can be quite striking, from the inspiring ***Symbols of Change,*** by Don Gensler, at 2110 Market St. to the psychedelic ***Larry Fine,*** by David McShane, at 3rd Street and South, to the nostalgic ***South Philly Musicians,*** by Peter Pagast, at Passyunk Avenue and Wharton Street. They range in size from small one-story designs like ***Fringe Festival,*** by Tom Judd at 35 N. 2nd St. to eight-story projects like ***Common Threads*** by Meg Fish Saligman, at Broad Street and Spring Garden. Each takes about 2 months to complete and costs from $15,000 to $25,000.

You can find a virtual gallery, with walking tour suggestions, and a schedule of trolley tours at www.muralarts.org or by calling ✆ **215/685-0745.** The 2-hour trolley tour takes place Wednesday, Saturday, and Sunday at 11am ($25 for adults, $23 for seniors 65 and over, $15 for children 3–10, and free for children 2 and under; tickets available at Independence Visitors Center). U. Penn has assembled a mural database at www.cml.upenn.edu/murals.

Here are more highlights:

- ***All Join Hands,*** by Donald Gensler, at Broad and Spring Garden streets, features faces and a poem titled "When the City Is at Peace," a collaboration of the artist, youths coming out of detention and long-term placement, and students at Ben Franklin High School.
- ***Children of Philadelphia,*** by Burt Dodge, at 16th Street and Fitzwater, depicts children with a preacher, with the city as a backdrop.
- ***Untitled,*** by Keith Haring, at 22nd Street and Ellsworth, features the artist's iconic colorful figures.
- ***Peace Wall,*** by Mural Arts Program director Jane Golden and Peter Pagast, at 29th and Wharton streets, lovingly portrays children's hands overlapping.
- ***Pride and Progress,*** by Ann Northrup, at 13th Street and Spruce, is a large, elaborate tribute to the gay community.
- ***Philadelphia on a Half Tank,*** by Paul Santoleri, near the airport at 26th Street and Penrose Avenue, is a vivid pastel portrait of the city on the side of an oil tank.

A fun aside: The ironworkers Local Union 401 that built the structure affixed a small William Penn figurine to the final beam. Their goal: Break the "curse of William Penn," which, according to local lore, was that Philadelphia's major pro teams couldn't win a championship after a Center City skyscraper was built higher than Penn's statue atop City Hall. It worked. The Phils captured the World Series a few months later.

1701 J.F.K. Blvd. www.comcast.com. Free admission. Daily. SEPTA: Suburban Station. Bus: 17.

Fisher Fine Arts (Furness) Library Like the Pennsylvania Academy of the Fine Arts building (see above), this citadel of learning has the characteristic chiseled thistle of Frank Furness, although it was built a decade later from 1888 to 1890. The use of 1890s leaded glass here is even richer than on the Pennsylvania Academy of the Fine Arts building. Originally the University of Pennsylvania's library, the building now houses, appropriately, the fine arts library. It's best viewed in a quick look while on Penn's Locust Walk.

220 S. 34th St. (at Locust Walk on U. Penn campus). ✆ **215/898-8325.** Free admission; photo ID required to enter; nonstudents may not enter evenings or Sat–Sun. Mon–Fri 9am–10pm during academic year; Mon–Fri 9am–5pm during summer. Bus: 44.

Pennsylvania Convention Center With the July 1993 opening of the Pennsylvania Convention Center (PCC), Philadelphia made it clear that the future of the area depends on its ability to accommodate tens of thousands of visitors weekly. Though the 440,000-square-foot, $522-million building is enormous, it's going to get bigger, and soon. The new center will go where old office buildings, a historic firehouse, and artists' studios stood as of press time. It will have 1 million square feet of saleable space, the largest contiguous exhibit space (541,000 sq. ft.) in the Northeast, and the largest convention center ballroom on the East Coast. (Let's hope it's worked out its many operational kinks by then.)

Unless you're one of the millions the PCC hopes to lure in for a meeting, you'll need to access the center via the Philadelphia Marriott's walkway, to an overlook of the Grand Hall. This cavernous, chilly, marble-covered space stars Judy Pfaff's vast kaleidoscopic *Cirque,* a network of airy steel and aluminum tubes over 70,000 square feet of space. Esplanades and corridors contain a veritable museum of 52 living artists (35 from Philadelphia).

This neighborhood is rife with chain restaurants. If you'd like to dine in a true Philly setting nearby, have breakfast, lunch, or an early supper at the Reading Terminal Market (p. 117), or explore the marvelous finds in Chinatown (p. 110).

Btw. 11th and 13th sts. and Market and Race sts. ✆ **215/418-4700.** www.paconvention.com. Enter at the northwest corner of 12th and Arch sts. Subway: Rail lines (including Airport Express) stop at Market East Station; SEPTA at 11th and Market and 13th and Market. Bus: PHLASH, 12, 17, 33, or 44. Car: Separate exit from I-676, btw. I-95 and I-76.

CEMETERIES

Christ Church Burial Ground ★★ This 1719 expansion of the original graveyard of Christ Church (see below) contains the graves of Benjamin Franklin and his wife, Deborah, along with those of four other signers of the Declaration of Independence and many Revolutionary War heroes. There are always pennies on Ben's grave; tossing them there (through an opening in the enclosing wall) is a local tradition that is supposed to bring good luck.

5th and Arch sts. ✆ **215/922-1695.** www.oldchristchurch.org. Closed to the public. Bus: PHLASH, 48, or 50.

Laurel Hill Cemetery ★ (Finds) How come you find Benjamin Franklin buried in a small, flat plot next to a church (see above), while Civil War general George Meade is buried in a bucolic meadow? Basically, the view of death and the contemplation of nature changed with the 19th-century romantic movement, and Laurel Hill reflects that romanticism. Laurel Hill, designated a National Historic Landmark in 1998, was the second American cemetery (after Mount Auburn in Cambridge) to use funerary monuments—

some are like small Victorian palaces. Set amid the rolling, landscaped hills overlooking the Schuylkill, its 78 acres also house plenty of tomb sculpture, pre-Raphaelite stained glass, and Art Nouveau sarcophagi. People picnicked here a century ago, but only walking is allowed now. Visitors are welcome, but are asked to respect those attending burials, as Laurel Hill remains a functional cemetery. Each year, the charity that helps keep up Laurel Hill holds a ritzy Gravediggers Ball at the Union League.

3822 Ridge Ave., E. Fairmount Park. ✆ **215/228-8200** or 228-8817. www.thelaurelhillcemetery.org. Free admission. Mon–Fri 8am–4:30pm; Sat 9:30am–5pm. Tours free–$30. Bus: 61. Car: Go north on E. River Dr., make a right on Ferry Rd., go 1 block to Ridge Ave., and turn right. The entrance is a half-mile down on the right.

Mikveh Israel Cemetery Philadelphia was an early center of American Jewish life, with the country's second-oldest synagogue (1740) organized by English and Sephardic Jews. While this congregation shifted location and is now adjacent to the Liberty Bell, the original cemetery—well outside the city at the time—was bought from the Penn family by Nathan Levy and later filled with the likes of Haym Solomon, a Polish immigrant who helped finance the revolutionary government, and Rebecca Gratz, the daughter of a fine local family, who provided the model for Sir Walter Scott's Rebecca in *Ivanhoe.*

Spruce St. (btw. 8th and 9th sts.). ✆ **215/922-5446.** www.mikvehisrael.org/thecemeteries. Summer Sun and Tues–Fri 10am–3pm. Free tours off season. Bus: 9 or 47.

CHURCHES

Arch Street Meeting House This plain brick building dates from 1804, but William Penn gave the land to his Religious Society of Friends in 1693. In this capital city of Quakers, the Meeting House opens its doors to 12,000 local Friends for worship during the last week in March each year. Quakers believe in direct, unmediated guidance by the Holy Spirit. There is little or no hierarchy among Friends. Worship is referred to as "meeting," a time when individuals come together and speak if so moved. This particular meetinghouse is spartan. There is no pulpit. Wooden benches face one another. Other areas of the Meeting House display Bibles, clothing, and implements of Quaker life past and present, along with a simple history of the growth of the religion and the life of William Penn.

4th and Arch sts. ✆ **215/627-2667** or 413-1804 for group tours. www.archstreetfriends.org. Suggested donation $2. Guided tours year-round Mon–Sat 10am–4pm. Services Wed 7pm and Sun 10:30am. SEPTA: Market-Frankford El, 2nd St. Station. Bus: PHLASH, 17, 33, 48, or 121.

Christ Church ★★ (Moments) The most beautiful Colonial building north of Market Street has to be Christ Church (1727–54). Its gleaming white spire can be seen from anywhere in the neighborhood, now that a grassy park and a subway stop have replaced the buildings to the south. The churchyard has benches, tucked under trees or beside brick walls.

Christ Church, dating from the apex of English Palladianism, follows the proud and graceful tradition of Christopher Wren's churches in London. As in many of them, the interior spans one large arch, with galleries above the sides as demanded by the Anglican Church. Behind the altar, the massive Palladian window—a central columned arch flanked by proportional rectangles of glass—was the wonder of worshipers and probably the model for the one in Independence Hall. The main chandelier was brought over from England in 1744. As in King's Chapel in Boston, seating is by pew instead of on open benches—Washington's seat is marked with a plaque.

With all the stones, memorials, and plaques, it's impossible to ignore history here. William Penn was baptized at the font, sent over from All Hallows' Church in London. Penn left the Anglican Church at age 23 (he spent most of his 20s in English jails because of it), but his charter included a clause that an Anglican Church could be founded if 20 residents requested it, which they did. Socially conscious Philadelphians of the next generations adopted Anglicanism then switched to Episcopalianism after the Revolution. The church's still-active Episcopalian congregation holds regular weekly services, so please schedule visits accordingly.

2nd St. (1/2 block north of Market St.). ✆ **215/922-1695.** www.christchurchphila.org. Donations welcome. Mon–Sat 9am–5pm; Sun 12:30–5pm. Services Mon–Fri 8am; Wed 9am; Sun 9am and 11am. Closed Mon–Tues in Jan–Feb. SEPTA: Market-Frankford El, 2nd St. Station. Bus: PHLASH, 5, 17, 33, or 48.

Gloria Dei (Old Swedes' Church) (Finds) The National Park Service administers this church, the oldest in Pennsylvania (1700). Inside the enclosing walls, you'll think you're in the 18th century, with a miniature parish hall, a rectory, and a graveyard amid the greenery. The one-room museum directly across from the church has a map of the good old days. The simple church interior has plenty of wonderful details. Everybody loves the ship models suspended from the ceiling: The *Key of Kalmar* and *Flying Griffin* carried the first Swedish settlers to these shores in 1638. And note the silver crown in the vestry; any woman married here wears it during the ceremony. This church, by the way, is Episcopal.

916 Swanson St. (near Christian Ave. and Columbus Blvd., aka Delaware Ave.) ✆ **215/389-1513.** www.old-swedes.org. Memorial Day to Labor Day daily 9am–4pm; off season Tues–Sun 9am–4pm. Call ahead to schedule tour. Sun services June–Aug 10am; Sept–May 9am and 11am. Bus: 57 or 64. Take Swanson St. under I-95 at Christian St. in Queen Village, opposite Pier 34, then turn onto Water St.

Mother Bethel African Methodist Episcopal Church ★ This National Historic Landmark is the oldest piece of land continuously owned by blacks in the United States. Richard Allen, born in 1760, was a slave in Germantown who bought his freedom in 1782, eventually walking out of St. George's down the street to found the African Methodist Episcopal order. The order today numbers some 2.5 million in 6,200 congregations, and this handsome, varnished-wood-and-stained-glass 1890 building is their mother church. Allen's tomb and a small museum, featuring his Bible and hand-hewn pulpit, are downstairs; open by appointment only.

419 S. 6th St. ✆ **215/925-0616.** Donations welcome. Church Tues–Fri 9am–2:30pm; tomb and museum by appointment only. Sun service 8am and 10:45am.

Old St. Joseph's Church (Finds) When it was founded in 1733, St. Joseph's was the only place in the English-speaking world where Roman Catholics could celebrate Mass publicly. The story goes that Benjamin Franklin advised Father Greaton to protect the church, since religious bigotry wasn't unknown even in this Quaker city. That's why the building is so unassuming from the street, a fact that didn't save it from damage during the anti-Catholic riots of the 1830s. Such French allies as Lafayette worshiped here. The present interior (1838, and renovated in 1985 to its late-19th-c. appearance) is Greek Revival merging into Victorian, with wooden pews and such unusual colors as mustard and pale yellow. The interior has also preserved a Colonial style unusual in a Catholic Church.

321 Willings Alley (near 4th and Walnut sts.). ✆ **215/923-1733.** www.oldstjoseph.org. Mon–Fri 9:30am–4pm; Sat 10am–6:30pm; Sun 7:30am–7:30pm. Mass Mon–Sat 12:05pm; vigil Mass Sat 5:30pm and Sun 7:30am, 9:30am, 11:30am, and 6:30pm. Bus: PHLASH, 9, 21, 42, or 47.

St. Peter's Episcopal St. Peter's (1761) was originally established through the bishop of London, and has remained continuously open since. Like all pre-Revolutionary Episcopal churches, St. Peter's started out as an Anglican shrine. But there was something wrong with Christ Church at 2nd and Market: mud. As a local historian put it, "the long tramp from Society Hill was more and more distasteful to fine gentlemen and beautiful belles."

Robert Smith, the builder of Carpenters' Hall, continued his penchant for redbrick, pediments on ends of buildings, and keystoned arches for gallery windows. The white box pews are evidence that not much has changed. Unlike most churches, the wineglass pulpit in St. Peter's is set into the west end and the chancel is at the east, so the minister had to do some walking during the service. George Washington and Mayor Samuel Powel sat in pew 41. The 1764 organ case blocks the east Palladian window. The steeple outside, constructed in 1842, was designed by William Strickland to house bells, which are still played.

Seven Native American chiefs lie in the graveyard, victims of the 1793 smallpox epidemic. Painter C. W. Peale, Stephen Decatur of naval fame, Nicholas Biddle of the Second Bank of the United States, and other notables are also interred here.

3rd and Pine sts. ✆ **215/925-5968.** www.stpetersphila.org. Mon–Fri 8:30am–4pm; Sat–Sun 8:30am–3pm. Sun service Sun 9am and 11am. Bus: PHLASH, 40, or 57.

HISTORIC BUILDINGS & MONUMENTS

Betsy Ross House ★ Kids One Colonial home everybody knows about is this one near Christ Church, restored in 1937, and distinguished by the Stars and Stripes outside. Elizabeth (Betsy) Ross was a Quaker needlewoman who, newly widowed in 1776, worked as a seamstress and upholsterer out of her home on Arch Street. Nobody is quite sure if no. 239 was hers, though. And nobody knows for sure if she made the original American flag of 13 stars set in a field of 13 red-and-white stripes, but she was commissioned to sew ships' flags for the American fleet to replace the earlier Continental banners.

The tiny house takes only a minute or two to walk through. The house is set back from the street, and the city maintains the Atwater Kent Park in front, where Ross and her last husband are buried. The upholstery shop (now a gift shop renovated in 1998) opens into the period parlor. Other rooms include the cellar kitchen (standard placement for this room), tiny bedrooms, and model working areas for upholstering, making musket balls, and the like. Note such little touches as reusable note tablets made of ivory, pine cones used to help start hearth fires, and the prominent kitchen hourglass. Flag Day celebrations are held here on June 14.

239 Arch St. ✆ **215/686-1252.** www.betsyrosshouse.org. Suggested donation $3 adults, $2 students and children 12 and under. Audio tour $5. Apr–Sept daily 10am–5pm; Oct–Mar Tues–Sun 10am–5pm. Bus: PHLASH, 5, 17, 33, 42, 48, or 57.

Carpenters' Hall ★★ Carpenters' Hall (1773) was the guildhall for—guess who?—carpenters. At the time, the city could use plenty of carpenters, since 18th-century Philadelphia was the fastest-growing urban area in all the Colonies and perhaps in the British Empire outside of London. Robert Smith, a Scottish member of the Carpenters' Company, designed the building (like most carpenters, he did architecture and contracting as well). He also designed the steeple of Christ Church, with the same subdued Georgian lines. The edifice is made of Flemish Bond brick in a checkerboard pattern, with stone windowsills, superb woodwork, and a cupola that resembles a saltshaker.

You'll be surprised at how small Carpenters' Hall is given the great events that transpired here. In 1774, the normal governmental channels to convey Colonial complaints to the Crown were felt inadequate, and a popular Committee of Correspondence debated in Carpenters' Hall. The more radical delegates, led by Patrick Henry, had already expressed treasonous wishes for independence, but most wanted to exhaust possibilities of bettering their relationship with the Crown first.

What's here now isn't much—an exhibit of Colonial building methods, some portraits, and Windsor chairs that seated the First Continental Congress. If some details seem to be from a later period, you're right: The fanlights above the north and south doors date from the 1790s, and the gilding dates from 1857. Hours are short because the Carpenters' Company still maintains the hall.

320 Chestnut St. ✆ **215/925-0167.** www.carpentershall.com. Free admission. Jan–Feb Wed–Sun 10am–4pm; Mar–Dec Tues–Sun 10am–4pm. SEPTA: Market-Frankford El, 2nd St. Station. Bus: PHLASH, 9, 21, or 42.

Declaration House (Graff House) ★ Bricklayer Jacob Graff constructed a modest three-story home in the 1770s, intending to rent out the second floor for added income. The Second Continental Congress soon brought to the house a thin, red-haired tenant named Thomas Jefferson, in search of a quiet room away from city noise. He must have found it, because he drafted the Declaration of Independence here in less than 3 weeks in late spring 1776.

The 1975 reconstruction used the same Flemish Bond brick checkerboard pattern (only on visible walls), windows with paneled shutters, and knickknacks that would have been around the house in 1775. Compared to Society Hill homes, it's tiny and asymmetrical, with an off-center front door. You'll enter through a small garden and see a short film about Jefferson and a copy of Jefferson's draft (which would have forbidden slavery in the United States had that clause survived debate). The upstairs rooms are furnished as they would have been in Jefferson's time. Hours vary according to season. Call ahead to confirm.

7th and Market sts. ✆ **215/965-7676.** www.nps.gov/inde/declaration-house.htm. Free admission. Daily in summer, times vary. SEPTA: Market-Frankford El, 8th St. Station.

Elfreth's Alley ★★ The modern Benjamin Franklin Bridge shadows Elfreth's Alley, the oldest continuously inhabited street in America. Most of Colonial Philadelphia looked like this: cobblestone lanes between the major thoroughfares, small two-story homes, and pent eaves over doors and windows, a local trademark. Note the busybody mirrors that let residents see who was at their door (or someone else's) from the second-story bedroom. In 1700, most of the resident artisans and tradesmen worked in shipping, but 50 years later haberdashers, bakers, printers, and house carpenters set up shop. Families moved in and out rapidly, for noisy, dusty 2nd Street was the major north-south route in Philadelphia. Jews, blacks, Welsh, and Germans made it a miniature melting pot in the 18th and 19th centuries. The destruction of the street was prevented in 1937, thanks to the vigilant Elfreth's Alley Association and a good deal of luck. The minuscule, sober facades hide some ultramodern interiors, and there are some restful shady benches under a Kentucky Coffee Bean tree on Bladen Court, off the north side of the street.

Number 126, the 1755 **Mantua Maker's House** (cape maker), built by blacksmith Jeremiah Elfreth, now serves as a museum. An 18th-century garden in back has been restored, and the interior includes a dressmaker's shop and upstairs bedroom. You can also buy Colonial candy and gifts and peek into some of the open windows on the street. On the first weekend in June all the houses are open for touring—don't miss this.

Off 2nd St. (toward Front St., btw. Arch and Race sts.). ✆ **215/574-0560.** www.elfrethsalley.org. Visitor center and gift shop free admission; Mantua Maker's House, garden, and 20-min. guided tour $5 adults, $1 children 6–18, free for children 5 and under; free for all July 4th. Mar–Oct Tues noon–5pm, Wed–Sat 10am–5pm, Sun noon–5pm; Nov–Feb Thurs–Sat 10am–5pm, Sun noon–5pm. Bus: PHLASH, 5, or 48.

Masonic Temple Quite apart from its Masonic lore, the temple—among the world's largest—is one of America's best on-site illustrations of the use of post–Civil War architecture and design. No expense was spared in the construction, and the halls are more or less frozen in time. Sitting directly across the street from City Hall, the historic megaplex houses seven lodge halls designed to capture the seven "ideal" architectures. Renaissance, Ionic, Oriental, Corinthian, Gothic, Egyptian, and Norman are all represented. This is the preeminent Masonic Temple of American Freemasonry. Many of the Founding Fathers, including Washington, were Masons, and the museum has preserved their letters and emblems. (For fun, ask the guard for the secret handshake.)

1 N. Broad St. ✆ **215/988-1917.** Admission $8 adults, $6 students with ID, $5 seniors and children 12 and under. Tours Mon–Fri 11am, 2pm, and 3pm; Sat 10 and 11am. Bus: 17, 33, 44, or 48.

Pennsylvania Hospital The original Pennsylvania Hospital, like so much in civic Philadelphia, owes its presence to Benjamin Franklin. This was the first hospital in the Colonies, and it seemed like a strange venture into social welfare at the time. Samuel Rhoads, a fine architect in the Carpenters' Company, designed the Georgian headquarters. The east wing, nearest 8th Street, was completed in 1755, and a west wing matched it in 1797. The grand Center Building by David Evans completed the ensemble in 1804. Instead of a dome, the hospital decided on a surgical amphitheater skylight. In spring, the garden's azaleas brighten the neighborhood and are a popular spot for wedding photos. The beautifully designed herb garden (highlighting plants used as medicines in the 18th c.) is very popular.

8th and Spruce sts. ✆ **215/829-5436.** www.pennhealth.com/pahosp. Free admission. Mon–Fri 8:30am–4:30pm. Self-guided tours available for 5 or fewer. Call for reservations. SEPTA: Market-Frankford El, 8th St. Station. Bus: PHLASH, 9, 12, 21, or 42.

Powel House ★★ If Elfreth's Alley (see above) leaves you hungry for a taste of more well-to-do Colonial Philadelphia, head for the Powel House. Mayor Samuel Powel and his wife, Elizabeth, hosted every Founding Father and foreign dignitary around. (John Adams called these feasts "sinful dinners," which shows how far Powel had come from his Quaker background.) He spent most of his 20s gallivanting around Europe, collecting wares for this 1765 mansion.

It's hard to believe that this most Georgian of houses was slated for demolition in 1930, because it had become a decrepit slum dwelling. Period rooms were removed to the Philadelphia Museum of Art and the Metropolitan Museum of Art in New York. But the Philadelphia Society for the Preservation of Landmarks saved it, and has gradually refurnished the entire mansion as it was. The yellow satin Reception Room, off the entrance hall, has some gorgeous details, such as a wide-grain mahogany secretary. Upstairs, the magnificent ballroom features red damask drapes whose design is copied from a bolt of cloth found untouched in a Colonial attic. There is also a 1790 Irish crystal chandelier and a letter from Benjamin Franklin's daughter referring to the lively dances held here. An 18th-century garden lies below.

244 S. 3rd St. ✆ **215/627-0364** or 925-2251. www.philalandmarks.org/powel.aspx. Admission $5 adults, $4 seniors and students, free for children under 6, $12 for a family. Guided tours only and by appointment. Last tour 4pm. Thurs–Sat noon–4pm; Sun 1–4pm. SEPTA: Market-Frankford El, 2nd St. Station. Bus: PHLASH, 9, 17, 21, 33, 42, 48, or 57.

LIBRARIES & LITERARY SITES

Athenaeum of Philadelphia *Finds* A 15-minute peek into the Athenaeum will show you one of America's finest collections of Victorian-period architectural design and also give you the flavor of private 19th-century life for the proper Philadelphian. The building, beautifully restored in 1975, houses almost one million library items for the serious researcher of American architecture. Visitors are welcome to view the changing exhibitions of rare books, drawings, and photographs in the recently reconstructed first-floor gallery; tours of the entire building or collections require an appointment.

219 S. 6th St. (Washington Sq. E.). ✆ **215/925-2688.** www.philaathenaeum.org. Free admission. Mon–Fri 9am–5pm; 1st Sat of each month 10am–2pm. Permission to enter and guided tours given on request. SEPTA: Market-Frankford El, 5th St. Station. Bus: PHLASH, 9, 12, 17, 21, 33, or 42.

Edgar Allan Poe National Historical Site The acclaimed American author, though more associated with Baltimore, Richmond, and New York City, lived here from 1843 to 1844. "The Black Cat," "The Gold Bug," and "The Tell-Tale Heart" were published while he was a resident. Just reopened following structural work, this is a simple place—after all, Poe was poor most of his life—and the National Park Service keeps it unfurnished. An adjoining building contains basic information on Poe's life and work, along with a reading room and slide presentation. The park service also runs intermittent discussions and candlelight tours on Saturday afternoon.

532 N. 7th St. (near Spring Garden St.). ✆ **215/597-8780.** www.nps.gov/edal. Free admission. Wed–Sun 9am–5pm. Bus: 43 or 47.

Free Library of Philadelphia Splendidly situated on the north side of Logan Circle, the Free Library of Philadelphia rivals the public libraries of Boston and New York for magnificence and diversity. The library and its twin, the Municipal Court, are copies of buildings in the Place de la Concorde in Paris (the library's on the left).

The main lobby and the gallery always have some of the institution's riches on display, from medieval manuscripts to exhibits of modern bookbinding. Greeting cards and stationery are sold for reasonable prices, too. The second floor houses the best local history, travel, and resource collection in the city. The local 130,000-item map collection is fascinating. The third-floor rare book room hosts visitors Monday through Friday from 9am to 5pm, with tours by appointment. If you're interested in manuscripts, children's literature, early printed books, and early American hornbooks, or you just want to see a stuffed raven, this is the place.

If you're hungry, the **Skyline Cafe** is a nice place for a snack and one of the only dining options on the parkway. There's an active concert-and-film series, and when Anne Lamott, Toni Morrison, or, um, Candace Bushnell comes to town for a reading, you can bet he or she will be speaking in the library's auditorium on a weekday night. Other notables participate in the library's regular lecture series. The library is also planning a 180,000-square-foot modern addition designed by Moshe Safdie.

1901 Vine St. (in the Central Library, Logan Circle). ✆ **215/686-5322.** www.library.phila.gov. Free admission. Mon–Wed 9am–9pm; Thurs–Sat 9am–5pm; Sun 1–5pm. Bus: PHLASH, 2, 7, 32, or 33.

Rosenbach Museum and Library *Finds* The Rosenbach specializes in books: illuminated manuscripts, parchment, rough drafts, and first editions. If you love the variations and beauty of the printed word, they'll love your presence.

The opulent town-house galleries contain 30,000 rare books and 270,000 documents. Some rooms preserve the Rosenbachs' elegant living quarters, with antique furniture and Sully paintings. Others are devoted to authors and illustrators: Marianne Moore's Greenwich Village study is reproduced in its entirety, and the Maurice Sendak drawings represent only the tip of his iceberg (or forest). Holdings include the original manuscript of Joyce's *Ulysses* and first editions of Melville, in the author's own bookcase. Small special exhibitions are tucked in throughout the house, and don't miss the shop behind the entrance for bargains in greeting cards and a nice collection of Sendak.

You are welcome to wander around the rooms unaccompanied, but you are not allowed to sit down and leaf through the books. For access to the books, you need to call and arrange special admission, granted for the most part only in conjunction with a specific scholarly purpose.

2010 Delancey Place (btw. Spruce and Pine sts). ✆ **215/732-1600.** www.rosenbach.org. Admission $10 adults, $8 seniors, $5 students; free for children 4 and under. Tues and Thurs–Sun 10am–5pm; Wed 10am–8pm. Guided tours on the hour 11am–4pm and Wed 6:30pm. Bus: 9, 17, 21, 40, or 42.

MORE MUSEUMS & EXHIBITIONS

Academy of Natural Sciences *Kids* If you're looking for dinosaurs, the academy is the best place to find them. Kids love the big diorama halls, with cases of various species mounted and posed in authentic settings. A permanent display, *Dinosaurs Galore* features more than a dozen specimens, including a huge *Tyrannosaurus rex* with jaws agape. The Dig (weekends only) gives you an opportunity to dig for fossils in a re-created field station. The North American Hall, on the first floor, has enormous moose, bison, and bears. A small marine exhibit shows how some fish look different in ultraviolet light and how the bed of the Delaware River has changed since Penn landed in 1682.

The second floor features groupings of Asian and African flora and fauna. Many of the cases have nearby headphones that tell you more about what you're seeing. Five or six live demonstrations using rocks, birds, plants, and animals are given here every day. The Egyptian mummy, a priest of a late dynasty, seems a bit out of place. Several daily demonstrations (called Eco Shows) are given on the second floor and in the auditorium downstairs.

Upstairs, Outside In is a touchable museum designed for children under 12, with a model campsite, fossils, minerals, and shells. Children can see, feel, hear, and smell live turtles, mice, bees in a beehive, and snakes (all caged), and wander around mock forests and deserts. An exhibit of live butterflies rounds out the picture, along with frequent films. There's a brown-bag lunchroom and vending area with drinks and snacks, or visit the Ecology Café.

19th St. and Benjamin Franklin Pkwy. ✆ **215/299-1000.** www.ansp.org. Admission $10 adults; $8 seniors, students with ID, military, and children 3–12; free for children 2 and under. Mon–Fri 10am–4:30pm; Sat–Sun and holidays 10am–5pm. Bus: PHLASH, 32, 33, or 38.

The African-American Museum in Philadelphia (AAMP) Built on land that once belonged to a historic black community, this 30-year-old museum pays tribute to African Americans—with a special focus on local history. The AAMP is easy to get to, but isn't easy to notice. It stands a few blocks northwest of the Liberty Bell, in an

Fun Facts Philadelphia's Oddball Museums

Philadelphia has an amazing assortment of small single-interest museums, built out of the passions of, or inspired by, a single individual. Maybe you and your family are ready for these!

- The Mummer's Parade on New Year's Day is uniquely Philadelphian; dozens of crews spend months practicing their musical and strutting skills with spectacular costumes. Mumming comes out of both Anglo-Saxon pagan celebrations and African dancing. The seriously worn, slightly fabulous **Mummers Museum,** South 2nd Street and Washington Avenue (✆ **215/336-3050**), is devoted to the history and display of this phenomenon. It's open Tuesday through Saturday from 9:30am to 4:30pm and Sunday from noon to 4:30pm. Tuesday in the summer, the museum stays open until 9:30pm for string band performances.
- In the northeast district of the city (yes, it's a schlep), Steve Kanya's **Insectarium,** 8046 Frankford Ave. (✆ **215/335-9500**), has taken off mostly as a school-class destination. The $6 admission lets you watch more than 40,000 assorted bugs and their predators (scorpions, tarantulas, and so on) scurry around. (The museum owner, by the way, is an exterminator.) It's open Monday through Saturday from 10am to 4pm.
- Not for the squeamish is the Philadelphia College of Physician's **Mutter Museum** ★ (p. 142), 19 S. 22nd St. (✆ **215/563-3737**), a collection of preserved human oddities assembled in the 1850s by a Philadelphia physician. Skeletons of giants and dwarves and row upon row of plaster casts of abnormalities inhabit this musty place.

unobvious modern building evocative of African mud housing. As you ascend the museum's five split levels, you follow a path leading from African-American continental roots and through a history of Africans living in the U.S., eventually becoming Americans.

Within the museum's four galleries are more than 500,000 images and documents. Utilitarian and domestic objects, fine and folk art, furnishings and costumes, and photographs and negatives are among the explorable exhibits. The second level of the gallery is a must-visit documentation of captivity and slavery. The upper three levels focus on black history and culture after emancipation. Black cowboys, inventors, athletes, spokespeople, and businesspeople are all presented, along with the history of the civil rights movement, up to the modern day.

7th and Arch sts. ✆ **215/574-0380.** www.aampmuseum.org. Admission $8 adults, $6 seniors and children. Tues–Sat 10am–5pm; Sun noon–5pm. SEPTA: Market-Frankford El, 8th St. Station. Bus: PHLASH, 17, 33, 38, 47, or 48.

American Swedish Historical Museum Deep in South Philly, not too far from the sports complexes, is this pretty place where visitors can learn about the history of Swedes in the Americas. The house itself is modeled after a 17th-century Swedish manor house. It contains 12 galleries, one devoted to the history of the region's New Sweden

Colony, one chronicling contributions of notable Swedish Americans such as women's rights activist Fredrika Bremer and soprano Jenny Lind, and another dedicated to Alfred Nobel and his famed prizes. Throughout are beautiful examples of Swedish art glass, sculpture, and paintings.

Traditional Swedish holidays are celebrated year-round, including *Valborgsmässoafton* (Spring Festival) in April, *Midsommarfest* in June, and the procession of St. Lucia and her attendants in December.

1900 Pattison Ave. ✆ **215/389-1776.** www.americanswedish.org. Admission $8 adults, $6 seniors and students, $5 children 5–11, free for children 4 and under and ASHM members; $1 off for AAA members. Tues–Fri 10am–4pm; Sat–Sun noon–5pm. Bus: 17.

Atwater Kent Museum This is the place to come to discover the finer points of Philadelphia's history. The small Atwater Kent Museum occupies an 1826 John Haviland building. With more artifacts than the Independence Visitor Center, it does a bang-up job of showing what Philadelphia was like from 1680 to today. Nothing, apparently, was too trivial to include in this collection, which jumps from dolls to dioramas, cigar-store Indians to period toyshops. Sunbonnets, train tickets, rocking horses, ship models, and military uniforms all fill out the display. A hands-on history laboratory lets you play with these historical objects.

15 S. 7th St. (btw. Market and Chestnut sts.). ✆ **215/685-4830.** www.philadelphiahistory.org. Admission $5 adults, $3 seniors and children 13–17, free for children 12 and under; free 1st Fri of every month 5–8pm. Wed–Sun 1–5pm. Group tours for 10 or more adults available by appointment, $6 per person. SEPTA: Market-Frankford El, 8th St. Station. Bus: PHLASH, 9, 17, 21, 33, 42, or 44.

Eastern State Penitentiary ★ Back when it opened in 1829, a visit to this medieval fortress–looking prison was no fun at all. These days, however, an audio-guided stroll through Eastern State's beautifully decrepit halls is creepily entertaining. The site, in the Fairmount section of the city, is north of Center City West, a few blocks east of the Philadelphia Art Museum. An hour-long tour provides a glimpse into solitary confinement "rehabilitation" cells (some in use until 1971). There are voyeuristically riveting tales of famous residents—robber Willie Sutton and superstar gangster Al Capone stayed here—thwarted escapes, romance behind bars, and incarcerated canines. And then there are the ghosts, who receive extra attention 5 weeks before Halloween. Terror Behind the Walls haunted tours require advanced tickets ($20–$30 each), and take place after dark (Mon–Thurs 7–10pm; Fri and Sun 7–11pm; Sat 7pm–midnight).

2124 Fairmount Ave. ✆ **215/236-3300.** www.easternstate.org. Admission $12 adults; $8 seniors, students, and children 7–12. Children 6 and under not admitted. Apr–Nov daily 10am–5pm (June–Aug Wed until 8pm). Last tour 4pm. Closed Dec–Mar. SEPTA bus: 7, 32, 33, 43, or 48.

Independence Seaport Museum ★ Kids Opposite Walnut Street, between the two dock areas, is this user-friendly maritime museum. The premier attraction of the city's waterfront, the Seaport Museum additionally boasts the docked cruiser *Olympia* and the submarine *Becuna*.

The museum is nicely laid out, blending a first-class maritime collection with interactive exhibits for a trip through time that engages all ages. The 11,000-square-foot main gallery is the centerpiece for exhibits, educational outreach, and activities that are jazzy and eye-catching without being noisy or obtrusive. Twelve sections mix the personal with the professional—call up interviews with river pilots, navy personnel, and shipbuilders. There are stories of immigrants who flooded Philadelphia between 1920 and 1970, and the rich reminiscences and memorabilia that make the past come to life. One of the museum's most attractive features is the **Workshop on the Water,** where you can watch classes in traditional wooden boat building and restoration throughout the year.

211 S. Columbus Blvd. (at Penn's Landing). ✆ **215/925-5439.** www.phillyseaport.org. Admission $10 adults, $7 seniors and children 3–12, $5 military, pay what you wish Sun 10am–noon. Daily 10am–5pm. Closed major holidays. SEPTA: Market-Frankford El, 2nd St. Station. Bus: PHLASH, 5, 17, 21, 33, 42, or 48.

Mutter Museum ★★ Finds Kids will be fascinated, possibly frightened, and definitely grossed out by this hugely entertaining collection of medical oddities in an appropriately dark, dank, Harry Potter–ish setting in a grand 19th-century building in Center City. Three operative words apply: *goiters in jars.* Or, as a friend of mine says, "you ain't seen nothin' 'til you've seen the giant colon." These and 20,000 other creepy objects fill the Mutter Museum, including the Secret Tumor of Grover Cleveland and plaster casts of famously conjoined twins Chang and Eng, housed in a paneled, double-height gallery within the College of Physicians. This medical institution was founded by Dr. Benjamin Rush, a signer of the Declaration of Independence; it's not an active medical school, but is an educational society with an important historical library. Everything in the Mutter, which began as a private collection in the 1850s, is very *Young Frankenstein:* 10,000 horrifying antique surgical implements, shelves of swollen brains floating in fluid in vintage glass jars, and even the thorax of John Wilkes Booth. Oh, and you can have private parties there, too. Like maybe your wedding.

19 S. 22nd St. ✆ **215/563-3737,** ext. 293. www.collphyphil.org. Admission $12 adults; $8 students with ID, seniors, and children ages 6–17. Sat–Thurs 10am–5pm; Fri 10am–9pm. Closed Thanksgiving, Dec 25, and Jan 1. SEPTA: Suburban Station. Bus: PHLASH, 21, or 42.

National Museum of American Jewish History This is the only museum specifically dedicated to preserving and presenting Jewish participation in the development of the United States. The museum was established in 1976. The congregation connected to it, Mikveh Israel, was established in Philadelphia in 1740. Enter close to 4th Street into a dark-brick lobby. The museum includes a fascinating permanent exhibition, *Creating American Jews,* combining reproductions of portraits and documents, actual diaries, letters, and oral histories from five diverse "snapshots" from today's six million American Jews and their predecessors. Smaller rotating exhibitions supplement this presentation, and there are moving and inspiring special events offered throughout the year. Attracting 40,000 visitors a year, the museum is usually cool and restful and makes a good break from a hot Independence Park tour. A small gift shop is attached. In 2006, the museum made plans to move across the street to 5th and Market. The move will be completed in late fall 2010.

55 N. 5th St. ✆ **215/923-3811.** www.nmajh.org. Free until new museum opens. Mon–Thurs 10am–5pm; Fri 10am–3pm; Sun noon–5pm. Bus: PHLASH, 17, 33, 48, or 50.

Physick House ★ Like the Powel House (p. 137), the Physick House combines attractive design and historical interest. The house is the area's most impressive—freestanding but not boxy, gracious but solid. Built during the 1780s boom, with money from importing Madeira wine, it soon wound up housing the father of American surgery, Philip Syng Physick (a propitious name for a physician). The usual pattern of neglect and renovation applies here, on an even grander scale.

All the fabric and wallpaper was fashioned expressly for use here, and the mansion as restored is an excellent illustration of the Federal style from about 1815. The drawing room opens onto a lovely 19th-century walled garden, and contains a Roman stool and 18th-century Italian art, collectibles that illustrate the excitement caused by the discovery of the buried city of Pompeii at that time. Look for an inkstand blessed by Ben Franklin's fingerprints. Dr. Physick treated Chief Justice Marshall, and Marshall's portrait and gift of a wine stand testify to the doctor's powers.

321 S. 4th St. ✆ **215/925-7866** or 925-2251. www.philalandmarks.org/phys.aspx. Admission $5 adults, $4 seniors and students. Thurs–Sat noon–4pm; Sun 1–4pm. Guided tours only. Bus: PHLASH, 9, 17, 21, 33, 40, 42, or 57.

Please Touch Museum ★★ Kids This hands-on, kids-centric attraction is anything but museum-like. Exhibitions are 100% hands-on: Everything is made to be jumped upon, entered in, bent, splashed, ridden, and otherwise played with. Oh yes, and it's educationally and culturally enriching, too, especially for children ages 3 to 12. In 2008, the museum relocated to historic Memorial Hall in Fairmount Park where it's no longer within walking distance to Center City, but it does allow for supereasy parking (for a fee). Also, the new space is many times bigger—and encompasses a 9,000-square-foot housing for a mint condition carousel (ca. 1824).

Enter between the Beaux Arts columns of Memorial Hall, site of the Centennial Exposition of 1876 (the first-ever world's fair)—and prepare to be impressed. A whopping $88 million went into the restoration of this grand structure. And, while it's seems a bit disproportionate to have a bunch of kids getting somewhat soaked while playing with plastic boats floating around waist-high pools in the River Adventures, climbing into a mini-SEPTA bus, fake shopping at a low-shelved supermarket, or play-working on a construction zone amid such architectural grandeur, the children sure don't seem to mind. Some exhibits are obviously tailored to toddlers; others, like the magically rendered Alice in Wonderland maze, seem better for children of reading age.

The larger facility allows for a nice little cafe that serves pizza, sandwiches, salads, and fruit—although if school's out, it's not quite large enough. It also offers an expanded space for daily activities such as storytelling and crafts. Grown-ups that grew up locally will likely appreciate the Philly-centric exhibits of an old monorail from John Wanamaker and the set of *Captain Noah.* But best of all is the staff: Everyone here is absolutely professional in the art of pleasing kids. During my last visit, I saw the carousel operator offer a free ride to a child without a ticket. The worker told the parent she didn't want to disappoint the child. They're pros, here, for sure, but they are definitely not day-care workers. Parents and guardians cannot simply drop the kids off and come back to pick them up in a couple of hours—and adults wouldn't want to. It's an absolute joy watching kids have so much fun together. It's also a great place to celebrate a child's birthday if you plan ahead.

4231 Ave. of the Republic (formerly N. Concourse Dr.). ✆ **215/581-3181.** www.pleasetouchmuseum.org. Admission $15 per person; free for children 1 and under. Mon–Sat 9am–5pm; Sun 11am–5pm. Stroller parking available at each exhibit zone. Bus: 38, 40, 43 or 64.

Rodin Museum ★★ Moments The beautiful, intimate Rodin Museum, in a 1929 Paul Cret building, exhibits the largest collection of the master's work (129 sculptures) outside the Musée Rodin in Paris. It has inherited its sibling museum's romantic mystery, making a very French use of space inside and boasting much greenery outside. Entering from the parkway, virtually across the street from the Franklin Institute (see earlier in this chapter), you'll contemplate *The Thinker,* then pass through an imposing arch to a front garden of hardy shrubs and trees surrounding a fishpond. Before going into the museum, study the *Gates of Hell.* These gigantic doors reveal the artist's power to mold metal with his tremendous imagination.

The main hall holds authorized casts of *John the Baptist, The Cathedral,* and *The Burghers of Calais.* Several of the side chambers and the library hold powerful erotic plaster models. Drawings, sketchbooks, and Steichen photographic portraits of Rodin are exhibited from time to time.

Benjamin Franklin Pkwy. (btw. 21st and 22nd sts.). ✆ **215/763-8100.** www.rodinmuseum.org. Suggested donation $3. Tues–Sun 10am–5pm. Free guided tours Tues, Thurs, Sun and 1st and 3rd Sat of each month 1:30pm. Bus: PHLASH, 7, 32, 38, 43, or 48.

U.S. Mint The U.S. Mint was the first building authorized by the government, during Washington's first term. The present edifice, diagonally across from Liberty Bell Pavilion, turns out about 1.5 million coins every hour. Free, self-guided, unreserved tours are available to the public, allowing regular folk to see coin in production—and to go home with a plastic goodie bag of shredded bills and some knowledge of our country's storied history of moolah. A visit should take about 45 minutes, and all this information will change if Homeland Security deems it necessary.

5th and Arch sts. ✆ **215/408-0114.** www.usmint.gov. Free admission. Reservations not necessary. Mon–Fri 9am–3pm. SEPTA: Market-Frankford El, 5th St. Station. Bus: 5 or 48.

University of Pennsylvania Museum of Archaeology and Anthropology ★ The 118-year-old museum got started early and well, and is endowed with Benin bronzes, ancient cuneiform texts, Mesopotamian masterpieces, pre-Columbian gold, and artifacts of every continent, mostly brought back from the more than 350 expeditions it has sponsored over the years. The taller structures that surround this museum give its Romanesque brickwork and gardens a secluded feel. The museum has had spectacular special exhibitions, including forays into ancient Iran, Roman glass, ancient Egypt, and works from ancient Canaan and Israel.

Exhibits are intelligently explained. The basement Egyptian galleries, including colossal architectural remains from Memphis and *The Egyptian Mummy: Secrets and Science,* are family favorites. Probably the most famous excavation display, located on the third floor, is a spectacular Sumerian trove of jewelry and household objects from the royal tombs of the ancient city of Ur. Adjoining this, huge cloisonné lions from Peking's (now Beijing's) Imperial Palace guard Chinese court treasures and tomb figures. The Ancient Greek Gallery in the classical-world collection, renovated in 1994, has 400 superb objects such as red-figure pottery—a flower of Greek art—and an unusual lead sarcophagus from Tyre that looks like a miniature house. Other galleries display Native American and Polynesian art and a small but excellent African collection of bronze plaques and statues. There's a very active schedule of events throughout the year.

3260 South St. (near Spruce St.). ✆ **215/898-4000.** www.museum.upenn.edu. Admission $8 adults, $5 seniors and students, free for children 5 and under. Tues–Sat 10am–4:30pm; Sun 1–5pm. Closed Sun from Memorial Day to Labor Day and holidays. SEPTA: Market-Frankford El, 34th St. Station. Trolleys: 11, 13, 34, or 36 to 33rd or 36th St. Bus: 21, 30 (from 30th St. Station), 40, or 42.

UNIVERSITY OF PENNSYLVANIA ★

You could call Philadelphia one big campus, with 27 degree-granting institutions within city limits and 50,000 annual college graduates. The oldest and most prestigious university is Penn. This private, coeducational Ivy League institution was founded by Benjamin Franklin and others in 1740. It boasts America's first medical (1765), law (1790), and business (1881) schools. Penn's liberal arts curriculum, dating from 1756, was the first to combine classical and practical subjects. The university has been revitalized in the last 30 years, thanks to extremely successful leadership, alumni, and fundraising drives. The West Philadelphia neighborhood where the core campus has been based since the 1870s has experienced a revitalization, too, thanks to former president Judith Rodin, and current president Amy Gutmann. Nowadays, Penn is a fun place for an afternoon of shopping or a night out. Sansom Commons, with Urban Outfitters, Douglas Cosmetics, and Pod restaurant, is across the street from campus. There are also the wonderful Inn at Penn, the Bridge de Lux cinema at 40th and Walnut streets, and the massive Barnes & Noble–run university bookstore.

The core campus features serene Gothic-style buildings and specimen trees in a spacious quadrangle. Visitors can hang out comfortably on the lawns and benches. More-modern buildings are results of the 20th-century expansion of the university to accommodate 22,000 students enrolled in four undergraduate and 12 graduate schools, in 100 academic departments. Sights of most interest to visitors include the University Museum of Archaeology and Anthropology, the Annenberg Center for the Performing Arts, and the always intriguing Institute of Contemporary Art, with its changing exhibits. 34th and Walnut sts. and surrounding neighborhood. ✆ **215/898-5000.** www.upenn.edu. Bus: 21, 30, 40, 42, or 90. Car: 30th St. exit from I-76 (Schuylkill Expwy.), 6 blocks west toward West Philadelphia.

A ZOO & AN AQUARIUM

Philadelphia Zoo ★★ Kids The Philadelphia Zoo, opened in 1874, was the nation's first. Today, the 42-acre zoo tucked into West Fairmount Park has become a national leader, with nearly 1,800 animals. The zoo celebrated its 125th anniversary with the opening of the **PECO Primate Reserve,** a breathtaking pavilion that blurs the line between visitors and its 11 resident species. Note that the basic admission (in season $17 for adults, $14 for children) does not include a lot of special attractions like the **Zooballoon,** a 15-minute ascent on a helium balloon that goes 400 feet high.

The 1½-acre **Carnivore Kingdom** houses snow leopards and jaguars, but the biggest attraction is the rare white lions. Feeding time is around 11am for smaller carnivores, 3pm for tigers and lions. The monkeys have a new home on four naturally planted islands, where a variety of primate species live together naturally.

In the magical **Jungle Bird Walk,** you can walk among free-flying birds. Glass enclosures have been replaced with wire mesh so that the birds' songs can now be heard from both sides. The **Treehouse** ($1 extra) contains six larger-than-life habitats for kids of all ages to explore—oversize eggs to "hatch" from, an oversize honeycomb to crawl through, and a four-story ficus tree to climb and see life from a bird's-eye view. The very popular Camel Rides start next to the Treehouse. A **Children's Zoo** portion of the gardens lets your kids pet and feed some baby zoo and farm animals; this closes 30 minutes before the rest of the zoo.

Other exhibits include polar bears; the renovated Reptile House, which bathes its snakes and tortoises with simulated tropical thunderstorms; and cavorting antelopes, zebras, and giraffes that coexist in the African Plains exhibit. Some animals you'll find missing as of spring of 2007 are the zoo's elephants, when the zoo's three African elephants, aged 50, 24, and 23, moved to Baltimore's Maryland Zoo. Soon thereafter, 42-year-old Asian elephant Dulary found new friends on the spacious grounds of Tennessee's Elephant Sanctuary.

A tip for those who are driving here: Try to arrive early in the day: It's a long hike from the more distant lots if you don't.

34th St. and Girard Ave. ✆ **215/243-1100.** www.philadelphiazoo.org. Admission adults $17 Mar–Nov, $13 Dec–Feb; children 2–11 $14 Apr–Nov, $13 Dec–Feb; free for children 1 and under. Zooballoon additional $10 Mon–Fri, $15 Sat–Sun. Feb–Nov daily 9:30am–5pm; Dec–Jan daily 9:30am–4pm (Children's Zoo closes at 4:30 and 3:30pm respectively.). Closed Thanksgiving, Dec 25, and Jan 1. SEPTA trolley: 15. Bus: 32 or 38. PHLASH: June 1–Sept 1 from Philadelphia Museum of Art. Car: Separate exit off I-76 north of Center City.

Adventure Aquarium ★ Kids The former New Jersey State Aquarium is seriously cool. The expansive facility has hippos you can watch bob for heads of lettuce, stingrays to touch in open tanks, jellyfish that morph before your eyes, performing penguins, and cavorting seals.

All in all, there are 2 million gallons of water in the place. While all the exhibits are impressive, there are a few things to look out for. Alligators cruise the West Africa River Experience. Rarely exhibited bluefin tuna zip past in the 760,000-gallon Ocean Realm. Let the kids take their time at the Touch a Shark tank. That's what they'll remember most. For additional fees, visitors age 18 and over can get even closer to the animals. The aquarium offers a variety of interactive packages; swimming with sharks in a 40-foot glass tunnel, feeding sea turtles, and training seals are among them.

1 Aquarium Dr., Camden, NJ. ✆ **866/451-2782** or 856/365-3300. www.adventureaquarium.com. Admission $19 adults, $15 children 2–12, free for children 1 and under. Daily 9:30am–5pm. Timed tickets and advanced reservations recommended. Round-trip ferry from Independence Seaport Museum at Penn's Landing $6 adults, $5 seniors and children; hourly arrivals/departures May–Oct. Car: From I-676 eastbound (Vine St. Expwy./Ben Franklin Bridge) or westbound from I-295/New Jersey Tpk., take Mickle Blvd. exit and follow signs.

4 PARKS, THE PARKWAY & PENN'S LANDING ★

BENJAMIN FRANKLIN PARKWAY ★

The parkway, a broad diagonal swath linking City Hall to Fairmount Park, wasn't included in Penn's original plan. In the 1920s, however, Philadelphians wanted a grand boulevard in the style of the Champs-Elysées. In summer, a walk from the visitor center to the "Museum on the Hill" is a flower-bedecked and leafy stroll. And year-round, various institutions, public art, and museums enrich the avenue with their handsome facades. Most of the city's parades and festivals pass this way.

Logan Circle, aka Logan Square, outside the Academy of Natural Sciences, Free Library of Philadelphia, and Franklin Institute, was a burial ground before becoming a park. The designers of the avenue cleverly made it into a low-landscaped fountain, with graceful figures cast by Alexander Stirling Calder. In June, look for students from neighboring private schools, getting a traditional graduation dunking in their uniforms. From this point, you can see how the rows of trees follow the diagonal thoroughfare, although all the buildings along the parkway are aligned with the grid plan.

The PHLASH bus goes up as far as Logan Circle every 12 minutes.

FAIRMOUNT PARK ★★

The northern end of the Benjamin Franklin Parkway leads into Fairmount Park (✆ **215/683-0200;** www.fairmountpark.org), the world's largest landscaped city park, with 8,700 acres of winding creeks, rustic trails, and green meadows, plus 100 miles of jogging, bike,

Belmont Mansion **9**
Cedar Grove **13**
Chamounix Mansion
(Youth Hostel) **8**
Japanese House **11**
Laurel Hill **4**
Laurel Hill Cemetery **7**
Lemon Hill **2**
Mann Music Center **10**
Please Touch Museum **12**
Mount Pleasant **3**
Philadelphia Museum of Art **1**
Philadelphia Zoo **15**
Strawberry Mansion **6**
Sweetbriar **14**
Woodford **5**

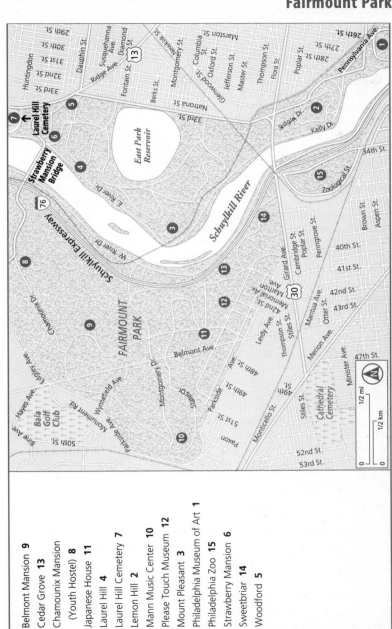

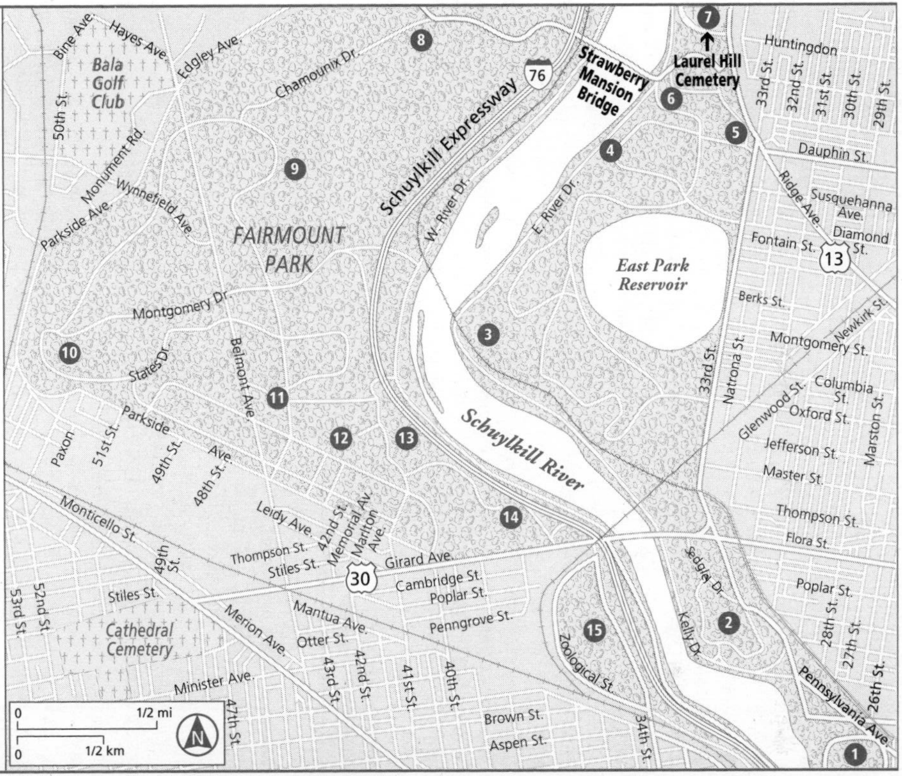

and bridle paths, including one that connects the park to Center City via entrances where Walnut Street and Locust Street meet the Schuylkill River. In addition, this park features more than a dozen historical and cultural attractions, including 29 of America's finest Colonial mansions (most are open year-round with some wonderful Christmas tours, and are run by the art museum; standard admission is $3), as well as gardens, boathouses, the Philadelphia Zoo (p. 145), a youth hostel, and a Japanese teahouse. Visitors can rent sailboats and canoes, play tennis and golf, swim, or hear free symphony concerts in the summer. See "Biking & Blading" later in this chapter for information on renting bikes and in-line skates for a couple of hours; they're cheap, and can get you in and out of the heart of the park quickly. A little pricier are the newly available **Segway i2 Gliders** (✆ **877-GLIDE-81** [454-3381]**;** www.iglidetours.com), whose tours depart from Eakins Oval March to November daily at 10am, 1:30, and 7pm. Daytime tours are 2½ hours and cost $69; evening tours are 1½ hours and are $49.

If you're driving, there are several entrances and exits off I-76, such as Montgomery Drive; the Kelly Drive and the West River Drive are local roads flanking the Schuylkill River.

The park is generally divided by the Schuylkill River into East and West Fairmount Park. Before beginning a tour of the mansions, stop by the **Waterworks Interpretive Center** (✆ **215/685-0723**). It is open daily Tuesday through Saturday from 10am to 5pm and Sunday from 1 to 5pm. Philadelphia set the waterworks up here in 1812 to provide water for the city. They set aside a 5-acre space around the waterworks, which became a park in 1822. This site also has an elegant restaurant, the **Water Works Restaurant and Lounge** (p. 100), that's worth a visit.

The Greek Revival mill houses behind the art museum and an ornamental post–Civil War pavilion connecting them have been restored. Also on the east bank, don't miss **Boathouse Row,** home of the "Schuylkill Navy" and its member rowing clubs. Now you know where Thomas Eakins got the models for all those sculling scenes in the art museum. These gingerbread Tudors along the riverbank look magical at night, with hundreds of tiny lights along their edges and eaves.

The four most spectacular Colonial houses are all in the lower east quadrant of the park. **Lemon Hill** (✆ **215/232-4337**), just up the hill from Boathouse Row, shows the influence of Robert Adam's architectural style, with its generous windows, curved archways and doors, and beautiful oval parlors. John Adams described **Mount Pleasant** (✆ **215/763-8100**), built for a privateer in 1763 and once owned by Benedict Arnold, as "the most elegant seat in Pennsylvania" for its carved designs and inlays. **Woodford** (✆ **215/229-6115**), the center of Tory occupation of the city in 1779, is not to be missed, both for its architecture and for the Naomi Wood Collection of Colonial housewares. Along with Winterthur (p. 226), this is the best place to step into 18th-century home life, with all its ingenious gadgets and elegant objects. The next lawn over from Woodford is the park's largest mansion, **Strawberry Mansion** (✆ **215/228-8364**), with a Federal-style center section and Greek Revival wings.

Just north of this mansion is bucolic **Laurel Hill Cemetery** (p. 132), but if you cross Strawberry Mansion Bridge, West Fairmount Park also has many charms. Located in West Fairmount Park, **Belmont Mansion** (✆ **215/878-8844**) hosted all the leaders of the revolutionary cause. South of this area, you'll enter the site occupied by the stupendous 1876 Centennial Exposition. Approximately 100 buildings were designed and constructed in under 2 years. Only two remain today: **Ohio House,** built out of stone from that state, and the rambling Beaux Arts **Memorial Hall** (✆ **215/683-0200**), now

Finds America's Oldest Botanical Garden

The story begins like this: 250 years ago, Quaker farmer John Bartram was plowing his field when he was stopped in his tracks by a single daisy. The simple beauty of the flower turned him from full-time farmer to self-taught botanist. His lab was his garden. Today, his botanical garden is a hidden gem off the Schuylkill River, not too far from the Philadelphia International Airport. If you're the kind of person (gardener, botanist, nature lover) that gets excited by the country's oldest living gingko tree, or delicate specimens of *Franklinia alatamaha,* which Bartram rescued from extinction and named for his good bud Ben, then you'll love this place. **Bartram's Gardens,** 54th Street and Lindberg Boulevard (✆ **215/729-5281;** www.bartramsgarden.org) is a rare slice of country life preserved within city boundaries. Parking and access to the grounds are free. It's a 15-minute drive from Center City and is accessible by SEPTA's no. 36 trolley. The gardens are open daily, except for city holidays. House tours last 45 minutes and depart at 12:10, 1:10, 2:10, and 3:10pm. Tour admission is $5 for adults, $4 for seniors and students, and free for children 12 and under. Group tours and historic garden tours are also available.

the park's headquarters and a recreation site. The **Japanese House and Gardens** (✆ **215/878-5097**), on the grounds of the nearby Horticultural Center, is a typical 17th-century Japanese scholar's house, with sliding screens and paper doors in place of walls and glass. It was originally presented to the Museum of Modern Art in New York. Since the Centennial Exposition had featured a similar house, it wound up here. The waterfall, grounds, and house are serene and simple and were extensively refurbished in 1976 by a Japanese team as a bicentennial gift to the city. It's open during the summer only, Tuesday through Sunday from 11am to 4pm.

Two more major homes lie south of the exposition's original concourses: **Cedar Grove** (✆ **215/878-2123**), a Quaker farmhouse built as a country retreat in 1748 and moved here in 1928, and **Sweetbriar** (✆ **215/222-1333**), a mixture of French Empire and English neoclassicism with wonderful river views. Continuing south past the Girard Avenue Bridge will bring you to the **Philadelphia Zoo** (see above), and then to Center City.

If you have some time and really want to get away from it all, **Wissahickon** and **Pennsylvania creeks** lie north of the park and don't allow access by automobile—only pedestrians, bicycles, and horses can tread here. The primeval trees and slopes of these valleys completely block out buildings and noise—right within the limits of the fifth-largest city in the United States. Search out attractions like the 340-year-old **Valley Green Inn** and the only **covered bridge** left in an American city.

PENN'S LANDING ★

Philadelphia started out as a major freshwater port, and its tourism and services are increasingly nudging it back to the water after 50 years of neglect (typified by the placement of the I-95 superhighway btw. the city and its port). Recent proposals for revitalization have been scrapped: The city now plans to let casinos come in and do their business. Before they do, take advantage of Penn's Landing's handful of safe, family-friendly options. For one, it's a pleasant place for a stroll on a nice day.

In 1945, 155 "finger" piers jutted out into the river; today, only 14 remain. The Delaware waterfront is quite wide, and the esplanade along it has always had a pleasant spaciousness. The challenge has been to give it the unified, cohesive sense of a destination. Since 1976, the city has added on parts of a complete waterfront park at Penn's Landing (✆ **215/629-3200;** www.pennslandingcorp.com), on Columbus Boulevard (formerly Delaware Ave.) between Market and Lombard streets, with a seaport museum and an assembly of historic ships, performance and park areas, cruise facilities, and a marina. Further additions include pedestrian bridges over I-95; wider sidewalks, improved lighting, additional kiosks along Columbus Boulevard, and the impressive riverside Hyatt Penn's Landing hotel.

You can access the Penn's Landing waterfront by parking along the piers or by walking across several bridges spanning I-95 between Market Street, at the northern edge, and South Street to the south. There are pedestrian walkways across Front Street on Market, Chestnut, Walnut, Spruce, or South streets; Front Street connects directly at Spruce Street. Bus nos. 17, 21, 33, and the purple PHLASH go directly to Penn's Landing; the stop for the Market-Frankford El and for bus no. 42 is an easy walk from 2nd Street across the Market Street bridge. If you're driving from I-95, use the Columbus Boulevard/Washington Street exit and turn left onto Columbus Boulevard. From I-76, take I-676 across Center City to I-95 south. There's ample parking available on-site.

Walking south from Market Street, you'll see an esplanade with pretty blue guardrails and charts to help you identify the Camden shoreline opposite. The hill that connects the shoreline with the current Front Street level has been enhanced with the addition of the festive **Great Plaza,** a multitiered, tree-lined space. In the other direction is a jetty/marina complex, perfect for strolling and snacking, anchored by the **Independence Seaport Museum,** the Hyatt hotel, and the Chart House restaurant. The lovely, sober 1987 **Philadelphia Vietnam Veteran Memorial** lists 641 local casualties. Nearby, you'll find the **International Sculpture Garden** with its obelisk monument to Christopher Columbus.

There's also plenty to do in and near the water. Just north of the Great Plaza at Columbus Boulevard and Spring Garden Street is Festival Pier. The Penn's Landing Corporation coordinates more than 100 events here annually, all designed to attract crowds with high-quality entertainment. Even on a spontaneous visit you're likely to be greeted with sounds and performances. Festival Pier is also the location of the Blue Cross RiverRink, Philadelphia's only outdoor skating rink, open daily from late November to early March.

Several ships and museums are berthed around a long jetty at Spruce Street, and the Independence Seaport Museum is slowly consolidating management of these attractions as the **Historic Ship Zone.** Starting at the north end, these attractions are the brig ***Niagara,*** built for the War of 1812 and rededicated as the official flagship of Pennsylvania in 1990; the **USS *Becuna,*** a guppy-class submarine, commissioned in 1944 to serve in Admiral Halsey's South Pacific fleet; and the **USS *Olympia,*** Admiral Dewey's own flagship in the Spanish-American War, with a self-guided three-deck tour. The harbor cruise boats ***Liberty Belle II*** (✆ **215/629-1131**) and ***Spirit of Philadelphia*** (✆ **215/923-1419;** www.spiritofphiladelphia.com), and the paddle-wheeler ***Riverboat Queen*** (✆ **215/923-BOAT** [2628]; www.riverboatqueenfleet.com), are joined by private yachts. In fact, Queen Elizabeth docked her yacht *Britannia* here in 1976. Anchoring the southern end is the **Chart House** restaurant, 555 S. Columbus Blvd. (✆ **215/625-8383**), open for lunch and dinner, and the restored **Moshulu** four-masted floating restaurant (p. 91) in Penn's Landing marina.

Another group of boats occupies the landfill directly on the Delaware between Market and Walnut streets. The ***Gazela Primiero,*** a working three-masted, square-rigged wooden ship launched from Portugal in 1883, has visiting hours on Saturday and Sunday from 12:30 to 5:30pm when it's in port, as does the tugboat ***Jupiter.*** All the boats are operated by the Philadelphia Ship Preservation Guild (✆ **215/238-0280**). Most are closed in winter. And, even in summer, it's a good idea to call before visiting.

If you want to get out onto the water, the ***RiverLink*** (✆ **215/925-LINK** [5465]), at the river's edge in front of the Independence Seaport Museum at Walnut Street, plies a round-trip route to the Camden attractions including the Adventure Aquarium, the Camden Children's Garden, and the battleship *New Jersey,* next to the Tweeter concert arena. The ferry crosses every hour on the hour between 9am and 5pm May to October. The trip takes 10 minutes, and the round-trip fare without museum admission on either end is $6 for adults and $4 for children.

5 ESPECIALLY FOR KIDS

Philadelphia is one of the country's great family destinations. It has a variety of attractions for different ages, and because it's so walkable and neighborhood based, a snack, a rest, or a new distraction is never far away. Since so many of the family attractions are explained in more detail elsewhere in this or other chapters, I'll restrict myself to a list of the basics.

The Independence Visitor Center, at 6th and Market streets (✆ **800/537-7676** or 215/965-7676; www.independencevisitorcenter.com), coordinates and sells several packages that combine free admission to many kid-friendly attractions with accommodations at hotels such as the Loews, Sheraton Society Hill, Four Seasons, and Holiday Inn. Contact the Greater Philadelphia Tourism and Marketing Corporation (✆ **215/599-0776;** www.gophila.org) for more family-oriented hotel packages.

MUSEUMS & SIGHTS

In Center City, you'll find **Franklin Institute** and **CoreStates Science Park** at Benjamin Franklin Parkway and 20th Street and the **Academy of Natural Sciences** at Benjamin Franklin Parkway and 19th Street. The **Free Library of Philadelphia Children's Department,** across Logan Circle at Vine and 19th streets, is a joy, with a separate entrance, 100,000 books, and computers in a playgroundlike space, with weekend hours. Around Independence Hall are the **Liberty Bell Center; Franklin Court,** between Market and Chestnut streets at 4th Street; the waterfront at **Penn's Landing,** off Front Street; the new **National Constitution Center** at Arch and 5th streets; and, of course, the guided tour of **Independence Hall.** You can also take the ferry from Penn's Landing and the great new **Independence Seaport Museum** to the **aquarium, children's garden,** and **battleship** in Camden, New Jersey. In West Fairmount Park, you'll find the **zoo.**

PLAYGROUNDS

Rittenhouse Square at 18th and Walnut streets has a small playground and space in which to eat and relax. Other imaginative urban playgrounds on this side of Center City are **Schuylkill River Park** at Pine and 26th streets, and at 26th Street and the Benjamin Franklin Parkway, opposite the art museum. Nearest Independence Hall, try **Delancey,** aka "Three Bears," **Park** at Delancey between 3rd and 4th streets (with lots of fountains and animal sculptures to climb on) or **Starr Garden** at 6th and Lombard streets. The best park in Fairmount Park is the **Smith Memorial.** It's got a giant wooden slide, weird things to climb on, and an indoor playground with plenty of toys to play with and spots to picnic (head north on 33rd St., then take a left into the park at Oxford Ave., near Woodford). Worth an afternoon is **Franklin Square Park,** between 6th and 7th on Race Street, with an old-fashioned carousel, a fountain (ca. 1825), a Philly-themed minigolf course, and a playground. Open daylight hours. The carousel costs $3 for adults and $2 for children. Minigolf costs $8 per adult and $6 per child. At press time, hours were limited to Friday, Saturday, and Sunday.

ENTERTAINMENT

There is lots of children's theater in Philadelphia. The **Arden Theatre** at 40 N. 2nd St. (© **215/922-1122;** www.ardentheatre.org) is one of a dozen companies that produces children's theater year-round. **Mum Puppettheatre** at 115 Arch St. presents a season of thought-provoking and enjoyable plays for all ages; call © **215/925-8686** or visit www.mumpuppet.org for schedule and details. The **Pennsylvania Ballet** (p. 189) also puts on matinee performances that make for a perfect early afternoon. Call © **215/551-7000** for more information.

The **Philadelphia Museum of Art** at 26th and Benjamin Franklin Parkway (bus: PHLASH, 21, or 42) has dedicated itself to producing Sunday-morning and early-afternoon programs for children, at minimal or no charge. Your kids could wind up drawing pictures of armor or watching a puppet play about dragons, visiting a Chinese court, or exploring cubism. Call © **215/763-8100,** or 684-7500 for 24-hour information.

OUTSIDE PHILADELPHIA

In Bucks County, there are *Sesame Street*–based rides and water slides at **Sesame Place** in Langhorne, and a restored antique carousel at **Peddler's Village** in Lahaska. To the northwest, try the 20th-century entertainment areas connected with **Franklin Mills,** and **Ridley Creek State Park** and its 17th-century working farm in Montgomery County. For Revolutionary War history in action, visit Valley Forge or Washington Crossing National Historical Parks. And for a fascinating experience, spend a couple of days in Lancaster County—you can even stay on a working Amish farm. See chapters 11 and 12 for directions and information.

6 ORGANIZED TOURS

BOAT TOURS

Recent years have expanded options for seeing Philly by boat. Spring through fall, **Ride the Ducks'** (p. 153) amphibious vehicles are nearly omnipresent, offering tours of Old City and a 20-minute splash in the Delaware River. In 2006, the ambitious **Schuylkill Banks** project (© **215/222-6030;** www.schuylkillbanks.org) opened up Philadelphia's tidal river to three narrated boat tours, one to Bartram's Gardens (p. 149); a "Jazz Cruise"; and a "Secrets of the Schuylkill" tour. At press time, future scheduling was still up in the air, but these programs will most like be in place May through October, with a 2-week hiatus in August. Make reservations online or by phone.

Penn's Landing's the ***Spirit of Philadelphia*** (✆ **866/211-3808**) at the Great Plaza combines brunch, lunch, or dinner with a cruise on a 600-person passenger ship, fully climate controlled, with two enclosed decks and two open-air decks. Reservations are suggested. Trips can be up to 3 hours and cost from $44 to $97. Popular among special events planners and promgoers, the tour involves an enjoyably (ironically) cheesy show and, if you sign up, a filling meal.

Across the dock, the slightly shabbier ***Riverboat Queen*** (✆ **215/629-1131**) also offers cruises and dining.

May to October, the ***RiverLink*** (✆ **215/925-LINK** [5465]) provides a 10-minute interstate crossing from landings just outside the Independence Seaport Museum and the Adventure Aquarium. The ferry is large inside, and the views of the Philadelphia skyline are great. Departures from Penn's Landing are on the hour, from Camden on the half-hour, from 9am to 5pm daily. Round-trip fares are $6 for adults and $4 for children. Packages including admission to various Camden attractions are a good deal and are available at the Independence Seaport Museum and attractions along the Philadelphia or Camden waterfront.

BUS & TROLLEY TOURS

Big Bus is a fleet of double-decker, British-style tour vehicles (✆ **866/324-4287** or 215/923-5008; www.bigbustours.com). Tours of historic areas, conducted by guides in the climate-controlled vehicles, leave from the visitor center at 5th and Market. The tours cost $27 for adults, $22 for seniors, and $10 for children.

Philadelphia Trolley Works and 76 Carriage Company ★★ (✆ **215/389-TOUR** [8687]; www.phillytour.com) offers 90-minute tours of the historic area in trolley-style buses. Trolley passes valid for 24 hours are $27 for adults, $25 for seniors, and $10 for children 4 to 12. The trolleys pick up at 5th and Chestnut streets. Seasonal Fairmount trolley tours are $20 for adults and $13 for seniors and children. There's also a discount zoo/trolley combination pass: $38 for adults, $21 for children 4 to 12. Short horse-drawn carriage tours start at $30.

The cheesiest touring fun you can have, however, is to hop a **Ride the Ducks ★★** land-to-water vessel, and cruise around town quacking on a plastic yellow duckbill. Modeled after World War II DUKW amphibious vehicles that carried soldiers and ammo ashore, the ducks operate mid-March through mid-December. They roam the historic district on their 70- to 80-minute tour, blaring oldies, and waving to pedestrians as the driver cracks jokes and eventually plunges the jalopy into the water, where the kids, loving every minute, take turns behind the wheel. Depending on demand, tours depart from 6th and Chestnut streets, near the ticket kiosk. Purchase tickets there, at the visitor center, by phone (✆ **877/887-8225** or 215/227-DUCK [3825]), or online (www.phillyducks.com). Prices are $26 for adults, $24 for seniors, and $16 for children 3 to 12.

HORSE & CARRIAGE TOURS

To get the feel of Philadelphia as it was (well, almost—asphalt is a lot smoother than cobblestones), try a narrated horse-drawn carriage ride. Operated daily by the **76 Carriage Company** (see above), tours begin at 5th and Chestnut streets in front of Independence Hall. They run Monday through Friday 9:45am to 6:30pm and Saturday and Sunday from 9:30am to 6:30pm. Fares range from $30 for 15 minutes to $80 for an hour. Evening tours from 6:30 to 10:30pm are available by appointment; call for rates. A word to the historically wise: It's not uncommon for these guides to stretch the truth.

If you do take a carriage ride, it's best to concentrate on the scenery you see—as opposed to the stories you hear.

WALKING TOURS

Chapter 8 offers self-guided walking tours. If you'd rather follow a guide, however, top marks go to summertime Old City walkabouts hosted by the Colonial characters of **Once Upon a Nation** (p. 122). April to October, **Old Original Walking Tours of Philadelphia** gives you an excellent 90-minute walking tour, for a mere $9. Go to www.oldoriginalwalkingtours.com to check out the variety of tours offered. Year-round, the **Independence Visitor Center** (p. 119) and www.gophila.com have information about special-interest tours such as African-American Philadelphia, Jewish sights of Society Hill, cultural centers of Chinatown, underground railroad stops in Germantown, and delicious stands of the Italian Market. Oh, and there's **Lights of Liberty** (p. 125), too.

7 OUTDOOR ACTIVITIES

I can't begin to make a complete list of all that you can do outdoors while in Philadelphia, so the following is merely a sample.

BIKING & BLADING

Lloyd Hall in **Fairmount Park,** the most southerly Boathouse Row building along the Schuylkill River, is the jumping-off spot for biking and blading activities. You can rent bikes and skates at the hall itself from Bikes, 1 Boathouse Row (✆ **888/901-9990**). Once you're on wheels, the paths along the Schuylkill on Kelly (East River) Drive, West River Drive, and off West River Drive to Belmont Avenue are pure pleasure. The lower half of West River Drive along the Schuylkill is closed to vehicular traffic most weekend hours in summer. Rent bicycles from $25 a day at **Bike Line** at 1028 Arch near the convention center (✆ **215/923-1310**). The ground is flat near the Schuylkill on either side but loops up sharply near Laurel Hill Cemetery or Manayunk. Anyone who enjoys cycling will love the outlying countryside, and you can rent bicycles in Lumberville, 8 miles north of New Hope on the Delaware, at the **Lumberville Store,** 3741 River Rd. (✆ **215/297-5388**). Bicycles may be taken free on off-peak SEPTA trains, but you might want to think twice before you tote your Schwinn into Suburban Station: Some transit riders don't take to cyclists.

Visit the **Bicycle Club of Philadelphia** at www.phillybikeclub.org for specific neighborhood recommendations. If you want my recommendation: Be careful if you decide to bike in town and always wear a bike helmet.

BOATING

Spring through fall, **Schuylkill Banks** rents kayaks from its location along the river between Locust and Walnut streets. Kayak rentals are $34 per person, $50 for the moonlight tour, and $75 to kayak on to Bartram's Gardens. Go to www.schuylkillbanks.org, or call ✆ **215/222-6030,** ext. 100, for more information. Outside of the city, try **Northbrook Canoe Co.,** north of Route 842 at 1810 Beagle Rd. W., in West Chester on Brandywine Creek (✆ **800/898-2279** or 610/793-2279; www.northbrookcanoe.com; reservations preferred), or **Bucks County River Country,** 2 Walter Lane in Point Pleasant, on Route 32, 7 miles north of the New Hope exit on I-95 (✆ **215/297-8823;** www.rivercountry.net) with canoeing, inner tubing, and rafting on the Delaware River.

FISHING

Pennypack Creek and **Wissahickon Creek** are stocked from mid-April to December with trout and muskie and provide good, even rustic, conditions. A required 1- or 3-day license is $27 and a 7-day license is $35, available online at www.fish.state.pa.us/license.htm. Outside the city, **Ridley Creek** and its **state park** (✆ **888/727-2757**) and **Brandywine Creek** at Hibernia Park of Chester County (✆ **610/383-3812**) are stocked with several kinds of trout.

GOLF

The quality and variety of public access golf is wonderful. The city of Philadelphia operates five municipal courses in the region. All have 18 holes, and current fees range from $15 to $25 Monday through Friday and $20 to $30 on Saturday and Sunday. Not everyone can get onto the legendary Pine Valley or Merion, but Hugh Wilson of Merion also designed the pretty and challenging **Cobbs Creek,** 7200 Lansdowne Ave. at Haverford Avenue (✆ **215/877-8707**). **Karakung** is the shorter 18-hole course, and preferred by seniors and juniors. **John F. Byrne,** 9550 Leon St. near the intersection of Frankford Avenue and Eden Street in North Philadelphia (✆ **215/632-8666**), has an Alex Findlay design with Torresdale Creek meandering through or beside 10 holes, and plenty of rolling fairways and elevations. **Walnut Lane,** Walnut Lane and Henry Avenue in Roxborough (✆ **215/482-3370**), places a premium on short game skills, with 10 par-3 holes and deep bunkers set into hills and valleys. There's also a driving range in East Fairmount Park.

Among the better township courses outside the city are **Pine Crest Club,** Route 202 (✆ **215/855-6112**); **Paxon Hollow Golf Club,** Paxon Hollow Road in Marple Township (✆ **610/353-0220**), under 6,000 yards and demanding accuracy; and **Valley Forge Golf Club,** 401 N. Gulph Rd., King of Prussia (✆ **610/337-1776**). Expect fees of $65 and up.

HIKING

Fairmount Park (p. 146) has dozens of miles of paths. The extensions of the park into the Wissahickon Creek area are quite unspoiled, with dirt roads and no auto traffic.

ICE-SKATING

November to early March—cold weather permitting—the **Blue Cross RiverRink at Festival Pier** is open for public skating near the intersection of Columbus Boulevard and Spring Garden Street daily. Admission for one 2-hour session is $8; skate rental, $3. Call ✆ **215/925-7465** or visit www.riverrink.com for details; the modest food court serves hot chocolate. One word of warning: This place can get way crowded on weekends. Across town, the indoor **Penn Ice Rink at the Class of 1923 Arena,** 3130 Walnut St. (✆ **215/898-1932;** www.business-services.upenn.edu/icerink), offers daily public skating sessions, usually from 1 to 3pm Sunday through Friday, and in early evening on Saturday (and sometimes Fri). Admission is $5.50 for daytime, $6.50 for evening; skate rental is $2.50. There are also weekly opportunities to freestyle and play open hockey games, and regular games from the women's and men's teams of Drexel and Penn.

RUNNING & JOGGING

Again, **Fairmount Park** has more trails than you could cover in a week. An 8.25-mile loop starts in front of the art museum, goes up the east bank of the Schuylkill, across the river at Falls Bridge, and back down to the museum. At the north end, Forbidden Drive along the Wissahickon has loops of dirt/gravel of 5 miles and more, with no traffic. The Benjamin Franklin Bridge path from 5th and Vine streets is 1.75 miles each way. Wherever you choose, go during daylight hours. The newest, and greatest, addition to the running scene is the completion of the riverside **Schuylkill Banks** trail, which stretches from Locust to Race Street, behind the art museum, where it connects with the east and west river drives (Martin Luther King Jr. is to the west; Kelly Dr. to the east). Entrances for this smooth, convenient trail are at Locust and Walnut streets.

SWIMMING

Many hotels have small lap pools, and, until late 2008, when the city announced major budgetary cutbacks, Philadelphia had 86 municipal pools. Time will tell which splash zones reopen in the summer of 2009. Hopefully, City Hall will preserve my favorites: **Cobbs Creek,** 63rd and Spruce streets, and **FDR Pool,** Broad and Pattison in South Philadelphia. Call © **215/686-1776** for updates and details.

TENNIS

Some 115 courts are scattered throughout **Fairmount Park**, first come, first served. You might also try the University of Pennsylvania's indoor courts at the **Robert P. Levy Tennis Pavilion,** 3130 Walnut St. (© **215/898-4741**). Hours are limited, but the cost for guests totals $32 per court/per hour spring through fall, $28 in winter.

8 SPECTATOR SPORTS

Even in these days of nomadic professional teams, Philadelphia fields teams in every major sport, and boasts two new outdoor stadiums and two indoor venues at the end of South Broad Street to house them all. The 43,000-seat **Citizens Bank Park** is a beautiful baseball stadium opened by the Phillies in 2004; the state-of-the-art **Lincoln Financial Field** seats 66,000 for Eagles games. The 21,000-seat **Wachovia Center** houses the Philadelphia Flyers pro hockey team and the Philadelphia 76ers basketball team. It couples with the 17,000-seat **Spectrum,** which functions as a rock-concert forum and hosts the U.S. Pro Indoor Tennis Championships and other one-of-a-kind events.

All these facilities are next to each other and can be reached via a 10-minute subway ride straight down South Broad Street to Pattison Avenue (cash fare is $2; tokens are $1.45 each, in packs of two and five). The same fare will put you on the SEPTA bus C, which goes down Broad Street more slowly but is the safer choice late at night.

Professional sports aren't the only game in town, though. Philadelphia has a lot of colleges, and **Franklin Field** and the **Palestra** dominate West Philadelphia on 33rd below Walnut Street. The Penn Relays, the first intercollegiate and amateur track event in the nation, books Franklin Field on the last weekend in April (p. 158). Regattas pull along the Schuylkill all spring, summer, and fall, within sight of Fairmount Park's mansions (p. 146).

A call to Ticketmaster (© **215/336-2000** in Philadelphia) can often get you a ticket to a game before you hit town.

BASEBALL

The **Philadelphia Phillies** (© **215/463-1000** or www.phillies.com for ticket information, or 463-5300 for daily game information), won the World Series in 1980, the National League pennant in 1993, and made the playoffs in 1995, and, at very long last, recaptured the World Series in 2008. Everyone has a favorite Phil: first basemen and home-run hitter extraordinaire Ryan Howard gets a whole lot of love, but second baseman Chase Utley, starting pitchers Cole Hamels and Jamie Moyer, and closer Brad Lidge aren't far behind, and shortstop Jimmy Rollins and center fielder Shane "Flyin' Hawaiian" Victorian are undeniably the team's heart and soul (not that I'm biased or anything). Anyway, the whole lot of them (including my secret favorite, catcher Carlos Ruiz) dominate **Citizens Bank Park,** where great local food options include Tony Luke's (p. 114), Bull's BBQ (owned by former Phillie Greg Luzinski, who signs autographs at games), and Peace-a-Pizza. There are even kiosks selling locally brewed beer. A giant lighted Liberty Bell rings after every Phillies home run. Fans come early (and stay late) to drink beer and listen to cover bands at lively McFadden's Pub behind the 3rd Base Gate. Day games usually begin at 1:05pm, regular night games at 8:05pm on Friday, 7:05pm on other days. When there's a twilight double-header, it begins at 5:35pm.

Box seats overlooking the field at Citizens Bank Park are $60, and the cheapest bleacher seats are $16 if you're 15 or over . Tickets are sometimes available on game days—less so when the Phils are on a winning streak.

BASKETBALL

The **Philadelphia 76ers** (www.sixers.com) play about 40 games at the Wachovia Center between early November and late April. Call ✆ **215/339-7676** for ticket information, or charge at ✆ **215/336-2000;** single tickets range from $25 to $125. A great thing about Sixers games is the crowds: They're generally better behaved (and better groomed) than Birds, Phils, or Flyers fans.

There are five major college basketball teams in the Philadelphia area, and the newspapers print schedules of their games. Philly's favorite young teams are the **Temple Owls** who play at home at the Liacouras Center, 1776 N. Broad St. (✆ **800/298-4200;** http://owlsports.cstv.com), and the **Hawks** of St. Joseph's University, home at the Alumni Memorial Fieldhouse, 54th St. and City Line Ave. (✆ **610/660-1712;** http://sjuhawks.cstv.com). Many college ballgames are played at Penn's **Palestra**, 235 S. 33rd St., between South and Walnut sts. Call ✆ **215/898-6151** for availability.

BIKING

The **U.S. Pro Cycling Championship,** held each June, is a top event in the cycling world. (Lance Armstrong is a former rider in this event.) The 156-mile race starts and finishes along the Benjamin Franklin Parkway. Watching the cyclists climb the torturous incline of "The Wall" in Manayunk is thrilling: The entire street throws house parties and cheers the straining riders onward and upward. Visit www.procyclingtour.com for this year's event information.

BOATING

From April to September, you can watch regattas on the Schuylkill River, which have been held since the earliest days of the "Schuylkill Navy" a century ago. The **National Association of Amateur Oarsmen** (✆ **215/769-2068**) and the **Boathouse Association** (✆ **215/686-0052**) have a complete schedule of races, one of the best known being the **Dad Vail Regatta** (p. 34).

FOOTBALL

Football is, without a doubt, Philadelphia's favorite sport, and current **Eagles** quarterback Donovan McNabb may be injury prone, but still is the spiritual backbone of the

Fun Facts The Eagles Cheer

If you ever find yourself in a bad spot in a bar, or if you'd like to win over some new friends, shout out the letters *E* and then *A*. Guaranteed everyone around you will chime in with a boisterous, "G, L, E, S: Eagles!" And, at last, you'll be popular. (If you'd like to lose friends in Philly, however, appear in a public place wearing a Dallas jersey—especially T. O.'s.)

team. For fans, the fun starts way before the kickoff, when the parking lot of Lincoln Financial Field turns into a giant tailgate party, with full bars, pig roasts, bands playing, and beer that flows freely. Getting stuck there for the duration of the game might not be a bad thing—and it might be your only choice. Virtually 100% of Birds' tickets are sold to season-ticket holders. Call © **215/463-5500** for ticket advice; you may be able to score pricey club seats. For team updates, visit www.philadelphiaeagles.com.

HORSE RACING

Home of Kentucky Derby underdog (and winner) Smarty Jones, **Philadelphia Park** (the old Keystone Track) is the only track left in the area, with races from June 15 to February 13, Saturday through Tuesday. (Post time is 12:35pm.) Admission, general parking, and a program are free. The park is at 3001 Street Rd. in Bensalem, half a mile from exit 28 on the Pennsylvania Turnpike. Call © **215/639-9000** for information.

The **Turf Club at Center City,** 7 Penn Center, 1635 Market St. (© **215/246-1556**), is on the concourse and lower mezzanine levels and features 270 color video monitors and an ersatz Art Deco design.

ICE HOCKEY

The Wachovia Center rocks to the **Philadelphia Flyers** (www.philadelphiaflyers.com) from fall to spring. As with the Eagles, Flyers tickets aren't easy to find—80% of tickets are sold by the season's start in October. Call © **215/735-9700** for ticket information; if you can get them, they'll cost between $26 and $96.

TRACK & FIELD

The city hosts the **Penn Relays,** the oldest and still the largest amateur track meet in the country, in late April at the University of Pennsylvania's Franklin Field. For tickets, contact the Penn Athletics box office at © **215/898-6151** or www.thepennrelays.com. The annual **Philadelphia Marathon** (© **215/683-2122;** www.philadelphiamarathon.com) fills hotels with strong-calved runners in November. September sees the increasingly world-class **Philadelphia Distance Run** (www.runphilly.com), a half marathon. My favorite, however, is May's **Broad Street Run** (© **215/683-3594;** www.broadstreetrun.com), a 10-miler (mostly downhill) beginning at North Broad Street's Central High School and ending at South Philadelphia's handsome Naval Yard.

8

City Strolls

by Lauren McCutcheon

Philadelphia is the most walkable major city in the United States. As you stroll its streets, you'll be fascinated by the physical illustration of the progress of the centuries, the juxtapositions of past and present. Many neighborhoods are still made up of tree-lined, intimate streets flanked by lovely Federal town houses, especially in Society Hill, along Pine Street's Antique Row, and the residential streets west of Rittenhouse Square, such as Spruce, Locust, and Delancey. You'll notice the nearer you are to the Delaware, the older (and smaller) the buildings are likely to be. The walking tours mapped out below are specifically designed to cover the most worthwhile attractions.

Note: It is important that you get individual (free) tickets for Independence Hall at the Independence Visitor Center (some are available in advance at www.reservations.gov for $1.50), as you will not be able to get tickets at the hall itself. Before you enter the Liberty Bell Center, Independence Hall, Congress Hall, and Old City Hall, you must pass through a security screening facility across from Independence Visitor Center; be sure to allow time to get through security when you are choosing timed tickets to Independence Hall during busy afternoon hours.

WALKING TOUR 1 — HISTORIC HIGHLIGHTS & SOCIETY HILL

START:	**Independence Visitor Center, 6th and Market streets.**
FINISH:	**City Tavern, 2nd and Walnut streets; optional extension to Penn's Landing.**
TIME:	**6 to 7 hours.**
BEST TIME:	**Start between 9 and 11am to avoid hour-long waits for Independence Hall tours.**
WORST TIME:	**Midafternoon.**

Start your tour at the:

1 Independence Visitor Center

The Independence Visitor Center (daily 8:30am–5pm, until 7pm July–Sept) is in Independence National Historical Park, on 6th and Market streets. This handsome brick building was built for the 21st-century renovation of Independence Mall. It maintains spotless restrooms, a cafe for that jump-start-your-day coffee, and a plethora of information about the park, the city, and the region. This is where you pick up tickets to get inside Independence Hall (whether you've reserved in advance or are counting on walk-up access). Tickets to the Bishop White and Todd houses (below) and information about special tours and daily events are also available here. The John Huston–directed film *Independence* is shown free of charge every half-hour. There is a handsome exhibition area and a substantial-quality gift shop and bookstore.

Just south of the visitor center is:

❷ Independence Hall

Independence Hall is grand, graceful, and one of democracy's true shrines (see p. 122 for a full description). Ranger-led 35-minute tours depart every 15 minutes or so, starting at 9am. (Remember, you must stay inside the secure area of the park, or you will need to go through the screening process again to enter Independence Hall.)

The two flanking buildings, **Old City Hall** (built to house the Supreme Court) and **Congress Hall,** were intended to balance each other, and their fanlight-adorned doors, keystone-decorated windows, and simple lines are appealing from any angle. They were used by a combination of federal, state, county, and city governments during a relatively short period.

Turn right as you exit Independence Hall and walk next door for a quick stop in:

❸ Old City Hall

Built in 1791, and located at the corner of 5th and Chestnut streets, Old City Hall was home to the third branch of the federal government, the U.S. Supreme Court, under Chief Justice John Jay, from 1791 to 1800. From 1800 to 1870, the building was used as the city hall. An exhibit here describes the first years of the judiciary branch of the U.S. government.

In back of this central trio of buildings is the tree-lined and hallowed:

❹ Independence Square

On July 8, 1776, John Nixon read the Declaration of Independence to the assembled city on this spot. At night, from April to October, the *Lights of Liberty* sound-and-light tour/show ends with projections on the back wall of Independence Hall.

Head back through Independence Hall and cross Chestnut Street to:

❺ The Liberty Bell

Decades ago, the famously cracked giant bell was located in Independence Hall. Today, it's in a shiny Liberty Bell Center on Market between 5th and 6th streets, between the visitor center and Independence Hall. There is a video presentation about the bell's history, and audio is offered in a dozen languages. You will need to pass through a security screening before entering this glass-walled center at 6th Street. See p. 125 for a full description.

Backtrack across the visitor center block with its new landscaping to:

> **TAKE A BREAK**
> The National Constitution Center's spacious, ground-floor **Delegates Restaurant** is open daily from 8:30am to 4pm, and serves simple salads, smoked salmon sandwiches, cheesesteaks, chicken fingers, and snacks.

❻ National Constitution Center

This is a generous half-block-long space that is dramatically modern, made of limestone, steel, and glass. The center, which opened in July 2003, explores the history of the framing of the Constitution in 1787, and also challenges visitors to think about the effect that this document has had on the lives of all Americans, from 1787 to the present day. Its designers, Pei Cobb Freed & Partners, have a great track record with the Holocaust Museum in Washington, D.C.; the Rose Planetarium in New York; and Cleveland's Rock and Roll Hall of Fame and Museum. Walk under a doorway inscribed "We the People," receive a "delegate's card," à la the Constitution's authors in 1787, and you'll find architecture and creative multimedia exhibits that are informative and entertaining, if ultimately a bit mind numbing. Families can split up during their visit to experience different parts of the center. The Epcot-esque multimedia introductory theater presentation isn't essential but will appeal to kids.

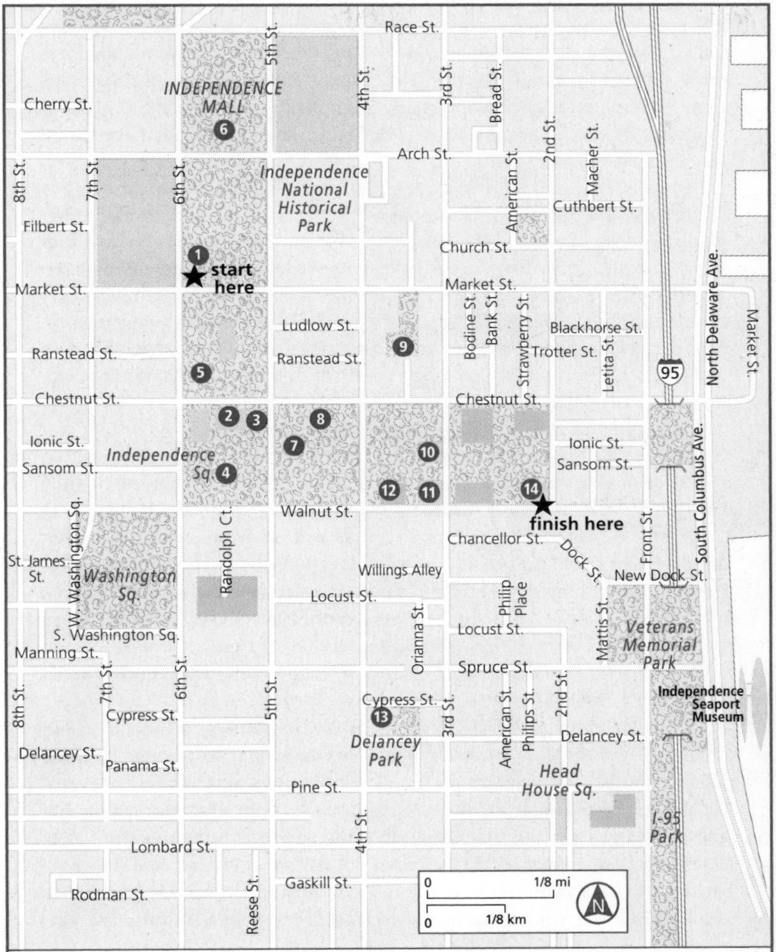

1 Independence Visitor Center
2 Independence Hall
3 Old City Hall
4 Independence Square
5 The Liberty Bell
6 National Constitution Center
7 Library Hall and Philosophical Hall
8 Second Bank of the United States
9 Franklin Court
10 First Bank of the United States
11 Bishop White House
12 Todd House
13 Physick House
14 City Tavern

Architectural ABCs

You'll enjoy your stroll around Society Hill and Queen Village even more if you know something about Colonial and Federal architecture, especially since many homes aren't open for individual tours. Brick is the constant, clay being abundant by the Delaware's banks—but construction methods have varied over the past 150 years.

Generally, houses built before the 1750s, such as the **Trump House** at 214 Delancey St., are two-and-a-half stories, with two rooms per floor and a dormer window jutting out of a steep gambrel roof (a gambrel roof consists of a roof with two slopes on each of the two sides, with the lower slope steeper than the upper). An eave usually separates the simple door and its transom windows from the second level. Careful bricklayers liked to alternate the long and short sides of bricks (called "stretchers" and "headers," respectively), a style known as Flemish Bond. The headers were often glazed to create a checkerboard pattern. Wrought-iron boot scrapers flank the doorsteps.

Houses built in Philadelphia's Colonial heyday soared to three or four stories—taller after the Revolution—and adopted heavy Georgian cornices (the underside of a roof overhang) and elaborate doorways. The homes of the truly wealthy, such as the **Powel House** at 244 S. 3rd St. and the **Morris House** at 235 S. 8th St., have fanlights above their arched brick doorways; the **Davis-Lenox House** at 217 Spruce St. has a simple raised pediment. Since the Georgian style demanded symmetry, the parlors were often given imaginary doors and windows to even things out. The less wealthy lived in "trinity" houses—one room on each of three floors, named for faith, hope, and charity. Few town houses were free-standing (most were row houses)—the **Hill-Physick-Keith House** at 321 S. 4th St. is an exception.

Federal architecture, which arrived from England and New England in the 1790s, is less heavy (no more Flemish Bond for bricks) and generally more graceful (more glass, with delicate molding instead of wainscoting). Any house like the **Meredith House** at 700 S. Washington Sq., with a half story of marble stairs leading to a raised mahogany door, was surely constructed after 1800. Greek Revival elements such as rounded dormer windows and oval staircases became the fashion from the 1810s on. Three Victorian brownstones at 260 S. 3rd St. once belonged to Michel Bouvier, Jacqueline Kennedy Onassis's great-great-grandfather.

If you're here in April through June, don't pass up the **Philadelphia Open House** to view the interiors of dozens of homes (volunteered by proud owners). Call ✆ **215/928-1188** or visit www.friendsofindependence.org for information.

Returning to Independence Square, walk behind Old City Hall. Along 5th Street and opposite, you'll find the:

7 Library Hall & Philosophical Hall

Library Hall is the 1954 reconstruction of Benjamin Franklin's old Library Company, which was the first lending library in the Colonies. The Library Company is now at 1314 Locust St., and today this graceful Federal building houses the library of the American Philosophical Society, across the street. The collection is fascinating, including Franklin's will, a copy of William Penn's 1701 Charter of Privileges, and Jefferson's own handwritten copy of the Declaration of Independence. Note, however, that not everything is on view at all times. The exhibits focus on the history of science in America. The library's hours follow the park schedule (Mon–Fri, 9am–5pm). **Philosophical Hall,** across the way, is the home of the American Philosophical Society (APS). The society, founded by Ben Franklin, is made up of a prestigious honor roll of America's outstanding intellects and achievers. In Franklin's day, philosophers were more often than not industrious young men with scientific and learned interests. Current members of the society include former senator Bill Bradley, violinist Itzhak Perlman, poet Rita Dove, and commentator Bill Moyers. The building's interior opened to the public in 2001 for the first time since Philadelphia artist, naturalist, and APS member Charles Wilson Peale closed his museum here in the 19th century. It's open Friday through Sunday, 10am to 4pm (and 5–8pm May 1 to Labor Day), and offers delightful seasonal exhibitions such as *From the Laboratory to the Parlor: Scientific Instruments in Philadelphia, 1750–1875.*

Next to Philosophical Hall is the:

8 Second Bank of the United States

Its strong Greek columns have worn away somewhat, but the beautiful bank still holds interest. The Second Bank was chartered by Congress in 1816 for a term of 20 years, at a time when the country felt that it needed reliable circulating money. The building (1818–24), designed like the Philadelphia Exchange by William Strickland, is adapted from the Parthenon, and the Greeks would have been proud of its capable director, Nicholas Biddle. An elitist to the core, he was the man Andrew Jackson and his supporters had in mind when they complained about private individuals controlling public government. "Old Hickory" vetoed renewal of the bank's charter, increasing the money supply but ruining Biddle and the bank.

The building was used as a Customs House until 1935. Now the National Park Service uses it as a portrait gallery of early Americans. The collection contains many of the oldest gallery portraits in the country, painted by Peale, Sully, Neagle, Stuart, and Allston. Admission is free. The building is open Wednesday to Saturday from 11am to 5pm. The portrait gallery is open sporadically: Independence National Park rangers suggest visitors contact the park or visitor center for details.

Walk east on Chestnut Street 1 block. The southern side of the block is 18th century all the way, passing New Hall Museum. Crossing the street brings you to a handsome collection of 19th-century banks and commercial facades, including the 1867 First National Bank at no. 315 and the Philadelphia National Bank at no. 323. Go into the marked alleyway to enter:

9 Franklin Court

Ben and Deborah Franklin's home is not much more than excavated foundations and outdoor privy wells encased by a reconstructed frame that delineates the structure's original dimensions. What's most interesting here are the exhibits: a mirrored room dedicated to Franklin's far-flung passions, phones where you can hear international luminaries' opinions of Franklin, and a cleverly staged doll drama in three acts. See p. 124 for a full description of this wonderful tribute to Benjamin Franklin.

You can cross through to Market Street to the north to buy some stamps from Ben's own re-created post office.

TAKE A BREAK

A few doors east of Ben Franklin's Post Office on Market Street is **Fork Etc.,** a great spot to grab an espresso, panini, or juice and take a load off while reading one of the cafe's many design-oriented magazines or metropolitan newspapers.

Society Hill

You may be surprised to learn that Society Hill wasn't named after the upper crust who lived here in Colonial times. Rather, the name refers to the Free Society of Traders, a group of businessmen and investors persuaded by William Penn to settle here with their families in 1683. The name applies to the area east of Washington Square between Walnut and Lombard streets. Many of Philadelphia's white-collar workers, clerics, teachers, importers, and politicos have lived and worked here over the years.

Looking at Society Hill's handsome Colonial facades, it's hard to imagine that a few decades ago, this part of town was considered blighted. The rescuing came about in the 1950s, when City Planner Edmund Bacon (father of actor Kevin) and Mayor Richardson Dilworth went about rescuing by blending new housing developments in with original Georgian neighbors.

Among these residences are Georgian and Federal public buildings and churches, from **Head House Square** and **Pennsylvania Hospital** to **St. Peter's** and **St. Paul's,** which may make you feel as if you've stumbled onto a movie set. But all of the buildings are used—and the area works as a living community today.

Return to Chestnut Street, and head south on 3rd Street for more history at the:

⑩ First Bank of the United States

This 1795 building is not open to the public but is a superb example of Federal architecture. This graceful edifice is the oldest surviving bank building in America. Initially, each of the new states issued its own currency. Dealing with 13 different currencies hampered commerce and travel among the states, so Alexander Hamilton proposed a single bank (originally in Carpenters' Hall) for loans and deposits. The classical facade, Hamilton's idea, is meant to recall the democracy and splendor of ancient Greece. The mahogany American eagle on the pediment over the Corinthian columns at the entrance is a famous and rare example of 18th-century sculpture.

The park service cleared many of the nonhistoric structures on the block behind the First Bank (and throughout the historical park area), creating 18th-century gardens and lawns.

A bit south of your present location, fine restaurants and charming stores cluster south of Lombard, especially around Head House Square (1803) at 2nd and Lombard streets.

Continuing on your tour from the greenery in back of the First Bank, you'll see very typically restored row houses along the southern side of Walnut Street between 3rd and 4th streets. At no. 309 Walnut Street is the:

⑪ Bishop White House

Tours (for 10 persons at a time) are the only way to see the house; free tickets (which include admission to the Todd House, below) can be obtained only at the Independence Visitor Center. This house is on one of the loveliest row-house blocks in the city, and it's a splendid example of how a pillar of the community lived in Federal America. Bishop White (1748–1836) was the founder of Episcopalianism, breaking with the Anglican Church. He was a good friend of Franklin, as you'll see from the upstairs library. Notice how well the painted cloth floor in the entrance hall survived muddy boots and 20 varnishings. Perhaps the most unusual interior feature is the "necessary," an uncommon amenity in Colonial Philadelphia. The library reveals the bishop's tastes, featuring Sir Walter Scott's Waverley novels, the *Encyclopaedia Britannica,* the Koran, and other traditional religious texts.

Farther east on Walnut at the corner of 4th and Walnut streets is the other park-run dwelling, the:

⑫ Todd House

Tours of the house (for 10 persons at a time) are required (you can't explore on your own), but free; tickets can be obtained at the Independence Visitor Center, where they come with a tour of the Bishop White House. John Todd, Jr., was a young Quaker lawyer of moderate means. His house, built in 1775, cannot compare to that of Bishop White, but it is far grander than Betsy Ross's. Todd used the ground-floor parlor as his law office and the family lived and entertained on the second floor. When Todd died in the 1793 epidemic of yellow fever, his vivacious widow Dolley married a Virginia lawyer named James Madison, the future president.

Continue for 2½ blocks down 4th Street to no. 321, the:

⑬ Physick House

This is possibly the finest residential structure in Society Hill. See p. 142 for a full description. Take a few steps east on adjoining Cypress Street to reach **Delancey Park,** more popularly known as "Three Bears Park," a delightful playground with places to play and a group of stone bears that are perfect photo props.

Continue south along 4th Street. More Georgian and Federal church facades appear at the corners of 4th and Pine streets. If you like, take a detour and keep going south on 4th Street to Lombard and South streets, where you'll find South Street's funky shopping and nightlife district. When you're through, head back to 3rd Street, which you'll take north to Walnut Street. Go right (east) on Walnut to 2nd Street and:

⑭ City Tavern

Built in 1773, demolished in 1854, and reconstructed in 1948, this was the most opulent and genteel tavern and social hall in the Colonies and the scene of many discussions among the Founding Fathers. Unlike most of the city's pubs, it was built with businessmen's subscriptions, to assure quality. George Washington met with most delegates to the Constitutional Convention for a farewell dinner here in 1787. The City Tavern (p. 88) now serves Colonial fare continuously from 11am. The back garden seating is shady and cool—perfect for a midafternoon break in warm weather.

If you choose to continue toward the Delaware via the pleasant pedestrian extension of Walnut Street and the staircase at its end, you'll pass between the Sheraton Society Hill hotel (p. 70) and the new incarnation of famous Bookbinder's restaurant (p. 89), winding up more or less in front of the wonderful Independence Seaport Museum and the new Hyatt Regency on the waterfront. See "Parks, the Parkway & Penn's Landing," in chapter 7 for more details on this area.

WALKING TOUR 2 OLD CITY

START:	**Franklin Court, 3rd and Chestnut streets.**
FINISH:	**Independence Square, 5th and Walnut streets.**
TIME:	**3 to 5 hours.**
BEST TIME:	**Start no later than 3pm to avoid museum closings. If contemporary art and socializing is your interest, the first Friday of every month brings special late hours for all galleries, cafes, and many historic attractions.**
WORST TIME:	**Afternoons.**

Old City is an intriguing blend of 17th- and 18th-century artisan row houses, robust 19th-century warehouses and commercial structures, and 20th-century rehabs of all of the above featuring artist lofts and galleries. Many of the cast-iron and brick buildings are being carefully restored and preserved; even if they are modern condos outside, their facades retain a sense of history.

---

❶ Franklin Court

This was Ben Franklin's final home, and is now a post office. See p. 124 for a full description.

Standing on Market Street, you can't miss the graceful spire of:

❷ Christ Church

Christ Church, with its restful benches and adjoining cemetery, has for centuries been Philadelphia's leading place of worship. See p. 133 for a full description.

> **TAKE A BREAK**
> It may be a bit early for a break, but the block of Church Street directly to the west of the church contains **Old City Coffee** at no. 221, a favorite place for marvelous coffee and light lunches. If the end of the day is approaching by the time you get here, duck underneath the Market Street ramp to I-95 at Front Street to reach **Panorama's** wine bar and bistro.

Walk east down Church Street and take a left at Front Street. Walk north along Front Street for 3 blocks to get the flavor of the 1830s warehouses, such as Girard at 18–30 N. Front St. and Smythe Stores at 101 Arch St. Take a left onto:

❸ Elfreth's Alley

Since 1702, this has been the oldest continuously occupied group of homes in America. See p. 136 for a full description of these tiny houses. Several courts are perfect for wandering into, and you can enter the house at no. 126 and shop at the gift boutique at no. 124.

Walk to the end of Elfreth's Alley and make a left back onto 2nd Street, with its china and restaurant-supply stores. Head south now and turn right on Arch Street, where you'll come to no. 239, the:

❹ Betsy Ross House

See p. 135 for full details on the apparent home of the first lady of flag making. The tour of the tiny dwelling is short, but there's a large garden to explore.

Continue west on Arch Street until you find 3rd Street. At the corner of 3rd Street, turn north (toward the Ben Franklin Bridge) to reach the:

❺ Old City Galleries & Shops

This stretch of 3rd Street is my favorite place to shop. Try the modern home goods at no. 117 **Minima** and the clothes and accessories at funky, pretty **Vagabond** at no. 37.

> **TAKE A BREAK**
> The blocks of 2nd and 3rd streets between Chestnut and Market contain lots of good, casual restaurants such as **Cuba Libre, Farmacia,** and **Society Hill Hotel and Restaurant.**

Cross 3rd Street to the Hoop Skirt Factory at 309–313 Arch St., dating from 1875, and the charming Loxley Court just beyond, designed by carpenter Benjamin Loxley in 1741. (It stayed within the family until 1901.) On the south side of Arch Street is the:

❻ Arch Street Meeting House

This is the largest Quaker meetinghouse in America, a simple 1805 structure with a substantial history. See p. 133 for details.

Walk west on Arch Street to the corner of 5th and Arch streets, where you'll find:

❼ Christ Church Burial Ground

This is the resting place of Benjamin and Deborah Franklin and other notables. Toss a penny—in honor (and defiance) of Ben's famous "A penny saved is a penny earned"—through the opening in the brick wall for luck.

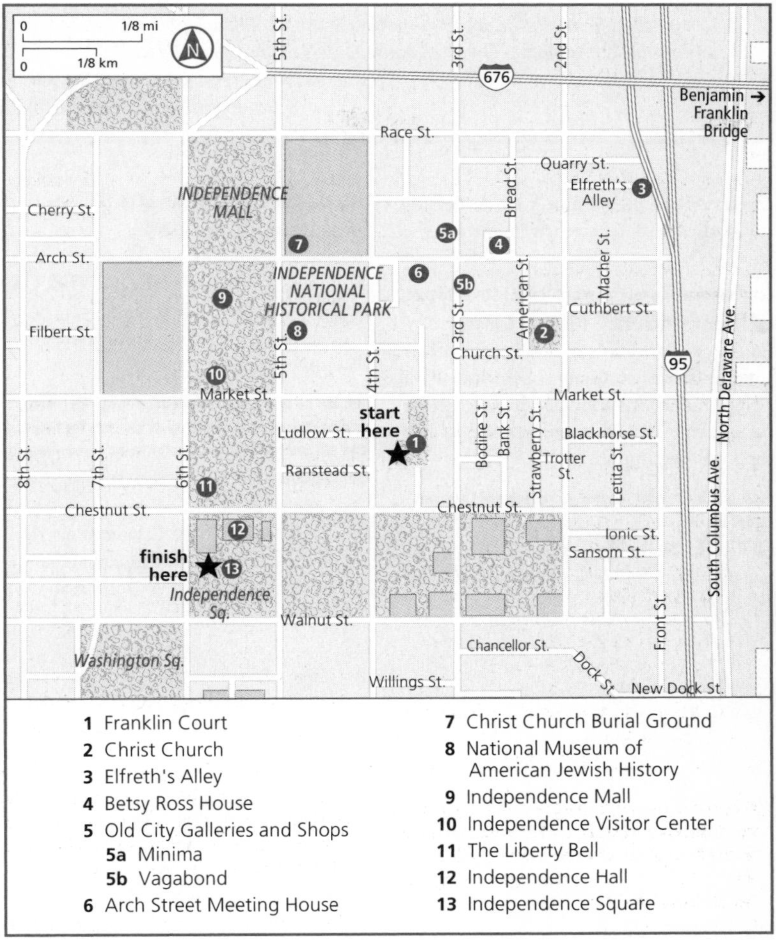

Walk south down 5th Street to 55 N. 5th St. to the:

8 National Museum of American Jewish History

The city of Philadelphia has a history of distinguished Jewish involvement in town affairs that's almost as long as the life of the city itself. This museum, connected to the city's oldest congregation, commemorates the history of Jews in America. The museum plans to relocate across the street to the current WHYY (local TV and radio station) building at 5th and Market streets in the fall of 2010. See p. 142 for a full description.

Across 5th and Market streets, you'll find the vast:

9 Independence Mall

Independence Mall is a swath of urban renewal that has recently been graced with

Impressions

[With its] streets of small, low, yet snug-looking houses . . . Philadelphia must contain in comfort the largest number of small householders of any city in the world.

—*London Times* reporter William Bussell,
My Diary North and South (1850)

the Independence Visitor Center, beautiful landscaping, and a new home for the Liberty Bell.

Continue walking south toward Market Street to the:

⑩ Independence Visitor Center

For a general rest stop, tickets to chief Independence National Historical Park sights, and information about the city and region, this facility is superb. See p. 119 for a full description.

Walk south, crossing Market Street toward Chestnut Street to:

⑪ The Liberty Bell

See p. 125 for a description and history of the bell.

Cross Chestnut Street, heading south to:

⑫ Independence Hall

Independence Hall and the two flanking buildings, **Congress Hall** and **Old City Hall** are described on p. 122. Tour hours and security-screening information are also given on this page.

Just on the other side of Independence Hall (north, toward Walnut St.) are plenty of benches for taking a load off and reviewing your whirlwind history lesson:

⑬ Independence Square

One of the quietest and nicest squares in the city, the site of the first, famous reading of the Declaration of Independence, is the perfect spot to end your excursion.

9

Shopping

by Lauren McCutcheon

Center City's shopping scene offers a refreshing antidote to big-box stores and all manner of malls. Here, shops seem to cluster in small, neighborhoody pockets. As you browse, you'll find many of the same chain stores that exist elsewhere in the United States, but those familiar names are interspersed with thoroughly unique, independently owned shops.

My favorite neighborhood for shopping is arty, stylish Old City, where a new boutique seems to open every season. Higher-end shops can be found on Walnut Street from Broad to 20th Street, aka "Rittenhouse Row." I love the handful of shops along 13th Street, too, between Walnut and Chestnut streets. The kid in me can't resist South Street's splash of sneaker parlors, vintage destinations, costume jewelry shops, and gift emporiums. And the grown-up in me savors walking along tree-lined Antique Row, an area of Pine Street between 9th and Broad streets.

For all its retail independence, Philly has shopping centers, too, albeit modest ones. You'll find them at the end of this chapter. But if you want to shop Bloomie's, Neiman's, Nordstrom, Crate & Barrel, or hundreds more familiar stores, you'll have to brave the traffic of the notoriously jammed Schuylkill Expressway (I-76W) to the Court, Plaza, and Pavilion in suburban King of Prussia, a mall comparable in size to Minnesota's sprawling Mall of America.

One more note, before you don the comfortable shoes and break out the plastic: In Pennsylvania, there is no sales tax on clothing. Other items are taxed at 7%. Most city stores are open daily from 10am to 6 or 7pm, often later on Wednesday and Friday.

1 SHOPPING A TO Z

ANTIQUES

With its tradition of fine furniture making since the 1700s, Philadelphia is a trove of antiques, which range from fine locally made chairs and desks to beautiful imports sold in intimate shops. Tree-lined Pine Street from 9th to 13th streets boasts a dozen or so antiques stores, some of which do their own refinishing and silver restoration (go to www.antique-row.org for listings). Old City stores mostly specialize in Art Deco and mid-20th-century modern pieces, and Germantown Avenue in Chestnut Hill also has fine antiques shops. As in any antiques market, you'll have to bring your own expertise to the store, and you'll have to trust your dealer. In April, several high-end antiques shows, including the prestigious **Philadelphia Antiques Show** (**© 215/387-3500;** www.philaantiques.com), are held at the Navy Yard, Philadelphia Cruise Terminal at Pier One, 5100 S. Broad St.

Antiquarian's Delight In a former synagogue just south of South Street, quirky vendors have stalls hawking everything from Bakelite bracelets to vintage Fiestaware to fur stoles to old fishing poles. Although this mishmash isn't exactly Freeman (see below), it's an odd, fun place to dig through merchandise, fall in love with a seashell brooch, and haggle. Closed Monday and Tuesday. 615 S. 6th St. (btw. South and Bainbridge sts.). ✆ **215/592-0256.**

Calderwood Gallery ★★★ Janet and Gary Calderwood are two of the country's foremost experts in very high-end French decorative arts (mostly Art Nouveau and Art Deco). Their impeccably restored furnishings are displayed beautifully in an impeccably renovated Rittenhouse Square town house. Though pieces run mostly $5,000 and up, the prices are reasonable compared to those in New York City. Open by appointment only on Sunday. 1622 Spruce St. ✆ **215/546-5357.** www.calderwoodgallery.com.

Freeman/Fine Arts of Philadelphia ★★ The dean of Philly's auction scene since 1805, Freeman specializes in Americana, and eBay has started streaming their sales in real time for online antiques lovers. Fully cataloged auctions for jewelry and fine furniture are held about once a month, often on Saturday. Regular auctions include antique and 20th-century modern home furnishings and some fine silver, rugs, jewelry, decorative arts, and, yearly, vintage fashions. 1808 Chestnut St. ✆ **215/563-9275.** www.freemansauction.com.

Gargoyles (**Value**) Among Society Hill antiques shops, Gargoyles stocks everything from toothpick holders to mantels and bars. Although much of the stock is American, there's also a delightful selection of English pub signs, dartboards, top hats, polo mallets, and the like. Several large items have been salvaged from 19th-century buildings and businesses. 512 S. 3rd St. ✆ **215/629-1700.** www.gargoylesltd.com.

John Alexander Ltd. ★★ Just off Germantown Avenue are 3,000 square feet holding one of the world's finest collections of British decorative arts furnishings (1860–1920). Dashing gallery owner John Levitties travels the globe in search of nearly priceless pieces, from Cotswold School cabinetry to delicate decanters. Open by appointment only on Sunday and Monday. 10–12 W. Gravers Lane (at Germantown Ave.). ✆ **215/242-0741.** www.johnalexanderltd.com.

M. Finkel and Daughter ★★ Just looking in the window of Morris and Amy Finkel's two-floor shop is a treat. On display are amazing, mint-condition schoolgirl samplers from the 17th through mid–19th centuries. The shop also sells marvelous folk art, furniture, and paintings. It is open weekends by appointment only; appointments are advised Monday through Friday. 936 Pine St. (at 10th St.). ✆ **215/627-7797.** www.samplings.com.

Mode Moderne ★★ Though not *officially* antiques, the wares at this Old City shop are vintage collectibles from the dawn of the modern era, such as Alan Gould's "string chair," Mies van der Rohe's Barcelona chaise, and starkly perfect tables by Paul McCobb and Eero Saarinen for Knoll. Mixed in are still-in-production pieces from the '50s and beyond, including George Nelson's classic atomic-age ball clock. 159 N. 3rd St. ✆ **215/627-0299.** www.modemoderne.com.

Moderne Gallery ★ Moderne is unique, specializing in vintage craft furniture. Owner Robert Aibel offers a very good selection of American and French ironworks—both furniture and decorative items. He's added inventory from the 1940s and 1950s, and features the world's largest selection of vintage pieces by renowned woodworkers such as George Nakashima. You'll also find books and fabrics with 20th-century designs. Closed Sunday and Monday. 111 N. 3rd St. (btw. Arch and Race sts.). ✆ **215/923-8536.** www.modernegallery.com.

Philadelphia Print Shop, Ltd. ★★ Fans of *Antiques Roadshow* might recognize Chestnut Hill shop owner and regular guest expert Donald Cresswell. The shop is a great source for antique maps, rare books, and old prints, with a nice under-$100 section of the latter. 8441 Germantown Ave. ✆ **215/242-4750.** www.philaprintshop.com.

W. Graham Arader III Gallery (Finds) Arader has become one of the country's leading rare-book, map, and print dealers in the past 20 years thanks to its aggressive purchasing techniques (which translates into high prices). You'll find a variety of interesting items here, including extra-rare prints from local naturalist John James Audubon. Closed Sunday. 1308 Walnut St. ✆ **215/735-8811.** www.aradergalleries.com.

ART GALLERIES

The line between art "galleries" and art "shops" is more blurred here than in many cities. Some galleries—mostly on and between 2nd and 3rd and Market and Race streets—stand out among the crowd for their superior quality. But it's fun to explore all of them on the "First Friday" night of every month, when they stay open late and draw crowds with free wine and snacks.

The Eyes Gallery Isaiah and Julia Zagar have presented a cheerful assortment of Latin American folk art, including *santos* and *retablos* (portable religious shrine panels and sculptures), for more than 30 years. Their shop is their showplace: Its walls are covered in Isaiah's omnipresent mosaic murals, which swath outside walls all over this part of town (the most famous of which is his *Magic Garden* at 10th and South sts.). Folksy clothing and sterling silver jewelry are also for sale. 402 South St. ✆ **215/925-0193.** www.eyesgallery.com.

Fleisher/Ollman Gallery This gallery is known for carrying fine, variable works by emerging contemporary and self-taught American artists such as Martin Ramirez. It is closed Sunday. 1616 Walnut St. ✆ **215/545-7562.** www.fleisher-ollmangallery.com.

Larry Becker Contemporary Art ★ An intimate Old City space for contemporary paintings and sculpture, Becker shows artists such as Steve Riedell and Stuart Arends. Appointments recommended Tuesday through Thursday. Closed Sunday and Monday. 43 N. 2nd St. (btw. Market and Arch sts.). ✆ **215/925-5389.** www.artnet.com/lbecker.html#.

Locks Gallery ★★★ This is a powerhouse gallery for paintings, sculptures, and mixed-media works, set in a Washington Square Beaux Arts building known for its serenity and elegance. You'll find works by artists such as Willem de Kooning, Warren Rohrer, David Hockney, and Robert Rauschenberg. Stylish owner Sueyun Locks aims "to help collectors get savvy," and there's more for the beginner than you might think. Closed Sunday and Monday. 600 Washington Sq. S. ✆ **215/629-1000.** www.locksgallery.com.

Newman Galleries ★ The oldest gallery in Philadelphia (founded in 1865), Newman Galleries has a strong representation of Bucks County artists, American sculptors, and traditional painters. Custom framing and art conservation work are also available. Signed, limited-edition prints start at $200. Closed Sunday. 1625 Walnut St. ✆ **215/563-1779.** www.newmangalleries.com.

Philadelphia Art Alliance ★ (Finds) Founded in 1915 in a striking mansion on Rittenhouse Square, the alliance now boasts exhibition space and performing/literary programs. The alliance's committee of laypersons and artists chooses the three floors of local talent displayed here. Closed Monday. 251 S. 18th St. (Rittenhouse Sq.). ✆ **215/545-4302.** www.philartalliance.org.

University of the Arts Rosenwald-Wolf Gallery This gallery in the heart of the Avenue of the Arts presents works by the University of the Arts faculty and students. It is open Monday through Friday from 10am to 5pm (Wed until 8pm) and Saturday and Sunday from noon to 4pm. 320 S. Broad St. ✆ **215/717-6480.** www.uarts.edu.

BOOKSTORES

AIA Bookstore and Design Center ★ This book and design store sells Aalto vases, lamps, journals, tabletop items, cards, and toys, along with architecture and design literature. Visit here at Christmas for the city's best selection of cards. The AIA also has an excellent downstairs gallery of architectural renderings, watercolors, and drawings. It is open Monday through Saturday from 10am to 6pm. 1218 Arch St. (in the Center for Architecture). ✆ **215/569-3188.** www.aiabookstore.com.

Barnes & Noble B&N's three floors (including a cafe) overlook Rittenhouse Square. The retailer stocks every imaginable tome and magazine (but not music). Visiting authors abound. 1805 Walnut St. ✆ **215/656-0716.** www.barnesandnoble.com.

Big Jar ★ (Finds) In Old City, you'd expect a used bookstore to have a sizable collection of trendy and substantive fiction and nonfiction supplemented by mouthwatering cookies, pastries, and espresso. It's all here. 55 N. 2nd St. (btw. Market and Arch sts.). ✆ **215/574-1650.**

Book Trader Relocated from South Street to Old City, the new Book Trader has even more room to display its impressive collection of discounted books. You can also find a good selection of secondhand and out-of-print books, used LPs, tapes, and CDs. 7 N. 2nd St. ✆ **215/925-0517.** http://phillybooktrader.googlepages.com.

Borders Center City's main Borders (there's a Borders Express in Liberty Place) spreads its magazines, cards, journals, CDs, coffee mugs, and, of course, books in a slightly confusing fashion throughout three floors of a historic building. 1 S. Broad St. (corner of S. Broad and Chestnut). ✆ **215/568-7400.** www.borders.com.

Cookbook Stall The space is tight at this cookbook shop in Reading Terminal Market, but the outstanding selection and helpful service draw many of Philly's top chefs. 12th St. (at Filbert St. in Reading Terminal Market). ✆ **215/923-3170.** www.thecookbookstall.com.

Head House Books ★★ (Finds) Opened in 2005, this cozy, neat-as-a-pin neighborhood bookstore stocks classics, bestsellers, and the best of the best children's books. It also hosts locals such as author Jennifer Weiner and Mural Arts Program director Jane Golden. 619 S. 2nd St. (btw. South and Bainbridge sts.). ✆ **215/923-9525.** www.headhousebooks.com.

Joseph Fox Bookshop ★ This tiny, walkup Rittenhouse-area shop is cozy, well organized, and always has what I want to read, whether it's George Eliot's *Middlemarch* or the new mystery by Janet Evanovich. Excellent for fiction and nonfiction, the shop often sponsors author signings at the Free Library. 1724 Sansom St. ✆ **215/563-4184.** www.foxbookshop.com.

The University of Pennsylvania Bookstore A 50,000-square-foot collaboration between U. Penn and Barnes & Noble, this store opened in 2000. It's a great academic bookstore, but you'll also find excellent selections of quality fiction and nonfiction and children's books; a 100-seat Starbucks cafe; a comprehensive music department with listening stations; last-minute accessories for a college interview; even sweatshirts that say PENN, NOT PENN STATE. 3601 Walnut St. (Sansom Commons). ✆ **215/898-7595.** www.upenn.bncollege.com.

CRAFTS

Philadelphia artisanship has always commanded respect. The tradition endures, both in small individual workshops and in cooperative stores. The Craft Show held every November at the convention center is one of the best in the country.

For outdoor crafts vendors, **Head House Square** bustles with booths from April to September, all day Saturday and Sunday afternoon. **Reading Terminal Market** has several booths devoted to tableware, wearable art, and South American and African crafts.

AIA Bookstore and Design Center ★ This book and design store specializes in small home furnishings, lighting, and drawings. Its also added custom framing to the list of services offered. In the fall, it becomes a gorgeous holiday shop and each spring, the center features Inuit sculpture and textiles. Connected to it is an excellent bookstore (see above). The store is open Monday through Saturday from 10am to 6pm. 1218 Arch St. (in the Center for Architecture). ✆ **215/569-3188.** www.aiabookstore.com.

Art Star ★★ Finds If you like the website Etsy, you'll adore this gallery-like Northern Liberties boutique, selling superfly handmade clothing, accessible fine art, amazing jewelry, and irresistible home accessories—all at amazing prices. Owners Megan Brewster and Erin Waxman are crafty artists, too; make sure to ask which awesome pieces are theirs. Open daily. 623 N. 2nd St. ✆ **215/238-1557.** www.artstarphilly.com.

The Black Cat ★ Finds Next door to University City's White Dog Café is a charmingly crafty boutique that's open late on weekends, so you can shop after dinner or before you head out to a birthday party. All items here—woven baskets, fragrant soaps, handcrafted jewelry, knitted caps, felted bags—are made according to socially responsible guidelines, many by international artisans paid fair wages, and many by local craftspeople. 3424 Sansom St. ✆ **215/386-6664.** www.blackcatshop.com.

Conspiracy Showroom ★ A 2006 pet project of the creatively powerful founding members of the Philly Craft Mafia, this loungey Northern Liberties boutique displays handmade jewelry, clothing, and handbags that are stylishly (and mostly locally) handmade—and definitely don't resemble anything handmade by your Aunt Gladys. 910 N. 2nd St. (north of Poplar St.). ✆ **215/925-2153.** www.conspiracyshowroom.com.

The Fabric Workshop and Museum Near the convention center is the only nonprofit arts organization in the United States devoted to creating, displaying, and selling new work in fabric and other materials. You'll find an abundance of finished fabric crafts on sale. The store also operates as a workshop center and collaborates with both emerging and recognized artists. Don't miss the Venturi and Red Grooms–designed bags, scarves, ties, and umbrellas. 1315 Cherry St., 5th Floor. ✆ **215/568-1111.** www.fabricworkshop.org.

Loop ★ Finds This beautiful, gallery-like knitting shop has a near spiritual reverence for yarn and the things that can be made with it. Skeins hang like precious sculpture along the white walls. Still, the help here couldn't be nicer, whether you're picking up a $12 wool or a $54 cashmere. Next door, adorable sister shop **Spool** sells fabrics, patterns, quilting projects, and more of equal cuteness. 1914 South St. ✆ **877/893-9939** or 215/893-9939. www.loopyarn.com. Spool: 1912 South St. ✆ 215/545-0755. www.spoolsewing.com.

Mew Gallery ★ Proof that the charms of South Philly are not lost on young artists and artisans lies in this gallery shop. Girly but tough, the chandelier-lit shop features bright silk-screened T-shirts, cool pet toys, funky jewelry, and objets d'art that you'll likely see replicated in Urban Outfitters next season. The gallery also holds craft workshops for kids and adults. Closed Monday. 906 Christian St. ✆ **215/625-2424.** www.mewgallery.org.

Rosie's Yarn Cellar This well-stocked, basement-level yarn store has fueled the knitting careers of hundreds of Philadelphians. A block from Rittenhouse Square, Rosie's gets busy during lunch hours and just after work. 2017 Locust St. ✆ **215/977-9276.** www.rosiesyarncellar.com.

DEPARTMENT STORES

Daffy's For the patient shopper, Daffy's offers value on name and house brands for men, women, and children in a beautiful 1920s Art Deco building (now a bit downscale) that once housed the luxurious Bonwit Teller store. Prices are 40% to 75% off regular retail, and men's Italian suits, children's clothing, and lingerie are particular bargains. Sometimes the selection is very picked over; occasionally it can be fun. 1700 Chestnut St. ✆ **215/963-9996.** www.daffys.com.

Macy's This landmark store was once Wanamaker's, a Philadelphia classic and one of the country's first great department stores. Now, Macy's is running things, offering stock that's a shadow of what existed back in the day. Still, the giant eagle—John Wanamaker's motif—stands tall in the center of the dazzling center courtyard, right between the Cosmetics and Men's departments. This Macy's is missing a Home Accessories Department, but does a fine job stocking widely available, mostly American, designers.

The time to stop by here is in December. The center courtyard presents a wonderful Christmas light show while the building's massive, 30,000-pipe organ plays carols. A small cafe overlooks the scene from a third-floor terrace. 1300 Market St. (entrances on Chestnut, 13th, and Juniper sts.). ✆ **215/241-9000.** www.macys.com.

FASHION

Center City has a **Banana Republic** at Broad and Walnut streets (✆ 215/751-0292), a **BCBG** at 1601 Walnut St. (✆ 215/665-1917), and a **bebe** at 1423 Walnut St. (✆ 215/569-2118). It has two **Benetton** stores, one at 1520 Walnut St. (✆ 215/546-9830) and the other in Liberty Place, 1625 Chestnut St. (✆ 215/864-0678). It has both **Brooks Brothers,** 1513 Walnut St. (✆ 215/564-4100), and **Burberry,** 1616 Walnut St. (✆ 215/545-6003). It has a **Club Monaco** at 1503 Walnut St. (✆ 215/567-7071), a **Coach** at 1703 Walnut St. (✆ 215/564-4558), and a **Cole Haan** at 1600 Walnut St. (✆ 215/985-5801). **Lucky Jeans, Jones New York, Ann Taylor, Talbot's,** and **Zara** are also all on Walnut. There's a **J. Crew** in Liberty Place, 1625 Chestnut St. (✆ 215/977-7335). A handsome **Ralph Lauren** is in the Bellevue, and **Gap** seems to be everywhere.

You could spend all day in these chains—and have fun doing it. For those of you who'd like to discover the more unique charms of Philadelphia's retail scene, here's a list of independently owned and/or locally significant Philadelphia shops.

Men's & Women's Fashion

Anthropologie Original to Philadelphia, the younger yet more mature sister of Urban Outfitters (see below) holds court in the decadently chic Van Rensselaer Mansion on Rittenhouse Square. The store is stocked from basement to third floor with pretty designer pieces and the store's own label. Both wearable and decorative merchandise are inspired by bazaars, artisan shops, and boutique finds in Europe, India, and right here in Philadelphia. The below-ground basement is home to amazing sale racks. 18th and Walnut sts. ✆ **215/568-2114.** www.anthropologie.com.

Boyd's This white wedding cake of a store has a grand entrance under a maroon canopy, a large valet parking lot across the street, and every major men's designer from Armani to Zegna. In recent years, the utterly gentlemanly (and, some might say, old gentlemanly)

Boyd's invited in high-end Govberg Jewelers, and expanded their Women's Department to include pieces by Dolce & Gabbana, Alice Temperly, Escada, and Manolo Blahnik.

Family owned, the place is intended for persons accustomed to luxury, from the gorgeous marble and columns to the omnipresent, never-ending, follow-you-around-the-store service. Boyd's has 65 tailors on-site, and a mezzanine cafe is overseen by French chef Georges Perrier. Sale periods are January and July. 1818 Chestnut St. ✆ **215/564-9000.** www.boydsphila.com.

H&M Philadelphia is home to two of these quick-turnover, fast-paced, low-cost fashion stores. The one on Chestnut Street aims at a younger, more budget-conscious shopper. The newer location on Walnut has slightly fatter wallets in mind. 1530 Chestnut St. (at 16th St.). ✆ **215/561-6178** and 1725 Walnut St. ✆ 215/563-2221. www.hm.com.

Lost & Found ★★ Value This buoyant Old City shop is run by a casually stylish mother and daughter. The look here is anything but buttoned down: easy printed T-shirts for both sexes, retro shirts for the guys, breezy skirts, long tops, stretchy dresses, Seychelles kicks, Orla Kiely bags, and pretty baubles for the ladies. Cost-conscious Lost & Found gets packed on weekends: If you see something you like, grab it today. It might not be here tomorrow. 133 N. 3rd St. ✆ **215/928-1311.**

Urban Outfitters This amazingly successful, ever-youthful chain started in these parts a while back, and eventually spread to college shopping areas and suburban malls the country over. Philly's two fun-to-explore locations offer clothes your parents wouldn't understand and dorm room accessories you've gotta have next semester. (There are two more in high-rent shopping districts in the city's environs: You could call them SubUrban Outfitters.) 1627 Walnut St. ✆ **215/569-3131** and 110 W. 36th St. ✆ 215/387-6990. www.urbanoutfitters.com.

Children's Fashion

Born Yesterday Right on Rittenhouse Square, this store outfits babies, boys to size 8, and girls to size 10 in current, stylish fashions. Trendy items such as adorable black velvet dresses with matching leggings are sold alongside traditional hand-knit baby sweaters, supersoft French onesies, and old-fashioned quilts. For the baby who has everything—and wants more. 1901 Walnut St. ✆ **215/568-6556.** www.bornyesterdayphila.com.

Children's Boutique All the high-end labels are here, plus luxurious party clothes, design-your-own cotton sweaters, and an excellent selection of adorable shoes, from classic to trendy. The store has a large Infant's Department and stocks some toys; sizes range up to 14 or 16. 1702 Walnut St. ✆ **215/732-2661.** www.echildrensboutique.com.

Genes ★ One of a handful of extrahip children's shops, this boutique offers the latest from Splendid, Ella Moss, C&C California, and other designers you didn't realize dressed pint-size fashionistas. Also for sale: Modern nursery furnishings, books, toys, and more. 122 S. 13th St. ✆ **215/735-4300.** www.shopgenes.com.

Lolli Lolli Pretty much the only place to outfit and gift wee ones in the greater Old City area, this darling walk-up shop stocks classic toys, cute place mats, and plenty of adorable garments for infants and children through age 12. 713 Walnut St. ✆ **215/625-2655.** www.lollilolli.net.

Piccolini ★ Rocker T-shirt dresses, chic changing tables, and organic burp cloths add up to just what any unsuspecting infant (read: stylishly minded parent) wants, and this sweet little shop is excellently suited to provide all of the above. 264 S. 20th St. ✆ **215/545-0395.** www.piccolinionline.com.

Spring Garden St.
Spring Garden
Philadelphia Museum of Art
FRANKLINTOWN
Eakins Oval
22nd St.
Hamilton St.
Rodin Museum
19th St.
18th St.
17th St.
16th St.
15th St.
Broad St.
Hamilton St.
Noble St.
Philadelphia Print Shop, Ltd.
To Manayunk and King of Prussia
John Alexander Ltd
Callowhill St.
The Benjamin Franklin Parkway
676
Schuylkill River
Winter St.
Logan Square
Race/Vine
Race St.
Pennsylvania Convention Center
Cherry St.
PARKWAY/MUSEUMS DISTRICT
Arch St.
30th Street Station
Suburban Station
Market East Station
JFK Blvd.
Philadelphia Stock Exchange
The Black Cat
15th
13th
Market St.
City Hall
City Hall
22nd
19th
One Liberty Place
University of Pennsylvania Bookstore
Ludlow
PENN CENTER
Juniper St.
13th St.
12th St.
Chestnut St.
Urban Outfitters
Sansom St.
Sansom St.
Walnut St.
Walnut St.
RITTENHOUSE SQUARE DISTRICT
Rittenhouse Square
Walnut/Locust
Locust St.
15th/16th
Merriam Theater
12th/13th
Schuylkill River Park
Spruce St.
Kimmel Performing Arts Center
Fitler Square
Delancey Pl.
UNIVERSITY OF THE ARTS
Pine St.
20th St.
Lombard/South
25th St.
24th St.
23rd St.
Lombard St.
GRADUATE HOSPITAL DISTRICT
South St.

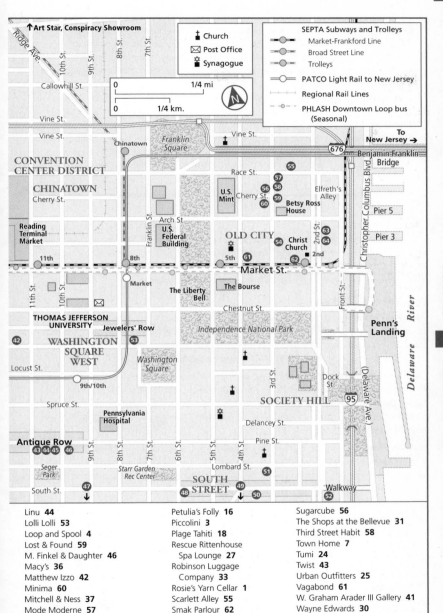

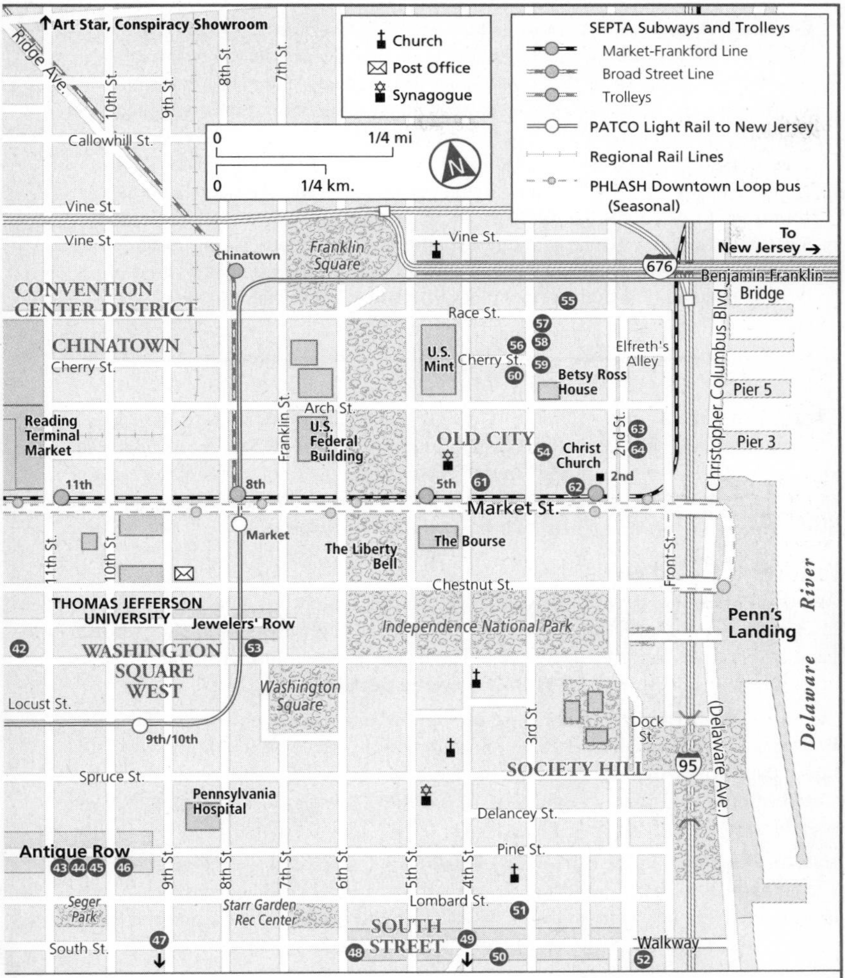

Linu **44**
Lolli Lolli **53**
Loop and Spool **4**
Lost & Found **59**
M. Finkel & Daughter **46**
Macy's **36**
Matthew Izzo **42**
Minima **60**
Mitchell & Ness **37**
Mode Moderne **57**
Open House **39**
Petulia's Folly **16**
Piccolini **3**
Plage Tahiti **18**
Rescue Rittenhouse Spa Lounge **27**
Robinson Luggage Company **33**
Rosie's Yarn Cellar **1**
Scarlett Alley **55**
Smak Parlour **62**
Sophy Curson **6**
Sugarcube **56**
The Shops at the Bellevue **31**
Third Street Habit **58**
Town Home **7**
Tumi **24**
Twist **43**
Urban Outfitters **25**
Vagabond **61**
W. Graham Arader III Gallery **41**
Wayne Edwards **30**

Finds Throwback Proball Jerseys, Jackets & Caps

Century-old Philly merchant **Mitchell & Ness,** 1318 Chestnut St. (✆ **267/765-0613;** www.mitchellandness.com), doesn't need to advertise its wares. The athletes who first wore them take care of that. The company, originally a traditional sporting goods shop, specializes in authorized reproductions of pro and college team get-ups. Almost every item is limited edition, which means if you want an exact copy of Wayne Gretzky's LA Kings road jersey (ca. 1993); Junior Seau's '94 alternate jersey from the Chargers championship game; Mickey Mantle's home shirt from '51 or '52, the Saints' '06 warm-up jacket, or a red, white, and blue wool Sixers team jacket, you'll have to buy it soon—and pay a pretty penny. Just about every pro athlete and hip-hop star collects Mitchell & Ness nostalgia. If you drop by during store hours but the door's locked, chances are a celebrity's doing some shopping.

Men's Fashion

Wayne Edwards ★ Prada loafers, Paul Smith shirts, and Jil Sander sportswear are among the finds at this spare and sleek metrosexual shop. Wayne Edwards's jet-setting shoppers are treated right, with cold drinks. They're paying for the service, but for the quality, too. 1525 Locust St. ✆ **215/731-0120.** www.wayne-edwards.com.

Women's Fashion

Adresse Fashionistas love this spare, unusual boutique, where you can find stylish investment pieces. Maybe a gorgeous Peter Som dress, a Givenchy skirt, a splurge-worthy Lambertson Truex handbag, or a piece of handmade jewelry is just what your wardrobe is missing. 1706 Locust St. ✆ **215/985-3161.** www.adressephiladelphia.com.

Echochic ★★ Finds If you're the type who covets Botkier handbags, See by Chloe, Bodybag, Twinkle, and Rachel Pally, you'll enjoy this party-minded, cutting-edge boutique, popular with bankrolled Penn students, visiting celebs, and certain unnamed writers prone to occasional spending sprees. 1700 Sansom St. ✆ **215/569-9555.** www.echochic.com.

Jacques Ferber In the market for a $60,000 sable coat, or a sheared-mink scarf for a few hundred dollars? Beyond the elegant Art Deco brass windows, this local family-owned furrier stocks white-mink ski parkas alongside full-length classics and Longchamps handbags. 1708 Walnut St. ✆ **215/735-4173.** www.jacquesferber.com.

Joan Shepp Boutique ★★★ This much-loved, bi-level store elegantly presents an eclectic, extrachic mix of Chloe bags, antique jewelry, Wolford hosiery, Miu Miu pumps, and especially clothing. Among the Yohji Yamamotos, Marnis, Dries Van Notens, and Junya Watanabes, you'll occasionally find spectacular bargains. On Wednesday, dressmaker Irina Sigal stops by to work her seam-changing magic. You can't miss everybody's favorite salesperson, Tuesday, the best-dressed person in Philadelphia. 1616 Walnut St. ✆ **215/735-2666.** www.joanshepp.com.

Knit Wit In a sleek spot with windows on Walnut Street, Ann Gitter's Knit Wit specializes in contemporary fashions and accessories from designers such as Miu Miu, Habitual, and Blumarine. The cases are filled with amazing estate jewelry. The tough-love salespeople are brutally honest when it comes to telling you exactly what you need. Sales come in March and September. 1721 Walnut St. ✆ **215/564-4760.** www.knitwitonline.com.

Petulia's Folly Finding the kind of fashions that grace the pages of *Lucky* is just a matter of walking in the door of this two-room shop. Rag and Bone, Jovovich-Hawk, Catherine Malandrino, and Phillip Lim are all here, as are pretty home goods. 1710 Sansom St. ✆ **215/569-1344.** www.petuliasfolly.com.

Plage Tahiti This tiny, selective, trend-minded store has original separates with an artistic slant from Theory, Ghost, and Garfield + Marks. The second-floor sale racks have some real steals in Betsey Johnson dresses and the like. As the name suggests, French bathing suits are a constant. 128 S. 17th St. ✆ **215/569-9139.**

Smak Parlour ★ Finds Old City's cutest boutique resembles its owners: pretty, perky, and creative. Fresh designers Abby Kessler and Katie Loftus design each hooded top, checkered sundress, and smart jacket in their girly Old City shop. Also for sale: bright Tarina Tarintino jewelry, kicky Jeffrey Campbell shoes, and boudoir necessities. 219 Market St. ✆ **215/625-4551.** www.smakparlour.com.

Sophy Curson ★★ There is something very Audrey Hepburn–ish about this dress shop (ca. 1929). At Sophy Curson, trying on a Lanvin frock or Lacroix gown isn't about skimming the racks. It's about the staff getting to know you, gauging your style, and then disappearing into the back to return with your couture options. All this fuss makes the boutique best suited for an older clientele, although it can be much fun for younger princesses, too. 19th and Sansom Sts. ✆ **215/567-6442.** www.sophycurson.com.

Sugarcube ★★★ Finds Not all of us are ready to invest seriously in fashion, but this Old City vintage-meets-new shop sure makes me want to. Owner Elisa Burrato—official candidate for friendliest Philadelphian—traffics in A.P.C., Veena, Wrangler, awesome one-of-a-kind jewelry, amazingly perfect secondhand cowboy boots, bright pumps, Prada sweaters, and dressy dress-ups. Most of all, she's awesome at summing up styles. 124 N. 3rd St. ✆ **215/238-0825.** www.sugarcube.us.

Third Street Habit ★ Old City's highest-end shop stocks an it list of designers: Cynthia Rowley, Burning Torch, Alex Woo, L.A.M.B., Splendid, and Gentle Fawn among them. The setup is stylishly familiar, with an old wooden floor and sweet tunes playing on the sound system. 153 N. 3rd St. ✆ **215/925-5455.** www.thirdstreethabit.com.

Finds Rescue Rittenhouse Spa Lounge ★★★

One floor above the din of bustling 17th Street is Philadelphia's most tranquil—and toniest—day spa. **Rescue Rittenhouse Spa Lounge,** 255 S. 17th St. (✆ **215/772-2766;** www.rescuerittenhousespa.com), has a devoted following among Philadelphia's most discerning spagoers. Patrons swear by the magical "biolift" facials (everyone who does skin here is amazing), ethereal massages, impeccable mani-pedis, and flawless makeup application. You'll crawl into one of the robes, sip a glass of cucumber-mint water, curl up on a cushy white sofa, and never want to leave—at least, not without a bagful of magical products from Biologique Recherche, Valmont, or Chantecaille.

Vagabond ★★★ The shop that started this whole Old City thing, Vagabond belongs to designers Megan Murphy and Mark Clark, a dressmaker and a knitter, respectively. Original plank flooring and exposed brick walls make the space feel just right for the neighborhood. A nice supply of yarns makes it feel crafty, as does an increasing stock of handmade cards and home gifts. But let's be honest: The ladies come here for the fashions—swingy hand-knit Stellapop sweaters (Mark's designs, also sold at Steven Alan, Barney's, and the like), ruched leather bags, fitted little black dresses, and great artisan-made jewelry. 37 N. 3rd St. ✆ **267/671-0737.** www.vagabondboutique.com.

FOOD

Also see the review of the **Reading Terminal Market** (p. 101) at 12th and Market streets, with its dozens of individual booths and cafes.

Assouline & Roth ★ An astonishing selection of oils, chocolates, caviar, and other delicacies greets you at this superb gourmet market. There's an excellent selection of gift baskets. The market is open Monday through Friday from 10am to 4pm. 2050A Richmond St. ✆ **215/627-3000.** www.assoulineandroth.com.

Chef's Market ★ (Finds) The premier gourmet store in Society Hill offers a staggering array of charcuterie, cookbooks, and condiments. Would you believe, breads and cakes from 20 different bakeries? (It's also a great place to pop by for a quick brunch or lunch.) 231 South St. ✆ **215/925-8360.** www.chefsmkt.com.

Di Bruno Bros. ★★ The original shop is in the Italian Market; now you can also go to Chestnut Street for this gourmet market, quick lunch spot, and cafe, the local version of Dean & DeLuca. The strongest suit here is the cheese selection, but I wouldn't turn down an offer of Carmella's pasta, stuffed peppers, or Le Bec-Fin-made pastry, either. 1730 Chestnut St. ✆ **215/665-9220.** www.dibruno.com.

Italian Market ★★ (Finds) The Italian Market feels like it's straight out of another era, with pushcarts and open stalls selling fresh goods, produce, and cheese Tuesday through Saturday (the end of the week is better). Many shops are open until noon on Sunday. Particular favorites are **Di Bruno Bros.** at 930 S. 9th St. (✆ **888/322-4337** or 215/922-2876) for cheese, **Sarcone's Bakery** at 758 S. 9th St. (✆ **215/922-0445**) for sesame-seeded Italian bread, **Isgro's** at 10th and Christian streets (✆ **215/923-3092**) for cannoli, and **Fante's** at 1006 S. 9th St. (✆ **215/922-5557**) for kitchenware. To reach the market, head 5 blocks south of South Street. 9th St. btw. Fitzwater and Wharton sts. Bus: SEPTA 47.

Whole Foods Market Whole Foods has a wonderful selection of the finest natural and organic foods, including a great assortment of prepared dishes and oven-baked goods. Generous samples in every aisle, too. 2001 Pennsylvania Ave. ✆ **215/557-0015** and 929 South St. ✆ 215/733-9788. www.wholefoodsmarket.com.

GIFTS & HOME GOODS

You will run into basic historic Philadelphia memorabilia all over Society Hill and Independence National Historical Park, beginning with the gift shop at the Independence Visitor Center at 6th and Market streets. Here are some spots for more unique gifts.

Blendo ★★ An amazing sidewalk sale announces this eclectic, fun, and often cramped shop, where you could find a vintage painting, retro ashtray, wooden toy, letterpress stationery, proper hat, enamel earrings, or an exact replica of your mother's old cocktail set, umbrella stand, or beach bag. If you don't see it, ask. It's probably there, among the shelves. Hours vary by season. 1002 Pine St. ✆ **215/351-9260.** www.shopblendo.com.

Foster's Homeware ★★ If you love modern home decor, you must visit Old City's Foster's for cool, whimsical wares ranging from Karim Rashid's light-up bowling pins and Ittala dishes to rubber ducks and Chilewich table runners. Great vases, plates, frames, clocks, cards, and toys fill out the space. 399 Market St. ✆ **800/734-8511** or 215/925-0950. www.shopfosters.com.

Hello World ★ At its locations on Antique Row and south of Rittenhouse Square, Hello World is the quintessential gift shop. The pretty freshwater pearl earrings, Hobo bags, reworked vintage furnishings, bright pillows, and French tablewares make great gifts for hosts (or for yourself). 1201 Pine St. ✆ **215/545-7060** and 257 S. 20th St. and 1201 Pine St. ✆ 215/545-5207. www.shophelloworld.com.

Linu (Finds) This Antique Row shelter shop easily converts shoppers to the European way of sleeping—on durable, soft linen. The owner imports much of her stock from cooperatives of weavers in Latvia, and sells the bedding and table linens alongside modern pottery, stone necklaces, candles, and vases. 1034 Pine St. ✆ **215/206-8547.** www.linuboutique.com.

Matthew Izzo ★★ Interior designer Matthew Izzo moved from New York to Philly in 2002—and the city hasn't been the same since. His spacious Walnut Street shop feels like an oversize living room, with plenty of Jonathan Adler couches, tables, and pottery, along with pod chairs, handmade candles, racks of clothes in back, and Izzo's own artwork. 1109 Walnut St. ✆ **215/829-0606.** www.matthewizzo.com.

Minima ★★ Lovers of modern design will find refuge in this spare, white furnishings gallery, where classic designs by Jasper Morrison, Piero Lissoni, Patrick Norguet, and Philippe Starck are displayed like individual works of art. 118. N. 3rd St. ✆ **215/922-2022.** www.minima.us.

OLC ★★ If you're just passing through, you might not have use for the design services of this impeccably modern lighting and art gallery, one of Old City's pioneers. Still, stop in for a look at one of the best collections of pieces from Knoll, Cassina, B&B Italia, Artemide, and Ingo Mauer on the East Coast. You'll want to move in. Closed Monday and Tuesday. 152–154 N. 3rd St. ✆ **215/923-6085.** www.olc152.com.

Open House ★★ This 13th Street shop is another place to find small gifts (wee bright vases in interesting shapes, seashell balls, espresso cups, and candles) and large ones (coffee tables, silk pillows, pottery trays, and bedding). The look is neither modern nor traditional, rustic nor sleek, but it's definitely today. Great for gifts. 107 S. 13th St. ✆ **215/922-1415.** www.openhouseliving.com.

Scarlett Alley ★ Close by the Betsy Ross House is a boutique that sells the best engagement and birthday gifts in Old City: Italian cordial glasses, hand-painted bowls, clocks, candlesticks, table linens, and more. Sniff the fresh flowers as you walk in and slowly take in all the colors and textures. 241 Race St. ✆ **215/592-2898.** www.scarlettalley.com.

Town Home ★★ Philadelphia society girl Dana Bank has made this Rittenhouse Square shop into a shopping destination among discerning shoppers. Cashmere blankets, crystal vases, shell bowls, baby goods, and gift baskets are all for sale—and very stylishly so. 126 S. 19th St. ✆ **215/972-1500.** www.townhomephila.com.

Twist ★ A contemporary shelter shop along Antique Row, Twist offers reworked vintage armchairs, bright African baskets, old European tower clocks, pretty tea sets, hefty tables, bright pillows, and light-as-air linens. The owners are designers in their own right and offer great advice. 1134 Pine. St. ✆ **215/925-1242.** www.twisthome.com.

JEWELRY & SILVER

Many of the city's jewelers can be found within a couple of city blocks at **Jeweler's Row,** centering on Sansom and Walnut streets and 7th and 8th streets, which touts itself as offering 30% to 50% off retail prices. This area contains more than 350 retailers, wholesalers, and craftspeople. Particularly notable is quirky **I Switt,** 130 S. 8th St. (✆ **215/922-3830**), for its trove of vintage and antique jewelry.

Halloween ★★★ Finds There's no sign outside Philadelphia's most unique jewelry store, just an orange business card in the window. Ring the bell, and descend into owner Henri David's real-life fantasy: wall-mounted cases dripping with strands of pearls, chunky Gothic silver, oversize opal pins, and gold chains galore. Some pieces are vintage, but most are made by David's team of artists—this is the spot to have your custom jewelry made. The place is named for the owner's favorite holiday, which he celebrates by throwing one of the largest and most lavish costume balls in existence. 1329 Pine St. ✆ **215/732-7711.**

Lagos Lagos is known for its striking, fashion-forward settings and unusually colored gems, like evergreen topaz. Oprah is a fan. 1735 Walnut St. ✆ **215/567-0770.** www.lagos.com.

Linde Meyer Gold & Silver ★ This nook on the ground-floor passage to the central atrium of Liberty Place presents contemporary designer jewelry from Niessing, Georg Jensen, and Henrich+Denzel in precious metals, along with an adjoining collection of estate jewelry and giftware. Meyer's taste in jewelry is impeccable. Trust it. 1625 Chestnut St. (Liberty Place). ✆ **215/851-8555.**

Niederkorn Silver Antique baby items, dressing-table adornments, napkin rings, picture frames, and Judaica are featured here. Also on display is Philadelphia's largest selection of period silver, including works of such fine crafters as Jensen, Tiffany, and Spratling. 2005 Locust St. ✆ **215/567-2606.** www.niederkornsilver.com.

Tiffany & Co. ★ The Philadelphia Tiffany & Co. feels special, especially since its renovation into two, contemporary floors. Although best known for their perfect diamonds, Tiffany also stocks designs by Frank Gehry, along with many items under $100. The sales staff here is wonderful and helpful. 1414 Walnut St. (the Bellevue). ✆ **215/735-1919.** www.tiffany.com.

LUGGAGE

Robinson Luggage Company At this recently expanded flagship of six regional locations, you'll find a great selection of leather gear, along with discounted travel accessories and briefcases. Broad and Walnut sts. ✆ **215/735-9859.** www.robinsonluggage.net.

Tumi It's worth noting that in 2008, this popular brand of stylishly durable luggage opened a store near Rittenhouse Square. 1733 Walnut St. ✆ **215/564-1317.** www.tumi.com.

MUSIC

A.K.A. Music ★★ Whether you want a line on the next big local band or would like to browse stacks of used CDs in peace, you can find what you're looking for at this Old

City shop. Knowledgeable salespeople won't look down on you for stocking up on greatest hits albums; nor will they shy away from making recommendations based on your current faves. A.K.A.'s also a great place to pick up concert info. 27 N. 2nd St. ✆ **215/922-3855.**

Borders A vast selection is sold at this supersize bookstore, from classical to jazz, pop, and rock, with all CDs available for previews at listening stations. 1 S. Broad St. ✆ **215/568-7400.** www.borders.com.

Cue Records ★ Finds From its modest, just-south-of-South digs, this music store serves up all manner of tunes. Hard-to-find music is easy to find at Cue, where you can score erstwhile sold-out soul 45s and 12-inch vinyl from A Tribe Called Quest, plus imports—Latin jazz, Latin, Icelandic hip-hop, whatever. 617 S. 4th St. ✆ **215/413-3525.**

Hideaway Music ★ Among Chestnut Hill's preppy boutiques and antiques stores, the owner of this friendly shop will special order that rare Wham import for you or gently push you toward new releases. 8428 Germantown Ave. ✆ **215/248-4434.**

Main Street Music This Manayunk repository is the go-to shop for fans of locally based, public independent music station WXPN. They've got a full stock of Flaming Lips, B. B. King, and John Mayer—and often show off local bands that deserve a listen. 4444 Main St. ✆ **215/487-7732.**

611 Records ★ Finds Across from Cue (above), this joint caters to DJs—the pros, man. You'll find drum and bass, techno, house, and electroclash cassettes, CDs, and vinyl here—plus the tools to play and tote them in. You won't, however, find much in the way of Dave Matthews. 611 S. 4th St. ✆ **215/413-9100.** www.611records.com.

Theodore Presser Music Store Known primarily as a piano store since 1900, this store (formerly called Jacobs Music Co.) is Center City's best source of sheet music for classical and pop musicians alike. 1718 Chestnut St. ✆ **215/568-0964.**

SHOES

Here is a list of specialty shoe stores. Philadelphia Runner and Rittenhouse Sports (see "Sporting Goods," below) sell sneakers. Joan Shepp, Vagabond, Lost & Found, Sugarcube, Smak Parlour, and Macy's (all reviewed elsewhere in this chapter) also sell shoes.

Benjamin Lovell Shoes ★★ Center City has two Benjamin Lovells—one in Rittenhouse, and the original, along South Street. The locally based chain (there are around a half-dozen elsewhere) focuses mainly on stylish comfort, so you'll find plenty of options from Merrell, Ugg, Ecco, Dansko, and Naot, as well as fresh kicks by Cole Haan, Michael Kors, and Camper. Ben's help is the best at fit and look. His South Street store is famous for its backroom sales. 119 S. 18th St. ✆ **215/564-4655** and 318 South St. ✆ 215/238-1969. www.benjaminlovellshoes.com.

Bus Stop Boutique ★★★ Finds Colorful Fabric Row (S. 4th St.) provides a kicky setting for this absolutely addictive ladies' shoe store, where Brit-born owner Elena Brennan specializes in hard-to-find Continental designers, plus locally made jewelry, Look of London tights, and irresistible handbags. Closed Monday and Tuesday. 750 S. 4th St. ✆ **215/627-2357.** www.busstopboutique.com.

Head Start Shoes ★★ This corner store offers major scores on European options, particularly Italian, whether tame (Via Spiga) or edgy (Ixos). The prices aren't cheap, but they're not outrageous, either—and are vastly improved by regular sales. 126 S. 17th St. (on Sansom St.). ✆ **215/567-3247.** www.headstartshoes.com.

Sherman Brothers Old-fashioned Sherman Brothers sells fine men's shoes from Cole Haan, Allen Edmonds, Clarks, and Rockport—even in difficult sizes. Everything is discounted 10% to 25% all the time. 1520 Sansom St. ✆ **215/561-4550.** www.shermanbros.com.

SPORTING GOODS

City Sports This full-service store for the urban runner, in-line skater, baseball or hockey player, swimmer, or racquet-ball player has captured the Center City market. 1608 Walnut St. ✆ **215/985-5860.**

Eastern Mountain Sports This superstore near U. Penn has a complete line for hiking, trekking, and camping. Brands include Timberland, Patagonia, Woolrich, and the excellent house EMS brand. 130 S. 36th St. ✆ **215/386-1020.** www.ems.com.

The Original I Goldberg ★ Value This classic army-navy store sells everything you need to spend the night outdoors: tents, camp stoves, sleeping bags, and pocketknives. The business has been around since 1919, and stock has shifted, through the years, from gas masks to khaki Dickies. But it remains the best place in town to stock up on hiking boots and inexpensive knit caps, wool socks, and undershirts. 1300 Chestnut St. ✆ **215/925-9393.**

Philadelphia Runner ★ More than 250 styles of running and walking shoes is what sets this runner-run shop apart. If you can name the brand, they carry it, along with running tights, socks, shorts, T-shirts, and jackets. This is also the home of the Philadelphia Running Club and a good place to find out about training with a group. 1601 Sansom St. ✆ **215/972-8333.** www.philadelphiarunner.com.

Rittenhouse Sports Specialties ★ This shoebox-size store really packs in the gear—and knows its stuff. Overpronators, underpronators, pro athlete, and lazybones are all cared for by an owner-athlete who knows feet. This is the spot to pick up a little bit of everything sporty. 1729 Chestnut St. ✆ **215/569-9957.**

TOBACCO & CIGARS

Harry's Smoke Shop Harry's has been puffing along since 1938 and retrocool has caught up with its historic location. Premium cigars like Arturo Fuente, Macanudo, and Partegas are the specialty. You'll find shaving accessories here also. 15 N. 3rd St. ✆ **215/925-4770.**

Holt's Cigar Co. Holt's is renowned throughout the country for its selection of pipes and tobaccos. There are enough fresh cigars here to fill every humidor on Wall Street, plus an excellent pen selection. The opulent location and late hours fit perfectly with the neighborhood, and there is an upstairs cafe and bar, one of the few places left where you can light up a stogie. 1522 Walnut St. ✆ **215/732-8500.**

WINE & LIQUOR

After the repeal of Prohibition, Pennsylvania decided not to license private liquor retailing but to establish a government monopoly on alcohol sales. You can buy spirits only in state stores, wine in state stores or Pennsylvania winery shops (such as **Blue Mountain Vineyards** [✆ **215/238-9022**] in Reading Terminal Market), and beer in distributors, licensed delis or convenience stores, and some bars, where you'll likely pay way above retail.

This situation (plus the relative lack of small-maker wines) makes most out-of-town drinkers growl, or at least roll their eyes. Relief is coming slowly: Some state stores are now open daily, expanding their regular Monday-through-Friday 9am-to-9pm hours to include Sunday from noon to 5pm. Stores open daily include centrally located 1218

Chestnut St. (✆ **215/560-4380**), Society Hill/Independence Park–area 326 S. 5th St. (✆ **215/560-7064**), Rittenhouse at 1913 Chestnut St. (✆ **215/560-4215**), and West Philadelphia's 4049 Market St. (✆ **215/823-4709**). For a complete listing of all state-run wine and liquor stores, visit www.lcb.state.pa.us.

For beer—especially interesting craft brews and imports—I recommend the **Foodery,** with corner locations along Antique Row at 10th and Pine (✆ **215/928-1111**) and in Northern Liberties at 2nd and Poplar streets (✆ **215/238-6077**).

2 SHOPPING CENTERS

The Bellevue The lower floors of the Park Hyatt Philadelphia at the Bellevue house a small, upscale collection of retailers. The Ralph Lauren store here is the third largest in the world, boasting three floors of mahogany-and-brass splendor. Other tenants include Tiffany & Co., with its extraordinary jewelry, silver, and accessories; Williams-Sonoma for gourmet snacks and high-end kitchen supplies; a just-right fashionable Nicole Miller; Pierre & Carlo Salon for blowouts and flawless manicures; Teuscher Chocolates of Switzerland; and Origins cosmetics. Dine at the Palm Restaurant, grab a soy latte at Starbucks, or pick up spring rolls or soup at the lower-level food court. Broad and Walnut sts. ✆ **215/875-8350.** www.bellevuephiladelphia.com.

Franklin Mills *Value* Fifteen miles northeast of Center City, on the edge of Bucks County is the city's hugely popular outlet mall, with 220 discount and outlet stores within 1.8 million square feet. Franklin Mills is a bargain shoppers' landmark, with designer clothing at outlets from Saks Fifth Avenue, Neiman Marcus, Kenneth Cole, and Marshall's Home Goods. If you are diligent, you can dig up off-priced Chanel, Manolo Blahnik, and Gucci—or at least a nice Banana Republic sweater. 1455 Franklin Mills Circle. ✆ **800/336-6255** or 215/632-1500. www.franklinmills.com. Follow the signs from I-95 (take exit 35, Woodhaven Rd.) or from the Pa. Tpk. (take exit 351 south). Bus: SEPTA 20, 67, or 84.

The Gallery at Market East The Gallery at Market East, next to the Pennsylvania Convention Center, features four levels and more than 170 stores. A big Kmart anchors one end, sleek Ubiq is a haven for Nike connoisseurs, and Old Navy, Aldo, and an indoor basketball free-throw competition get a lot of traffic. The site inspired the Fresh Prince and Jazzy Jeff's adolescent diatribe "Parents Just Don't Understand," and Philly's teens continue to keep this place vibrant and cool. 8th to 11th and Market sts. ✆ **215/625-4962.** www.galleryatmarketeast.com.

King of Prussia Court and Plaza Aptly named, this is retail royalty: King of Prussia is, by some accounts, the largest mall in the country, impeccably designed and marketed, with more than 400 places to exercise your plastic in three connected tiers. The major stores include Bloomingdale's, JCPenney, Lord & Taylor, Neiman Marcus, Nordstrom, Macy's, and Sears. Other top-quality shops: Hugo Boss, Versace, Williams-Sonoma, Hermès, Sephora, Cartier, Thomas Pink, and Tiffany & Co. Restaurants here—California Pizza Kitchen, Cheesesteak Factory, California Café, Morton's—always seem to have lines out the door. The 126 acres of parking can make finding your car a postshopping adventure, while the drive in and out can be downright frustrating. Near junction of U.S. 202 and Pa. 422. ✆ **610/265-5727.** www.kingofprussiamall.com. Half-mile south of the Pennsylvania Tpk. Valley Forge exit 326, take Rte. 202 north; 3 miles south of Valley Forge National Historical Park via Rte. 422.

186 **The Shops at Liberty Place** (Kids) Liberty Place, the steely, 60-story tower that supplanted City Hall as the city's tallest spire, has a bi-level shopping area that contains 70 stores and stalls laid out in a sunbeam shape around a soaring, glass-domed rotunda. A food court occupies the second level. Retailers include J. Crew and Express for clothing, Nine West and Aldo for shoes, and Douglas Cosmetics. **Linde Meyer** (p. 182) is one of the center's local retailers. 1625 Chestnut St. (btw. 16th and 17th sts.). ✆ **215/851-9055.** www.shopsatliberty.com.

Philadelphia After Dark

by Lauren McCutcheon

Not so long ago, if you were exploring Philly after sunset, you were probably up to no good. These days, the Avenue of the Arts (S. Broad St. btw. Market and Pine sts.), Rittenhouse Square, Old City, and Northern Liberties come to life as the hour grows later and there are plenty of fun ways to occupy yourself.

For complete listings of what's going on and week-of discounts (called "Philly Fun Savers"), visit the **Greater Philadelphia Cultural Alliance** listings website, **Philly Fun Guide** at www.phillyfunguide.com, or call ✆ **215/557-7811.** Another all-inclusive website, www.gophila.com, offers a marvelous overview of Philadelphia's cultural landscape.

For commercial attractions such as large concerts, **Ticketmaster** (✆ **215/336-2000;** www.ticketmaster.com) is your best bet. Local ticket brokers such as the **Philadelphia Ticket Office,** 1500 Locust St. (✆ **215/735-1903** or 545-1527), or **Ticket Warehouse** (✆ **888/252-8499;** www.ticketwarehouse.com) are also reliable. Out-of-state brokers may have better selections, though their prices could be exorbitant.

1 THE PERFORMING ARTS

Music, theater, and dance are presented regularly all over the city. I have restricted the venues below to those in Center City and West Philadelphia, where you'll be most of the time, and where the quality of entertainment tends to be highest. Although the Philadelphia Orchestra and the Pennsylvania Ballet finish their seasons at the end of May, they continue limited performances off season, often in outdoor venues such as the Mann Music Center.

Most cultural attractions keep their box offices open until curtain time. Many performing arts companies and venues—the Kimmel Center for the Performing Arts, the Philadelphia Orchestra, the Pennsylvania Ballet, and the Philadelphia Chamber Music Society—have assigned their telephone box office to **Ticket Philadelphia,** which levies a surcharge and can be reached at ✆ **215/893-1999** and www.ticketphiladelphia.org. Also check out **UPSTAGES** (✆ **215/569-9700**), the city's nonprofit box-office service, representing smaller dance companies and theaters such as the Adrienne. They take phone orders Monday through Friday from 10am to 6pm and Saturday and Sunday noon to 5pm. The principal walk-up location is at the Prince Theater, at 1412 Chestnut St.; the box office is open daily noon to 5pm. There's a small service charge.

Classical Music Groups

The Chamber Orchestra of Philadelphia ★ This excellent orchestra, made up mostly of Curtis Institute of Music graduates (such as music director Ignat Solzhenitsyn), and talent from New York, performs chamber music at the **Perelman Theater,** the smaller hall within the **Kimmel Center.** 1520 Locust St. ✆ **215/545-5451.** www.chamberorchestra.org. For tickets: ✆ 215/893-1999 or www.ticketphiladelphia.org. Tickets $24–$81.

Philadelphia Chamber Music Society ★ Value This is a wonderful homegrown series: Director Tony Cecchia knows all of the classical music greats from his time at the Marlboro Music Festival and brings renowned international soloists, chamber musicians, and jazz and popular artists to the city. Most concerts take place at the Pennsylvania Convention Center's 600-seat hall, or the Perelman Theater of the Kimmel Center. Ticket prices are exceptionally low for the quality of the performances. 1616 Walnut St., Ste. 1600. ✆ **215/569-8080** box office or 569-8587 office. www.philadelphiachambermusic.org. Tickets $15–$27.

The Philadelphia Orchestra ★★ For many people, a visit to Philadelphia isn't complete without hearing a concert given by the smooth, powerful Philadelphia Orchestra. Though the group has seen an incredible string of 20th-century leaders—Leopold Stokowski, Eugene Ormandy (for 44 legendary years), Riccardo Muti, Wolfgang Sawallisch, and, most recently, Christoph Eschenbach—at press time, it was still searching for a conductor. The ensemble has built a reputation for virtuosity and balance that only a handful of the world's orchestras can match. Verizon Hall, their modern home designed by Rafael Vinoly, has a soaring glass-roofed lobby, and the concert hall is built of warm, dark woods, with curved spaces, and plush seats ringing the stage.

Concerts are most Tuesday, Thursday, Friday, and Saturday evenings, and Friday and Sunday afternoons. More tickets to individual performances are available than in the past, with certain dress rehearsals open and fewer subscriptions sold. Try to buy tickets well in advance for the best seats. In summer, the orchestra moves to Mann Music Center for 4 weeks of concerts (see Mann Music Center, later in this chapter). Ticket prices can be as low as $10 for a family concert, and above $100 for first-tier seats for the opening night and New Year's Eve concerts. The regular season is September to May. Verizon Hall in the Kimmel Center, Broad and Spruce sts. www.philorch.org. For tickets: ✆ **215/893-1999.** www.ticketphiladelphia.org. Tickets $10–$100.

Relâche Ensemble ★ This contemporary-music group, with a particular affinity for young composers, strikes a refreshing balance between the interesting and the intellectual. The dozen or so instrumentalists often perform new works. Relâche's Sonic Cinema series accompanies silent films at Penn's International House (p. 211). Other performance spaces include the Annenberg Center (p. 192), the Prince Music Theater (p. 194), the National Constitution Center (p. 126), and various churches around the city. Tickets at door only. Office at 715 S. 3rd St., Ste. 208. www.relache.org.

DANCE COMPANIES

Local troupes perform alongside such distinguished visitors as White Oak Dance Project, Pilobolus, and the Dance Theater of Harlem.

Headlong Dance Company ★ Described by one critic as "not your mother's dance company," Headlong is dead-on when it comes to accessible, insightful modern dance. The five-member group was founded in 1993 and uses a rotating roster of choreographers to keep performances fresh. Headlong usually performs at the Philadelphia Fringe Festival and elsewhere throughout the year. Some of its more recent and fun works have included *Hotel Pool* (performed in a real hotel pool) and *Mixed Tape for a Bad Year.* Studio and office at 1170 S. Broad St. ✆ **215/545-9195.** www.headlong.org. Tickets $4–$18.

Koresh Dance Company ★ Roni Koresh's organization performs a handful of times a year in the city. The company's hallmarks are colorful athleticism and deep-seated passion. Israeli by birth, Koresh juxtaposes themes of the Holocaust and war with country dances and an interpretation titled "Day Old Coffee." Hmmm. Office and studio at 2020 Chestnut St. ✆ **215/751-0959.** www.koreshdance.org. Tickets: $5–$15.

Pennsylvania Ballet ★★ Founded in 1963, this nationally renowned, 42-member company has seen great success under the leadership of Roy Kaiser, a former principal dancer. The company is known for diverse classical dance (with Merce Cunningham and Christopher Wheeldon choreography occasionally in the mix) and a Balanchine backbone. They perform at the Academy of Music and Merriam Theater during the annual season. The Christmas-season performances of Tchaikovsky's *Nutcracker,* with the complete Balanchine choreography, are a beloved city tradition. Each of the company's dozens of performances, held from September to June, offers something old, something new, and always something interesting. 1101 S. Broad St. at Washington Ave. ✆ **215/551-7000** Academy of Music box office. www.paballet.org. For tickets: ✆ 215/893-1999 or www.ticketphiladelphia.org. Tickets $24–$129 at the Academy of Music; $22–$127 at the Merriam; $24–$129 for the Nutcracker.

Philadanco ★★ If you're in town when Philadanco is performing, don't miss it: This is one of the most innovative ensembles on the Philadelphia dance scene today. Philadanco founded the International Conference of Black Dance Companies and the International Association of Blacks in Dance to address the special needs of African Americans in the dance community. They're the only dance company that claims residence in the Kimmel Center, and have grown from a community arts group to 17 dancers blending African-American, ballet, jazz, and cutting-edge styles. Philadanco tours frequently, but shows off at home in November and May. Box office at 9 N. Preston St. Performances at Kimmel Center, S. Broad and Spruce sts. ✆ **215/387-8200.** www.philadanco.org. For tickets: ✆ 215/893-1999 or www.ticketphiladelphia.org. Tickets $34–$46; limited discounted rush seats.

Rennie Harris Puremovement ★★ One of the country's first professional hip-hop dance companies has made audiences all over the world rise to their feet. Founder and director Rennie Harris hails from North Philly, and he takes much of his thematic inspiration from the urban African-American experience. His best-known repertory work is *Rome & Jewels,* a modern, street take on Shakespeare's *Romeo & Juliet.* Other performances are throughout the city. Box office at 1500 Market St., 12th Floor. ✆ **215/665-5718.** www.rhpm.org. Tickets: $10–$15.

OPERA COMPANIES

Academy of Vocal Arts (AVA) ★ This exclusive, 70-plus-year-old opera school housed in a beautiful town house presents small but expertly produced full operas starring the AVA's 30 students, many of whom go on to join the Met and other renowned companies after graduation. The AVA performs throughout the city, including the Kimmel Center's Perelman Theater. But if possible, catch a performance or recital at the town house's theater, an intimate and ornate setting (Oct–May). 1920 Spruce St. ✆ **215/735-1685.** www.avaopera.org. Tickets $28–$83.

The Curtis Opera Theater ★ Students in the vocal arts program at the renowned Curtis Institute of Music (p. 192) regularly show off their talents around town. These 25 singers, ages 18 to 28, present fully staged performances and concert productions at the Prince Music Theater and Kimmel Center, as well as in the beautiful studio and Field Hall of their Rittenhouse Square school. 1726 Locust St. ✆ **215/893-7902** box office or 893-5252 main number. www.curtis.edu. Tickets $5–$36.

Opera Company of Philadelphia ★★ The Opera Company is the star tenant of the Academy of Music, and benefited in 2002 from a renovation that restored the theater to her original glory as a premier opera house. English translations are projected in superscript above the stage. The company presents four fully staged operas a year, mostly classics like *La Bohème, Falstaff,* and *Porgy and Bess.* In 2009, the company will be performing *Turandot* and *The Rape of Lucretia.* Offices at 1420 Locust St., Ste. 210. ✆ **215/732-8400.** www.operaphilly.org. For tickets: ✆ 215/893-1999 or www.ticketphiladelphia.org. Tickets $7–$210; $5 and up to half-price amphitheater tickets available on day of performance for students.

THEATER COMPANIES

At any given time there will be at least one Broadway show in Philadelphia, on its way into or out of New York. There are also student repertory productions, professional performances by casts connected with the University of Pennsylvania, small-theater offerings in the various neighborhoods of Center City, and cabaret or dinner theater in the suburbs.

Arden Theatre Company One of the city's most popular professional theaters offers a veritable soup-to-nuts of all things theatrical. Plays—often world premières or clever adaptations of masterpieces—are staged in two performance spaces (one with 360 seats, the other with 175). Recent productions have included Conor McPherson's *The Seafarer,* an adaptation of Voltaire's *Candide,* and, for the kids, *James and the Giant Peach.* (The theater augments its five seasonal productions with two popular children's shows.) 40 N. 2nd St. ✆ **215/922-1122** box office or 922-8900 administrative office. www.ardentheatre.org. Tickets $29–$48.

InterAct Theatre Company InterAct was founded in 1988 as a theater with a social conscience, mirroring today's world. All plays are new to Philadelphia audiences, with four contemporary productions mounted annually between September and June. Performances are at the Adrienne Theater. 2030 Sansom St. ✆ **215/568-8077.** www.interacttheatre.org. Tickets $14–$28 ($10 student rush).

Philadelphia Theatre Company ★ This company combines fine regional talent with Tony Award–winning actors and directors. Since its inception in 1974, the company has produced more than 100 world and Philadelphia premières, including Broadway-bound productions like *Master Class* and *Side Man,* and, in 2009, Tony Award–winning *Grey Gardens.* Suzanne Roberts Theatre, S. Broad and Lombard sts. ✆ **215/985-0420** box office or 985-1400. www.philadelphiatheatrecompany.org. Tickets $46–$70.

Walnut Street Theatre ★ This National Historic Landmark theater has been in business, incredibly, since 1809. The 1,052-seat home to the regional Walnut Street Company is the country's oldest playhouse. The resident company presents five plays from September to June. Most are familiar such as *Hairspray, State Fair,* and *A Streetcar Named Desire.* The theater frequently puts on children's shows, such as *Nate the Great* and *The Berenstain Bears' Family Matters.* Newer and more experimental works play in smaller

Finds Philadelphia's Film Festivals

Philadelphia hosts two major film festivals annually. The largest is the **Philadelphia Festival of World Cinema.** For 2 weeks in April, the popular Ritz Movie Theaters, the Prince Theater, and Penn's International House host screenings and premières of all manner of independent films. Notable festival showings have included *Friends with Money, Akeelah and the Bee,* and *My Architect.* Actors and directors are often in attendance—Susan Sarandon! Laurence Fishburne! Will Shortz!—and stick around to answer the audience's questions when the film ends. The other big movie deal is the **Philadelphia International Gay and Lesbian Film Festival,** which takes place 2 weeks in July and draws major crowds to the theaters—and to the notoriously amazing after parties. For more info on both, visit www.phillyfests.org.

adjoining studio spaces. 9th and Walnut sts. ✆ **215/574-3550.** www.walnutstreettheatre.org. Tickets $10–$70.

Wilma Theater ★ Philly's premier modern-theater company can thank directors Blanka and Jiri Zizka for its national acclaim. Playwright Tom Stoppard has debuted works here, as have Sarah Ruhl and Ken Ludwig. These productions are mounted in a beautiful, state-of-the-art 300-seat theater, designed by Hugh Hardy. You'll recognize it in the heart of the Avenue of the Arts district by the jagged neon logo. 265 S. Broad St. ✆ **215/546-7824.** www.wilmatheater.org. Tickets $35–$50.

PERFORMING ARTS VENUES

In addition to musical performances held at the following major institutions, look out for concerts presented in churches, especially around Rittenhouse Square. Ticket prices can vary wildly for these venues; check with the box office for specific event prices.

Academy of Music ★★★ In the early 19th century, building an opera house/symphony hall was a proposal much discussed by the cultural movers and shakers in Philadelphia. At the time, opera was the hallmark of culture, and in 1852, Philadelphia followed New York and Boston in constructing a hall specifically equipped to handle opera. The Academy of Music opened in 1857, a model of La Scala in Milan. The "Grand Old Lady of Locust Street" is grand, ornate, and, some critics contend, acoustically problematic. The academy underwent a major multimillion-dollar overhaul ending in 2002, with construction of a level extended stage, replacement of an old bowl-shaped floor with a raked one, and better seating and lighting. The spectacular 5,000-pound crystal chandelier stayed. To me, it's the most special place in town to watch any manner of show. (Prince played here once. It was perfect.) After all its work, the academy remains a symphony of Victorian crimson and gold, with well-loved brick and original gaslights still flaming at the Broad Street entrance.

When the Philadelphia Orchestra (owner of the building and chief resident since 1900), moved to the Kimmel Center (see below) in 2001, the Academy of Music's calendar became a patchwork of performances by the Pennsylvania Ballet, the Opera Company of Philadelphia, and Broadway shows. Broad and Locust sts. ✆ **215/893-1935.** www.academyofmusic.org. For tickets: ✆ 215/893-1999 or www.ticketphiladelphia.org. Advance sales are through the Kimmel Center box office, S. Broad and Spruce sts. Daily 10am–6pm. Academy of Music box office open only 1 hr. before performances to a half-hour after performance begins.

Annenberg Center at the University of Pennsylvania ★ On the beautiful University of Pennsylvania campus and easily reached by bus or subway, the roomy, modern Annenberg Center presents a wide variety of performances by American and international companies from September to June. Of the two stages, the Harold Prince Theater generally has the more intimate and more avant-garde productions. The Zellerbach Theater can handle the more demanding lighting and staging needs. There is also a small studio theater.

Since U. Penn established Penn Presents in 1999 as the professional performing arm of the campus, they've expanded the programming mix to include classical, world, and jazz music; Philadelphia's leading contemporary dance series, Dance Celebration; and each April, the International Children's Festival, with dance, theater, and music. 3680 Walnut St. ✆ **215/898-3900** box office. www.pennpresents.org. Box office weekdays 10am–6pm.

Arts Bank One of the cornerstones of the Avenue of the Arts, the Arts Bank was a gift of the William Penn Foundation, which realized that there wasn't enough quality, affordable performance space in Center City. The 230-seat theater (a former bank, of course) is owned and operated by the nearby University of the Arts and serves a large, diverse constituency. The stage has a sprung (bouncy) wood floor and state-of-the-art computerized lighting and sound. This is the place for excellent, inexpensive student dance and theater. 601 S. Broad St. (at South St.). ✆ **215/545-1664** box office, 545-0590 venue, or 717-6000 University of the Arts. www.uarts.edu.

Curtis Institute of Music ★★ Value The most famous touring concert pianist in the world, 22-year-old Lang Lang, trained at the Curtis, one of the country's finest music schools, housed in a rambling historic limestone mansion with its own theater. Eighteen percent of the principal chairs in America's leading orchestras—and musical directorships of three major orchestras—are held by alumni. Nearly half of the players in the Philadelphia Orchestra are alumni, too. Curtis itself has a small hall just off Rittenhouse Square that's excellent for chamber works. Free student recitals are Monday, Wednesday, and Friday evenings at 8pm from October through May. Both the Curtis Opera Theater and the Curtis Symphony Orchestra present full-scale productions at the school, the Prince Music Theater, and the Kimmel Center. 1726 Locust St. ✆ **215/893-5252.** www.curtis.edu.

The Forrest ★ Of Philadelphia's commercial theaters, the Forrest—owned by the Shubert Organization—is the best equipped to handle big musicals like *Phantom of the Opera* and *Pippin,* several of which take place here during the year. The venue is nothing short of spectacular. It should be: It was built for $2 million in 1927, a whopping sum back in those days. Gilbert and Sullivan and Yiddish Theatre launched productions at the Forrest. Today, it serves primarily as a roadhouse, although smaller and short-run acts do perform. Performances are usually Tuesday through Saturday at 8pm (occasionally Sun night as well) and Wednesday, Saturday, and Sunday at 2pm. 1114 Walnut St. ✆ **215/923-1515.** www.forrest-theatre.com. For tickets: ✆ 800/447-7400, www.telecharge.com, or in person at the theater box office Mon–Sat 10am–6pm.

Kimmel Center for the Performing Arts ★★★ Opened with tremendous fanfare in December 2001, Rafael Vinoly's dramatic glass-and-steel vault along the Avenue

Value Good Shows, Good Deals

Not all, but a few good venues offer performances free of charge. The Avenue of the Arts's **Kimmel Center** (p. 192) often hosts free performances in its ground-level Commonwealth Plaza, especially around the Kimmel's birthday in mid-December. Another option is Rittenhouse Square's beautiful **Curtis Institute of Music** (p. 192) where mightily talented 18- to 25-year-olds give weekly afternoon concerts. Who knows? You might encounter the next Yo-Yo Ma.

Seniors can receive discounts of about 10% or $5 per ticket or more at many theaters, including the **Annenberg Center** and **Wilma Theater.** Concert halls generally make rush or last-minute seats available to students at prices under $10; these programs sometimes extend to adults as well. Groups can generally get discounts of 20% to 50% by calling well in advance.

of the Arts encompasses **Verizon Hall,** a 2,500-seat cello-shaped concert hall built specifically to house the Philadelphia Orchestra; and **Perelman Theater,** a 650-seat hall for chamber music, dance, and drama with a turntable stage. Other features at Kimmel include an interactive education center; "black box" theater space; a daytime cafe and gift shop in the plaza along Spruce Street; and parking and restaurant facilities. Above all, there is space, acres and acres of it—space designed to sparkle and amaze, unlike anything else in the area.

With its comfortable mahogany interior, four levels of seating, and excellent acoustics, Verizon Hall is a pleasure. Perelman's design is also nice, with a metal-clad exterior and light woods and warm fabrics within.

Most of the jewels in Philadelphia's cultural crown—the city opera, orchestra, and ballet companies—perform either at Kimmel or at the historic Academy of Music (which is affiliated with Kimmel and located 1 block north). Visiting talent in music and dance and an incredible jazz series presented by the Kimmel Center also use the venue frequently. Tickets for *both* locations are sold during the day only at the Kimmel Center box office. The Kimmel also presents frequent free performances by jazz artists, DJs, singing groups, folk ensembles, and more in its main Commonwealth Plaza, usually in the early evening or afternoon. 300 S. Broad (at Spruce St.). ✆ **215/790-5800** or 670-2300. www.kimmelcenter.org. For tickets: ✆ 215/893-1999 or www.ticketphiladelphia.org. Advance sales at the box office, daily 10am–6pm, until 30 min. past the last performance.

Mann Music Center ★ An evening concert at the Mann is one of summer's delights. Located at one end of Fairmount Park, this open-air theater has covered seating and space for picnicking on the grass. The Mann presents annual performances by the Philadelphia Orchestra and showcases artists such as Yo-Yo Ma, James Taylor, R.E.M., and the Gipsy Kings. There is also a Young People's Series, and regular performances by the Philly Pops.

Special SEPTA buses travel from Center City and plenty of paid parking is available in nearby lots. Concerts are usually at 8pm. Tickets for the covered amphitheater seats may be purchased at the box office there, if available, or by calling ahead.

You can also enjoy music under the stars, on the grassy slopes above the orchestra, where picnicking is encouraged. From here, you'll have a great view of the city skyline.

Seating is unassigned, but tickets are required. The food stall choices range from fine and ethnic to fast, and wine and beer are available. Don't forget the blankets and insect repellent. 5201 Parkside Ave. (off Belmont Ave.). ✆ **215/546-7900.** www.manncenter.org. For tickets: ✆ 215/893-1999 or www.ticketphiladelphia.org.

Merriam Theater The Merriam, belonging to the University of the Arts, hosts many of Broadway's top touring shows such as *Chicago* and *Into the Woods.* Popular artists like Patti LaBelle and Mandy Patinkin perform there, as does the Gilbert and Sullivan International Festival. The Merriam is an ornate turn-of-the-20th-century hall with 1,668 seats. During the vaudeville era, Al Jolson took the stage here. 250 S. Broad St. ✆ **215/732-5997.** www.merriamtheater.org. For tickets: ✆ 215/336-1234 or www.ticketmaster.com.

Painted Bride Art Center ★★ It's hard to know what to call the wonderful, welcoming, and often edgy Painted Bride Art Center, located near the entrance to the Benjamin Franklin Bridge. This spot set the trend of cultural activity in Old City starting 36 years ago. It's an art gallery catering to contemporary—okay, more left-wing—tastes, but it also hosts folk, electronic, and world music, plus Philadelphia's longest running jazz series, dance, and theater events. 230 Vine St. ✆ **215/925-9914.** www.paintedbride.org.

Prince Music Theater ★ Founded in 1984 by visionary Marjorie Samoff as the American Music Theater Festival, the Prince is a renovated 450-seat picture palace that hosts original productions. Musical theater is presented in all major forms—opera, musical comedy, cabaret, and experimental theater, along with film. *Time* magazine has called the Prince Music Theater the foremost presenter of new and adventurous music theater in the country. I like to go to see movies here, when they're playing. 1412 Chestnut St. (btw. Broad and 15th sts.). ✆ **215/972-1000.** For tickets: ✆ 215/569-9700 or www.princemusictheater.org.

Society Hill Playhouse Just north of South Street this two-stage, venue (ca. 1960) describes itself as "the theatre for people who don't like theatre." The main stage is upstairs and has 223 seats (not wheelchair accessible); the first-floor, 99-seat Red Room hosts independent-minded local productions. 507 S. 8th St. ✆ **215/923-0210.** www.societyhillplayhouse.org.

Suzanne Roberts Theatre The splashy new home to the Philadelphia Theatre Company (see above) is heralded by a scarf-shaped marquee, standing on the first floor of a very pink building along the Avenue of the Arts. Inside, the space is laid out on the principles of universal access, and is one of the easiest venues in town to navigate. The 370-seat playhouse also hosts performances by Koresh Dance Company (see earlier in this chapter) and out-of-town visitors. It's named for former playwright, actress, and director Suzanne Roberts, the wife of Comcast cable founder Ralph Roberts. 480 S. Broad St. (at Lombard St.). ✆ **215/985-1400.** www.philadelphiatheatrecompany.org.

2 THE CLUB & MUSIC SCENE

Luckily for those of us who rise and shine when the sun goes down, Philadelphia's nightlife scene has evolved over the years. The city offers plenty of dance clubs that invoke scenes from party-hearty reality shows, pubs for chilling out over a few pints, subdued martini lounges, and excellent DJ scenes. The minimum legal drinking age in Pennsylvania is 21. Bars may stay open until 2am; establishments that operate as private clubs can serve until 3am. Dance clubs often have rules prohibiting sneakers, but most are okay with unfaded jeans.

THE LAY OF THE LAND

Here's a quick-and-dirty rundown of what's happening where, with exceptions all around.

DELAWARE AVENUE/COLUMBUS BOULEVARD Not the scene it used to be, this high-traffic, four-lane city strip is nonetheless dotted with a popular spots—just not enough to allow you to walk among them. There are a couple of places on the river, a pair of strip clubs (one male, one female), and a dance club or two.

NORTHERN LIBERTIES A few blocks north of Old City, across the Vine Street expressway, this once dodgy neighborhood has been discovered. And then some. The nightlife corridor generally stretches along 2nd and 3rd streets, between Callowhill Street and Girard Avenue. Anchor bar Standard Tap is no longer the secret it once was, so the owners opened a second place, even farther north, called Johnny Brenda's—and now even that place is getting gentrified. New additions include bars Deuce and Bar Ferdinand, both in the recently opened Liberties Walk, and North Bowl, a stylish bowling alley.

OLD CITY By day, historic sites and boutiques. By night, restaurants, bars—and more bars, the most in Philly. While there are a few quiet nooks where one can enjoy adult conversation, Old City's going-out scene is mostly loud and lusty (in both senses of the word). It also seems to grow more bridge-and-tunnelish by the weekend. (For evidence, see the full garages and parking lots—and the traffic jams along 2nd and 3rd sts.) A ton of well-heeled Penn students party here, as do young, hetero professionals in ironed, tucked-out shirts (the men) and the latest skimpiest styles (the women). In winter, no one, apparently, needs a coat.

RITTENHOUSE SQUARE A slightly more mature crowd patronizes the less-crowded nightlife scene of this park-centric neighborhood. Although Rittenhouse Square has a dollop of bump 'n' grind—Denim, for example—it definitely welcomes a preening cocktail crowd—Rouge, Continental Mid-Town. Its many restaurant-attached bars are more couple friendly. Yet the neighborhood's edges still offer laid-back settings (like Monk's and Good Dog) for hanging out with friends.

SOUTH STREET Center City's southern border has downtown's most diverse going-out scene, with beer bars, starter bars (for folks for whom catching a buzz is still a novelty), the city's coolest dance club, sports bars, gastropubs, and teen hangouts. A little farther south into Bella Vista has restaurants with bars serving boutique wines.

UNIVERSITY CITY You might think there'd be a ton of watering holes in the across-the-river section of West Philly, but you'd be wrong. You can find a few popular pubs—New Deck, the bar at the White Dog, and "Pennstitution" Smokey Joe's—and lounges—Marathon, the bar at Pod—but many students go elsewhere to party, or do it in their social clubs.

WASHINGTON WEST Just east of Broad Street (before you hit Old City), this eclectic neighborhood comprises the bars and dance clubs of the "Gayborhood," the emerging 13th Street corridor (El Vez, Vintage), and the city's oldest continuously operational bar (McGillin's), with a few casual taprooms, a swanky new bowling alley, and a dive or two in between. It's not as sceney as either of the above, but it's near the convention center, and fits the bill if you're not planning an oversize pub-crawl.

Philadelphia Bars, Clubs & Lounges

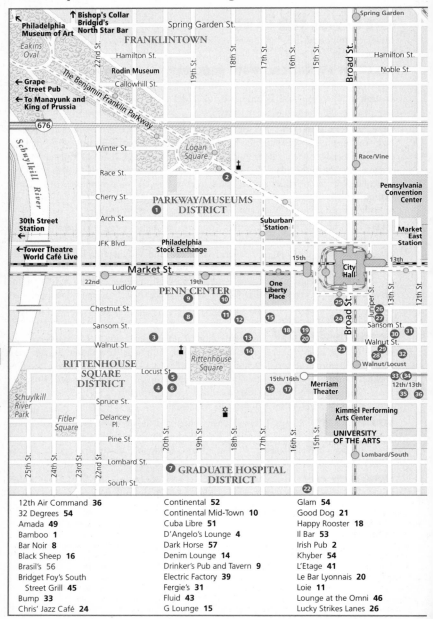

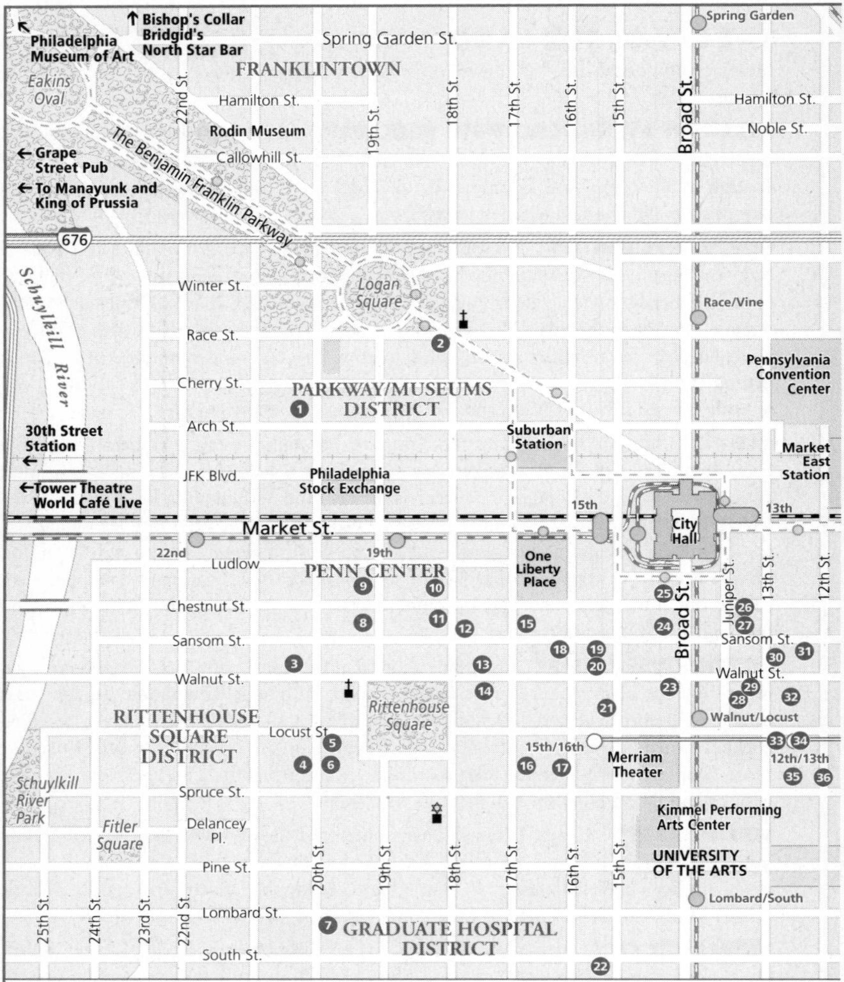

12th Air Command **36**
32 Degrees **54**
Amada **49**
Bamboo **1**
Bar Noir **8**
Black Sheep **16**
Brasil's 56
Bridget Foy's South Street Grill **45**
Bump **33**
Chris' Jazz Café **24**
Continental **52**
Continental Mid-Town **10**
Cuba Libre **51**
D'Angelo's Lounge **4**
Dark Horse **57**
Denim Lounge **14**
Drinker's Pub and Tavern **9**
Electric Factory **39**
Fergie's **31**
Fluid **43**
G Lounge **15**
Glam **54**
Good Dog **21**
Happy Rooster **18**
Il Bar **53**
Irish Pub **2**
Khyber **54**
L'Etage **41**
Le Bar Lyonnais **20**
Loie **11**
Lounge at the Omni **46**
Lucky Strikes Lanes **26**

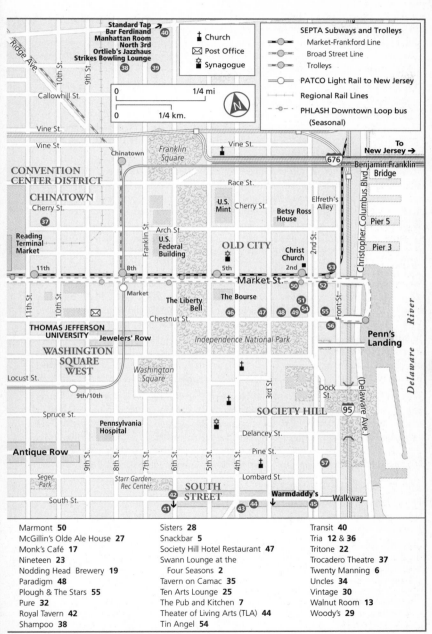

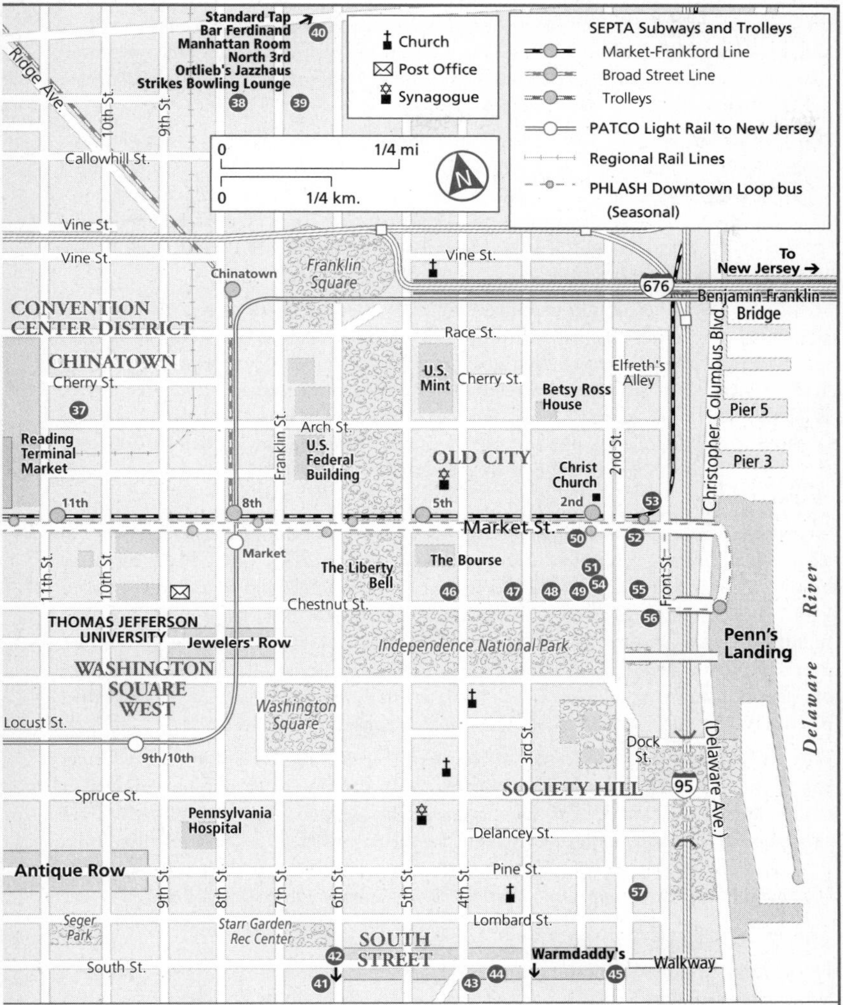

Marmont **50**
McGillin's Olde Ale House **27**
Monk's Café **17**
Nineteen **23**
Nodding Head Brewery **19**
Paradigm **48**
Plough & The Stars **55**
Pure **32**
Royal Tavern **42**
Shampoo **38**
Sisters **28**
Snackbar **5**
Society Hill Hotel Restaurant **47**
Swann Lounge at the Four Seasons **2**
Tavern on Camac **35**
Ten Arts Lounge **25**
The Pub and Kitchen **7**
Theater of Living Arts (TLA) **44**
Tin Angel **54**
Transit **40**
Tria **12** & **36**
Tritone **22**
Trocadero Theatre **37**
Twenty Manning **6**
Uncles **34**
Vintage **30**
Walnut Room **13**
Woody's **29**

DANCE CLUBS

Brasil's Brasil's compact, upstairs dance floor is the best place in Old City to show off—or to learn—salsa moves. Plenty of regulars hit the floor hard on Wednesday, Friday, and Saturday nights. This was the first place in town to serve refreshing and sweet mojitos and caipirinhas. Free salsa lessons are offered 9 to 10:30pm, before the crowd arrives. 112 Chestnut St. ✆ **215/413-1700.** Cover $5–$10.

D'Angelo's Lounge Just off Rittenhouse Square, the dance floor of D'Angelo's Ristorante Italiano conjures a happy party scene from *The Sopranos.* (Think Vesuvio, with a DJ.) The crowd is generally older, and may include a goomar or two. Early in the evening, DJ Inga starts off slow and smooth—Frank Sinatra, Barry White—before moving into hits by OutKast, the Bee Gees, and Miami Sound Machine. 256 S. 20th St. ✆ **215/546-3935.** www.dangeloristorante.com.

Fluid ★★ Finds This quintessential Philly club has love for all musical genres—and all manner of talented DJs. King Britt, Josh Wink, and ?uestlove (the Roots' drummer) spin here regularly. The second-floor space is small, but somehow, everyone seems to fit. Techno, rock, punk, glam, new wave, hip-hop, and electronic music all have their nights, as do accessible funk, Motown, soul, and reggae mixed with house music. The entrance is an unmarked door in the alley just off 4th Street, above the **Latest Dish** (p. 206). 613 S. 4th St. (btw. South and Bainbridge sts.). ✆ **215/629-0565.** www.fluidnightclub.com. Cover $5–$10.

Shampoo This thumping maze of a spot seems to be all things (dance-club wise) to all people. On any given night, Shampoo's eight bars and three dance floors might be hosting a Goth party; an '80s tribute; a dance mix of R&B, hip-hop, and reggae; or Latin, Greek, or Asian gatherings. Friday nights have been a social staple of the gay community for years—if you're into drag queen–watching, this is the place to be. In summer, a tented courtyard holds patio furniture, a Jacuzzi, and an extra DJ. On the first Sunday of every month, Shampoo hosts Baby Disco, an afternoon dance party for tots and their parents. 417 N. 8th St. ✆ **215/922-7500.** www.shampooonline.com. Cover $7–$12.

Transit Nightclub On the edge of Northern Liberties, this cavernous, musty former bank attracts a young, sometimes fashionable crowd that doesn't need to hear each other to communicate. By virtue of size alone (three floors, six bars, three dance floors), Transit is popular, especially its regular Making Time party, where DJs spin everything from Brit pop to neosoul to techno. It's open until 3am—and, a few times a year—daylight. 600 Spring Garden St. (at 6th St.). ✆ **215/925-8878.** www.transitnightclub.com. Cover $5–$10.

JAZZ & BLUES CLUBS

Philadelphia has long been one of the great American hot spots for jazz. It's the one-time home of greats Billie Holiday and John Coltrane. And while Philly-born bassist Christian McBride has left for New York, sax phenom Grover Washington, Jr., lives in the city and drummer Mickey Roker still appears weekly for sets at Ortlieb's Jazzhaus. In addition to the clubs listed below, the Kimmel Center hosts a popular jazz series and the Philadelphia Museum of Art offers live jazz most Wednesday and Friday evenings. Lastly, tune into WRTI, FM 90.1, Temple University's public classic and jazz music station.

Chris' Jazz Cafe ★ Finds Dwarfed by a neighborhood of imposing buildings, and tucked into three cozy rooms, this bar feels nearly clandestine. Chris's modestly hosts acts both big and small—and somehow makes them all seem local. Ten coveted bar stools make great seats for watching, as do front-and-center tables. A menu of sandwiches and ribs is served until 1am on weekends. 1421 Sansom St. ✆ **215/568-3131.** www.chrisjazzcafe.com. Cover $3–$30.

Ortlieb's Jazzhaus ★★ Finds Northern Liberties' longtime jazz hangout in a former brewery is the real, dark, bare-bones deal. If you can, come when Mickey Roker (Dizzy Gillespie's drummer) heads up the "Hausband." Noshes include popcorn shrimp, fried pork chops, and blackened catfish. 847 N. 3rd St. ✆ **215/922-1035.** www.ortliebsjazzhaus.com. Cover Fri–Sat $10–$15.

Warmdaddy's ★★ It's worth the cab fare to the warmly sleek new South Philadelphia location of this popular blues club and restaurant. Koko Taylor, Cee Cee Collins, and the Blind Boys of Alabama have all taken the stage. The Southern soul menu matches the music: collards, corn bread, and fried green tomatoes along with rib-eye steaks and crab cakes. Warmdaddy's stage and sound system are first-rate, and the ambience is both sexy and familial. Closed most Mondays. 1400 S. Columbus Blvd. ✆ **215/462-2000.** www.warmdaddys.com. Cover from $10 Sat–Sun.

ROCK CLUBS & CONCERT VENUES

The biggest concerts in town—Dave Matthews Band, the Rolling Stones, Veggie Tales on Ice—happen in South Philadelphia's stadiums: Wachovia Center and the Spectrum, mostly. In summer, larger acts also perform across the river at Camden's Tweeter Center on the Waterfront. The following is a list of small to midsize year-round (mostly rock) music venues.

Electric Factory On a warehousey stretch of 7th Street between Old City and Northern Liberties sits this 2,500-capacity concert hall, a favorite for bands like the Killers. The standing-room-only place feels like the factory it once was, with ceilings that stretch up to infinity. Most shows are appropriate for all ages. A large mezzanine accommodates the 21-and-over crowd. Parking can be a challenge, so most drivers entrust their cars to the dudes waving flags up and down the street—these lots accept cash only. 42 N. 7th St. ✆ **215/627-1332.** www.electricfactory.info. For tickets: ✆ **215/336-2000** or box office at 111 Presidential Blvd., Bala Cynwyd, PA.

The Khyber ★★ Philadelphia's oldest (but not oldest continuously operated) bar puts on rock shows nightly on a small stage that backs up to 2nd Street. The venue fills when local bands like Audible and Burning Brides play. It also hosts out-of-town touring groups (Garbage was once one of these). Enter into a timeworn, English-feeling taproom with its walls of concert flyers and carved gargoyles. The no-nonsense (translation: no Jell-O shots) bar maintains taps of local and imported beers, and gladly serves bottles ranging from Miller Lite to Chimay Premiere. The crowd largely depends on the band, and it's always easy to pick out who's accidentally wandered in, mistaking this spot for Glam or Cuba Libre. Upstairs is a low-key, rock DJed dance club that's way less dressed-up than its neighbors. 56 S. 2nd St. ✆ **215/238-5888.** www.thekhyber.com. Cover $5–$12.

Manhattan Room ★ The latest spot for indie bands—and emerging DJs—to do their stuff borders Northern Liberties and Fishtown. The M Room is a simple, bipartite spot, with a bar to chill in and a stage to rush up to. 15 W. Girard Ave. ✆ **215/739-5577.** www.themanhattanroom.com. Cover $5–$8.

North Star Bar ★ The North Star, located at the edge of the Fairmount–art museum area, is the place Supersuckers, Fall Out Boy, and the Yeah Yeah Yeahs play. It's small, but not cramped, with a front bar and poolroom that lead to a dimly lit, lodgelike concert space. The bar menu is inexpensive, with burgers, nachos, and other no-utensils-required fare. The crowd depends on the band, but tends to be stylishly grubby 20-somethings. 2629 Poplar St. ✆ **215/787-0488.** www.northstarrocks.com. Cover $8–$20.

Theater of the Living Arts (TLA) The marquee over this converted movie house announces all sorts of musicians: funk bands, world music collaborators, hip-hop acts, and rockers all perform to crowds of up to 1,000. The bare-bones TLA is GA (general admission) and SRO (standing room only), although patrons who arrive early may score one of the few cafe tables at the side bar. Tickets for hot, locally connected acts like the Roots often sell out quickly. 334 South St. ✆ **215/922-1011.** For tickets: www.livenation.com or from 10am at the box office.

Tin Angel ★ Old City on a Saturday night might be the last place you'd expect to see a quiet acoustic show by Amos Lee, Dar Williams, or a bluegrass trio, but I swear, it happens here all the time. The second-floor Tin Angel feels more like a big coffeehouse than a cafe, and once the night's performer takes the small stage, the room hushes. Seats are general admission, so come early if you want to score. Downstairs, Serrano restaurant does a nice job with international fare. 20 S. 2nd St. ✆ **215/928-0978** box office. www.tinangel.com. For tickets: www.ticketweb.com or at the box office (noon–10pm).

Tower Theatre ★ All post-Depression-era gilt and scrollwork, the Tower is the jewel of West Philly's 69th Street corridor. (It's officially in Upper Darby.) After all these years, the 3,500-seat venue remains one of the most special places in town to catch Damien Rice, Fiona Apple, or, if you're extra lucky, Philly's own Hall & Oates. 69th and Ludlow sts. ✆ **610/352-2887** box office (open days of show at 4pm). SEPTA: Market-Frankford El to 69th St. Terminal.

Trocadero Theatre ★★ Of Montreal, Ladytron, Lil' Kim, and the Psychedelic Furs have all performed beneath the timeworn vaulted ceilings of this once-ornate house of vaudeville and burlesque. Not all acts are that big, however. The Troc's best known for its brash rock, Goth, and punk acts, and has a devoted all-ages clientele. If you're into any sort of music and are staying around the convention center, this is the place to check out first; it's just a block away, in the heart of Chinatown. Monday is movie night, with big-screen showings of *Pee-Wee's Big Adventure, Animal House,* and seasonal flicks. 1003 Arch St. ✆ **215/922-6888.** Box office Mon–Fri 11:30am–5pm; Sat 11:30am–6pm. www.thetroc.com.

World Café Live ★★ The University of Pennsylvania's acclaimed independent/alternative public radio station 88.5 FM/WXPN moved to an impressive, music multi-tasking venue in 2004. Just across the Walnut Street bridge at the edge of University City, the modern, art-splashed site houses the radio station itself at ground level, a cafe with a stage, and, downstairs, a larger, two-level, 1,000-capacity venue for concerts by Josh Rouse, They Might be Giants, and other singer-songwriter performers. 3025 Walnut St. ✆ **215/222-1400.** www.worldcafelive.com.

3 THE BAR SCENE

LOUNGES

Bamboo This clubby upstairs lounge hides a few blocks north of Rittenhouse Square above a grungy first-floor piano bar. The music is usually low-key, and clients usually on the younger side of 21. Though it's not the place to break a sweat with your running man, it's perfectly acceptable here to turn your head bob into a fanny shake. Exposed

Ben Franklin: "Bottoms Up!"

Believe it or not, Ben Franklin approves of your Philly bar-crawl. Franklin was a wine and beer enthusiast and occasional winemaker, who coined drinking proverbs still quoted in Philadelphia taverns:

- *There cannot be good living where there is not good drinking.*
- *Beer is proof that God loves us and wants us to be happy.*
- *Wine makes daily living easier, less hurried, with fewer tensions and more tolerance.*

Just remember that Franklin also valued moderation:

- *Take counsel in wine, but resolve afterwards in water.*
- *Eat not to dullness; drink not to elevation.*

brick walls lend a historical feel, while petite chandeliers conjure earbobs befitting Marie Antoinette. Supermodel-friendly cocktails include pineapple-infused vodka and sake drinks. 101 N. 20th St. ✆ **215/636-0228.**

Bar Noir Phillies ladies' man Pat Burrell was once photographed dancing on the bar at this basement-level Rittenhouse Square hangout. Narrow little Bar Noir, with its film-poster decor and house DJ who's been known to spin oldies and punk in the same set, is a casual let-you-be spot that sometimes verges on wild as 2am approaches. Never a cover, but occasionally a queue. 112 S. 18th St. ✆ **215/569-1160.** www.barnoir215.com.

Denim Lounge Beyond a velvet rope on Walnut Street, a jeans-covered elevator whisks VIP guests to a Philippe Starck–style series of rooms; $300 bottles of vodka are among the top-shelf libations. Members of the Flyers and Eagles often make appearances at this hot spot (in the off season only, of course). While most people come to drink (nonbottle buyers will pay up to $15 for a martini), there's a nice menu of international tapas, too. DJs spin louder as the night goes on, and the scene is definitely about getting noticed on the dance floor—and going home with a new groupie. Open Thursday through Saturdays 9pm to 3am; after 10pm, tables are bottle service only. 1712 Walnut St. ✆ **215/735-6700.** www.denimlounge.com. Cover $10.

Glam In Old City central, this two-story lounge does a whole lot in a little space. Downstairs, a TV-laden bar slings relatively inexpensive cocktails (very inexpensive during an extended happy hour). Upstairs, a ruggedly clubby lounge offers pricey bottle service to patrons seated on plush banquettes. On busy weekends, there's a line to enter—and, if you're lucky, shot girls. Hurray! 52 S. 2nd St. ✆ **267/671-0840.** Cover $5–$10 Sat–Sun.

G Lounge If you're over 30, stop reading. G is a nightclub for those of us that can spend 3 hours getting dressed to go out—and then stay out for three times 3 hours. Strict bouncers, big DJs, VIP rooms, bottle service, a no T-shirts dress code, one of the best sound systems in town, and a whole lot of attitude make this the in spot for the in crowd. Open Thursday and Friday 5pm to 2am, Sunday 9pm to 2am. 111 S. 17th St. ✆ **215/564-1515.** www.thebestlounge.com. Cover $10–$20 Sat–Sun.

L'Etage ★ Finds This vaguely Art Deco, South Street–area lounge is the sister act to downstairs **Beau Monde** (p. 92). L'Etage has a handsome horseshoe bar, a small dance floor, banquette seating, an excellent little wine list, and an all-inclusive, welcoming vibe. It's a great spot to groove out to a retro DJ while sipping a nice glass of pinot, or to relax

Tips: Quizzo: Philly's Favorite Bar Game

Quizzo, a weekly, team-based trivia competition, allows hundreds of Philadelphia bar patrons to exercise their brains—even as they destroy their brain cells. The game started way back at Fergie's (where it's now held twice a week; p. 203), and it works like this. You go to a bar with a group/team of friends. At an appointed time, an emcee announces a series of trivia questions. (Examples: "Who is buried in Grant's tomb?" "What are the four original Lucky Charms shapes?") You write down answers to these important questions, submit your answers to the emcee, and possibly win a gift certificate to use in the bar.

into a cushy leather seat while a cabaret singer croons above the low din. Lighting is low, just as it should be. 624 S. 6th St. (entrance on Bainbridge St.). ✆ **215/592-0656.** Cover $10 Fri–Sat from 10pm.

Paradigm One of Old City's first trendy bars, Paradigm sets itself apart with a single gimmick: the see-through doors on its restrooms' stalls. Like a joke that never gets old, these doors (which, to everyone's relief, fog up when locked), have become a rite of passage for bar hoppers. On paper, blue-lit Paradigm is also a gourmet restaurant, but the kitchen is hit-or-miss at best. Most patrons stick to the mocha carameltinis. 239 Chestnut St. ✆ **215/238-6900.** www.paradigmrestaurant.com.

32 Degrees There's usually a line to enter this plain little upstairs lounge in the heart of Old City. The big deal here: bottle service. At $250 a pop, the Dom Perignon is a bestseller. Those who order it will be treated to low, white-leather cube stool seating at a VIP table. Those who don't can order by the glass at one of two bars. One tip: If you want to hang out longer, order the more stretchable $200 bottle of Stoli, which comes with a full complement of mixers. (Request 32's signature ice shot glasses.) One more fun fact: The lounge accepts euros as payment (but counts them as dollars). Dancing is permitted and rather de rigueur. 16 S. 2nd St. (btw. Market and Chestnut sts.). ✆ **215/627-3132.** www.32lounge.com.

Walnut Room This red, narrow, upstairs martini lounge is an appealing spot for a drink early in the evening—and becomes a crowded, pulsating scene best experienced with many drinks as the night rolls on. DJs Jazzy Jeff and King Britt have spun here, and weekly parties feature reggaeton, soul, and funk. Past the one bar, the small dance floor quickly gets cramped; loungers take refuge in a small alcove overlooking Walnut Street. 1709 Walnut St., 2nd Floor. ✆ **215/751-0201.** www.walnut-room.com. Cover $5–$10 Sat–Sun.

PUBS

Bishop's Collar I know someone who stops into this corner pub—named for the foam head and inky liquid of a perfectly poured pint of Guinness—after a jog on Kelly Drive. The Bishop's Collar is casual (and close) enough to do it, too, just a couple blocks east, on Fairmount Avenue. It's a wood-covered place, with old church pews for seats and a simple menu of $10-and-under entrees. Like most taverns of its ilk, it crowds up on weekend nights. 2349 Fairmount Ave. ✆ **215/765-1616.** www.thebishopscollar.citysearch.com.

Black Sheep Another cozy Irish pub in the Rittenhouse Square area, the Black Sheep occupies three floors of an old Colonial town house. Whenever it's open (always), it's busy (always). The crowd is mostly young and apparently professional. Although the Irish-inspired fare is decent, more people are interested in drinking than in dining. 247 S. 17th St. ✆ **215/545-9473.** www.theblacksheeppub.com.

Bridgid's This tiny, friendly, horseshoe-shaped art museum–area bar stocks a superb collection of Belgian beers, including an array of fruit-to-hops-originated brews. Open lunch (weekdays) through dinner, the bar posts inexpensive dinner specials that sell out nightly. Menu served until 11pm Monday to Saturday and until 10pm Sunday. 726 N. 24th St. ✆ **215/232-3232.** www.bridgids.com.

Dark Horse This traditional English pub has more rooms than you can shake a stick at. Downstairs, just off South Street's Headhouse Square, is the grown-ups' bar. Upstairs is a dining room, a more youthful bar area, and a few smaller bars that open during busy nights or for private parties. The kitchen's specialties are Irish breakfasts, shepherd's pie, and bangers and mash. The best time to go here is during a football (soccer) match, when Philly's many expats gather to cheer on their teams. 421 S. 2nd St. ✆ **215/928-0232.** www.darkhorsepub.com.

Drinker's Tavern and Pub "Never has a bar in Philly been so aptly named," says one patron. These two taverns (one in Old City, one in Rittenhouse Sq.) share a theme of diveyness. Which is to say, they're both relatively new, but look—and act—triumphantly grungy. Dollar shotgun "ripcords" of Pabst Blue Ribbon, $2 shots of Jaegermeister ($30 buys shots for the whole bar), and a rock-heavy jukebox are selling points. The crowd is a mix of lightly tattooed or pierced college and just graduated. 124 Market St. ✆ **215/351-0141** and 1903 Chestnut St. ✆ 215/564-0914. www.drinkers215.com.

Fergie's ★ Finds This cozy, candlelit Irish pub serves craft and standard brews, and is a great, hidden escape from the nearby convention center. Like its sister bar Monk's (below), Fergie's doesn't have a TV. It does, however, have tasty mussels, fries, burgers, potpies, and fish and chips. The downstairs bar relies on a jukebox for tunes. Upstairs hosts the most popular quizzo game in town on Tuesday and Thursday, and music on weekends. Fergie's is open daily for lunch. Menu served until midnight. 1214 Sansom St. ✆ **215/928-8118.** www.fergies.com.

Good Dog ★ This Standard Tap (see below) of Center City offers some great grub—the *Philadelphia Inquirer's* restaurant critic calls their burger the best in the city—and way-above-average taproom atmosphere. Downstairs is a long bar with tall-backed booths. Upstairs are cafe tables, Ms. Pac Man, and darts. Menu served until 1am. 224 S. 15th St. ✆ **215/985-9600.** www.gooddogbar.com.

Irish Pub This Rittenhouse Square stalwart for motivated drinkers packs in hundreds of college kids and young professionals on its busiest nights. Early on, there's Irish and American folk music in the front, and a quieter area in the back. Later on, a PA system

Tips Drink Like a Founding Father

If you want a taste of what our first representatives drank at the end (and sometimes in the middle) of their work day, try a glass of **Madeira,** a mixture of wine and brandy originally from an island off of Portugal. Madeira was considered a tasty, healthy drink that didn't spoil easily.

announces specials on lemon drops. The pub has a second, quieter location on the other side of Broad Street. Both places are good for game. 2007 Walnut St. ✆ **215/568-5603.** Cover $2 Fri–Sat. Also at 1123 Walnut St. ✆ 215/925-3311. www.irishpubphilly.com.

McGillin's Olde Ale House Tucked into the best known of Center City's side streets is the oldest continuously operating tavern in Philadelphia. The Khyber (p. 199) predates it, but stopped serving during Prohibition. McGillin's is popular with everyone, really, but its best customers are college age or just beyond. A decent mix of local microbrews and imports are on tap and available in pitchers. The best seats are downstairs. Upstairs has a little less personality. Nightly specials include $5 pitchers of Pabst on karaoke Friday nights. 1310 Drury St. ✆ **215/735-5562.** www.mcgillins.com.

Monk's Café ★★ This narrow taproom is the city's premier local dispenser of flavorful craft beer. The first in the country to import kegs of Chimay White, Monk's specializes in Trappiste, small-maker brews—including a unique Flemish sour ale it has custom brewed in Belgium. Though you'd think its evolved beer list and lack of TVs would keep the kids away, it doesn't. Monk's packs 'em in nightly, from back bar, past wooden booths, to front bar. Mussels and fries star on a nice menu. No reservations. Menu served until 1am. 264 S. 16th St. ✆ **215/545-7005.** www.monkscafe.com.

Nodding Head Brewery and Restaurant This cozy brew house opened in the late 1980s as an offshoot of the Sansom Street Oyster House downstairs, but now has its own identity. Six beers are regularly brewed right here: three light to dark, and three seasonal ales. Try to secure one of the spacious booths opposite the bar. Menu served until midnight Sunday to Thursday and until 1:30am Friday and Saturday. 1516 Sansom St., 2nd floor. ✆ **215/569-9525.** www.noddinghead.com.

Plough & The Stars Old City's spacious Irish pub is a cozy place to kick off a night. Sit by the fire, chill out with a Harp, and watch as the 20-something crowd packs the bar, two, three, then four deep. Tall sidewalk tables offer nice vantage points for people-watching. Sunday afternoon, Irish musicians perform. 123 Chestnut St. (entrance on 2nd St. btw. Chestnut and Market sts.). ✆ **215/833-0300.** www.ploughstars.com.

Royal Tavern ★ Bella Vista's best neighborhood pub is exactly the bar you wish was on your own corner. It's got interesting beer and wine lists, above-average cocktails, and a menu that does bar fare right. Although there's always a game on the tube above the ancient mahogany bar and great music blaring from a jukebox, not too many people are paying attention. They'd rather just hang out. Menu served until 1am. 937 E. Passyunk Ave. ✆ **215/389-6694.** www.royaltavern.com.

Standard Tap ★★ This Northern Liberties gastropub has long anchored its neighborhood, and draws a casual, convivial crowd 7 nights a week. Downstairs, a jukebox blares indie rock, including many local bands. Upstairs is a small pub plus a large dining area and deck. Great grub is posted on chalkboard menus (p. 111), and don't expect anything less in the beverage department, as the beers are regional and mostly craft brews. The closest you'll get to a Bud is a Yuengling Lager, from Philadelphia's (and America's) oldest continuously operating brewery. No TV here. Menu served until 1am. Corner of 2nd and Poplar sts. ✆ **215/238-0630.** www.standardtap.com.

Tritone Across the street from the famed Bob & Barbara's (p. 209), this dimly lit, retro joint fits into more than one bar category. Tritone serves decent pirogi, red beans and rice, and the odd fried candy bar; and hosts music and events (rock-themed quizzo, soul DJs, indie rock bands). Tritone is a little divey, a little posh, and has a most excellent jukebox. 1508 South St. ✆ **215/545-0475.** www.tritonebar.com.

HOTEL BARS

Also see the description of **Il Bar** on p. 208.

Lounge at the Omni This lounge is a pleasant, quiet spot, with dark woods and Oriental carpets, a crackling fireplace, a player piano, and large picture windows surveying Independence National Historical Park across the street. It's good if you're looking for a sophisticated backdrop to conversation, and it stays open past midnight on weekends. 401 Chestnut St. ✆ **215/925-0000.** www.omnihotels.com.

Nineteen ★★ Though known for its cozy, fireside atmosphere and ample upholstery, the bar that leads to Nineteen's dining room pretty much always draws a crowd. I can't blame them, though. The size is just right, the crowd is dressed up, and the martinis are to die for. 200 S. Broad St. (at Walnut St. in the Park Hyatt at the Bellevue, 19th floor). ✆ **215/790-1919.** www.nineteenrestaurant.com.

Swann Lounge at the Four Seasons ★★★ There's something about having a hostess lead you to a plush couch near a fireplace, or near the window overlooking the fountain, that turns cocktail hour into a very refined happening indeed. Beyond the hotel lobby and connected to the fine Fountain Restaurant (p. 95), the Swann serves delicate cheese straws, afternoon tea, flawless martinis, cheesesteak spring rolls—and just about anything else you can dream up. 1 Logan Sq. (on 18th St.). ✆ **215/963-1500.** www.fourseasons.com/philadelphia.

10 Arts Lounge ★ Art Deco and delightful, the lobby lounge formerly (and more formally) known as the Rotunda serves noshes from Eric Ripert's menu and changes dramatically from family gathering spot by day to post business dinner nightcapery late at night. 20 S. Broad St. (in the Ritz-Carlton Philadelphia). ✆ **215/523-8273** or 523-8221. www.10arts.com.

BARS TO EAT IN, TOO (INCLUDES RESTAURANTS WITH GREAT BARS)

Amada ★★ If you can score a bar stool at this popular Old City Spanish restaurant, count yourself lucky, and bunker down. Amada's bar is a great spot to get tipsy on fruit-filled sangria, and to nibble the *jamón* (ham) and Manchego that slide off the antique slicer. It's also an excellent place to have a meal (p. 85). Menu served until 11:45pm Friday and Saturday. 217–219 Chestnut St. ✆ **215/625-2450.** www.amadarestaurant.com.

Bar Ferdinand ★ Finds This Northern Liberties bar became an instant favorite when it opened in 2006, serving tapas, Alhambra beer, and homemade sangria in a rustic gold-and-wood setting. The crowd is artsy and stylish, the sort that could live just on the bar's $2 wine specials and tiny Spanish platters of smoked fish, cured ham, and spiced almonds. The wine list is 100% Spanish, and there's always a $1 draft beer. Menu served until 1am. 1030 N. 2nd St. ✆ **215/923-1313.** www.barferdinand.com.

Bridget Foy's South Street Grill This classy bar and restaurant has been serving top-shelf martinis and bottles of beer, spicy Buffalo wings, and straightforward filet mignon to South Street neighbors for years. There's no pressure to socialize if you don't feel like it, but plenty of company to keep you entertained if you do. Bridget Foy's occupies the lower corner of Head House Square, and opens its above-sidewalk cafe tables in summer. Menu served until midnight Sunday to Friday and until 1am Saturday. 200 South St. ✆ **215/922-1813.** www.bridgetfoys.com.

Continental Mid-Town ★ The larger, more colorful crosstown expansion of Continental Restaurant and Martini Bar offers three floors and bars (including a popular rooftop deck). In warm weather, Mid-Town's deck is a huge scene: Around happy hour, a line waiting for elevator access forms on 18th Street. Menu served until 11pm Sunday through Wednesday and until midnight Thursday through Saturday. 1801 Chestnut St. ✆ **215/567-1800.** www.continentalmidtown.com.

Continental Restaurant and Martini Bar ★ This Old City vintage diner, with olive-shaped lamps and inventive cocktails, is one of the coolest spots in the city for sharing big plates of Szechuan fries and enjoying cocktails. The bar itself is long but not huge; your best bet is to wait for a table. Menu served until 11pm Sunday through Wednesday and until midnight Thursday through Saturday. 138 Market St. ✆ **215/923-6069.** www.continentalmartinibar.com.

Cuba Libre By day and into the early evening, this mammoth Havana-goes-to-Vegas restaurant is great for splurging on *ropa vieja* and empanadas. But once the sun's been down for an hour or so, Cuba Libre cranks up the salsa music and cranks out the Red Bull mojitos, with a selection of 60 rums. Menu served until 1am. 10 S. 2nd St. ✆ **215/627-0666.** www.cubalibrerestaurant.com.

Happy Rooster ★ This handsome, brassy bar has stood on the corner of 16th and Sansom for ages, first as a gentleman's city retreat for Russian vodka and caviar, now as a neighborhood refuge for marvelous dirty martinis, steaks, and caviar scrambled eggs. Roosters adorn the walls and shelves. Business folk and restaurant workers adorn the booths and bar stools. Menu served until 11pm on weekends. 118 S. 16th St. ✆ **215/963-9311.** www.thehappyrooster.com.

Latest Dish ★★ Downstairs from Fluid (p. 198), this unpretentious, hip restaurant and bar serves South Street's most stylish and eclectic crowd. Diners sit at the copper-top bar or tables, noshing amazing mac and cheese, and downing microbrews and cocktails made with Jack. Menu served until 11pm Sunday through Tuesday, until midnight Wednesday and Thursday, and until 1:30am Friday and Saturday. 613 S. 4th St. ✆ **215/629-0565.** www.latestdish.com.

Le Bar Lyonnais Downstairs from famed Le Bec-Fin restaurant (p. 95), you'll find this crowded, intimate, favorite hangout of those with high bank balances, hormones, and/or hopes. This is also the spot to sample Le Bec's menu a la carte. 1523 Walnut St. ✆ **215/567-1000.** www.lebecfin.com.

Loie Although handsome Loie's Parisian doors open to the sidewalk, and its lunch and dinner menus feature brasserie-style burgers à cheval, this Rittenhouse-area spot functions mostly as a hangout for a business-school crowd. Weekend nights, the packed front bar is quite a scene. Around 9pm, the back dining room makes do as a dance floor. In late 2006, Loie added an upstairs lounge. 128 S. 19th St. ✆ **215/568-0808.** www.loie215.com.

Marmont Marmont is a swank little Old City bar and restaurant, serving burgers and steaks early in the night, and hosting the occasional DJ. Though it's grown quieter through the years, it still is a nice, low-lit spot to bring a date, and offers cafe seating on the sidewalk in summer. 222 Market St. ✆ **215/923-1100.** www.marmont.net.

North 3rd ★ This colorful corner bar is cheerful and noisy—and one of the most popular hangouts in Northern Liberties. Cafe tables fill the sidewalk until the weather makes it absolutely unbearable to be outside. Inside, booths and bar always seem to be busy with groups filling up on burgers, mussels, falafel salads, and pints of locally brewed

Late-Night Eats

When the bars close, the grubbing begins. Here's where everyone goes to get a late-night/early-morning junk-food fix.

- South Street: **Lorenzo's & Son's,** 305 South St. (✆ **215/627-4110**). For floppy, oversize triangles of slippery, satisfying pizza, $2.50 a slice. Open until 4am (until 3am Sun—really Mon morning).
- Old City: **Sonny's Famous Steaks,** 228 Market St. (✆ **215/629-5760**). It's not a South Philly cheesesteak, but it's close enough tastewise, and much closer distancewise. Open until 3am on weekends. See p. 115.
- South Philly: **Pat's** and **Geno's,** intersection of Wharton, E. Passyunk, and 9th Street. They're open 24 hours, but somehow, the bargoers seem to be in a rush. Cosmi's closes at 9pm, unfortunately. See p. 115.
- Rittenhouse Square: **Little Pete's,** 219 S. 17th St. (✆ **215/545-5508**). This modest 24-hour diner, complete with counter seats, chocolate milkshakes, and skinny grilled cheeses packs 'em in come 2:15am, just like Rouge (p. 98) did, 3 hours earlier.
- Washington West: **Midtown II,** 122 S. 11th St. (✆ **215/627-6452**). All the Gayborhood seems to gather at this friendly diner (open 24/7) around 3am, to nosh spinach and feta omelets and BLTs—and to give up on flirting.

beer. Did I mention it's noisy in here? Menu served until 1am Monday to Friday and until midnight Sunday. 801 S. 3rd St. ✆ **215/413-3666.** www.norththird.com.

The Pub and Kitchen ★★ This relative newbie deftly fills its neighborhood's niche for great microbrews, delicious wine, and a gourmet menu—mostly of foods that you can eat with your hands. Oh, and a couple of TVs tuned to sports, too. It's the sort of place where you'd feel completely comfortable wearing jeans or a tux. Have the goat cheese pirogi, the bacon burger, the fish and chips, or the cheese plate. 1946 Lombard St. ✆ **215/545-0350.** www.thepubandkitchen.com.

Snackbar ★★ If it's pub fries and a double burger you seek, look elsewhere. This stylishly tiny Rittenhouse spot puts the word *snack* before *bar,* because that's just what its precious comestibles are, for the most part: tiny, delicious snacks—think four-piece shrimp cocktail, wee gnocchi with eggplant, cheese plates—not dinner. Try a few. The crowd, the wine, the food: All absolutely fabulous. 253 S. 20th St. ✆ **215/545-5655.** www.snackbarltd.com.

Society Hill Hotel Restaurant ★ You'll find no bar-top dancing at this handsomely restored corner bar. Instead, you'll find adults (imagine those?) savoring delicious French dip sandwiches, whole grilled fish, and a clever mix of French-fried yams and russet potatoes. Still, the thing here, beyond the tall tables and windows that open to the sidewalk, is the long, mahogany bar, pouring all manner of local ales and carefully mixed libations. The hotel (upstairs) has four rooms that range from $90 to $160 per night. Interested? Ask the bartender for a tour. Menu served until 1am. 301 Chestnut St. ✆ **215/923-3711.** www.phillyhotelbar.com.

Impressions

I have never observed such a wealth of taverns and drinking establishments as are in Philadelphia. . . . There is hardly a street without several and hardly a man here who does not fancy one his second home.

—Thomas Jefferson, letter to a Virginia friend (1790)

Twenty Manning With its windows opening out onto a leafy corner, and a long, modern bar, this is a living-room-style spot for professionals in their 20s through 40s. In the back are black leather sofas for canoodling, and the outdoor tables are a favorite dinner-date destination. The Asian-influenced cuisine and wine list are nice, but the noise level can get downright outrageous. 261 S. 20th St. ✆ **215/731-0900.** www.twentymanning.com.

WINE BARS

Il Bar ★★ Wine bar enthusiasts, this one's for you. The ground-floor bar at the Penn's View Hotel features an impressive *cruvinet* system that preserves up to 150 different bottles after they've been opened. Every selection is available by the glass, most for around $8, or by the taste (3 oz.). You can also order "flights" of five 1.5-ounce glasses, which makes for a convivial learning experience. Piano entertainment accompanies your sipping and swirling, and you can order from the stellar menu of the adjoined Ristorante Panorama (p. 92). 14 N. Front St. ✆ **215/922-7800.** www.pennsviewhotel.com.

Tria ★ This pair of small, narrow bars looks more New York than Philly, with their neutral colors, handsome light fixtures, and stylish patrons. Wines by the glass are categorized as Bold, Bubbly, and Zippy. Also on the menu: boutique beers, cheeses, and great little tapas in the forms of bruschetta, salads, and panini. 123 S. 18th St. ✆ **215/972-8742** and 12th and Spruce streets ✆ 215/629-9200. www.triacafe.com.

Vintage The most casual (but still not that casual) in this category is this narrow, loftlike spot, announced by a corkscrew on its door, which overlooks the 13th Street corridor. Exposed brick walls, a chandelier made from wine bottles, a list of 200 vintages (60 by the glass), and a nice menu of small plates (and one yummy bacon burger with truffled smoked tomato aioli) make Vintage popular among a crowd of aspiring oenophiles. 129 S. 13th St. ✆ **215/922-3095.** www.vintage-philadelphia.com.

4 THE GAY & LESBIAN SCENE

The area between Walnut and Locust streets south of the convention center—roughly from 9th Street to 13th Street—is known as the "Gayborhood." The heart of gay and lesbian Philadelphia is full of social services, bookstores, clubs, bars, and restaurants. Pick up a copy of *Philadelphia Gay News* at **Giovanni's Room** bookstore, 345 S. 12th St. (✆ **215/923-2960**) for suggestions of places that cater to a variety of niches and subniches.

Bump ★ This space-agey bar has warm orange lighting, sleek white booths, grass-green cocktails, and cute, multicolored guys. Bump busies up early on for the $3 martini

Moments Dive Bars

There's something slightly chic about these timeworn neighborhood joints, the kind of places where you'll feel comfortable in biker gear, tuxedo pants, sweat pants, or, if the occasion should call for it, no pants at all. Some of them even have exemptions from the nonsmoking law. (By the way, I was kidding about the no-pants thing.)

- **Bob & Barbara's,** 1509 South St. (✆ **215/545-4511**). There are many drinks here, but only one $3 "special," consisting of a shot of Jim Beam and a Pabst Blue Ribbon. Drink it. Then admire the old light fixtures. Or the collection of vintage Pabst ads papering the wall. Bob & Barbara's gets extra points for being gay friendly, especially during its famous Thursday-night drag shows.
- **Dirty Frank's,** 347 S. 13th St. (✆ **215/732-5010**). No sign outside. Just a mural of famous "Franks." Inside, it's art gallery meets ashtray, plus booth seating and intermittently friendly barkeeps. Skip the mixed drinks and the draft beer. Order bottles. Play darts. If you find yourself here New Year's Day, be sure to dance on the tables.
- **McGlinchey's,** 259 S. 15th St. (✆ **215/735-1259**). Ms. Pac Man tables. Mixed crowd that tends toward the down and out. Grumpy bartenders. 25¢ hot dogs. Cheap, cheap, cheap pints, the cheapest in the city. Nicer beer, too. And shots. Lots of 'em.
- **Oscar's Tavern,** 1524 Sansom St. (✆ **215/972-9938**). Oscar's is the textbook spot to hide from your boss—and to stay there until 2am. Don't be afraid of the dirt-cheap roast beef sandwiches. Or, for that matter, the cheap beer, or the hits-centric jukebox.
- **Ray's Happy Birthday Bar,** 1200 E. Passyunk Ave. (✆ **215/365-1169**). Right around the corner from the cheesesteak stands, this South Philly joint has been discovered by irony-peddling hipsters, but isn't that much the worse for it. Lou runs things behind the bar, and will be seriously disappointed if you didn't call ahead to tell him it's your birthday (so he can get you a cake). The original purpose of the trough that circles the bar is less than sanitary. But best of all is Ray's slogan: "You can't drink all day if you don't start in the morning."

specials (Mon–Sat, 5–7pm), and, on Sunday, for a $9.95 brunch with $3 champagne cocktails. Later on, some of Philly's fave DJs spin the tunes that give this place its name. Bump is definitely for beautiful people, including friendly heteros. In summer, a pretty courtyard out back offers more tables and quiet. 1234 Locust St. ✆ **215/732-1800.** www.bumplounge.com.

Pure ★★ With three lavishly decorated floors, room for 1,000, and a lineup of some of the best DJs on the East Coast, Pure is the Gayborhood's hottest (literally) nightlife scene. Among the fake zebra fur, baroque red-velvet curtains, and chandeliers, drag queens serve cocktails and glistening boys go shirtless. This place is after hours, so if you're planning on going late, make sure you've gotten on the guest list by calling ahead or signing yourself up online. 1221 St. James St. ✆ **215/735-5772.** www.purephilly.com.

Sisters Unfortunately, this is the only game in town for single lesbians, but Sisters delivers big: three bars over three floors, covering over 5,000 square feet, with a diverse clientele of lipstick, buzz-cut, professional, and student women—and a handful of the gay boys, too. The biggest nights are Thursday (karaoke) and Saturday (single dance party). Music ranges from house to pop to hip-hop to country. The business is run by women—for proof, take a peek into the sparkling and spacious restrooms. 1320 Chancellor St. ✆ **215/735-0735.** www.sistersnightclub.com. Cover $6–$10.

Tavern on Camac ★ **Finds** This unassuming, nearly hidden, 60-year-old pub—one of oldest gay bars in the U.S.—is most famous for its Friday and Saturday singalongs in its downstairs piano bar (so brush up on your show tunes). More recently, the Tavern has opened its upstairs for weekend night dance parties. The crowd here tends to be slightly more grown-up, if not in age, then in attitude, in the way that a dirty martini is more mature than a Cosmo. 243 S. Camac St. ✆ **215/545-0900.** www.tavernoncamac.com.

12th Air Command This neighborhood staple is a deck-top cookout, an arcade, a disco dance hall, a karaoke scene, and a lounge (complete with hunky barkeeps) rolled into one. Each night has its theme—Mexican fiesta, Asian drag show, college party (17 to enter, 21 to drink). The crowd is as diverse as they come: older guys, younger women, tailored suits, leather jackets. You'll find it all. No credit cards. 254 S. 12th St. ✆ **215/545-8088.** www.12thair.com. Cover $3 Fri, $5 Sat.

Uncles The bartenders and their mature male patrons are on a first-name basis at this small, menuless neighborhood bar, which comes complete with pale pink walls and slightly tacky tinsel decor. Younger crowds gather on weekends, but weekdays locals come to listen to the jukebox and watch the street scene pass by the bar's large folding windows. 1220 Locust St. ✆ **215/546-6660.**

Woody's This jumbo corner bar has anchored the neighborhood since the '70s, when most of its clientele was still in elementary school. Woody's does a respectable job of pleasing crowds. It's got a cybercafe, a straightforward downstairs bar and sandwich counter, and an upstairs bar where *trompe l'oeil* Atlases hold up a roof of stars. Nights follow themes: karaoke on Monday, all ages on Wednesday, Latin on Thursday, dancing on Saturday—and country line dancing early on Friday and Sunday nights. The spot is open to everyone, but women can have a hard time scoring a drink from bartenders. 202 S. 13th St. ✆ **215/545-1893.** www.woodysbar.com. Cover varies.

5 OTHER NIGHTTIME ENTERTAINMENT

BOWLING

Lucky Strikes Lanes One of a national chain of swank alleys, this centrally located hot spot spreads its 24 lanes over two floors, charges $45 to $65 per hour plus $4 for shoe rental—and, yet, there is a wait to play on weekends. The large, low-slung lounge makes for a nice waiting space, and serves buckets of beer along with sliders, cheeseburger fries, and sweet-tart cocktails. 1336 Chestnut St. ✆ **215/545-2471.** www.bowlluckystrike.com.

North Bowl ★ Northern Liberties' hip bowling alley opened in 2006 and has become one of the most fun nights out in all of the city. There are 17 lanes, two bars, and per-game pricing of $4 to $6. The decor is retrochic, with a mezzanine lounge with four private lanes. The menu stars tater tots, corn dogs, and local beers. 909 N. 2nd St. ✆ **215/238-BOWL** (2695). www.northbowlphilly.com.

Strikes Bowling Lounge University City's earlier version of North Bowl has a slightly less ritzy reputation, but it gets the job done with 12 lanes, Bud on tap, $45 per-hour rates, and discounts to students with valid IDs. 4040 Locust St. ✆ **215/387-2695.** www.strikesbowlinglounge.com.

CINEMA

Center City isn't a movie a minute, but it's getting better by the year. Old City has three nice **Ritz Cinemas,** and all of them tend toward Miramax style, small (but not that small) films, both domestic and foreign. The Ritzes share a phone number (✆ **215/925-7900**) and website (www.ritztheaters.com). There's the five-screen **Ritz 5 Movies,** 214 Walnut St.; the five-screen **Ritz at the Bourse,** 4th and Ranstead streets just off Chestnut Street behind the Omni Hotel; and the **Ritz East,** on 2nd Street between Chestnut and Walnut streets, with two screens. The Rittenhouse area's petite, slightly spartan, two-screen **Roxy Theatre** (✆ **215/923-6699**) shows first-run movies and occasional old-timers.

South Philly's **United Artist Riverview,** 1400 S. Columbus Blvd. (✆ **215/722-2219**), shows blockbusters to an often talkative crowd. The Franklin Institute's **Tuttleman IMAX Theater,** 222 N. 20th St. (✆ **215/448-1111;** www.fi.edu), shows adventure and nature movies *(Deep Sea, Roving Mars, Ant Bully)* on its four-story, domed screen.

In University City, there are first-run blockbusters at the **Bridge Cinema de Lux,** 230 S. 40th St. (✆ **215/386-3300;** www.thebridgecinema.com). Foreign film series, political documentaries, and other indie movies show at **Penn's International House,** 3701 Chestnut St. (✆ **215/387-5125**).

READINGS

The main branch of the **Free Library of Philadelphia,** a beautiful limestone temple at 1901 Vine St. (✆ **215/686-5415;** www.library.phila.gov), has regular author readings with writers like Toni Morrison and John Grogan. **Borders,** 1 S. Broad St. (✆ **215/568-7400**), runs one of the country's top series of author readings in an elegant setting across the Avenue of the Arts from the Ritz-Carlton. Readings are usually at 7:30pm weekdays and 2pm weekends. **Barnes & Noble** in Rittenhouse Square, 1805 Walnut St. (✆ **215/665-0716**), offers semiregular 7pm readings.

SALON

Several spots around town have started catering to the large pool of intellectually curious. Judy Wicks at the **White Dog Café,** 3420 Sansom St. (✆ **215/386-9224;** www.whitedogcafe.com), has instituted "table talk" dinners with local academics, artists, and activists. While tucking into locally farmed and raised fare, diners learn about issues such as domestic and foreign policy, the arts, and social movements. The salon talks include a three-course dinner that usually goes for $36 per person. Reservations are recommended.

SPECTACLES

The **Benjamin Franklin Bridge** has been outfitted with special lighting effects by the noted architectural firm Venturi, Rauch, and Scott Brown. The lights are triggered into mesmerizing patterns by the auto and train traffic along the span. Lighting plays on most of the major monuments and bridges leading in and out of Center City and on City Hall as well.

May through October, from dusk until 11:15pm, Independence National Historical Park becomes the backdrop for the mesmerizing ***Lights of Liberty*** show. Wearing special headsets, you hear stereophonic sound and see 50-foot projections and surprising special effects that illustrate the struggle toward America's independence. See p. 125 for details.

11

Side Trips from Philadelphia

by Lenora Dannelke

In less than an hour, you can drive north from Philadelphia to tranquil Bucks County or southwest to the green and beautiful Brandywine River Valley and find enchanting farms, classic stone farmhouses, antiques galleries, and art museums. The same boats that brought Penn's Quakers to Pennsylvania also brought the pioneers that fanned out into the Delaware Valley to the south, Bucks County to the north, and what is now Pennsylvania Dutch Country to the west. This chapter covers Bucks County and the Brandywine area; chapter 12 guides you through the Amish heartland of Lancaster County.

Many of these areas remain lush and unspoiled, although, of course, development has encroached where land preservationists have not been able to save open space. The major attractions of the Bucks and Brandywine countryside are historical and cultural: Colonial mansions, early American factories, incredible gardens and museums, and Revolutionary War battlegrounds. Both areas are known for inspiring renowned painters, also. Along with the New Hope School of Impressionist Art, the Brandywine is and was home to three generations of Wyeths, the late N. C. and Andrew as well as Jamie.

1 BUCKS COUNTY & NEARBY NEW JERSEY

Bucks County, at most an hour by car from Philadelphia, is bordered by the Delaware River to the east and Montgomery County to the west. Historic estates and sights, antiques stores, and country inns abound. The natural beauty here, which has survived major development so far, has inspired many artists and authors, including Oscar Hammerstein II, Pearl Buck, and James Michener, and draws as many New Yorkers on weekends as it does Philadelphians. With dozens of county and state parks, the lush landscape is great for gentle outdoor activities. Nearby New Jersey also offers scenic routes for bicycling and walking, plus enjoyable restaurants. The rural-but-sophisticated area, especially the bustling village of New Hope, is also very gay friendly.

ESSENTIALS

GETTING THERE The best automobile route into Bucks County from Center City is I-95 (north). Pa. 32 (which intersects I-95 in Yardley) runs along the Delaware past Washington Crossing State Park to New Hope, which connects to Doylestown by U.S. 202. By train, the R5 SEPTA commuter rail ends at Doylestown.

From New York, take the New Jersey Turnpike to I-78 west; follow to exit 29 and pick up Route 287 south to Route 202, which crosses the Delaware River at Lambertville, straight into New Hope. To stay a bit more north and rural, depart I-78 at exit 15 in

Clinton and take Route 513 south 12 tranquil miles, crossing the Delaware at picturesque Frenchtown, New Jersey.

VISITOR INFORMATION Get details on attractions, events, and lodgings, plus discounts and packages, from the **Bucks County Conference & Visitors Bureau,** 3207 Street Rd., Bensalem, PA 19020 (✆ **800/836-2825;** www.bccvb.org). A new **Bucks County Visitors Center, Peddler's Village** (shop #165) in Lahaska (✆ **215/794-3130**), operates during local store hours (which fluctuate season to season; see www.peddlersvillage.com). You can also visit the **New Hope Visitors Center,** 1 W. Mechanic St., New Hope, PA 18938 (✆ **215/862-5030;** www.newhopevisitorscenter.org), open 7 days a week, hours varying seasonally.

Along with the specific accommodations listed below, contact the **Bucks County Bed and Breakfast Association,** PO Box 154, New Hope, PA 18938 (✆ **215/862-7154;** www.bbonline.com/pa/buckscounty), which includes inns located in the wonderful New Jersey towns of Lambertville, Stockton, and Frenchtown. Also visit www.bedandbreakfast.com or www.ilovenewhope.com for more suggestions.

ATTRACTIONS IN BUCKS COUNTY

Fallsington When William Penn was in residence at Pennsbury Manor (see below) and wished to worship, he'd go to Fallsington, 6 miles north of his estate. This Colonial village, grouped around the Quaker meetinghouse, has been preserved virtually intact. Guided tours are mandatory to enter the buildings, but a free pamphlet outlining a self-guided walking tour of the grounds is available.

Tyburn Rd., Fallsington, PA. ✆ **215/295-6567.** www.historicfallsington.org. Admission $5 adults, $4 seniors, $2 children. Mid-May to mid-Oct Tues–Sat 10:30am–3:30pm; Mid-Oct to Mid-May Tues–Fri 10:30am–3:30pm. Free open-house days in May and Oct. Take Pa. 13 north to Tyburn Rd. (Pa. 9), then turn right and follow the road, or south off U.S. 1 at Tyburn Rd.

Pennsbury Manor The reconstructed country estate of Pennsylvania's founder, William Penn, was built in 1939 and is beautifully situated on 43 acres along the Delaware River, just 24 miles north of Philadelphia. Visitors can experience 17th-century life through the furnished manor house, stables, bake and brew house, outbuildings, and formal and kitchen gardens. The site comes alive with costumed interpreters and period farm animals. Programs include the Colonial Crossroads Festival, Holly Nights, and Sundays at Pennsbury. Visitor services include tours, exhibits, an orientation film, and a museum store.

Morrisville, PA. ✆ **215/946-0400.** www.pennsburymanor.org. Admission to buildings (by guided tour only) $7 adults, $6 seniors, $4 children 6–17, free for children 5 and under. Admission to grounds $3. Tues–Sat 9am–5pm; Sun noon–5pm. Call or check the website for tour times and special events. Take Pa. 9 (Tyburn Rd.) from U.S. 1 (intersects I-95) or U.S. 13.

Sesame Place ★★ Kids The more than 60 physical play stations and water rides at the nation's only theme park based on the award-winning television show *Sesame Street* are perfect for any family with 3- to 15-year-olds. The park is 30 minutes from Center City and 90 minutes from New York City. My kids and millions of others have happily explored it—climbing through three stories of sloping, swaying fun on the Nets and Climbs, splashing in the water, and enjoying the daily interactive musical parade starring Big Bird, Elmo, Bert and Ernie, and the rest. Count's Splash Castle, a huge new multilevel interactive water-play attraction, features 90 play elements. The popular Elmo's World features three fun rides and dining with an assortment of characters (reservations

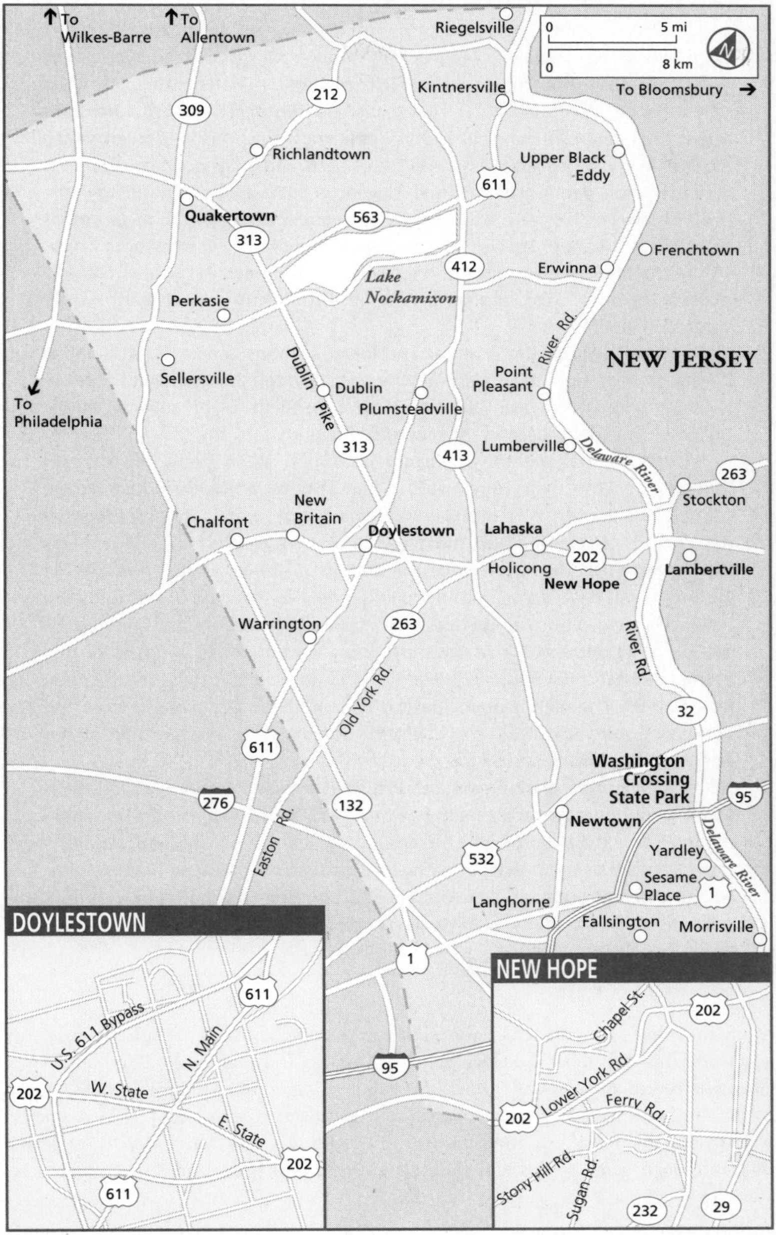
To Wilkes-Barre
To Allentown
Riegelsville
0 5 mi
0 8 km
N
To Bloomsbury
Kintnersville
309
212
Richlandtown
Upper Black Eddy
611
Quakertown
563
313
Frenchtown
412
Erwinna
Lake Nockamixon
Perkasie
River Rd.
NEW JERSEY
Sellersville
Dublin Pike
Dublin
Point Pleasant
Plumsteadville
To Philadelphia
313
413
Lumberville
Delaware River
263
Stockton
New Britain
Chalfont
Doylestown
Lahaska
202
Holicong
New Hope
Lambertville
Warrington
263
River Rd.
Old York Rd.
32
611
Washington Crossing State Park
276
132
95
Newtown
Easton Rd.
Delaware River
Yardley
532
Sesame Place
1
Langhorne
Fallsington
Morrisville
DOYLESTOWN
1
NEW HOPE
611
U.S. 611 Bypass
N. Main
202
W. State
E. State
202
611
95
Chapel St.
202
Lower York Rd.
Ferry Rd.
202
Stony Hill Rd.
Sugan Rd.
232
29

Fun Facts Where Washington Crossed the Delaware

A trip along the Delaware via Route 32 through Morrisville and Yardley will bring you to **Washington Crossing Historic Park** in Pennsylvania, 500 acres that are open year-round (there's a separate **Washington Crossing State Park** across the river in New Jersey). Most people know that Washington crossed a big river in a small boat on Christmas Eve of 1776, and many people are familiar with the heroic painting depicting this event, with Washington standing in the boat, his eyes on the far shore. This was the spot, and a copy of the enormous painting by Emanuel Leutze is on display at the visitor center, where a new 15-minute film provides a good orientation to the park. An annual reenactment of the historic crossing takes place here at Christmas. There's also a well-stocked museum store.

The park is divided into upper and lower sections separated by 4 miles; Washington left from the lower site, where you can tour **McConkey's Ferry Inn** (1752), where Washington ate before he crossed the river; several historic buildings in Taylorsville; and the Memorial Building.

A lovely alternative to driving to the lower park site is biking the towpath that connects the areas. Here, you can tour **Thompson-Neely House,** where General Washington, Brigadier General Stirling, and Lieutenant James Monroe decided on the year-end push into New Jersey. On a nearby hilltop, **Bowman's Hill Tower,** a 125-foot stone structure built in 1931—now equipped with an elevator—will reward you with a stunning view of this part of the Delaware Valley. Washington Crossing State Park, PO Box 103, Washington Crossing, PA 18977 (✆ **215/493-4076;** www.ushistory.org/washingtoncrossing), is located at the intersection of Route 32 (River Rd.) and Route 532, 3 miles north of I-96 from exit 31. The park is open Tuesday through Saturday 10am to 4pm and Sunday noon to 4pm (call to check since hours may vary). Tickets are $5 for adults, $4 for seniors, and $2 for ages 6 to 17.

Once part of the park, **Bowman's Hill Wild Flower Preserve** (✆ **215/862-2924;** www.bhwp.org) adjacent to Bowman's Hill Tower, now operates independently. This enchanting 134-acre arboretum, nature center, and botanical preserve features more than 24 paths that wind through diverse habitats, illustrating different botanical wonders. Grounds are open daily 8:30am to sunset. Admission is $5 for adults, $3 for seniors and students, and $2 for ages 4 to 14.

required). Bring swimsuits for 13 age-safe water rides including Sky Splash, the five-story water adventure; Rubber Duckie; Slimey's Chutes; and Big Bird's Rambling River. Changing rooms are provided. Older kids will love Vapor Trail, the park's roller coaster. All of the best-loved *Sesame Street* characters perform in shows at Big Bird Theater and are available for photo opportunities at 1-2-3 Smile with Me. Indoors, you'll find air-conditioned game rooms and shops. Lockers, wheelchairs, and stroller rentals are available.

100 Sesame Rd., Langhorne, PA. © **866/464-3566** or 215/752-7070. www.sesameplace.com. Admission $50 per person; free for children 1 and under. May 1 to day before Memorial Day Fri–Sun; Memorial Day to Labor Day daily; day after Labor Day to Oct 31 Sat–Sun. Hours subject to change: Call to check. Junction of Rte. 1 and I-95.

NEW HOPE & LAMBERTVILLE

Four miles north of Washington Crossing on River Road (Pa. 32), which is punctuated by hilly, lovely farmland (as opposed to U.S. 202's factory outlets), you'll come upon New Hope, a former Colonial town turned artists' colony. Although it's now something of a tourist mecca—the weekend crowds are fierce and parking is cramped (see parking map at www.newhopevisitorscenter.org)—once you're here you'll enjoy the specialty shops, restaurants, and galleries. Lambertville, across the Delaware in New Jersey, feels more sophisticated, with its fine antiques stores and restaurants.

NEW HOPE AREA ATTRACTIONS

Bucks County Playhouse The center of New Hope entertainment, this gristmill-turned-theater has featured Broadway hits, musical revivals, and dramas since 1939, and now also offers numerous Children's Theatre shows.

70 S. Main St., New Hope, PA. © **215/862-2041.** www.buckscountyplayhouse.com. Tickets $23–$25; Children's Theatre $8. Apr–Dec Thurs–Fri 8pm; Sat 4pm and 8pm; Sun 2pm.

Parry Mansion Museum One of the loveliest old homes in town, this mansion was erected in 1784 by the elite of New Hope. The Parry family lived in this 11-room Georgian until 1966, and the rooms are decorated in different period styles ranging from 1775 (whitewash and candles) to 1900 (wallpaper and oil lamps).

Main and Ferry sts., New Hope, PA. © **215/862-5652.** www.parrymansion.org. Admission $5 adults, $4 seniors and students, $1 children 11 and under. Late Apr to early Dec Sat–Sun 1–5pm.

Peddler's Village Five miles south of New Hope, on Route 202, Peddler's Village is a quaintly styled outdoor shopping mall, though most merchandise in the 70 specialty shops is contemporary. The village synergy kicks in with eight restaurants, an inn, and **Giggleberry Fair,** a lively family entertainment center with a restored 1922 carousel, three-story obstacle course, game room, and interactive Discovery Land (all-inclusive admission package $13 for adults and $15 children). The newest restaurant is **Sweet Lorraine's Café & Bar**, which is opening as we go to print. For an elegant steak-and-seafood dining experience, try **Earl's Prime** (**© 215/794-4020**). Specialties of the rustic **Cock 'n Bull** include a massive buffet on Thursday and a lavish Sunday brunch. The 70 well-appointed rooms and suites in the kid-friendly **Golden Plough Inn** are scattered across the village, and many feature Jacuzzis and fireplaces. Rates range from $160 to $420 per night.

U.S. 202 and Rte. 263, Lahaska, PA. © **215/794-4000.** www.peddlersvillage.com. Most stores Sun–Thurs 10am–6pm; Fri–Sat 10am–9pm. Giggleberry Fair Sun 10am–7pm; Mon–Thurs 10am–6pm; Fri–Sat 10am–10pm.

OUTDOOR ACTIVITIES IN THE NEW HOPE & LAMBERTVILLE AREA

BIKING & COUNTRY WALKING Walking or riding along the Delaware River or along the canals built for coal hauling on either side of the river can be the highlight of a summer. The following two routes are particularly convenient: The first is between Lumberville and the point, 3 miles south, where Route 263 crosses the Delaware into

Moments Horsing Around in Bucks County

With admission a mere five bucks a carload, **Tinimcum Park Polo Club** (www.tinicumpolo.org) matches are a bargain-priced family outing. Boys will relish the excitement of the arduous physical sport, while girls will be thrilled by the equine ballet. Matches are played at **Tinimcum Park,** 963 River Rd., Erwinna, from 2 to 4pm on Saturday, mid-May to early October, conditions permitting (call the Polo Hot Line on Sat morning; ✆ **908/996-3321**). You can park on the sidelines and tailgate; there's also a snack bar and a tent with chairs available to the general public. Crowds here are fun and friendly.

New Jersey. The towpath along the canal on the Pennsylvania side is charming, and Lumberville's historic (and newly renovated) **Black Bass Hotel** (✆ **215/297-5770;** www.blackbasshotel.com) is a great riverside destination for breakfast or lunch, as well as dinner or an overnight stay.

The second route, also just south of Lumberville, follows River Road (Rte. 32) south and west to Cuttalossa Road, which winds past an alpine chalet, creeks, ponds, and grazing sheep clanking their antique Swiss bells. In Frenchtown, New Jersey, the fleet of bikes for hire by the hour or day at **Cycle Corner of Frenchtown,** 52 Bridge St. (✆ **908/996-7712;** www.thecyclecorner.com), includes sport/mountain, tandem, and recumbent models, plus kid-friendly trailers and trail-a-bikes; call for hours and prices.

CANOEING & TUBING The award for relaxing family fun goes to **Bucks County River Country,** 2 Walters Lane, off Route 32, Point Pleasant (✆ **215/297-5000;** www.rivercountry.net). You can drift down the Delaware—which stays above 70°F (21°C) all summer and moves at a leisurely 1½-mph pace—from Upper Black Eddy and Riegelsville back to headquarters 8 miles north of New Hope. Rates are $18 to $45 per person for activities that include tubing, canoeing, rafting, and kayaking (novices can opt for the new single and double sit-on-top kayaks).

DRIVING TOURS Find details on self-guided driving tours of the area's 11 remaining covered bridges or 10 wineries at the Bucks Country Conference & Visitors Bureau website, www.bccvb.org. Notable oenophile stops include **Crossing Vineyards and Winery,** 1853 Wrightstown Rd., Washington Crossing (✆ **215/493-6500;** www.crossingvineyards.com), and **Sand Castle Winery,** 755 River Road, Erwinna (✆ **800/722-9463;** www.sandcastlewinery.com), with incredible 17-mile views.

STEAM RAILWAY TOUR The **New Hope & Ivyland Railroad,** 32 W. Bridge St., New Hope (✆ **215/862-2332;** www.newhoperailroad.com), steam railway chuffs a 45-minute loop between New Hope and Lahaska, and offers dinner and special Christmas, Easter, and Halloween trips.

SHOPPING

Penn's Purchase Factory Outlet Stores Adjacent to Peddler's Village, this sprawling shopping complex—one of the few area retailers open on a Sunday morning—straddles Route 202 between Doylestown and New Hope, and contains 45 outlets for stores such as **Coach, Bose, Osh Kosh, Geoffrey Beene, Bass,** and **Orvis.** For those immediate travel needs, there are clean restrooms and an ATM. Grab a snack at **Dairy Queen** or relax over an excellent rustic Italian meal at **Villaggio.**

Rte. 202, Lahaska, PA. © **215/794-0300.** www.pennspurchase.com. Mon–Fri 10am–8pm; Sat 9am–8pm; Sun 9am–6pm.

Rice's Market This is the real thing—a 30-acre country market that started selling farm-fresh foods in 1860 and is now famed for bargains on a huge spectrum of new merchandise, ranging from furniture to footwear. Amish wares, antiques, and collectibles are sold in the main building, and up to 1,000 outdoor stalls have vendors. There are indoor bathrooms, ATMs, and paved walkways for strollers and wheelchairs. Get here early to beat the enormous crowds.

6326 Greenhill Rd., New Hope, PA. © **215/297-5993.** www.ricesmarket.com. Jan–Feb Tues 7am–1:30pm; Mar–Dec Tues 7am–1:30pm, Sat 7am–1:30pm. Go 1 mile north of Peddler's Village on Rte. 263, then turn left by the Victorian gazebo onto Greenhill Rd.; Rice's is 1 mile ahead on the right.

WHERE TO STAY

Country Inns

New Hope and its New Jersey neighbor across the Delaware River, Lambertville, have well-deserved reputations for their country inns and restaurants. Many frown on children and most require 2-day stays on weekends, though it's worth checking for last-minute openings. The listings here only scratch the surface: Romantic choices include the cozy **Inn at Phillips Mill,** 2590 River Rd., New Hope (© **215/862-2984;** www.theinnatphillipsmill.com), and Upper Black Eddy's gorgeously appointed **1836 Bridgeton House on the Delaware,** 1525 River Rd. (© **888/892-2007;** www.bridgetonhouse.com), where most rooms feature a private riverfront balcony or patio. Luxurious, bucolic inns include **Barley Sheaf Farm Estate & Spa,** 5281 Old York Rd., Holicong (© **215/794-5104;** www.barleysheaf.com), with lavishly appointed suites in a vintage manor house and stone bank barn, and tranquil mansion rooms and very posh carriage house cottages at the **Woolverton Inn,** 6 Woolverton Rd., Stockton, NJ (© **609/397-0802;** www.woolvertoninn.com), complete with Frette linens and pet sheep. Located less than a mile from downtown Doylestown, **Highland Farm Bed & Breakfast Inn,** 70 East Rd. (© **215/345-6767;** www.highlandfarmbb.com), the lovingly restored home of Oscar Hammerstein, could put a song in your heart. Each room is tastefully decorated to reflect a different Rogers and Hammerstein musical, and guests are invited to play the Pranberry grand piano in the Sound of Music Room, where wine and cheese is served in the evening. Amenities include a swimming pool and tennis court, and children are welcome.

For convenient, in-town digs with premium style, there's the handsomely restored 1812 **Lambertville House,** 32 Bridge St. (© **609/397-0200;** www.lambertvillehouse.com). In New Hope, **Porches on the Towpath,** 20 Fisher's Alley (© **215/862-3277;** www.porchesnewhope.com), originally an 1830s granary, provides charming, peaceful seclusion right in the heart of town.

Centre Bridge Inn ★ Situated beside the Delaware River 3½ miles north of New Hope, the current building is the third since the early 18th century. Many of the lovely guest rooms have canopy, four-poster, or brass beds; wall-high armoires; modern private bathrooms; outside decks; and views of the river or countryside. The inn also has a pretty restaurant overlooking the river.

2998 N. River Rd. (intersection of Rte. 32 and Rte. 263), New Hope, PA 18938. © **215/862-9139.** www.centrebridgeinn.com. 12 units. $99–$265 double. Rates include continental breakfast. AE, DISC, MC, V. **Amenities:** Restaurant; lounge w/fireplace. *In room:* A/C, TV, Wi-Fi, no phone.

Inn at Bowman's Hill ★★ You'll feel like pampered royalty ensconced in this spectacular, gated, 5-acre country estate, which counts celebrities among its clientele. Stroll the beautiful grounds and gardens, lounge by the pool or under the Vine Terrace, soak in the hot tub, or just relax in the plush comforts of your elegantly furnished room in the main building or carriage house, complete with romantic lighting options, custom draperies, beautiful rugs, gas fireplace, plasma TV, and spacious Italian tile bathroom with a whirlpool and separate shower. My favorite room is the Orchard Retreat, with its secluded second-floor veranda and lovely views of the property. Cheery, warm, and attentive hosts Michael and Lynne Amery can arrange for a massage or even coordinate a proposal in the Orchid Room conservatory. Sumptuous breakfasts are worth waking up for—whether enjoyed in the intimate dining room or in your king-size feather bed.

58 Lurgan Rd. (just off Rte. 32, 2 miles south of New Hope), New Hope, PA 18938. ✆ **215/862-8090.** www.theinnatbowmanshill.com. 6 units. $325–$405 double; $455–$525 suite. Higher rates for holidays. Rates include breakfast. AE, DISC, MC, V. **Amenities:** Outdoor pool; hot tub; gardens. *In room:* A/C, TV/DVD, Wi-Fi, fridge, coffeemaker, hair dryer, iron, heated towel rack, CD player, private veranda (in some).

Hotels

For gay-friendly accommodations and an exhilarating social scene, head for the **Nevermore,** 6426 Lower York Rd., New Hope (✆ **215/862-5221;** www.thenevermorehotel.com), operated by an owner of the former Raven Resort. Along with 140 updated rooms, there's a full-service restaurant, pool and cabana bar, piano lounge and cabaret, plus DJ dance parties every Friday and Saturday night. If you prefer historic elegance, the **Inn at Lambertville Station,** 111 Bridge St., Lambertville (✆ **609/397-4400;** www.lambertvillestation.com), offers fine, antiques-laden lodgings in a wonderful waterfront location. The 45-room boutique hotel, housed in a meticulously restored Victorian train station, features an excellent restaurant and pub, plus a beautiful Canal Side outdoor dining area and bar in season.

Sheraton Bucks County Hotel (Kids) This festive, modern, 14-story hotel is right across the street from Sesame Place. The guest rooms have oversize beds and quilted fabrics, and there's no charge to put a cot in the room for kids. Facilities include a health club, an indoor swimming pool and sauna, and a full-service restaurant.

400 Oxford Valley Rd., Langhorne, PA 19047. ✆ **800/325-3535** or 215/547-4100. www.sheraton.com/buckscounty. 186 units. $139–$209 double. AE, DC, DISC, MC, V. Some dogs accepted. **Amenities:** Restaurant; lounge; indoor pool; fitness facility; sauna; Sesame Place shuttle; laundry service. *In room:* A/C, TV w/pay movies, Wi-Fi, coffeemaker, hair dryer.

WHERE TO DINE

With the staggering array of restaurants in this area, there's a dining spot to suit every mood, taste, and budget. In Lambertville, a local favorite is **Siam** ★, 61 N. Main St. (✆ **609/397-8128**), an unpretentious, cash-only BYOB that serves fantastic Thai fare at moderate prices. On the New Hope side, try the **Landing,** 22 N. Main St. (✆ **215/862-5711;** www.landingrestaurant.com), for regional American cuisine and a picturesque riverside setting; offbeat, seasonal **Zoubi** ★, 7 Mechanic St. (✆ **215/862-5851;** www.zoubinewhope.com), for amazing fusion fare; or funky **John and Peter's,** 96 S. Main St. (✆ **215/862-5981;** www.johnandpeters.com), for burgers and great live music. Across the street, the lively patio at **Havana,** 105 S. Main St. (✆ **215/862-9897;** www.havananewhope.com) is a great spot for cocktails, snacks, and people-watching. Heat lamps keep the outdoor action going all year long.

The Freight House NEW AMERICAN It's hard to believe that the building housing this stylish, upscale restaurant and lounge was once used for livestock. Located next to the SEPTA station, the vintage structure has been outfitted with a sensually undulating bar, curvy banquettes and intimate booths upholstered in leather, and striking contemporary artwork. The high-protein menu features premium seafood and steaks, and the brunch menu is varied and extensive. Premise-made infusions and extracts, crafted primarily from local fruit and herbs, flavor such state-of-the-art cocktails as apricot-rosemary martinis and watermelon-cilantro mojitos. There's live piano and vocals on Wednesday evenings, and dancing Thursday through Saturday nights packs the house.

194 W. Ashland St., Doylestown, PA. ✆ **215/340-1003.** www.thefreighthouse.net. Main courses $20–$49. AE, DISC, MC, V. Sun–Wed 4pm–midnight; Thurs–Sat 4pm–1am; Sun 10am–2pm (brunch).

Hamilton's Grill Room ★★ AMERICAN This insiders' spot, just across the bridge from New Hope in upscale Lambertville, is tucked away down a gravel alley by the canal, across from a wonderful bar in a former boathouse. You need to pick up your own bottle of wine (go to Welsh's Wines, 8 S. Union St. in the center of town), and reserve well in advance, but you'll be delighted by the cool crowd, and excellent, Mediterranean-seasoned grilled steaks or lamb eaten on a chic banquette inside, or under a beautiful white tent in the courtyard outside in summer months. The salads, small pastas, and savory fish dishes here are as good as any you'd find in Manhattan or in the countryside of Tuscany.

8 Coryell St., Lambertville, NJ. ✆ **609/397-4343.** www.hamiltonsgrillroom.com. Reservations required. Main courses $25–$35; half-portions from $13. AE, DC, DISC, MC, V. Mon–Sat 6–10pm; Sun 5–9pm.

Marsha Brown's CREOLE/STEAKHOUSE From the owner of Philly's Ruth's Chris Steak House, this grandly stylish spot is set in a 125-year-old lofty stone church with gorgeous lighting through clerestory windows and lavish murals. The crowd is well dressed and lively, with big families celebrating fun occasions, and romantic couples (both straight and gay). Expect generous plates of flavorful steakhouse classics, plus Creole-inflected dishes, courtesy of family recipes from dynamic proprietor Marsha Brown. Crab cakes are a robust, no-filler-used classic and meats are as well aged and enormous as you would expect.

15 S. Main St., New Hope, PA. ✆ **215/862-7044.** www.marshabrownrestaurant.com. Main courses $22–$38. AE, DC, MC, V. Mon–Thurs 5–10pm; Fri 5–11pm; Sat 2–11pm; Sun 2–9pm.

DOYLESTOWN

Authentic small-town charm shines throughout the picturesque community of Doylestown, the county seat. Inviting downtown streets are lined with specialty shops and loads of restaurants. There's even a vintage art-house cinema, the **County Theater,** 20 E. State St. (✆ **215/345-6789;** countytheater.org). It's a marvelous town to just walk around, but three interesting collections invite you indoors. All were endowed by Dr. Henry Chapman Mercer (1856–1930), an eccentric and avid collector, archaeologist, and master of pottery techniques. The **James A. Michener Art Museum,** housed in a splendidly renovated historic county jail at 138 S. Pine St. (✆ **215/340-9800;** www.michenerartmuseum.org), is another worthwhile stop. Motorists should exit the Pennsylvania Turnpike at the Willow Grove Interchange (exit 27) and follow Route 611 north to the Doylestown exit. Drive through scenic Doylestown and turn right onto Route 313 (Swamp Rd.).

DOYLESTOWN AREA ATTRACTIONS

Fonthill Museum ★ Everyone can call their home a castle, but Dr. Mercer could say it and mean it. The core of his wondrous castle, built from reinforced concrete in Mercer's own design in 1908, has towers, turrets, and tiles piled on beyond belief. Each room is a different shape and each is fully adorned with tiles, some antique and some made in Mercer's own tile works across the driveway.

E. Court St. (off Swamp Rd. [Rte. 313]), Doylestown, PA. ✆ **215/348-9461.** www.fonthillmuseum.org. Admission $9 adults, $8 seniors, $4 children 5–17. Mon–Sat 10am–5pm; Sun noon–5pm (last tour at 4pm). Guided tours only; reservations recommended.

Mercer Museum ★★ Mercer Museum displays thousands of early American tools, vehicles, cooking pieces, looms, and even weather vanes. Mercer had the collecting bug in a big way, and you can't help being impressed with the breadth of his collection and the castle that houses it. It rivals the Shelburne, Vermont, complex for Americana—and that's 35 buildings on 100 acres! The open atrium rises five stories, suspending a Conestoga wagon, chairs, and sleighs as if they were Christmas-tree ornaments. A log cabin is open periodically for costumed Colonial life demonstrations. Kid-friendly fun includes a scavenger hunt and embossing station based on animal images in the collection. Animals on the Loose, a hands-on, participatory adventure, encourages children ages 3 to 8 to search for curious creatures, like a rabbit chocolate mold and owl-shaped andiron. A major expansion, adding 10,000 square feet for changing exhibitions (plus additional parking), will be completed by 2010.

Pine St. at Ashland St., Doylestown, PA. ✆ **215/345-0210.** www.mercermuseum.org. Admission $8 adults, $7 seniors, $4 children 5–17, free for children 4 and under. Sun noon–5pm; Mon and Wed–Sat 10am–5pm; Tues 10am–9pm.

Moravian Pottery & Tile Works Down the road on Pa. 313, the sprawling Spanish mission–style Moravian Pottery & Tile Works was Dr. Mercer's first big project. Tiles and mosaics made here adorn the state capitol in Harrisburg and other notable buildings worldwide. At this living history museum, watch ceramists craft exquisite tiles and mosaics sold at the museum shop.

Swamp Rd., Doylestown, PA. ✆ **215/345-6722.** www.buckscounty.org/departments/tileworks. Admission $3.50 adults, $3 seniors, $2 children. Daily 10am–4:45pm. Tours available every 30 min. until 4pm. Closed major holidays.

2 EXPLORING THE BRANDYWINE VALLEY

The Brandywine Valley, bridging Pennsylvania and Delaware, makes a great 1- to 3-day excursion into rolling country filled with Americana from Colonial days through the Gilded Age.

Many of the farms that kept the Revolutionary troops fed have survived to this day. There are 15 covered bridges and 100 antiques stores in Chester County alone. Be sure to get off the highway and wander some country roads: Scenery simply doesn't get any better than this, and spring and fall are particularly colorful seasons. However, Route 100 between Route 141 and Route 1 is breathtaking even in winter. Delaware's tax-free shopping is a nice bonus.

The valley is rich in history. Without the defeat at Brandywine, Washington would never have ended up at Valley Forge, from which he emerged with a competent army. When the du Pont de Nemours family fled post-Revolutionary France, they wound up owning powder mills on the Brandywine Creek. Every pioneer needed gunpowder and iron, and the business grew astronomically, expanding into chemicals and textiles. The du Ponts controlled upper Delaware as a virtual fiefdom, building splendid estates and gardens. Most of these, along with the original mills, are open to visitors. The fabulous

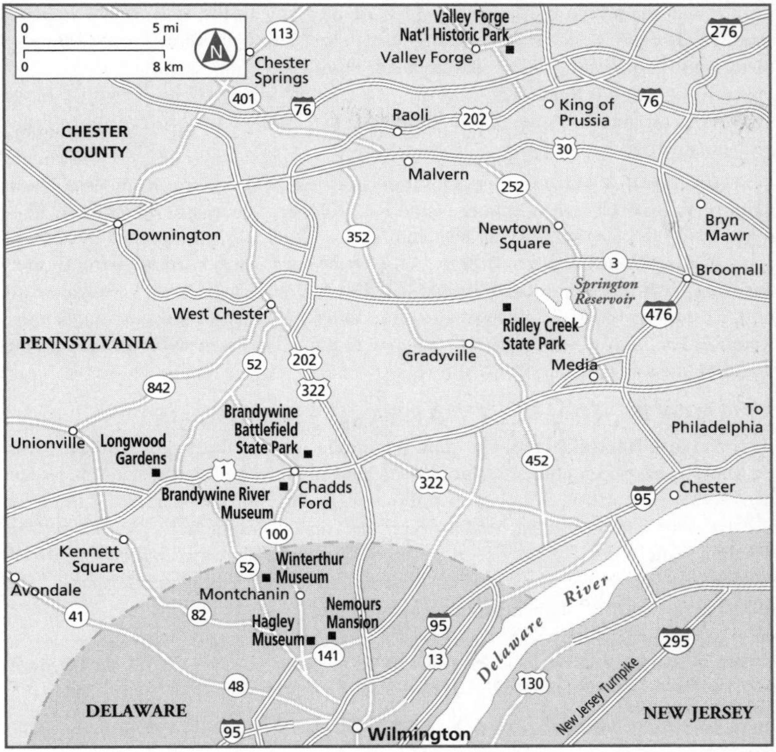

Nemours Mansion & Gardens, 1600 Rockland Rd., Wilmington, DE (✆ **302/651-6912;** www.nemours.org/mansion) recently reopened after a $39-million restoration.

Experience the region's beautiful landscape at the 650-acre **Tyler Arboretum,** 515 Painter Rd., Media (✆ **610-566-9134;** www.tylerarboretum.org), with fantastic horticultural collections, historic buildings, and extensive hiking trails. Get a taste of the area's agricultural heritage at **Linvilla Orchards,** 137 W. Knowlton Rd., Media (✆ **610/876-7116;** www.linvilla.com), a big, bustling, kid-friendly farm market with seasonal events, or sample your way along the **Brandywine Valley Wine Trail** (www.bvwinetrail.com).

Spend an afternoon exploring the one-of-a-kind shops, galleries, and cafes of such beautiful history-laden towns as **Kennett Square, Phoenixville,** and **West Chester,** which is home to the **American Helicopter Museum,** 1220 American Blvd. (✆ **610/436-9600;** www.helicoptermuseum.org), a popular family attraction. Less than a mile away you can take a popular **QVC Studio Tour,** 1200 Wilson Dr. (✆ **800/600-9900;** www.qvc.com), and get a new view of the world's largest electronic retailer. At the **Wendell August Forge,** 103 Woodcutter St., Exton (✆ **610/363-2426;** www.wendellaugust.com), visitors can watch skilled artisans handcraft metal giftware in aluminum, bronze, pewter, and silver, and find exclusive pieces at the retail store.

ESSENTIALS

GETTING THERE I-95 South from Philadelphia has various exits north of Wilmington marked for specific sites, most of which are off exit 7 to Pa. 52 North. If you have time, Pa. 100 off Pa. 52 North, linking West Chester to Wilmington, passes through picturesque pastureland, forest, and cropland. From New York, take exit 2 off the New Jersey Turnpike onto Route 322 West over the Commodore Barry Bridge into Pennsylvania, and continue on Route 322 to Route 452; take Route 452 north 4 miles to Route 1, the main artery of the valley.

VISITOR INFORMATION Get helpful details for planning a trip from the **Chester County Visitors Center,** 300 Greenwood Rd., Kennett Square (✆ **800/228-9933** or 610/388-2900; www.brandywinevalley.com/visitorscenter.asp), located just outside the gates of **Longwood Gardens** off Route 1, or **Delaware County's Brandywine Conference and Visitors Bureau** (✆ **800/343-3983** or 610/565-3679; www.brandywinecvb.org). For motorists on I-95, a Delaware visitor center, just south of Wilmington, between Route 272 and Route 896, operates from 8am to 8pm. **TheBrandyWine.com** is a wonderful online source of area information.

BRANDYWINE VALLEY AREA ATTRACTIONS

Brandywine Battlefield Park This picturesque park, 2 miles east of Chadds Ford on Route 1, has no monuments, since British general Howe snuck north outside present park borders to outflank Washington and eventually take Philadelphia. But Washington and Lafayette's reconstructed headquarters, the Gideon Gilpin house, marks the site, which in September 1777 saw one of the few full-army clashes between the Continentals and the British troops and mercenaries. The fields are excellent for picnicking and hiking; special events and reenactments bring history to life.

Rte. 1, east of Chadds Ford, PO Box 302, Chadds Ford, PA. ✆ **610/459-3342.** www.ushistory.org/brandywine. Grounds and visitor center free admission. House admission $5 adults, $3.50 seniors, $2.50 children ages 6–17, free for children 5 and under. Tues–Sat 9am–4:30pm; Sun noon–4:30pm. Last tour at 3pm.

Brandywine River Museum ★★ This 19th-century gristmill, set within the idyllic Brandywine Conservancy grounds, has been restored and joined by a dramatic spiral of brick and glass. The museum showcases American painters from the Brandywine school and other schools, and contains an unparalleled collection of works by three generations of Wyeths, including N. C., Carolyn, Andrew, and Jamie, who found inspiration in the astounding beauty of this area. Exhibits include wonderful displays of book and magazine illustration at its pretelevision zenith by such artists as Howard Pyle and Maxfield Parrish, and the incredible *Capturing Nureyev: James Wyeth Paints the Dancer* exhibition. There's separate admission for tours of N. C. Wyeth's house and studio, and the Kuerner Farm, where Andrew Wyeth found endless subjects in the people, buildings, and landscapes. Transportation to sites is by museum shuttle bus only.

Rte. 1 and Rte. 100, Chadds Ford, PA. ✆ **610/388-2700.** www.brandywinemuseum.org. Museum admission $8 adults; $5 seniors, students with ID, and children 6–12; free for children 5 and under. House and farm tour an additional $5; available Apr–Nov Tues–Sun. Museum daily 9:30am–4:30pm. Closed Christmas. Museum shop and self-service restaurant 11am–3pm.

Hagley Museum ★★ Since the early 1800s, this has been du Pont country, and the Hagley Museum, on 235 beautiful acres, shows how and when the family got its start. It's a wonderful illustration of early American industrialism and manufacturing.

Hagley has four parts: the Visitor Center, Workers' Hill, Powder Yard, and Eleutherian Mills, the du Pont ancestral home and gardens. The Visitor Center explains the early harnessing of the Brandywine River's power, used to operate flour mills. The du Ponts, who made their first fortune in gunpowder, found ready access to the water power and willow charcoal necessary for this industry. Company founder E. I. du Pont, who lived in Eleutherian Mills, had experience in France with gunpowder and supervised the delicate production process.

On Workers' Hill, part of the workmen's community has been restored. A visit through the Gibbons House reveals the lifestyle of a typical family, from food to furniture. Nearby is the school the children attended, complete with lesson demonstrations. At the base of Workers' Hill, a restored 1880s machine shop offers a fascinating demonstration of change in the workplace, from the quiet, painstaking hand-tooling of early artisans to the later din of power tools.

The wisteria-covered Georgian residence of the du Ponts was renovated by a member of the fifth generation, Mrs. Louis Crowninshield, who lived here until her death in 1958. Empire, Federal, and Victorian styles of furniture are highlighted in various room settings. As with all du Pont residences, the gardens and espaliered trees are superb, and there are flowers throughout the year.

The Belin House on Workers' Hill offers light lunches and drinks.

Rte. 141 (200 Hagley Rd.), Wilmington, DE. ✆ **302/658-2400.** www.hagley.org. Admission $11 adults, $9 seniors and students, $4 children 6–14, free for children 5 and under. Mid-Mar to Dec daily 9:30am–4:30pm; Jan to mid-Mar Sat–Sun 9:30am–4:30pm. Tour Mon–Fri 1:30pm. Transportation available on grounds. From Pennsylvania, take Rte. 52 to Rte. 100, go to the junction of Rte. 100 and Rte. 141, then follow directions on Rte. 141.

Longwood Gardens ★★★ Longwood Gardens is simply one of the world's great garden displays. Pierre S. du Pont devoted his life to horticulture. He bought a 19th-century arboretum to preserve the trees and then created the ultimate estate garden on 1,050 acres. You should plan at least half a day here.

Following a multimedia briefing on the gardens in the visitor center, head left toward the Main Fountain Garden, which has special water shows on Thursday, Friday, and Saturday evenings from June to September, usually preceded by hour-long concerts. Spectacular fireworks and fountain displays are featured on select summer evenings. Wrought-iron chairs and clipped trees and shrubs overlook the jets of water that rise up to 130 feet from the fountains. Near here, a topiary garden of closely pruned shrubs surrounds a 37-foot sundial.

The 4 acres of massive bronze-and-glass conservatories, renovated in 1996, 1997, and between 2000 and 2005 are among the finest and largest in the country. The Orangery displays are breathtaking. African violets, bonsai trees more than 100 years old, hibiscus, orchids, and tropical plants are among the specialties, but expect anything from Easter lilies to scarlet begonias to poinsettias, depending on the season. Special collections range from silver desert plants to roses. Exhibited only at their peak, plants are constantly replaced from the extensive growing houses.

A parquet-floor ballroom was added later, connected to the greenhouses, along with a 10,000-pipe organ, a magnificent instrument that's under renovation until 2010. A new Indoor Children's Garden features 3,000 square feet of child-friendly plants, 17 splash fountains, two mazes, a secret room, a grotto cave, and more.

Ahead and to the right of the visitor center, more gardens and fountains await, along with the Longwood Heritage Exhibit inside the Peirce du Pont House, the founder's residence. This exhibit illustrates the history of the property with artifacts from 2,000-year-old Native American spear points to du Pont family movies. The restaurant offers cafeteria-style dining year-round and full-service dining from mid-April to December, both with surprisingly good meals.

1001 Longwood Rd. (near Rte. 1), Kennett Square, PA. ✆ **610/388-1000.** www.longwoodgardens.org. Admission $16 adults, $14 seniors 62 and over, $6 ages 5–22, $2 ages 6–15, free for children 4 and under. Daily (including holidays) 9am–5pm (until 6pm Apr–Aug), open late for special events and displays.

Winterthur Museum & Country Estate ★★★ A later home of the du Ponts now provides the setting for the nation's best collection of American decorative arts. Henry Francis du Pont, a great-grandson of E. I. du Pont, was typical of wealthy Americans of the time who furnished their houses with fine European pieces. But after seeing a simple pine cupboard filled with Staffordshire transferware ceramics in 1923, and other American antiques, he decided to form his own collection and create more of an American home. Du Pont collected American furniture, decorative objects, and the interior woodwork of houses primarily from the 18th and early 19th centuries. From 1928 to 1930 he added over 110 rooms to Winterthur for the display of his collection and for hosting country house parties. Because the museum started out as a private home, the rooms have a unique richness and intimacy.

The Main Museum, which offers in-depth guided tours, displays the bulk of the collection and includes complete interiors from every Eastern seaboard colony. Special landmarks include the famous Montmorenci Stair Hall, two Shaker Rooms, fine examples of Pennsylvania Dutch decorative art, and the du Pont dining room. The Dorrance Gallery houses the Campbell Soup Tureen collection, displaying over 100 items. In addition to changing exhibitions, there's a kid-friendly, hands-on Touch-It Room that's fun to explore at any age.

In spring, the extensive Winterthur Garden explodes into an abundance of blossoms. Of particular note are the March Bank and Azalea Woods. Also featured is a 3-acre Enchanted Woods garden for children. At Christmastime, the house is ornately decorated in a variety of period styles for yuletide tours. Garden tram rides through the grounds are available when weather permits. There are two superb gift shops selling a selection of licensed reproductions, gifts, books, jewelry, and plants. The Visitor Pavilion's cafeteria serves lunch and snacks from 10am to 4pm; the Cappuccino Cafe next to the museum offers beverages and lighter fare.

Rte. 52, 6 miles northwest of Wilmington, Winterthur, DE. ✆ **800/448-3883** or 302/888-4600. www.winterthur.org. Admission (includes house tour, Garden Tram tour, self-guided museum galleries, and self-guided garden walk) $18 adults, $16 seniors and students, $5 children 2–11. 1 and 2-hr. tours available for an additional $12 or $22 (reservations required). Yuletide tours additional $4. Tues–Sat 10am–5pm; Sun noon–5pm (also Mon during yuletide season). Closed major holidays.

WHERE TO STAY

Distinctive, historic lodgings are scattered throughout the Brandywine Valley. A few highlights include **Hamanassett,** 115 Indian Springs Dr., Chester Heights (✆ **610/459-3000;** www.hamanassett.com), featuring sumptuous candlelight breakfasts; **Pennsbury Inn,** 883 Baltimore Pike, Chadds Ford (✆ **610/388-1435;** www.pennsburyinn.com), with gracious gardens; and **Sweetwater Farm,** 50 Sweetwater Rd., Glen Mills (✆ **610/459-4711;** www.sweetwaterfarmbb.com), a peaceful 50-acre estate. Check the **Brandywine Valley Bed & Breakfasts** website (www.bvbb.com) for more information on town and country B&Bs.

Brandywine River Hotel This modern hotel blends contemporary amenities with country inn character and is just steps from the prime Brandywine restaurants. Several suites have working fireplaces and Jacuzzis. Service is friendly and guest rooms are decorated with Queen Anne cherrywood furnishings, brass fixtures, chintz fabrics, and local paintings. Breakfast is served in an attractive hospitality room with a fireplace. Wine, beer, and cordials are available in the Fireside Lobby Bar. Room service is now available from neighboring Brandywine Prime Seafood & Chops.

Rte. 1 and Rte. 100, PO Box 1058, Chadds Ford, PA 19317. ✆ **800/274-9644** or 610/388-1200. www.brandywineriverhotel.com. 40 units. From $129 double; from $169 suite; Specials and packages available. Rates include European-plus breakfast and afternoon tea. Children stay free in parent's room. AE, DISC, MC, V. **Amenities:** Fitness room; business center. *In room:* A/C, TV, high-speed Internet, fridge (in suite), coffeemaker (on request), hair dryer.

Fairville Inn ★ With an 1827 main house and exquisitely comfortable lodgings (think matelassé coverlets and oversize canopied beds) in a carriage house and springhouse, this inn perfectly combines antiques-filled loveliness with modern amenities, like great bathrooms and satellite TV. It's set on a pretty stretch of Route 52, between the Brandywine River Museum and Winterthur, and offers excellent breakfasts and afternoon tea. You'll enjoy privacy in an intimate setting (especially in that wonderful carriage house).

506 Kennett Pike (Rte. 52), Chadds Ford, PA 19317. ✆ **877/285-7772** or 610/388-5900. www.fairvilleinn.com. 15 units. $160–$275 double. AE, DISC, MC, V. No children 11 and under. *In room:* A/C, TV, Wi-Fi, hair dryer, iron/ironing board.

Inn at Montchanin Village ★★ Originally part of the neighboring Winterthur estate, this exquisite inn is comprised of 11 meticulously restored vintage buildings, including former homes of gunpowder mill workers and the 1850 Dilwyne Barn, featuring a spectacular "gathering room" lounge with a huge fireplace. The buildings spread throughout this beautifully landscaped hamlet now offer enough luxurious comforts to capture the number-one spot on *Travel + Leisure*'s 2006 list of "World's Best Hotels for $250 or Less." Individually decorated rooms feature fine furnishings, from elegant period to whimsical contemporary pieces, fireplaces, gorgeous (usually huge) bathrooms, and a porch or patio for soaking up the scenery. Krazy Kats Restaurant, located in a renovated blacksmith shop complete with an original forge, is equally notable for excellent eclectic cuisine and a striking decor that's accented with animal prints and anthropomorphic feline portraits. The new on-site spa offers an alluring assortment of posh treatments and soothing massages for men and women.

Rte. 100 and Kirk Rd., PO Box 130, Montchanin, DE 19710. ✆ **800/269-2473** or 302/888-2133. www.montchanin.com. 28 units. $192–$244 double; $290–$399 suite. AE, DC, DISC, MC, V. **Amenities:** Restaurant; fitness room; spa, lounge w/fireplace and complimentary evening bar and snacks. *In room:* A/C, TV, dataport, high-speed Internet, microwave, wet bar, fridge (w/complimentary beverages), coffeemaker, hair dryer, iron, heated towel rack, soaking tubs for 2 (in most).

WHERE TO DINE

There's no shortage of fine restaurants in the well-heeled Brandywine Valley, including the **Gables,** Route 1, Chadds Ford (✆ **610/388-7700;** www.thegablesatchaddsford.com), and **Simon Pearce on the Brandywine,** 1333 Lenape Rd., West Chester (✆ **610/793-0948;** www.simonpearce.com). **Brandywine Prime Seafood & Chops,** at Route 1 and Route 100, Chadds Ford (✆ **610/388-8088;** www.brandywineprime.com), featuring in-house dry-aged local beef and an extensive wine selection, recently opened a more casual restaurant next door. The menu and decor at **Bistro on the Brandywine** (✆ **610/388-8090;** www.bistroonthebrandywine.com) are contemporary and appealing, and a separate "Bistro to Go" entrance simplifies takeout. In Kennett Square, famed "mushroom capital of the world," the local delicacy is highlighted at the **Orchard,** 503 Orchard Ave. (✆ **610/388-1100;** www.theorchardbyob.com), a former mushroom-packing house. Scoring dinner at **Talula's Table,** 102 W. State St., Kennett Square (✆ **610/444-8255;** www.talulastable.com) is mission impossible for casual travelers: The single farmhouse table is booked each morning for 1 year in advance. However, stop by this inviting little market from 7am to 7pm daily for coffee and pastries, then shop for incredible premise-made breads, pasta, charcuterie, and other gourmet goodies.

Dilworthtown Inn ★ CONTINENTAL Another old inn, this 1758 tavern saw the last phase of the Battle of Brandywine (specifically, the British victory). It has as cozy a mood and decor as you'll find this side of the Revolutionary War, with a roaring fireplace that you could stand up in and candlelit tables amid thick plaster walls. The restaurant, which also hosts cooking classes, is very fine, with exotic local mushroom dishes and premium meats. The wine cellar is one of the most extensive and admired in the Philadelphia region. A neighboring 18th-century general store was recently transformed into a companion restaurant, the **Blue Pear Bistro,** 275 Brintons Bridge Rd. (✆ **610/399-9812;** www.bluepearbistro.com), with a modern American focus.

1390 Old Wilmington Pike, West Chester, PA. ✆ **610/399-1390.** www.dilworthtowninn.com. Reservations recommended. Jacket preferred. Main courses $24–$47. AE, DC, DISC, MC, V. Mon–Fri 5:30–9:30pm; Sat 5–9:30pm; Sun 3–8:30pm.

Farmhouse FRENCH/AMERICAN Far off the beaten tourist path at the Loch Nairn Golf Club, this insider's spot offers a quintessential Brandywine Valley dining experience: an intimate, vintage farmhouse brimming with refined country elegance. You'll find all the right components—fireplaces, candlelight, plank floors, and a profusion of antiques—and a seasonally driven menu that features the finest local ingredients. Service can be slow, but standout dishes like signature crab cakes and rack of lamb will reward your patience. In summer, dinner is also served on a patio overlooking beautifully manicured greens. The wine list is substantial and varied. The spacious adjacent Greathouse offers a more casual dining option.

514 McCue Rd., Avondale, PA. ✆ **610/268-2235.** www.lngolf.com/farmhouse. Main courses $20–$40 dinner, $7–$17 lunch. AE, DISC, MC, V. Tues–Sat 11:30am–3pm and 5–9pm. Mon lunch and dinner and Sun brunch served at the Greathouse.

12

Lancaster County: The Amish Country

by Lenora Dannelke

Fifty miles west of Philadelphia is a beautiful region of rolling hills, neatly cultivated farms, covered bridges, and towns with picturesque names like Paradise and Bird-in-Hand. This is the gorgeous Amish Country, also known as Pennsylvania Dutch Country, an area of 7,100 square miles centered in Lancaster County, which is an easy day trip or overnight excursion from Center City Philadelphia. Made even more famous in the Harrison Ford film *Witness,* the Amish, Mennonites, and Brethren of Dutch Country (see "Meet the Amish," below, for an explanation of the differences) represent over 75,000 of Lancaster County's 500,000 residents. It's a small group that continues to live a gentle life centered on family cohesiveness and religious worship.

The preservation of the world of the Pennsylvania Dutch evokes feelings of nostalgia, respect, and curiosity. The word *Dutch* is derived from the word *Deutsch,* meaning German, as the community is of mostly German descent, though that description isn't restricted to "Plain People." The Old Order Amish offer a rare yardstick for measuring the distance that our own "outside" world has progressed over the past few centuries.

Pennsylvania Dutch Country offers agreeably varied pleasures to visitors. The verdant countryside is laced with tranquil rural roads for driving or cycling. You'll find opportunities to meet Amish and Mennonites on farms that have opened their quaint doors for commerce. Tourism trade has actually promoted continued excellence in quilt and furniture making, and crafts. There are historical sites, pretzel and chocolate factories, covered bridges, and bustling farmer's markets, plus modern diversions like movie theaters, amusement parks, and great outlet-mall shopping. And, of course, Pennsylvania Dutch smorgasbord and family-style restaurants are unique, all-you-can-eat experiences.

1 INTRODUCING THE PENNSYLVANIA DUTCH COUNTRY

This area has been a major farming region since German settlers came across its limestone-rich soil and rolling hills 3 centuries ago. Lancaster County boasts the most productive nonirrigated farmland in the United States, and it's the nation's seventh-largest dairy-producing county. The natural abundance of the region, the ease of getting goods to market in Philadelphia, and the strong work ethic of area residents have preserved major portions of the land for farming. In its day, Lancaster was a leading center of commerce, culture, and politics. The largest inland city in the United States from 1760 to 1810, it was even a contender in the choice of the new nation's capital. Agriculture, however, is now under threat from suburban sprawl as the county has become an increasingly popular suburb of Harrisburg and Philadelphia. Placid fields are being replaced with the housing developments and strip malls demanded by a mushrooming population.

TOURIST DOLLARS VERSUS STRIP MALLS: THE AMISH TODAY

It wasn't until the mid-1950s that the Amish became a "tourist attraction." As the rest of America rushed to embrace the growing presence of technology in everyday life, the Amish tenacity in maintaining traditional customs and values made them seem both exotic and intriguing. For better or worse, the reclusive Amish, who reject all forms of "worldliness," spawned a major tourist industry.

Most people, including many Amish, saw tourism in a positive light. Money flowed into the county, and the Amish found a growing market for such goods as quilts, wood furniture, metalwork, crafts, and foodstuffs—with customers literally appearing at their doors. However, less-benign consequences of development are becoming increasingly apparent. The growing Amish population has more than doubled to 28,000 in the past 2 decades (following the biblical edict to "be fruitful and multiply," families may have seven or more children), but as outsiders flock to Lancaster County, the non-Amish population has grown to about 500,000. Their need for housing is driving up land prices and attracting developers. In past years when Amish families looked to buy farmlands for their children, they turned to non-Amish farmers. Today, those non-Amish farmers can get much higher prices from developers.

This means that many Amish have been forced to leave their farms, build new houses (you can tell an Amish home by its dark green window shades), and set up nonfarming businesses. The construction industry in Lancaster County includes many Amish workers, and women who traditionally worked at home on the farm are increasingly running restaurants and shops or overseeing quilting and craft enterprises. Despite the injunction to remain separate from wider society, many families aggressively exploit the cachet that "Amish-made" gives to foods, craft objects, furniture, hex signs, and other souvenirs and products.

MEET THE AMISH

In the early 18th century, a time of persecution in Europe, William Penn's "holy experiment" of religious tolerance—plus word-of-mouth reports about the region's fertile farmlands—drew thousands of German-speaking immigrants to Pennsylvania. They were lumped together as Pennsylvania "Dutch"—a corruption of *Deutsch,* meaning German. Mennonite sects, particularly the Amish, became the most famous of the immigrants, but the Colonial period also saw a mixture of Scotch-Irish Presbyterians, French Protestants, English from Maryland, and Jews from Iberia arrive in the region. The ethnic makeup of the county changed little between 1796 and the late 20th century.

The religions of the Pennsylvania Dutch are part of the Anabaptist strand of the Protestant Reformation. Anabaptism is a Christian faith that emerged during the 16th century, and Anabaptists believe in the literal interpretation of the Bible, in baptism only for adults mature enough to choose this rite of transformation, and in remaining separate from larger society. Menno Simons, a Catholic priest from Holland, joined the Anabaptists in 1536 and united the various groups, whose members came to be called Mennonites. In 1693, Jacob Amman, a Mennonite bishop who found his church too tolerant of lax sinners, broke away to establish the Amish Church.

- Amish Farm & House **8**
- Central Market **12**
- Downtown Visitor Information Center **13**
- Dutch Wonderland **7**
- Ephrata Cloister **2**
- Hans Herr House **9**
- Heritage Center Museum **12**
- Kitchen Kettle Village **11**
- Lancaster County Convention Center **13**
- Lancaster Quilt & Textile Museum **12**
- Landis Valley Museum **4**
- Mennonite Information Center **7**
- Pennsylvania Dutch Convention & Visitors Bureau **6**
- Railroad Museum of Pennsylvania & Strasburg Railroad **10**
- Rockvale Square Outlets **8**
- Sturgis Pretzel Bakery **3**
- Wheatland **5**
- Wilbur Chocolate Company **3**

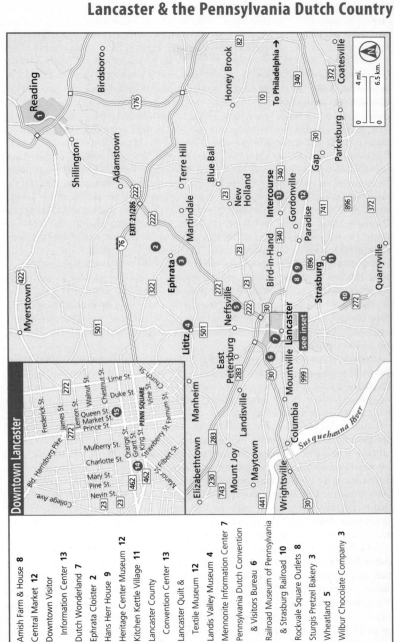

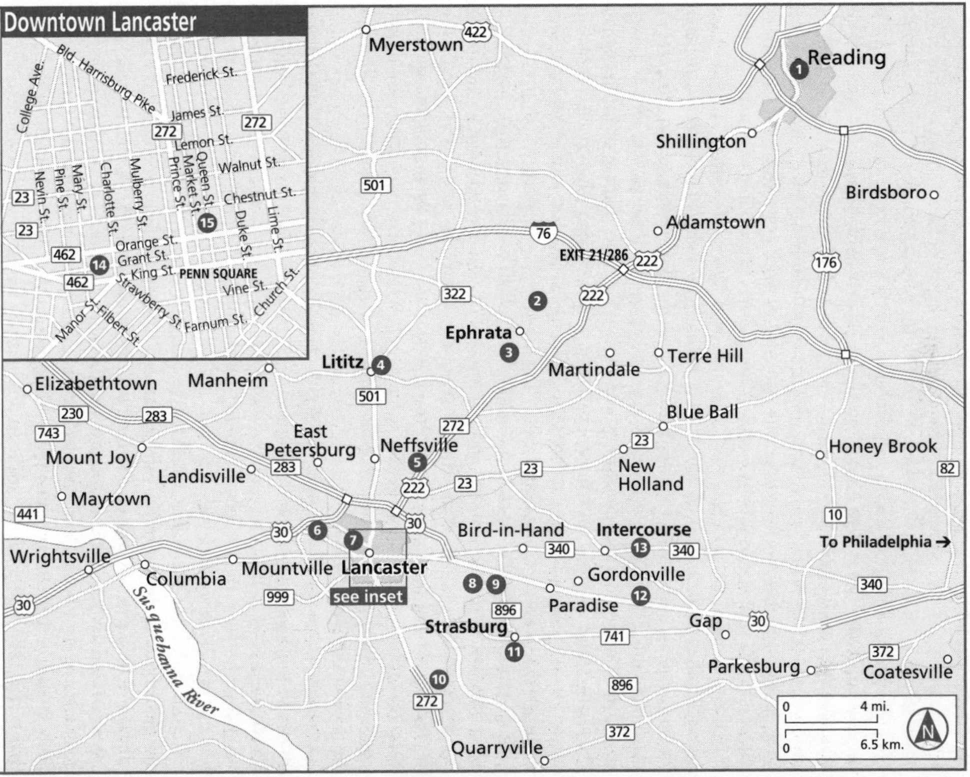

The three major sects in Lancaster County, the Amish, the Brethren (also called the Dunkards), and the Mennonites (there are numerous orders), share many beliefs, including those concerning adult baptism, nonresistance, and basic Bible doctrine. They differ in matters of dress, use or avoidance of technology, degree of literal interpretation of the Bible, and form of worship. For example, the Amish conduct worship services at home, while the Mennonites hold services in churches, which range from small and simple to large and majestic. The Amish do not proselytize, while Mennonites have a strong tradition of missionary work.

Today, the Amish reside in 21 states and in Canada. In Lancaster County, most continue to work on farms where fields are still plowed with horses or mules instead of tractors. While you won't spot any electrical lines (this energy source represents a dependent connection to the "outside" world), Amish farm existence is neither primitive nor ascetic. Homes are furnished comfortably (if quaintly by today's tastes), propane lamps provide ample illumination, and propane or air compressors power stoves, refrigerators, and other appliances. They are a trilingual people, speaking Pennsylvania Dutch (a German dialect) at home, High German at worship services (the German of Luther's Bible translation), and English with members of the larger society. Non–Plain People are referred to as "the English"—a reference to language rather than ethnic heritage—and worldly styles or practices are described as "Englishy."

Since family is the vital social unit among the Amish and large families the norm, more than half of their booming Lancaster County community is under the age of 18. Dozens of mailboxes are marked with the names Zook, Stoltzfus, and Zinn—a testimony to prolific extended families. The practice of "shunning"—an Old Testament–sounding excommunication from family relations for Amish who marry outsiders, violate basic tenets, or leave the church *after* baptism—is still enforced, though relatives will sometimes talk when unobserved.

Children attend school in simple one-room schoolhouses, built and maintained by the Amish, through the eighth grade. There are over 200 such schools in Lancaster County. Students, who are taught only the basics by an unmarried teenage Amish girl with an 8th-grade education and no special training, are exempt from the standard state curriculum and may leave school by age 16.

To the visitor, the two most distinctive characteristics of the Amish are their clothing and their use of horse and buggy rather than cars. Both these features are linked to their religious beliefs. The distinctive clothing worn by more than 35,000 "Plain People" in Lancaster County is meant to encourage humility and modesty as well as separation from larger society. Amish men and boys wear dark-colored suits, straight-cut coats without lapels, broadcloth trousers, suspenders, solid-colored shirts, black socks and shoes, and black or straw broad-brimmed hats. Men wait to grow beards until they are married, and do not grow mustaches. Women and girls wear modest, solid-colored dresses with long sleeves and long full skirts, covered by a cape and an apron. They never cut their hair, but gather it in a bun on the back of the head, concealed by a white prayer covering. Amish women do not wear printed fabrics or jewelry, even wedding rings. Single women in their teens and 20s wear black prayer coverings on their heads for church services. After marriage, a white covering is worn.

The Amish are reluctant to accept any technology that could weaken the family structure. Their horse-drawn buggies help keep them close to home by limiting distances that can be traveled in a day, and every boy receives his own "courting buggy" upon turning

16. Telephones, needed to conduct business, are located in roadside shelters rather than homes, and are shared by neighboring families. As new ideas emerge, each congregational district (about 100 families) evaluates them and decides what to accept or reject. The fundamental criterion is that an innovation should not jeopardize the simplicity of their lives or the strength of the family unit. Amish teens do sometimes succumb to sampling worldly temptations such as listening to rock music or changing into "English" clothes and sneaking off to movies—behavior that's forgivable prior to baptism. In fact, this normally rebellious teen stage of life has been sensationalized, exaggerated, and distorted by several TV shows on the Amish rite of passage called *rumspringa* (run wild). Even after getting a taste of "English" culture, the vast majority of Amish elect to remain in their tight-knit community—often dying in the same house where they were born.

There are a number of excellent books on the Amish way of life. The classic is John Hostetler's *Amish Society* (Johns Hopkins, 1993). A more impassioned, personal take is *After the Fire: The Destruction of the Lancaster County Amish* (UPNE, 1992) by Randy-Michael Testa. Children's books include *Growing Up Amish* (Atheneum, 1989) by Richard Ammon and Raymond Bial's *Amish Home* (Sandpiper, 1995), with wonderful photographs. Since Amish do not permit photography, film depictions are bound to be compromised, as was the case with both the crime-drama *Witness* (1985) and the farcical *For Richer or Poorer* (1997). For an entertaining read that's a perfect Lancaster vacation mood setter, pick up any of Tamar Myers's delightful Pennsylvania Dutch mysteries with recipes (www.tamarmyers.com), such as *Thou Shalt Not Grill* (Signet, 2005).

2 ESSENTIALS

The heart of Pennsylvania Dutch Country centers on wedges of land to the east and slightly west of Lancaster. The Susquehanna River to the west and the Maryland border and Mason-Dixon line to the south form the area's borders.

GETTING THERE

Lancaster County is 57 miles or 90 minutes west of Philadelphia, directly on Route 30. From the northeast, the easiest route is to take I-95 south from New York City onto the New Jersey Turnpike, then take exit 6 onto the Pennsylvania Turnpike (I-76), continuing to exit 266 or 286 on either side of Lancaster. You'll still be about 10 miles north of the town: From exit 286, follow Route 222 into the city; from exit 266, Route 72. Travel time is 2¼ hours, and tolls amount to $9 from New York City. From the south, follow I-83 north for 90 minutes from Baltimore, then go east on Route 30 from York into the county. Brandywine Valley sites are only minutes from Amish farms in Gap, via Route 41 and Route 741.

By train, Amtrak (✆ **800/872-7245**) takes about 70 minutes from 30th Street Station in Philadelphia to the great old Lancaster station, 53 McGovern Ave. (✆ **717/291-5080**), 10 blocks from Penn Square. The adult fare is $15 to $22 one-way, and 14 trains run daily. Three Capitol Trailways or Greyhound buses run daily from the Greyhound Terminal at 10th and Filbert streets in Philadelphia ($24 one-way; $46 round-trip), taking about 2 hours (with a change in King of Prussia) to arrive at the train station in Lancaster (✆ **800/231-2222** or 717/397-4861).

VISITOR INFORMATION

Before you set out, get in touch with the **Pennsylvania Dutch Convention & Visitors Bureau,** 501 Greenfield Rd., Lancaster, PA 17601 (✆ **800/PA-DUTCH** [723-8824] or 717/299-8901; www.padutchcountry.com). Its website offers a variety of printable coupons and package deals. The office is off the Route 30 bypass east of Lancaster, Greenfield Road exit. Staff can provide an excellent map and visitors' guide to the region, answers to specific questions or help with special interests, and a wealth of brochures. A film provides a good overview of the county. The office hours are Monday to Saturday 8am to 6pm and Sunday 9am to 5pm June through October, and Monday to Saturday from 8:30am to 5pm and Sunday 9am to 5pm off season.

Near the Tanger Outlet Center the **Mennonite Information Center,** 2209 Millstream Rd., Lancaster, PA 17602 (✆ **800/858-8320** or 717/299-0954; www.mennoniteinfoctr.com), has a lot of the same information but specializes in linking you with Mennonite guesthouses and church worship, and arranging personal tours (see "Organized Tours," below). Every half-hour the film, *Who Are the Amish?* is shown and there is a tabernacle tour given on-site. The center is open Monday through Saturday from 8am to 5pm April through October, and Monday through Saturday from 8:30am to 4:30pm November through March.

GETTING AROUND

Lancaster County's principal artery is Route 30, which runs from Philadelphia to York and Gettysburg. But beware: Major roads like Route 30 and Route 222 at Lancaster, and Route 340 from Intercourse to Lancaster, are crowded, especially in the summer with the onslaught of bus tours. The 25,000 horse-drawn vehicles in the county tend to stick to quieter back roads, but some highways cannot be avoided. And please be careful; the past few years have seen several horrible rear-end crashes in which tourists killed Amish families in buggies. AAA members who are in a jam can call ✆ **717/397-6135** for emergency road service.

Red Rose Transit Authority, 45 Erick Rd. (✆ **717/397-4246;** www.redrosetransit.com), serves Lancaster County, with fares ranging from $1.50 to $2.70. An all-day, all-zone pass costs $5. There's also a Historic Downtown Trolley Bus that loops Lancaster city. An information center is located at 225 N. Queen St.

ORGANIZED TOURS

The **Amish Experience,** on Route 340 in Intercourse (✆ **717/768-3600;** www.amishexperience.com), offers three attractions that provide an authentic illustration of Amish life, past and present. Tickets for a 40-minute multimedia show, an interpretive tour of a contemporary-style Amish home, and a guided back-road bus tour may be purchased separately, though a combination package is the best deal ($39 for adults, $19 for children). The show runs hourly between 9am and 5pm; house tours are conducted between 9:45am and 4:15pm; and bus tours during high season are at 10:30am and 2pm daily (11:30am only in Nov and Sat–Sun only Dec–Mar). They last 2 hours and include stops at Amish farms selling crafts or foods (though not on Sun) and pass by one-room schoolhouses. Reservations are recommended, and tickets may be purchased online (check the website for coupons) or at some local hotels. A new V.I.P. (Visit In Person) Tour escorts small groups of guests to three Amish farms for friendly, interactive personal experiences and costs $40 for adults and children. The Plain and Fancy Farm Restaurant and Aaron and Jessica's Buggy Rides are on the same premises.

Tips A Note on Etiquette

There aren't too many settings in the world where an entire native population is a tourist attraction. Pennsylvania Dutch country is one of them, but that doesn't mean that the Amish are there as theme-park characters. They are hardworking people leading busy lives. Your courtesy and respect are especially vital because their lifestyle is designed to remove them as much as possible from your fast-paced 21st-century focus.

First, *do not trespass* onto Amish farms or especially onto school grounds. We've listed several settings where you can visit a working farm, take a carriage ride, or even stay on a farm. Although these are not operated by the most orthodox Amish, you will certainly get a taste of the Amish lifestyle.

Second, if you're dealing with Amish directly, *don't even think of photographing them,* and *always ask before taking any photographs at all.* The Amish have a strongly held belief that photographic images violate the biblical injunction against graven images and promote the sins of personal vanity and pride. Taking pictures of their land and animals is permissible (though it's still polite to ask first); taking pictures of them is *not.*

Third, *watch the road.* What passes for moderate suburban speed in a car can be life threatening in this area. Roads in Lancaster County have especially wide shoulders to accommodate horses, carriages, and farm tractors, and these are marked with red reflective triangles and lights at night. It's preferable, if only to better see the sights, to slow down to Amish paces. And honking disturbs the horses. If you have the time, this is superb country for bicycling, punctuated by farm stands for refreshment and quiet conversations with Amish families—though expect some territorial farm dogs to run out and greet you.

Brunswick Tours (© **717/397-7541;** www.brunswicktours.com) can lead you on tours throughout Lancaster County and into Hershey and Gettsyburg, but your best bet for an intimate view of Amish Country is an in-car tour guide. The **Mennonite Information Center** (see "Visitor Information," above) has a group of friendly Mennonite and Amish guides on call who will ride with you in your car throughout Intercourse, Strasburg, and Bird-in-Hand, stopping in the towns or touring through the farmland. They personalize the tour to your interests—they'll make stops at Amish farm shops, or take you shopping for quilts or freshly made root beer. Call ahead or drop by to book 2-hour tours priced at $44 per car, for up to seven people.

3 EXPLORING AMISH COUNTRY

Amish Country attractions are spread out over a large area in and around Lancaster, so you'll need to plan ahead to make the best use of your time. Consider our itineraries, then note the highlights in each town.

SUGGESTED ITINERARIES

If You Have 1 Day

Start in the town of Intercourse, where you can shop for quilts, food, and more in the 36-stand marketplace of **Kitchen Kettle Village** (p. 237). Head west into Lancaster to visit the lovely **Wheatland** estate (p. 236), once home to President James Buchanan. Then drive 20 minutes northeast to the bucolic and historic **Ephrata Cloister** (p. 238) and, if it's a Friday, to the **Green Dragon Market** (p. 238) for its transactions featuring live animals and local wares.

If You Have 2 Days

Follow the itinerary above for Day 1. On Day 2, head west to **Hershey, PA** (p. 240). This drive affords you beautiful views of serene-looking farms where great quantities of milk are produced by the Amish (whom you'll be passing in their modest black buggies). Once in Hershey, the kids will want to visit **Hershey's Chocolate World** for a demonstration of how the treats are made. In season, they'll enjoy the rides and animals of **Hersheypark** and **Zoo America;** you'll wander the rose garden and check out the spa at the **Hotel Hershey.**

If You Have 3 Days or More

On Days 1 and 2, follow the itineraries given above. On Day 3, spend the morning in **Adamstown** at the excellent **flea and antiques markets** (p. 242) there: Renninger's, Shupp's Grove, and Stoudt's Black Angus. The latter has an adjacent **beer garden and restaurant**. Next, you can prepare for your reentry into the real world by shopping at the stylish outlets of **Rockvale** and the **Tanger Outlet Center** (p. 243).

LANCASTER

While Lancaster (pronounced "*lank*-uh-stir") is still the most important city in the region, it hit its peak in the Colonial era and as an early-20th-century urban beehive; this is reflected in the architecture and attractions. The basic street grid layout, copied from Philadelphia's, centers at Penn Square: the intersection of King (east-west) and Queen (north-south) streets. You won't see too many Plain People venturing into town anymore, since they can buy provisions and equipment more easily at regional stores, but they still sell at the bustling **Central Market.** Erected just off Penn Square in 1889 but operating since the 1730s, this is the nation's oldest continuously operated farmer's market, with more than 80 stalls. You can savor and purchase regional produce and foods, from sweet bologna and scrapple to breads, cheeses, egg noodles, shoofly pie (a concoction of molasses and sweet dough), and schnitzel or dried apple. The market is open Tuesday and Friday from 6am to 4pm and Saturday from 6am to 2pm.

Beside the market is the **Heritage Center Museum** in the old City Hall, with a collection of Lancaster County crafts and historical artifacts. Its new self-guided Family Walking Tour puts an entertaining spin on local history. The museum is free and open Tuesday through Saturday from 10am to 5pm and Sunday noon to 5pm. The nearby **Lancaster Quilt & Textile Museum** ★, a colorful collection housed in a magnificent 1912 Beaux Arts bank building, has undergone a recent expansion and is open Monday through Saturday, 9am to 5pm. Admission is $6 for adults, $4 for students, and free for ages 17 and under. The Heritage Center of Lancaster County (✆ **717/299-6440;** www.lancasterheritage.com) operates both. Less than 2 miles west is **Wheatland,** 1120

Tips: Amish Country on Two Wheels

Cycling enthusiasts can find bike gear and route suggestions at the following:

- The store **Green Mountain Cyclery,** 285 S. Reading Rd., Ephrata, PA 17522 (✆ **717/859-2422;** www.greenmtncyclery.com), attracts everyone from serious riders to casual cyclists.
- The website **www.lancasterbikeclub.org** is a resource for routes that range from 7 miles (around the town of Lancaster and through Buchanan Park) to serious, 50-mile-plus rides into the hills.

Marietta Ave., Route 23 (✆ **717/392-8721;** www.wheatland.org), the gracious Federal mansion and gardens of the 15th U.S. president, James Buchanan. It features costumed guides and is open April through October, Monday through Saturday 10am to 4pm; open select days in November and December (call for hours). Admission is $8 for adults, $7 for seniors, $6 for students, and $3 for children 6 to 11.

Four miles south of town near Willow Street rests the 1719 **Hans Herr House,** 1849 Hans Herr Dr., off Route 222 (✆ **717/464-4438;** www.hansherr.org), the oldest building in the county, restored and furnished to illustrate early Mennonite life, with a historic orchard and outdoor exhibit of agricultural tools. You can visit from April to November, Monday through Saturday from 9am to 4pm; admission, including a tour, is $5 for adults and $2 for children 7 to 12.

The eastern side of town explodes with a commercialized welter of faux Amish attractions and amusements like Dutch Wonderland and Running Pump Mini-Golf, fast-food restaurants, and outlet stores on Route 30. The **Amish Farm and House,** 2395 Lincoln Hwy. (✆ **717/394-6185;** www.amishfarmandhouse.com), offers guided tours of a historical 10-room Amish house, a new one-room schoolhouse, farm buildings with live animals, and exhibits including a water wheel outside. It's open daily April through October 8:30am to 5pm and November through March 8:30am to 4pm. Admission is $7.95 for adults, $7.25 for seniors, and $5.25 for children 5 to 11. Don't be put off by its odd location, sandwiched between a Target and a strip mall: This worthwhile attraction epitomizes the survival of old ways amid rampant development.

INTERCOURSE

Intercourse's suggestive name refers to the intersection of two old highways, the King's Highway (now Rte. 340 or Old Philadelphia Pike) and Newport Road (now Rte. 772). The Conestoga wagons invented a few miles south—unusually broad and deep wagons that became famous for transporting homesteaders all the way west to the Pacific Coast—were used on the King's Highway.

The town, in the midst of the wedge of country east of Lancaster, is a center of Amish life in the county. There are about as many commercial attractions, which range from the schlocky to good quality, as there are places of genuine interest along Route 340. Of the commercial sites, try **Kitchen Kettle Village,** on Old Philadelphia Pike, Route 340 (✆ **800/732-3538** or 717/768-8261; www.kitchenkettle.com), with 40 stores selling quilts, crafts, and homemade edibles, grouped around Pat and Bob Burnley's 1954 jam and relish kitchen. Their Lapp Valley Farms ice-cream store, with 18 all-natural flavors, is much more convenient than the original farm stand near New Holland. Buggy rides

Tips The Bridges of Lancaster County

Pennsylvania is the birthplace of the covered bridge, with some 1,500 built between the 1820s and 1900. Today, 217 bridges remain, mostly on small country roads, and you can actually drive (slowly!) through most of them. Lancaster County has the largest concentration, with 30, including one on the way to Paradise, a village east of Lancaster city. Bridges were covered to protect the trusses from the weather. Does kissing inside one bring good luck? The only way to find out is to try: Their one-lane width allows for a certain amount of privacy. The Pennsylvania Dutch Convention & Visitors Bureau map indicates all covered bridge locations. Five driving tours are listed on their website; call ✆ **800/PA-DUTCH** (723-8824) or visit **www.padutch country.com** for more information. The following bridges are interesting and easy to find:

- **Hunsecker's Mill Bridge:** This is the largest covered bridge in the county, built in 1975 to replace the original, which was washed away in Hurricane Agnes. From Lancaster, drive 5 miles north on Route 272. After you pass Landis Valley Farm Museum, turn right on Hunsecker Road and drive 2 miles.
- **Eshleman's Mill/Paradise Bridge:** This bridge is in the midst of Amish cornfields and farms. An oversize truck put it out of commission in the 1980s, but it has been restored. Drive north 1 mile on Belmont Road from Route 30, just east of the center of Paradise.
- **Kauffman's Distillery Bridge:** Drive west on Route 772 from Manheim, and make a left onto West Sunhill Road. The bridge will be in front of you, along with horses grazing nearby.

are available and festivals are held throughout the year. Comfortable rooms and suites are scattered in different buildings around the village.

EPHRATA

Ephrata, near exit 21 off I-76 northeast of Lancaster, combines a historic 18th-century Moravian religious site with a pleasant country landscape and the area's largest farmer's market and auction center. **Ephrata Cloister,** 633 W. Main St. (✆ **717/733-6600;** www.ephratacloister.org), near the junction of Route 272 and Route 322, housed one of America's earliest communal societies, which was known for its *fraktur*—an ornate, medieval German lettering you'll see on inscribed pottery and official documents. Ten austere wooden 18th-century buildings (put together without nails) remain in a grassy park setting. The cloister is open Monday through Saturday from 9am to 5pm and Sunday from noon to 5pm (closed Mon Jan–Feb and select holidays); admission is $7 for adults, $6.50 for seniors, and $5 for children 6 to 17.

The main street of Ephrata is pleasant for strolling and features an old rail car on the place where the train line used to run. On North State Street, 4 miles north of town, is the wonderful **Green Dragon Market & Auction** (✆ **717/738-1117;** www.greendragon market.com), open Friday from 9am to 9pm. Seven market buildings, with over 400 local growers, merchants, and artisans, include an auction house for hay and small animals. A flea market and arcade have sprung up outdoors, with plenty of cotton candy, clams on the half shell, and fresh corn.

LITITZ ★

Founded in 1756, this town, 6 miles north of Lancaster on Route 501, is one of the state's most charming. The cottage facades (now packed with wonderful shops and cafes) along East Main Street (Rte. 772) haven't changed much in the past 2 centuries. One interesting sight is the **Linden Hall Academy,** founded in 1794 as the first school for girls in the United States. There are several Revolutionary War–era churches and buildings on the grounds of the school. Across the street is the **Julius Sturgis Pretzel Bakery,** 219 E. Main St. (✆ **717/626-4354;** www.juliussturgis.com). Founded in 1861, the oldest such bakery in the country launched Lititz's reputation as "the Pretzel Town." An entertaining 20-minute guided tour lets you try your hand at rolling and twisting dough, and see the original ovens and bake shop. Tours, $3 for adults, $2 for ages 4 to 12, are offered Monday through Saturday, 9am to 5pm (reduced hours Jan to mid-Mar). Stock up on assorted goodies in the gift shop. Down the street, the **Lititz Museum** at 145 E. Main St. (✆ **717/627-4636;** www.lititzhistoricalfoundation.com) has permanent collections tracing the history of the town, and currently features an amazing exhibition of vintage toys. Hours are 10am to 4pm Monday through Saturday, Memorial Day through October; and select weekends in May, November, and December. Donations are accepted. Even if you don't have time for a meal, at least make a quick stop at the terrific, organic-focused **Café Chocolate** at 40 E. Main St. (✆ **717/626-0123;** www.chocolatelititz.com) for a decadent dessert or a "Turbo" (classic hot chocolate plus a shot of espresso) to go.

At the junction of Route 501 and Main Street is **Wilbur Chocolate Company's Candy Americana Museum & Store,** 48 N. Broad St. (✆ **888/294-5287** or 717/626-3249; www.wilburbuds.com). Famous for its "Wilbur buds" (bite-size chocolates that preceded the foil-wrapped Hershey Kiss), the factory provides a delightful nostalgic peek at the process and history of chocolate making, with samples, plus a store selling cooking or gift chocolate in a turn-of-the-20th-century atmosphere. Next door is the **Lititz Springs Park,** with a lovely duck-filled brook flowing from the 1756 spring, and the historic **General Sutter Inn** (p. 247).

STRASBURG

This little town, named by French Huguenots, is southeast of Lancaster on Route 896 and is a paradise for rail buffs. Until the invention of the auto, railroads were the major mode of fast transport, and Pennsylvania was a leader in building and servicing thousands of engines. The **Strasburg Rail Road** (✆ **717/687-7522;** www.strasburgrailroad.com) winds over 9 miles of preserved track from Strasburg to Paradise and back, as it has since 1832; wooden coaches and a Victorian parlor car are pulled by an iron steam locomotive. The railroad head is on Route 741 east of town and is open daily from mid-March to November and December 26 to December 31 and on weekends February to mid-March. Fares start at $12 for adults, $6 children ages 3 to 11, and free for children age 2 and under; prices vary for the numerous special events and tours. Other attractions include the **Railroad Museum of Pennsylvania** (✆ **717/687-8628;** www.rrmuseumpa.org), displaying dozens of stationary engines right across from the Strasburg Rail Road; the **National Toy Train Museum** (✆ **717/687-8976;** www.nttmuseum.org) on Paradise Lane off Route 741, one of the world's largest and most prestigious such collections,

Fun Facts — Some Facts About Pennsylvania Dutch Country

- The Pennsylvania Dutch Country hosts eight million visitors a year.
- Lancaster was the nation's capital for a day, when Congress fled from Philadelphia on September 27, 1777.
- In-line skates and scooters are considered acceptable forms of transportation among the Amish, though bicycles are not permissible.

featuring five huge push-button operating layouts; and **Choo Choo Barn–Traintown USA** (✆ **717/687-7911;** www.choochoobarn.com), a 1,700-square-foot miniature Amish Country landscape filled with animated trains and figures, which enact activities such as parades and circuses; an authorized Thomas Trackside Station store is a bonus. If you eat and sleep trains, then the **Red Caboose Motel & Restaurant** (✆ **888/687-5005;** www.redcaboosemotel.com), with its refurbished 25-ton caboose rooms and 80-ton P-70 coach dining car, offers lodgings that are right on track.

4 ESPECIALLY FOR KIDS

With the exception of beaches, Pennsylvania Dutch Country has everything for families, including rainy-day entertainment. In addition to the suggestions below and the above-mentioned **Julius Sturgis Pretzel House** in Lititz and the various **railroad attractions** in Strasburg, try the **Lancaster Science Factory,** 454 New Holland Ave., Lancaster (✆ **717/509-6363;** www.lancastersciencefactory.com). Dozens of farm activities, numerous special events, and an incredible, seasonal 5-acre corn maze make **Cherry Crest Adventure Farm,** 150 Cherry Hill Rd., Ronks (✆ **866/546-1799** or 717/687-6843; www.cherrycrestadventurefarm.com), fun for both kids and adults.

Driving along a country lane in a horse-drawn carriage not only sounds irresistible but fits right in with the speed of Amish life. **Ed's Buggy Rides** (✆ **717/687-0360;** www.edsbuggyrides.com) on Route 896, 1½ miles south of Route 30 in Strasburg, operates daily from 9am until dusk. Allow at least 1 hour for the 3-mile ride ($10 for adults and $5 for children); a visit to a working Amish farm can be arranged.

Amish Country is spectacular from the air, with its rural landscapes and generally clear weather. It's undeniably pricey at $179 per person minimum for a 1-hour flight, but the **U.S. Hot Air Balloon Team** (✆ **800/763-5987** or 717/299-2274; www.balloonflights.com) lifts off for the first and last 2-hour stretches of daylight. The local departure pad is at the Netherlands Inn & Spa in Strasburg.

HERSHEY ★

Hershey is technically outside the county, 30 minutes northwest of Lancaster on Route 422, but the assembly of amusements in a storybook setting makes the sweetest town on earth worth the trip. Milton Hershey set up his town at the turn of the 20th century to reflect his business and philanthropy, and it is a magical spot for kids (and for adults, since there is excellent golf and a wonderful spa here at the luxe Hotel Hershey). Start with the website (www.hersheypa.com), or just head for **Hershey's Chocolate World,** Park Boulevard (✆ **717/534-4900;** www.hersheyschocolateworld.com), where an array of diversions can easily fill an afternoon, including the special effects–filled Great American Chocolate Tour ride, the interactive Factory Works Experience, the Really Big 3D Show, and an entertaining guided trolley tour through Chocolate Town. A huge new immersive environment museum, the **Hershey Story,** 111 W. Chocolate Ave. (✆ **717/534-3439;** www.hersheystory.org), illustrates the rags-to-riches story of philanthropist and innovator Milton Hershey. Along with interactive exhibits, a hands-on Chocolate Lab offers classes on tempering, molding, or making chocolate from scratch, and an international Chocolate Tasting is available at the Café Zooka.

Hersheypark, a huge 110-acre theme park at the junction of Route 743 and Route 422 (✆ **800/HERSHEY** [437-7439] or 717/534-3090; www.hersheypark.com), offers more than 65 rides and attractions including water rides, 11 roller coasters, more than 20 kiddie rides, and music theaters. The Boardwalk, a hugely popular water-play area that's a nostalgic nod to the old-fashioned pleasures of Coney Island, Atlantic City, and other seaside towns, gets two splashy new attractions in 2009: the Shore, a nearly 378,000-gallon wave pool, and the Intercoastal Waterway, a relaxing individual raft float down a "lazy river." Also on-site is the 11-acre **ZooAmerica,** with more than 200 animals native to this continent and a new education building for special programs. Look for exciting celebrations during the zoo's centennial in 2010. Hersheypark is open daily from May to Labor Day; call for operating hours for the date you want to visit. ZooAmerica is open year-round except for Thanksgiving, Christmas, and New Year's Day. Daily admission prices for 2009: $52 for ages 9 to 54; $31 for ages 3 to 8 as well as seniors 55 to 69; $21 for seniors 70 and older; and free for ages 2 and under. Value-priced season passes range from $130 to $185.

The logical place to stay is the **Hershey Lodge,** West Chocolate Avenue and University Drive (✆ **717/533-3311;** www.hersheylodge.com), with miniature golf and tennis courts. And if you're tempted to sneak away without the kids, Hershey does have superb gardens, 72 holes of championship golf, and the palacelike **Hotel Hershey** (✆ **717/533-2171;** www.thehotelhershey.com) up the mountain, offers an extensive array of signature chocolate and Cuban-themed treatments at their luxurious, splurge-worthy spa. Elements of a massive "grand expansion," to be completed by the end of 2009, will be ready by summer, including a new restaurant and 10 premium multibedroom guest cottages in the woods behind the hotel.

Dutch Wonderland That ersatz castle you see heading east on Lincoln Highway (Rte. 30) out of Lancaster is the headquarters for a 44-acre amusement park with a large water-play area and entertainment such as storytelling and theatrical high diving. There's a moderately wild roller coaster and a flume ride, but most of the 32 rides are perfect for young families. Special themed weekends include Happy Hauntings in mid-October and Winter Wonderland from late November through Christmas.

2249 Lincoln Hwy. E., Lancaster, PA 17602. ✆ **717/291-1888.** www.dutchwonderland.com. Unlimited rides $31 ages 3–59, $26 ages 60–69, $19 ages 70 and up, free for ages 2 and under. Hours vary; park generally opens 10am and closes 6pm, 7pm, or 8:30pm.

Landis Valley Museum This large outdoor museum of Pennsylvania German culture, folk traditions, decorative arts, and language had its start when George and Henry Landis established a small museum here in the 1920s to exhibit family heirlooms. After the state acquired the Landis Valley Museum in the 1950s, it blossomed into a 21-building "living arts" complex. The costumed practitioners—clockmakers and clergymen, tavern keepers and tinsmiths, storekeepers, teachers, printers, weavers, and farmers—are experts in their fields and are generous with samples, which are also for sale in the shop. Check the website for fun-filled special events throughout the year.

2451 Kissel Hill Rd., Lancaster, PA 17601. ✆ **717/569-0401.** www.landisvalleymuseum.org. Admission $10 adults, $8 seniors, $7 for children 6–17. Mon–Sat 9am–5pm; Sun noon–5pm. Follow Oregon Pike (Rte. 272) north from Lancaster for 5 miles.

National Christmas Center The National Christmas Center offers a staggering array of self-guided exhibits, from a storybook village for kids to a nostalgic recreation of an F.W. Woolworth Co. 5 and 10 Cent Store (which originated in Lancaster). Even the biggest Grinch (like me) can find something to smile about in the 20,000 square feet of enchanting displays, plus a gift shop. Hours are expanded during the holiday season.

3427 Lincoln Hwy. (Rte. 30), Paradise, PA 17562. ✆ **717/442-7950.** www.nationalchristmascenter.com. Admission $11 adults, $5 children 3–12. May–Dec daily 10am–6pm; Mar–Apr Sat–Sun 10am–6pm.

5 SHOPPING

There are many reasons to keep your credit card handy in Lancaster County. Quilts and other craft products unique to the area are sold in dozens of small stores and out of individual farms, but keep cash or checks on hand for some Amish merchants. The thrifty Pennsylvania Dutch have saved old furniture and objects in their barns and attics for 300 years, so antiquing is plentiful here. Fine pieces tend to migrate toward New Hope and Bucks County for resale, where you compete directly with dealers at the many fairs and shows. If antiques aren't your bag, numerous outlet centers provide name-brand items at discounts of 30% to 70% along Route 30 east of Lancaster and in Reading.

ANTIQUES

Two miles east of exit 286 off I-76, Route 272, is Adamstown, self-proclaimed "Antiques Capital U.S.A." (www.antiquescapital.com). It's the undisputed local center of Sunday fairs, with numerous competitors within 5 miles. The largest are **Stoudt's Black Angus Antique Mall** and **Renninger's Antique and Collectors Market,** both with more than 300 indoor dealers and hundreds more outdoors; seasonal **Shupp's Grove** is smaller and mostly outdoors.

FARMER'S MARKETS

Most farmer's markets in Lancaster County today are shedlike buildings with stalls at which local farmers, butchers, and bakers vend their produce, eggs, cheese, baked goods, and meat products like sausage and scrapple. Since farmers can only afford to get away once or twice a week (to sell at Philadelphia's Reading Terminal, for example), more commercial markets supplement the local goods with stalls selling everything from deerskin to souvenirs. The low-ceilinged, air-conditioned commercial markets lack the flavor of, say, **Central Market** (p. 236) in Lancaster, with its swirling fans and 1860 tiles, or Friday at **Green Dragon Market & Auction** (p. 238), on North State Street in Ephrata.

A notable contemporary market is the **Bird-in-Hand Farmers Market** on Route 340 (✆ **717/393-9674;** www.birdinhandfarmersmarket.com). It's open from 8:30am to 5:30pm Friday and Saturday year-round, plus Wednesday and Thursday in season. **Root's Country Market and Auction,** just south of Manheim on Route 72 (✆ **717/898-7811;** www.rootsmarket.com), is a very complete market on Tuesday. The historic riverside **Columbia Market** at 308 Locust St. in Columbia (✆ **717/684-5767**) operates on Thursday and Friday from 9am to 6pm.

Moments **Shopping Like the Amish**

For an authentic Amish shopping experience that provides remarkable insights into everyday lives, stop by **Fisher's Houseware & Fabric,** on Route 372 near Georgetown (no phone). You'll park next to the buggies of locals buying essentials like fabrics, toys, books, snacks, clothespins, and glassware "fancies" in this wonderful general store (no credit cards accepted). Prices are extremely reasonable and the dishware and cookware selections are great.

Among the treats at the dozens of roadside stands that you'll pass, try the homemade root beer, ice cream, whoopee pies, and other local delicacies at **Countryside Road-Stand** at 2966 Stumptown Rd. near Ronks (✆ **717/656-9206**), open 8am to 8pm Monday through Saturday. Take a right turn from Route 772 heading west out of Intercourse and follow Stumptown for 1/2 mile. **Fisher's Produce**, on Route 741 between Strasburg and Gap (✆ **717/442-3078**), sells delicious baked goods and wonderful seasonal produce.

OUTLET CENTERS

With over 100 stores, **Rockvale Outlets,** Route 30 East at the intersection with Route 896 (✆ **717/293-9595;** www.rockvalesquareoutlets.com), is Lancaster's largest outlet mall, and includes a hotel, six restaurants, and courtesy shuttle service on its grounds. Brand names like Reebok, Bose, and Lenox are represented. Hours are Monday through Saturday from 9:30am to 9pm and Sunday from 11am to 5pm. The 60-plus store **Tanger Outlet Center,** 2200 Lincoln Hwy. E. (✆ **800/408-3477** or 717/392-7260; www.tangeroutlet.com), has shops like Coach, Fossil, and Kenneth Cole, and is slightly closer to Lancaster and more compact. Tanger is open Monday through Saturday from 9am to 9pm and Sunday from 10am to 6pm.

Home Furnishings Outlet, on Route 10 South in Morgantown at the junction of exit 298 off the Pennsylvania Turnpike (✆ **610/286-2000**), has 18 furniture stores, including Natuzzi Leather, and is open Monday through Saturday from 10am to 9pm and Sunday from noon to 5pm. A Holiday Inn is attached to the property.

I have neither the space nor the adjectives to fully describe the original "Outlet Capital of the World" in **Reading,** housed mainly in former textile mills along the Schuylkill. Some three million shoppers are drawn here annually to over 100 separate outlet stores offering name brands like Nautica, Lee, and JanSport. It's 30 minutes from Lancaster or 75 from Philadelphia, via I-76 to I-176 north to Route 422. The largest destination is **VF Outlet Village,** 801 Hill Ave. (✆ **800/772-8336** or 610/378-0408; www.vffo.com), just west of the city in Wyomissing.

QUILTS

Quilts occupy a special place in Lancaster County life. Quilting can be a time for fun and socializing, but it also affords an opportunity for young girls to learn the values and expectations of Amish life from their elders. German immigrant women started the tradition of reworking strips of used fabric into an ever-expanding series of pleasant, folkloric designs. Popular patterns include Wedding Ring, with interlocking sets of four circles; the eight-pointed Lone Star radiating out with bursts of colors; Sunshine and Shadow, virtuoso displays of diamonded color; and herringbone Log Cabin, squares with multicolored strips. Contemporary quilters have added free-form designs to these traditional patterns.

Color palettes and designs of quilts created for retail sale have a different sensibility from Amish-intended quilts. Amish women select patterns using careful calculations, based on the availability of gem-toned fabrics in green, red, blue, and purple left over from dressmaking, usually with a border or background of black (which can result in a single, oddly mismatched patch when a certain material runs out). They would never dream of buying whole fabric simply to express creativity or to capture an artistic impression of a spider web or a sunset. Extravagant "English" custom orders may be accompanied by a brief lecture on Amish thriftiness, in hopes that these frugal Amish values might "rub off" a bit.

The quilting process is laborious and technically astounding—involving choosing, cutting, and affixing thousands of pieces of fabric, then filling in the design with intricate needlework patterns on the white "ground" that holds the layers of the quilt together. Interestingly, though all quilts require a great deal of sewing by hand, the Amish have used sewing machines (usually treadle, though sometimes powered by air compressors) since their introduction in the 1800s for quilt backings. Within communities, a sort of "assembly line" often exists among farmhouses, in which one woman is skilled at cutting fabric, another at piecing, another at batting or backing the finished quilt top. Expect to pay at least $700 for a good-quality quilt and $25 and up for runners, bags, and throw pillows.

The **Old Country Store** (✆ **800/828-8218** or 717/768-7101; www.theoldcountrystore.com) in Intercourse has a knowledgeable sales staff and an excellent inventory of quilts, plus crafts, fabrics, and books. On the second floor, their dazzling **People's Place Quilt Museum** (www.ppquiltmuseum.com) provides an excellent overview of this art form, free of charge. The **Quilt Shop at Miller's,** located at the famed smorgasbord on Route 30 1 mile east of Route 896 (✆ **717/687-8439;** www.millerssmorgasbord.com/quiltshop.htm), has hundreds of handmade examples from local artisans, and is open daily. Demonstrations are offered from 2 to 4pm on weekends. Emma Witmer's mother was one of the first women to hang out a shingle to sell quilts 30 years ago, and she continues the business with more than 100 patterns at **Witmer Quilt Shop,** 1070 W. Main St. in New Holland (✆ **717/656-9526**). The shop is open from 8am to 6pm Tuesday through Thursday and Saturday and from 8am to 8pm Monday and Friday.

The county's back roads are dotted with simple signs indicating places where quilts are sold; prices are slightly lower, though choices are more limited. **Hannah Stoltzfoos** offers a good selection, plus custom work, at her home on 216 Witmer Rd. (✆ **717/392-4254**), just south of Route 340 near Smoketown. Katie Stoltzfuz operates **Country Lane Quilts** at 221 S. Groffdale Rd. in Leola (✆ **717/656-8476**). She also has a three-bedroom, two-bathroom guesthouse with solar-panel electricity on her picturesque farm. Rates start at $100 per night.

OTHER CRAFTS

Amish and Mennonites have created their own baskets, dolls, furniture, pillows, toys, wall hangings, and hex designs for centuries, and tourism has led to a healthy growth in production. Much of this output is channeled into the stores lining Route 340 in Intercourse and Bird-in-Hand, such as the Amish-owned **Quilts and Fabric Shack,** 3137 Old Philadelphia Pike (✆ **717/768-0338**). The **Weathervane Shop** at Landis Valley Museum (see "Especially for Kids," earlier in this chapter) has a fine collection of work from tin and pottery to caned chairs, produced by its own craftspeople. Find traditionally crafted salt-glazed stoneware and redware at **Eldreth Pottery** in Oxford (✆ **888/811-4313;** www.eldrethpottery.com). On the contemporary side, the **Pennsylvania Arts Experience** (✆ **717/917-1630;** www.paartsexperience.com) helps serious collectors connect with the many fine artists and artisans of the Susquehanna Valley Artist Trail.

6 WHERE TO STAY

Lancaster County lodgings vary from campsites and intimate inns to luxury resorts and bedrooms in working Amish farmhouses. Reservations are recommended in summer—especially at farms with only a few rooms available. Find farm lodgings at www.afarmstay.com, www.padutchcountry.com, or www.mennoniteinfoctr.com.

HOTELS & MOTELS

Incorporating the stately facade of the former Watt & Shand department store, the new **Lancaster County Convention Center,** 3 E. Vine St. (✆ **866/503-3786;** www.lancasterconventioncenter.com), brings an adjoining **Marriott Lancaster,** with 300 upscale rooms, and two more restaurants to historic downtown Lancaster. A museum will be added to the state-of-the-art complex in 2010.

Best Western Revere Inn & Suites ★ Eight miles east of Lancaster, the original inn is built off a historic 1740 post house now used as a restaurant and lounge. The main building, constructed in 1999, houses 66 oversize rooms, plus there's a recently renovated 24-room Amish-built annex and an attractive, restored farmhouse that was built in 1790 (try to snag a room there). Some of the 12 suites include such luxurious touches as fireplaces and Jacuzzis. Just across the parking lot is the all-comedy Rainbow Dinner Theater, with matinees and evening shows.

3063 Lincoln Hwy. (Rte. 30), Paradise, PA 17562. ✆ **800/429-7383** or 717/687-7683. www.revereinn.com. 95 units. $70–$130 double; $110–$180 suite. Rates include continental breakfast. Children 17 and under stay free in parent's room. 10% AAA and AARP discount. AE, DC, DISC, MC, V. Free parking. **Amenities:** Restaurant; lounge; 2 pools (1 indoor); exercise room; Jacuzzi; game room, coin-op laundry. *In room:* A/C, TV, Wi-Fi, fridge, coffeemaker, hair dryer, iron.

Bird-in-Hand Family Inn & Restaurant (Kids) This motel's location puts you directly in the heart of Amish Country. With plenty of kid-friendly diversions on-site, from minigolf and a petting zoo to scooter rentals and hot-air balloon rides, it's a great place for families. I prefer the back building, with a spacious lounge and rooms off an indoor hallway, to the front building's motel setup. Some of the 10 suites feature private patios and jetted tubs. The Bird-in-Hand Corporation operates several companion lodging facilities nearby, including the **Bird-in-Hand Village Inn & Suites,** an upscale country inn listed on the National Register of Historic Places: Check www.bird-in-hand.com for details and property descriptions. The recently expanded restaurant serves meals from the menu, but the superhungry should opt for the generous smorgasbord. Grandma Smucker's Bakery offers a wide assortment of treats, including shoofly pie. From June to October, popular weekly "socials" enable guests to talk with local Amish residents.

Rte. 340, Bird-in-Hand, PA 17505. ✆ **800/665-8780.** www.bird-in-hand.com. 125 units. $59–$149 double; $139–$229 suite. Packages available. Children 15 and under 16 stay free in parent's room. AE, DISC, MC, V. Free parking. **Amenities:** Restaurant; 3 pools (2 indoor); minigolf; 2 lighted tennis courts; Jacuzzi (indoor); game room; playground, petting zoo; coin-op laundry service; free 2-hr. bus tour of country roads. *In room:* A/C, TV, dataport, fridge, coffeemaker, hair dryer.

The Inn at Leola Village ★ In a cozy setting just 4 miles outside Lancaster, the six antique barns and buildings of an early-19th-century farm have been refurbished and expanded into a lovely hotel and restaurant with 21st-century comforts. Those who like their country with plush touches will appreciate the attractive decor of the roomy guest rooms and suites, with their beige-and-green color scheme, down comforters, TVs, and antiques and antique reproduction furniture. Breakfast is included, with quiche, muffins, and fruit on the buffet, and there's a fitness center and spa. The on-site Restaurant Mazzi presents sophisticated Italian- and French-influenced cuisine in a casually elegant setting. Check for package deals on lodging and treatments for women, men, and couples at Destinations Hair Salon & Day Spa.

38 Deborah Dr. (Rte. 23), Leola, PA 17540. ✆ **717/656-7002** or 877/669-5094. www.theinnatleolavillage.com. 63 units, including 12 suites and 1 cottage. $170 doubles; $200–$290 suites; $200 cottage. Rates include full breakfast. AE, DISC, MC, V. **Amenities:** Restaurant; outdoor pool; lounge; fitness center; salon/spa; billiards room. *In room:* TV/DVD, Wi-Fi, kitchenette, coffeemaker, hair dryer, iron/ironing board, whirlpool tub (in some suites).

INNS & BED & BREAKFASTS

As the second-largest and most diverse B&B community on the East Coast, Lancaster County encompasses a wonderful assortment of romantic to family-friendly lodgings in quaint villages and idyllic country locales. Among the most appealing destinations is the Victorian mansion–style **Hurst House Bed & Breakfast,** 154 E. Farmersville Road, Ephrata (✆ **800/603-9227** or 717/355-5151; www.hursthousebandb.com), with enchanting hilltop views from the wraparound porch. Each period-furnished room includes a private bathroom, balcony, fireplace, microwave, fridge, cable TV/DVD, and Wi-Fi, and there's an elevator to all floors.

Alden House ★ This elegant 1850 brick Victorian house is at the center of the town's historic district. There are private bathrooms in all rooms. Two suites can be accessed either through the house or via an outdoor spiral staircase to the second-floor porch. A new Carriage House Suite offers privacy and extra amenities like heated floors and a rainfall shower with body sprays. The morning brings a bountiful breakfast served in the dining room or overlooking the charming gardens outside.

62 E. Main St. (Rte. 772), Lititz, PA 17543. ✆ **800/584-0753** or 717/627-3363. www.aldenhouse.com. 6 units. $99–$130 double and suite. Rates include full breakfast. AE, DISC, MC, V. Free parking. *In room:* A/C, TV/VCR/DVD, Wi-Fi, fridge, microwave, bar sink (Carriage House only).

Cameron Estate Inn and Restaurant The wide front porch alone is reason to visit this gracious 1805 mansion on 15 green acres, with beautiful, formal antiques-filled rooms that range in style from French toile–canopied suites to serene hideaways under the eaves on the third floor. All rooms have their own bathrooms, and nine have wood-burning fireplaces. Since the excellent restaurant, open Wednesday to Sunday evenings, is open to the public, make reservations when booking your stay.

1855 Mansion Lane, Mount Joy, PA 17552. ✆ **717/492-0111** or 888/422-6376. www.cameronestateinn.com. 17 units. $129–$299 double. Rates include a fixed-menu hot breakfast. AE, DISC, MC, V. **Amenities:** Restaurant. *In room:* Wi-Fi, whirlpool tub (in 2).

Churchtown Inn Bed & Breakfast This completely restored 1735 stone inn has evening cocktail hours in the Victorian parlor, serves opulent breakfasts in a glassed-in porch overlooking the garden, and hosts periodic Murder Mystery parties. Guest rooms all have private bathrooms and lovely Amish quilts, and innkeepers Jim and Chris Farr can arrange dinner invitations with nearby Amish families. Although children 15 and under are not permitted at the inn (a rule that bends occasionally), there are two cozy stone cottages on the property that are both kid and pet friendly.

Main St. (Rte. 23), Churchtown, PA 17555. ✆ **800/637-4446** or 717/445-7794. Fax 717/445-0962. www.churchtowninn.com. 9 units. $95–$150 double. Rates include full breakfast. 2-night weekend minimum. AE, MC, V. Children and pets accepted in cottage only. *In room:* A/C, TV/VCR, CD player, fireplace.

General Sutter Inn ★ The General Sutter has operated continuously since 1764 at the charming intersection of Route 501 and Route 772. The inn boasts such niceties as verandas overlooking a fountain and marble-topped tables. Most of the rooms occupy the original building (wings have been added), and are decorated in Victorian style with folk-art touches. There is a coffee shop for breakfast and lunch, and the dining room offers a notable Sunday brunch and a solid Continental gourmet menu.

14 E. Main St. (junction of Rte. 501 and Rte. 772), Lititz, PA 17543. ✆ **717/626-2115.** Fax 717/626-0992. www.generalsutterinn.com. 16 units. $95–$129 double; $125–$150 suite. Rates include continental breakfast. AE, DISC, MC, V. Free parking. Pets $10. **Amenities:** 2 restaurants; lounge. *In room:* A/C, TV, Wi-Fi.

Historic Smithton Inn This inn, near Ephrata Cloister, is a pre–Revolutionary War stagecoach stop. Dorothy Graybill, the owner, has painstakingly decorated each room with canopy beds and collector-quality quilts, working fireplaces, sitting areas, and leather upholstered chairs. Triple-pane windows, magazines, and fresh flowers are typical thoughtful touches; the grounds have lovely gardens and a gazebo.

900 W. Main St., Ephrata, PA 17522. ✆ **717/733-6094.** www.historicsmithtoninn.com. 8 units. $95–$165 double. Rates include full breakfast and afternoon snacks. MC, V. Children welcome by prior arrangement, $20 extra ages 6–12; $35 ages 13 and up. **Amenities:** Golf nearby. *In room:* A/C, fridge, hair dryer (upon request), iron (upon request), Jacuzzi (in some), fireplace, feather bed (upon request).

The Inns at Doneckers ★ These lovely (and surprisingly affordable) accommodations are located in two vintage homes. The Guest House, where visitors check in, features simple but cozy rooms as well as luxury suites that come with fireplaces and Jacuzzis. The 1777 House, built by a clockmaker member of Ephrata Cloister, is more stately and distinguished. Rooms feature such original details as stained-glass windows and inlaid wood floors.

322 N. State St. (near junction of Rte. 322 and Rte. 222), Ephrata, PA 17522. ✆ **717/738-9502.** Fax 717/738-9554. www.doneckers.com. 31 units. $75–$125 double; $150–$250 suite. AE, DC, DISC, MC, V. Free parking. *In room:* A/C, TV, Wi-Fi (in Guest House), hair dryer, iron/ironing board, radio/CD player, Jacuzzi (in suite), fireplace (in suite).

Historic Strasburg Inn ★ Kids This attractive kid- and pet-friendly country inn is set on 18 acres, and surrounded by Amish farmlands. It has a good-size outdoor pool and hot tub, exercise room, and an inviting Fireside Tavern restaurant and lounge, but still manages to feel like an inn. Rooms are Colonial themed, some with poster beds, handmade floral wreaths, and handsome chair rails.

1 Historic Dr., Strasburg, PA 17579. ✆ **800/872-0201** or 717/687-7691. www.historicinnofstrasburg.com. 102 units. $109 double; $129–$169 suite. Packages and AAA/AARP discount available. AE, DC, DISC, MC, V. Free parking. **Amenities:** Restaurant; lounge; heated outdoor pool; exercise room; Jacuzzi; sauna; bike rentals (seasonally); children's playground; concierge; laundry service; dry cleaning. *In room:* A/C, TV, Wi-Fi, coffeemaker, hair dryer, iron.

FARM VACATION BED & BREAKFASTS

What better way to get the flavor of Amish life than by staying with a farm family? The **Pennsylvania Dutch Country Convention & Visitors Bureau** (✆ **800/PA-DUTCH**

[723-8824]; www.padutchcountry.com) has a complete listing of about 40 working farms that take guests. Reservations are recommended since most offer only three to five rooms. Expect simple lodgings, hall bathrooms, and filling, family-style breakfasts, all at less than motel rates. Dinners with the family are sometimes offered at an additional charge. You'll be able to chat with the women in the family (the men start and end their days with the sun) and get suggestions on local routes, walks, and crafts producers. Even day-trippers can get an entertaining, hands-on taste of farm life for an hour or two as a "Farmer's Apprentice" at **Verdant View Farm Bed & Breakfast,** 429 Strasburg Rd. (✆ **888/321/8110** or 717/687-7353; www.verdantview.com). One tip: Stay away from dairy and poultry farms if you have a sensitive nose!

Green Acres Farm Bed & Breakfast Wayne and Yvonne Miller can sleep 26 people in this lovely 150-year-old farmhouse, with private bathrooms in all rooms. It's a corn and soybean farm but also offers hay wagon rides, farm pets, a playhouse, swings, and a major-league trampoline for kids. All rooms have one queen-size bed plus bunk beds. There's no smoking, but you're allowed to bring your own alcohol. Well-behaved dogs permitted with carriers.

1382 Pinkerton Rd., Mount Joy, PA 17552. ✆ **717/653-4028.** Fax 717/653-2840. www.thegreenacresfarm.com. 7 units. $110 per room, up to 4 guests. Additional child $5. Rates include family-style breakfast. Secure reservation with MC or V, pay with cash or check only. Follow driving directions on website; GPS will take you to a neighbor's home. Dogs accepted. *In room:* A/C.

Rayba Acres Farm Ray and Reba Ranck offer clean, quiet rooms on a working sixth-generation farm. (You're welcome to visit with the animals or just wander the grounds.) Each room has a private bathroom, satellite TV, microwave, and fridge. The motel-like units have separate entrances, and four are on the first floor. Outside is a pretty pergola and gardens.

183 Black Horse Rd., Paradise, PA 17562. ✆ **717/687-6729.** Fax 717/687-8386. www.raybaacres.com. 6 units. $83–$88 double. DISC, MC, V. From Paradise center, go south from Rte. 30 onto Black Horse Rd. for 2 miles. *In room:* A/C, TV, fridge, coffeemaker.

RESORTS

Best Western Eden Resort & Suites ★ The amenities of this freshly renovated hotel are somewhat hard to reconcile with the surrounding region; that is, the hotel provides comforts like plush rooms (request poolside, with a balcony) and family-size suites, and a tropically landscaped atrium and pool. If you want a respite from the minimalist style of Amish life, this is great place to hang out. Pets under 35 pounds are welcome and Doggie Daycare is a popular service.

222 Eden Rd. (Rte. 30 and Rte. 272), Lancaster, PA 17601. ✆ **800/528-1234** or 717/569-6444. Fax 717/569-4208. www.edenresort.com. 276 units. From $99 double; from $140 suite. Up to 2 children 17 and under stay free in parent's room. 10% AAA and AARP discount. AE, DC, DISC, MC, V. Free parking. Pets under 35 lb. accepted. **Amenities:** 2 restaurants; lounge; 2 pools (1 heated indoor); tennis and basketball courts; health club; Jacuzzi; sauna; shuffleboard; business center; game room, laundry service; dry cleaning. *In room:* A/C, HDTV w/pay movies, Wi-Fi, kitchenette or full kitchen (in some suites), fridge, coffeemaker, hair dryer, iron/ironing board, safe.

Willow Valley Resort & Conference Center (Kids) This recently renovated Mennonite-owned resort (no drinking permitted on premises) started as a farm stand in 1943 and now combines a very complete set of modern comforts on 307 acres—a 9-hole golf course, lighted tennis courts, indoor water park, and indoor and outdoor pools—with nice touches like a bakery with local specialties. A skylit atrium is home to two smorgasbords and a restaurant. Free Amish Country bus tours offered Monday through Saturday in season and select days in winter.

2416 Willow St. Pike (3 miles south of Lancaster on Rte. 222), Lancaster, PA 17602. ✆ **800/444-1714** or 717/464-2711. www.willowvalley.com. 342 units. Double from $99, $119 with breakfast; suite from $149, $169 with breakfast. Rates increase in summer. Packages available. Children 11 and under stay free in parent's room. AE, DISC, MC, V. Free parking. **Amenities:** Restaurant; 3 pools (2 indoor); water park; 9-hole golf course; lighted tennis and basketball courts; fitness center; sauna; children's playground; prayer chapel. *In room:* A/C, TV/pay movies, Wi-Fi, fridge, coffeemaker, hair dryer, iron/ironing board.

7 WHERE TO DINE

While Ben Franklin would probably be staggered at the size of a modern Pennsylvania Dutch meal or smorgasbord, he'd recognize everything in it—you'll find the same baked goods, meat and poultry, and fruits and vegetables that were offered here in Colonial times. The Amish way of life calls for substantial, long-cooking dishes, rich in butter and cream. Don't look for crisp vegetables—if they're not creamed, they're thoroughly boiled. The baked goods are renowned, with shoofly pie, a crumb-topped concoction of molasses and sweet dough (hence its attraction to flies), being the most famous.

Included here are representative family-style and smorgasbord dining spots, as well as restaurants that update local ingredients. Family style means that you'll be eating with a group of 10 or 12, and heaping platters of food will be delivered to your long table, course after course. At a smorgasbord, you fill your own plate at central food stations, with unlimited refills. Prices are fixed per person at both.

And when looking for a meal, don't neglect the signs along the road, or "Community Event" listings in the Thursday "Weekend" section of the *Lancaster New Era* (or check the "Entertainment" link at www.lancasteronline.com), for church or firehouse breakfasts or dinners. These generally charge a minimal amount for an abundance of homestyle food, and they're great chances to meet the locals. Annual festivals include the Sertoma Club's enormous chicken barbecue at Long's Park in Lancaster (www.lancaster sertomabbq.com) and New Holland's **Summer Fest,** featuring the Pennsylvania State Championship BBQ cook-off (www.nhsummerfest.org). Downtown Lancaster restaurants offer everything from tasty California mission–style burritos at **Senorita Burrita** (✆ **717/283-0940**) to exquisitely artful contemporary cuisine at **Effie Ophelia** (✆ **717/397-6863;** www.effieophelia.com).

FAMILY STYLE/SMORGASBORD

Good 'N' Plenty Restaurant PENNSYLVANIA DUTCH They've added the 500-seat Dutch Room to the original 110-seat farmhouse here. The location is very convenient, and tables seat 10 to 12 for family-style dining. Expect waits at peak dining hours: Tables must be fully seated before they're filled with platters, though the maximum time is usually only 10 minutes. The menu changes daily, and you can purchase baked goods and other gift items on the premises.

Rte. 896 (1/2 mile south of its intersection with Rte. 340 and north of intersection with Rte. 30), Smoketown. ✆ **717/394-7111.** www.goodnplenty.com. Reservations not accepted. Adults $19, children $9.25 for ages 4–12, free for children 3 and under. MC, V. Mon–Sat 11:30am–8pm.

The Underground Railroad

The pastoral Lancaster County village of Christiana was the scene of what could be considered the first battle in the Civil War—long before states started seceding from the Union. Violence erupted here in 1851 when the Fugitive Slave Law of 1850 was put to the test: A deadly conflict between slave bounty hunters and local abolitionists became known as the Christiana Resistance, and a landmark court decision signaled that the North would not comply with legislation contrary to human rights. The new **Underground Railroad Center at the Historic Zercher Hotel,** at 11 Green St. in Christiana illustrates this area's contribution to African-American heritage, and is one of many destinations on the **Quest for Freedom Trail** that stretches from Philadelphia to Gettysburg (see www.questforfreedom.org for more information). Another highlight is the historic **Bethel African Methodist Episcopal Church,** 450–512 E. Strawberry St. in Lancaster (© 717/393-8379; www.livingtheundergroundrailroad.com), which offers *Living the Experience* performances, a poignant reenactment of the struggle for freedom, told through story, song, and audience participation.

Throughout the region, courageous abolitionists provided safe houses, known as "stations," for fugitive slaves, and several homes that provided refuge are now guesthouses, including **Rocky Acre Farm B&B,** 1020 Pinkerton Rd., Mount Joy, PA 17552 (© **717/653-4449;** www.rockyacre.com), and **Across the Way B&B at the Fassitt Mansion,** 5061 Old Philadelphia Pike, White Horse, PA 17527 (© **888/984-3929;** www.acrossthewaybb.com).

You can catch a glimpse of another station—this one literally underground—at **Bube's Brewery,** 102 N. Market St., Mount Joy, PA 17552 (© **717/653-2056;** www.bubesbrewery.com). This remarkably intact 19th-century brewery offers tours of the vast building's original brewing facilities, including "catacombs" 43 feet below the earth, where beer was stored and slaves hidden. The Catacombs is now one of three diverse and wonderful restaurants on the property, where live music, playful-themed feasts, and murder-mystery parties are featured. Bube's Brewery will have 10 original hotel rooms, refurbished in a uniquely theatrical style, ready for adventurous guests by the time you read this.

Miller's Smorgasbord PENNSYLVANIA DUTCH/SMORGASBORD In 1929, Anna Miller prepared chicken and waffles for truckers while Enos Miller repaired their vehicles. For millions of people since then, Miller's has been the definitive Pennsylvania Dutch smorgasbord, offering homemade chicken corn soup; slow-roasted carved beef, turkey, and ham; chicken potpies; a bevy of desserts; and so much more—including health-conscious choices. You can even order wine, beer, or a cocktail with your meal (a rarity at this type of restaurant). Breakfast is served 7 days a week, with both a big buffet and an a la carte menu. On-site stores include a gallery, a bakery, and furniture and quilt shops. Check the website for numerous coupons.

Rte. 30 at Ronks Rd. (5 miles east of Lancaster and 1 mile east of Rte. 896). © **800/669-3568** or 717/687-6621. www.millerssmorgasbord.com. Reservations accepted. Full smorgasbord dinner $23 adults (with partial options starting at $9.95), $5.95–$9.95 children 4–12; breakfast buffet $12 adults, $6.95 children 4–12. AE, DISC, MC, V. Breakfast Mon–Sat 7:30–10:30am, Sun 7:30–11:30am; lunch and dinner daily noon–9pm.

Plain & Fancy Farm Restaurant PENNSYLVANIA DUTCH This 51-year-old family-style restaurant started out as a barn (you can still see the original posts), and has expanded into a recently renovated complex that includes shops, buggy rides, a theater, homestead and farmland tours, and the luxurious 50-unit Amish View Inn & Suites. A recipient of *USA Today's* Great Plate Award, the restaurant now complements the Family-Style Feast with an a la carte menu. Don't miss the crisp and flavorful fried chicken. Check the website for entertainment and coupons, or to reserve a behind-the-scenes kitchen tour.

Rte. 340 (7 miles east of Lancaster), Bird-in-Hand, PA. ✆ **717/768-4400.** www.plainandfancyfarm.com. Reservations recommended. Family-style dinner $19 adults, $9.95 children 4–12. AE, DISC, MC, V. Daily 11:30am–7pm.

Shady Maple Smorgasbord & Farm Market Value SMORGASBORD This is somewhat north of most of the attractions, but it does an enormous business, with waits of up to 30 minutes on Saturday for one of the 1,700 seats. Tourist buses have their own entrance and seating. The Pennsylvania Dutch buffet is a mind-boggling 140 feet long, with 46 salads, 14 vegetables, eight meats, eight breads, 27 desserts, and a make-your-own-sundae station. Breakfast includes everything you've ever imagined eating at that hour. There's a touristy gift shop and a fast-food version (why bother?) downstairs. The starting dinner price of $16 includes tax, tip, and all nonalcoholic beverages Different nightly specials, such as prime rib and seafood, range up to $22.

Rte. 23 (1 mile east of Blue Ball, at intersection with Rte. 897), E. Earl, PA. ✆ **717/354-8222.** www.shady-maple.com. Reservations not accepted. Dinner $16–$22; lunch $12; breakfast $9.30. Half price for children 4–10. 10% discount for seniors. AE, DC, DISC, MC, V. Mon–Sat 5am–8pm.

MORE DINING CHOICES

Of the many fine eateries found in downtown Lancaster, standouts include **Carr's Restaurant,** across from Central Market at 50 W. Grant St. (✆ **717/299-7090;** www.carrsrestaurant.com), featuring creatively prepared local meats and produce and an extensive

Tips Dining with the Amish

Joining an Amish family for dinner is a wonderful, enlightening experience that can personally acquaint you with these hospitable people. You'll be treated to lively, informative conversation and hearty, home cooking that's likely to include handcrafted pickles and baked goods. Remember, these are people's homes, not restaurants, so you can't just call for reservations (that would be *illegal*). However, some country innkeepers who are friendly with their Amish neighbors can arrange a dinner "invitation" for *registered guests,* and you may discreetly offer an envelope with a cash "gift" to your Amish hosts. Places with such Amish connections include the elegant and romantic **E. J. Bowman House,** 2672 Lititz Pike (Rte. 501; ✆ **877/519-1776** or 717/519-0808; www.ejbowmanhouse.com), and the more bucolic **Eby's Pequea Bed & Breakfast Farm** with two locations in Gordonville, one at 345 Belmont Rd. and the second at 459a Queen Rd. (✆ **717/768-3615;** www.ebyfarm.com).

The Arts Scene

Think that Pennsylvania Dutch country art is restricted to hex signs and Amish quilts? Then the burgeoning and quite sophisticated arts scene that has blossomed in Lancaster and Berks counties over the past few years will come as a wonderful surprise. There are more than 80 galleries within a 5-block area in downtown Lancaster, ranging from fun-and-funky home furnishings at **Metropolis,** 154 N. Prince St. (✆ **717/572-9961;** www.metropolis-store.com), to changing exhibits at **Red Raven Art Company,** 139 N. Prince St. (✆ **717/299-4400;** www.redravenartcompany.com), plus loads of great (non-Dutch) cafes and bakeries, including **Rachel's Café & Creperie,** 309 N. Queen St. (✆ **717/399-3515**). The city is also home to the **Pennsylvania College of Art & Design,** 204 N. Prince St. (✆ **717/396-7833;** www.pcad.edu) and the **Demuth Museum,** 120 E. King St. (✆ **717/299-9940;** www.demuth.org), housed in the historic home of early-20th-century artist Charles Demuth.

For artistic lodgings, check into the superb **Lancaster Arts Hotel** ★, 300 Harrisburg Ave. (✆ **866/720-ARTS** [2787] or 717/431-3266; www.lancasterartshotel.com), an incredibly stylish, art-bedecked boutique hotel with high-end amenities and gorgeous individually decorated rooms and suites. The property features architectural elements from its former life as a tobacco warehouse, and its cutting-edge restaurant, **John J. Jeffries,** specializes in fine local and seasonal cuisine. (A signature on an old tobacco inspection slip found during renovation inspired the name.) At nearby **Checkers Bistro,** 300 W. James St. (✆ **717/509-1069;** www.checkersbistro.com), local artists who often paint at a mid–dining room easel add to the lively ambience.

Art energy peaks during festive, well-attended **First Friday** celebrations; visit www.lancasterarts.com or www.figlancaster.com for more information. Another alliterative arts event, **Second Sunday,** is hosted 30 miles northeast at the **Goggleworks,** 201 Washington St. (✆ **610/374-4600;** www.goggleworks.org) in Reading. Housed in a huge, multibuilding former goggle factory site, this vibrant, comprehensive center for the arts—the largest facility of its kind in the nation—is packed with five stories of galleries, studios, and classrooms, and includes an art-house film theater, a gift shop, and a casual restaurant. A voluminous hot-glass studio has stadium seating so you can observe the fiery spectacle of molten glass being transformed into fragile masterpieces. Open daily, there's no admission fee, and parking is free.

wine selection, and **Character's Pub,** tucked in an alleylike side street at 38 N. Christian St. (✆ **717/735-7788**), well worth tracking down for its sophisticated casual fare and fun atmosphere. If you're looking for restaurants with a great nightlife, try the **Belvedere Inn,** 402 N. Queen St. (✆ **717/394-2422;** www.belvedereinn.biz). The second floor of this opulent grand Victorian restaurant is home to Crazy Shirley's, a sexy, red-drenched piano bar and lounge with fabulous cocktails and live jazz or blues on weekends. Mediterranean-influenced **Gibraltar,** 931 Harrisburg Pike (✆ **717/397-2790;** www.keares restaurants.com/gibraltar), notable for outstanding seafood and an award-winning wine list, also presents weekend jazz at the chic Aqua Lounge. **Annie Bailey's,** a delightfully traditional Irish pub at 28–30 E. King St. (✆ **717/393-4000;** www.anniebaileysirishpub.com), offers a variety of live bands and an enormous deck that draws happy crowds in summer. Brewpub fans can head for the recently opened branch of **Iron Hill Brewery & Restaurant,** 781 Harrisburg Pike (✆ **717/291-9800;** www.ironhillbrewery.com/lancaster) or a hometown favorite, **Lancaster Brewing Company,** 302 N. Plum St. (✆ **717/391-6258;** www.lancasterbrewing.com), with excellent food and finely crafted flagship and seasonal brews served in a rustic former tobacco warehouse.

Dans Restaurant ★ NEW AMERICAN When the mood for fine dining strikes, this tiny gem of a restaurant—located in a center city walk down—will dazzle you with exquisite fare and flawless service. The decor is crisp, clean, and simple, and the food presentation elegant and uncluttered. A French accent on the seasonally driven menu isn't surprising since the youthful executive chef, Jason Hook, honed his skills under culinary superstars Alain Ducasse and Georges Perrier. In fact, the sophisticated cuisine could be likened to Le Bec Fin's—but at a fraction of the price. Hook demonstrates exceptional talent for marrying flavors and highlighting natural tastes, from foie gras with roasted white peaches and fresh honeycomb to tilapia with truffles and golden chanterelles. Fixed-price multicourse tasting menus provide excitement for gastronomic adventurers.

1049 Penn St., Reading, PA. ✆ **610/373-2075.** www.dansrestaurant.com. Reservations recommended Sat–Sun. Main courses $18–$35; brunch $9–$17. AE, DISC, MC, V. Wed–Sat 5–9:30pm; Sun noon–7pm (brunch noon–3pm). Parking behind apartments across the street.

Stoudt's Black Angus Restaurant & Pub STEAKHOUSE/BREWPUB Stoudt's German-style lagers, ales, heavyweights, and seasonal brews, all crafted here, make a perfect conclusion to a Sunday of antiquing at the market next door. The steakhouse, specializing in aged prime beef, includes such sophisticated options as a seafood bar, tapas, and cheese plates with artisanal bread and summer chutney. An agreeable pub dishes up a nice variety of sausages, alongside burgers, soups, and salads. The restaurant has a 1928 Packard in the lobby, and hosts many special events and festivals.

Rte. 272 (1 mile north of exit 21 from I-76), Adamstown, PA. ✆ **717/484-4385.** www.stoudtsbeer.com. Reservations recommended. Main courses $17–$35; brewpub $6.95–$12. AE, DC, DISC, MC, V. Mon–Thurs 4:30–10pm; Fri–Sat noon–10pm; Sun 11:30am–8pm.

Tips Showtime in Dutch Country

Local theatrical venues cater to a variety of tastes. **Sight & Sound Millennium Theatre** (✆ **717/687-7800;** www.sight-sound.com) specializes in Christian musical entertainment, while the grand Victorian **Fulton Theatre** (✆ **717/397-7425;** www.thefulton.org) stages Broadway caliber musicals and plays. **American Music Theatre** (✆ **717/397-7700;** www.amtshows.com) hosts a wide spectrum of celebrity concerts and a great family-oriented holiday extravaganza. Professional performers and a live orchestra present new and classic shows at **Dutch Apple Dinner Theatre** (✆ **717/898-1900;** www.dutchapple.com), and **Rainbow Dinner Theatre** (✆ **717/687-4300;** www.rainbowdinnertheatre.com) is the nation's only all-comedy dinner theater.

Appendix: Fast Facts, Toll-Free Numbers & Websites

1 FAST FACTS: PHILADELPHIA

AMERICAN EXPRESS There is an Amex office at 16th Street and John F. Kennedy Boulevard (✆ **215/587-2300**).

AREA CODES Philadelphia's telephone area codes are **215** and **267.** Bucks County and half of Montgomery County share these codes, but the Brandywine Valley area of Delaware County and half of Montgomery County (the Main Line) have switched to **610, 484, or 835.** Lancaster County and the Pennsylvania Dutch region use area code **717.**

ATMS & CASHPOINTS See section 5, "Money & Costs," in chapter 3.

BUSINESS HOURS Banks are generally open Monday through Friday from 9am to 5pm, with some open Saturday from 9am to noon. **TD Banks** offer extended hours and are open Sunday. Most bars and restaurants serve food until 10 or 10:30pm. Those near Rittenhouse Square and in Old City tend to stay open later, and some Chinatown places stay open until 3am. Bars must close at 2am. Offices are open Monday through Friday from 9am to 5pm. Stores are open daily from about 10am to 7pm; most Center City shops keep doors open later on Wednesday evenings. Old City, Rittenhouse Square, South Street, Northern Liberties, and Manayunk are the most active late-night districts. Some SEPTA "Night Owl" routes run all night, but the frequency of buses and trolleys drops dramatically after 8pm (except subways coming back from the stadiums on game or event nights).

CAR RENTALS See "Toll-Free Numbers & Websites," later in this chapter.

DRINKING LAWS The legal age for purchase and consumption of alcoholic beverages is 21; proof of age is required and often requested at bars, nightclubs, and restaurants, so it's always a good idea to bring ID when you go out. In Philadelphia and throughout Pennsylvania, wine and liquor are sold at state stores called Wine and Spirits Stores, which are controlled by Pennsylvania's Liquor Control Board. Find these stores' locations and hours at www.lcb.state.pa.us; several are closed Sunday. Beer to go is sold at licensed convenience stores, permitted bars, and beer distributors.

Do not carry open containers of alcohol in your car or in any public area that isn't zoned for alcohol consumption. The police can fine you on the spot. And nothing will ruin your trip faster than getting a citation for DUI (driving under the influence), so don't even think about driving while intoxicated.

DRIVING RULES See section 4, "Getting There & Getting Around," in chapter 3.

ELECTRICITY Like Canada, the United States uses 110–120 volts AC (60 cycles), compared to 220–240 volts AC (50 cycles) in most of Europe, Australia, and New Zealand. Downward converters that change 220–240 volts to 110–120 volts are difficult to find in the United States, so bring one with you.

EMBASSIES & CONSULATES All embassies are located in the nation's capital, Washington, D.C. Some consulates are located in major U.S. cities, and most nations have a mission to the United Nations in New York City. If your country isn't listed below, call directory information in Washington, D.C. (✆ **202/555-1212**) or check **www.embassy.org/embassies**.

The embassy of **Australia** is at 1601 Massachusetts Ave. NW, Washington, DC 20036 (✆ **202/797-3000**). The embassy of **Canada** is at 501 Pennsylvania Ave. NW, Washington, DC 20001 (✆ **202/682-1740;** www.canadianembassy.org). Other Canadian consulates are in Buffalo (New York), Detroit, Los Angeles, New York, and Seattle.

The embassy of **Ireland** is at 2234 Massachusetts Ave. NW, Washington, DC 20008 (✆ **202/462-3939;** www.irelandemb.org). Irish consulates are in Boston, Chicago, New York, San Francisco, and other cities. See the website for a complete list.

The embassy of **New Zealand** is at 37 Observatory Circle NW, Washington, DC 20008 (✆ **202/328-4800;** www.nzembassy.com). New Zealand consulates are in Los Angeles, Salt Lake City, San Francisco, and Seattle.

The embassy of the **United Kingdom** is at 3100 Massachusetts Ave. NW, Washington, DC 20008 (✆ **202/588-7800;** www.britainusa.com). Other British consulates are in Atlanta, Boston, Chicago, Cleveland, Houston, Los Angeles, New York, San Francisco, and Seattle.

EMERGENCIES To contact police, fire, and rescue in an emergency, dial ✆ **911.** In case of accidental poisoning, call ✆ **800/222-1222** or 215/386-2100. For 24-hour pet emergencies, call the Matthew J. Ryan Veterinary Hospital at the University of Pennsylvania at ✆ **215/898-4685.** (Care here tends to be more expensive than it would be at a standard vet, but this facility is considered to be one of the best of its kind—anywhere.)

GASOLINE (PETROL) At press time, the cost of gasoline (also known as gas, but never petrol), is in great flux. Gasoline in Philadelphia averages from $2 to $3 per gallon, more if you opt for full-service (wherein an attendant pumps your gas). Just across the bridge, New Jersey offers cheaper gasoline and does not permit self-service. Taxes are already included in the printed price. One U.S. gallon equals 3.8 liters or 0.85 imperial gallons. Fill-up locations are known as gas or service stations.

HOLIDAYS Banks, government offices, post offices, and many stores, restaurants, and museums are closed on the following legal national holidays: January 1 (New Year's Day), the third Monday in January (Martin Luther King Day), the third Monday in February (Presidents' Day), the last Monday in May (Memorial Day), July 4 (Independence Day), the first Monday in September (Labor Day), the second Monday in October (Columbus Day), November 11 (Veterans Day/Armistice Day), the fourth Thursday in November (Thanksgiving Day), and December 25 (Christmas). The Tuesday after the first Monday in November is Election Day, a federal government holiday in presidential-election years (held every 4 years, and next in 2012).

For more information on holidays see "Philadelphia Calendar of Events," in chapter 3.

HOSPITALS Medical care in Philadelphia is world renowned. Major hospitals include Children's Hospital, 34th Street and Civic Center Boulevard (✆ **215/590-1000;** www.chop.edu); Hahnemann University Hospital, Broad and Vine streets (✆ **215/762-7000;** www.hahnemann hospital.com); University of Pennsylvania Hospital, 3400 Spruce St. (✆ **215/662-4000;** www.pennhealth.com); Pennsylvania Hospital, 8th and Spruce streets (✆ **215/829-3000;** www.pennhealth.com/pahosp); and Thomas Jefferson University Hospital, 11th and Walnut streets (✆ **215/955-6000;** www.jeffersonhospital.org).

HOT LINES People with thoughts of suicide or other mental health issues can speak to someone 24/7 at Philadelphia Behavior Health by calling ✆ **215/686-4420.** For nonbiased advice on reproductive issues or sexual health, call the Choice Hot Line at ✆ **800/848-3367** or 215/985-3300.

INSURANCE **Medical Insurance** Although it's not required of travelers, health insurance is highly recommended. Most health insurance policies cover you if you get sick away from home—but check your coverage before you leave.

International visitors to the U.S. should note that unlike many European countries, the United States does not usually offer free or low-cost medical care to its citizens or visitors. Doctors and hospitals are expensive, and in most cases require advance payment or proof of insurance before they render their services. Good policies will cover the costs of an accident, repatriation, or death. Packages such as **Europ Assistance's Worldwide Healthcare Plan** are sold by European automobile clubs and travel agencies at attractive rates. **Worldwide Assistance Services, Inc.** (✆ **800/777-8710;** www.worldwide assistance.com) is the agent for Europ Assistance in the United States. Though lack of health insurance may prevent you from being admitted to a hospital in nonemergencies, don't worry about being left on a street corner to die: The American way is to fix you now and bill the daylights out of you later.

If you're ever hospitalized more than 150 miles from home, **MedjetAssist** (✆ **800/527-7478;** www.medjetassistance.com) will pick you up and fly you to the hospital of your choice in a medically equipped and staffed aircraft 24 hours day, 7 days a week. Annual memberships are $225 for individuals and $350 for families; you can also purchase short-term memberships.

Canadians should check with their provincial health plan offices or call **Health Canada** (✆ **866/225-0709;** www.hc-sc.gc.ca) to find out the extent of their coverage and what documentation and receipts they must take home if they are treated in the United States.

Travelers from the U.K. should carry their European Health Insurance Card (EHIC), which replaced the E111 form as proof of entitlement to free/reduced cost medical treatment abroad (✆ **0845/606-2030;** www.ehic.org.uk). Note, however, that the EHIC only covers "necessary medical treatment," and for repatriation costs, lost money, baggage, or cancellation, travel insurance from a reputable company should always be sought. Try www.travelinsuranceweb.com.

Travel Insurance The cost of travel insurance varies widely, depending on the destination, the cost and length of your trip, your age and health, and the type of trip you're taking, but expect to pay between 5% and 8% of the vacation itself. You can get estimates from various providers through **InsureMyTrip.com**. Enter your trip cost and dates, your age, and other information, for prices from more than a dozen companies.

U.K. citizens and their families who make more than one trip abroad per year may find an annual travel insurance policy is cheaper. Check **www.moneysupermarket.com,** which compares prices across a wide range of providers for single- and multitrip policies.

Most big travel agents offer their own insurance and will probably try to sell you their package when you book a vacation. Think before you sign. **Britain's Consumers' Association** recommends that you insist on seeing the policy and reading the fine print before buying travel insurance. The **Association of British Insurers** (✆ **020/7600-3333;** www.abi.org.uk) gives advice by phone and publishes *Holiday Insurance,* a free guide to policy provisions and prices. You might also shop around for better deals: Try **Columbus Direct** (✆ 0870/033-9988; www.columbusdirect.net).

Trip-Cancellation Insurance Trip-cancellation insurance will help retrieve your money if you have to back out of a trip or depart early, or if your travel supplier goes bankrupt. Trip cancellation traditionally covers such events as sickness, natural disasters, and State Department advisories. The latest news in trip-cancellation insurance is the availability of **expanded hurricane coverage** and the **"any-reason"** cancellation coverage—which costs more but covers cancellations made for any reason. You won't get back 100% of your prepaid trip cost, but you'll be refunded a substantial portion. **TravelSafe** (✆ **888/885-7233;** www.travelsafe.com) offers both types of coverage. Expedia also offers any-reason cancellation coverage for its air-hotel packages. For details, contact one of the following recommended insurers: **Access America** (✆ 866/807-3982; www.accessamerica.com); **Travel Guard International** (✆ 800/826-4919; www.travelguard.com); **Travel Insured International** (✆ 800/243-3174; www.travelinsured.com); and **Travelex Insurance Services** (✆ 888/457-4602; www.travelex-insurance.com).

INTERNET ACCESS It's harder to find a Center City coffee shop *without* wireless Internet access than it is to find a coffee shop with one. Wi-Fi abounds at all manner of cafes, in neighborhoods from University City to Northern Liberties. Cybercafes that provide computers to work on are not quite as easy to find, but they do exist. **ING Direct Café** at 17th and Walnut streets (✆ **215/731-1410;** http://home.ingdirect.com) offers inexpensive coffee and a kiosk. Branches of the **Free Library of Philadelphia** (✆ **215/686-5322;** www.freelibrary.org) have Web-connected computers, too. For additional help, see section 10, "Staying Connected" in chapter 3.

LAUNDROMATS **U-Do-It Laundry & Dry Cleaning** at 1513 Spruce St. (✆ **215/735-1255**) is open from 7am until 9 or 10pm most days, and is the biggest such operation in Center City. **Quick & Clean Coin Laundry** at 320 S. 10th St. (no phone) is a popular laundromat on the other side of Broad Street.

LEGAL AID If you are "pulled over" for a minor infraction (such as speeding), never attempt to pay the fine directly to a police officer; this could be construed as attempted bribery, a much more serious crime. Pay fines by mail, or directly into the hands of the clerk of the court. If accused of a more serious offense, say and do nothing before consulting a lawyer. Here the burden is on the state to prove a person's guilt, and everyone has the right to remain silent, whether he or she is suspected of a crime or actually arrested. Once arrested, a person can make one telephone call to a party of his or her choice. International visitors should call their embassy or consulate.

LOST & FOUND Be sure to tell all of your credit card companies the minute you discover your wallet has been lost or stolen and file a report at the nearest police precinct. Your credit card company or insurer may require a police report number or record of the loss. Most credit card companies have an emergency toll-free number to call if your card is lost or stolen;

they may be able to wire you a cash advance immediately or deliver an emergency credit card in a day or two.

Visa's U.S. emergency numbers are ✆ **800/847-2911** and 410/581-9994. American Express cardholders and traveler's check holders should call ✆ **800/221-7282.** MasterCard holders should call ✆ **800/307-7309** or 636/722-7111. For other credit cards, call the toll-free number directory at ✆ **800/555-1212.**

If you need emergency cash over the weekend when most banks and American Express offices are closed, you can have money wired to you via **Western Union** (✆ **800/325-6000;** www.westernunion.com).

If you lose something on a SEPTA train, bus, or subway, try the stationmaster's office in Suburban Station (✆ **215/580-7800**).

MAIL At press time, domestic postage rates were 27¢ for a postcard and 42¢ for a letter. For international mail, a first-class letter of up to 1 ounce costs 94¢ (72¢ to Canada and Mexico); a first-class postcard costs the same as a letter. For more information go to **www.usps.com** and click on "Calculate Postage."

If you aren't sure what your address will be in the United States, mail can be sent to you, in your name, c/o General Delivery at the main post office of the city or region where you expect to be. (Call ✆ **800/275-8777** for information on the nearest post office.) The addressee must pick up mail in person and must produce proof of identity (driver's license, passport, and so on). Most post offices will hold your mail for up to 1 month, and are open Monday to Friday from 8am to 6pm, and Saturday from 9am to 3pm.

Always include a zip code when mailing items in the U.S. If you don't know a zip code, visit www.usps.com/zip4.

MEDICAL CONDITIONS If you have a medical condition that requires **syringe-administered medications,** carry a valid signed prescription from your physician; syringes in carry-on baggage will be inspected. Insulin in any form should have the proper pharmaceutical documentation. If you have a disease that requires treatment with **narcotics,** you should also carry documented proof with you—smuggling narcotics aboard a plane carries severe penalties in the U.S.

For **HIV-positive visitors,** requirements for entering the United States are somewhat vague and change frequently. For up-to-the-minute information, contact **AIDSinfo** (✆ **800/448-0440** or 301/519-6616 outside the U.S.; www.aidsinfo.nih.gov) or the **Gay Men's Health Crisis** (✆ **212/367-1000;** www.gmhc.org).

NEWSPAPERS & MAGAZINES Philadelphia has two main print journals, both owned by the same firm. You'll want to check out the Friday "Weekend" supplement of the *Philadelphia Inquirer* for listings and prices of entertainment, as well as events and tours. The *Philadelphia Daily News* has more local news. Find them at newsstands, corner pay boxes, and convenience stores. Visit both papers online at www.philly.com. The *Metro* is a free daily offered at SEPTA stations. Free alternative weeklies *PW (Philadelphia Weekly)* and *City Paper* offer a glimpse of the younger side of city life; you'll find them in street-corner boxes. *Philadelphia* magazine is the city's upscale magazine and is sold at bookstores and newsstands. It is available online at www.phillymag.com. For the most complete selection of local and international journals and newspapers, try **Avril 50,** 3406 Sansom St. (✆ **215/222-6108**), in University City. Center City has a **Barnes & Noble** at 1805 Walnut St. (✆ **215/665-0716**), a **Borders** bookstore at 1 S. Broad St. (✆ **215/568-7400**), and a **Borders Express** on the mezzanine level of Liberty Place at 1625 Chestnut St. (✆ **215/557-8443**).

PASSPORTS The websites listed below provide downloadable passport applications as well as the current fees for processing applications. For an up-to-date, country-by-country listing of passport requirements around the world, go to the "International Travel" tab of the U.S. State Department website at **http://travel.state.gov**.

International visitors to the U.S. can obtain a visa application on the same website. ***Note:*** Children are required to present a passport when entering the United States at airports. More information on obtaining a passport for a minor can be found at http://travel.state.gov. Allow plenty of time before your trip to apply for a passport; processing normally takes 4 to 6 weeks (3 weeks for expedited service) but can take longer during busy periods (especially spring). And keep in mind that if you need a passport in a hurry, you'll pay a higher processing fee.

For Residents of Australia You can pick up an application from your local post office or any branch of Passports Australia, but you must schedule an interview at the passport office to present your application materials. Call the **Australian Passport Information Service** at ✆ **131-232,** or visit the government website at www.passports.gov.au.

For Residents of Canada Passport applications are available at travel agencies throughout Canada or from the central **Passport Office,** Department of Foreign Affairs and International Trade, Ottawa, ON K1A 0G3 (✆ **800/567-6868;** www.ppt.gc.ca). ***Note:*** Canadian children who travel must have their own passport. However, if you hold a valid Canadian passport issued before December 11, 2001, that bears the name of your child, the passport remains valid for you and your child until it expires.

For Residents of Ireland You can apply for a 10-year passport at the **Passport Office,** Setanta Centre, Molesworth Street, Dublin 2 (✆ **01/671-1633;** www.irlgov.ie/iveagh). Those 17 and under and 66 and over must apply for a 3-year passport. You can also apply at 1A South Mall, Cork (✆ **21/494-4700**) or at most main post offices.

For Residents of New Zealand You can pick up a passport application at any New Zealand Passports Office or download it from its website. Contact the **Passports Office** at ✆ **0800/225-050** in New Zealand or 04/474-8100, or go to www.passports.govt.nz.

For Residents of the United Kingdom To pick up an application for a standard 10-year passport (5-year passport for children 15 and under), visit your nearest passport office, major post office, or travel agency or contact the **United Kingdom Passport Service** at ✆ **0870/521-0410** or search its website at www.ukpa.gov.uk.

For Residents of the **United States** Whether you're applying in person or by mail, you can download passport applications from the U.S. State Department website at **http://travel.state.gov**. To find your regional passport office, either check the U.S. State Department website or call the **National Passport Information Center** toll-free number (✆ **877/487-2778**) for automated information.

POLICE The emergency telephone number is ✆ **911.**

Smoking A citywide smoking ban applies to enclosed workplaces and public places—including restaurants and most bars, with a few corner taprooms providing the exception. Smoking is permitted in private and outside, but it is considered polite to ask a host or companion's permission before lighting up in his or her presence. The legal age for purchasing cigarettes is 18.

TAXES The United States has no value-added tax (VAT) or other indirect tax at the national level. Every state, county, and city may levy its own local tax on all purchases, including hotel and restaurant checks and airline tickets. These taxes will not appear on price tags.

At press time, the hotel tax adds 14% onto room rates, 6% for state tax, and 8% city surcharge. There is a 7% tax on restaurant meals and general sales, and a 10% tax on liquor. Clothing and food bought in groceries is tax-free.

TELEPHONES Many convenience groceries and packaging services sell **prepaid calling cards** in denominations up to $50; for international visitors these can be the least expensive way to call home. Many public pay phones at airports now accept American Express, MasterCard, and Visa credit cards. **Local calls** made from pay phones in most locales cost either 25¢ or 35¢ (no pennies, please). Most long-distance and international calls can be dialed directly from any phone. **For calls within the United States and to Canada,** dial 1 followed by the area code and the seven-digit number. **For other international calls,** dial 011 followed by the country code, city code, and the number you are calling.

Calls to area codes **800, 888, 877,** and **866** are toll-free. However, calls to area codes **700** and **900** (chat lines, bulletin boards, "dating" services, and so on) can be very expensive—usually a charge of 95¢ to $3 or more per minute, and they sometimes have minimum charges that can run as high as $15 or more.

For **reversed-charge or collect calls,** and for person-to-person calls, dial the number 0 then the area code and number; an operator will come on the line, and you should specify whether you are calling collect, person-to-person, or both. If your operator-assisted call is international, ask for the overseas operator.

For **local directory assistance** ("information"), dial © 411; for long-distance information, dial 1, then the appropriate area code and 555-1212.

TELEGRAPH, TELEX & FAX **Telegraph and telex services** are provided primarily by **Western Union** (© **800/325-6000;** www.westernunion.com). You can telegraph (wire) money, or have it telegraphed to you, very quickly over the Western Union system, but this service can cost as much as 15% to 20% of the amount sent.

Most hotels have **fax machines** available for guest use (be sure to ask about the charge to use it). Many hotel rooms are wired for guests' fax machines. A less-expensive way to send and receive faxes may be at stores such as the **UPS Store.**

TIME Philadelphia adheres to Eastern Standard Time (EST), one of **four time zones** in the continental United States: Eastern Standard Time (EST), Central Standard Time (CST), Mountain Standard Time (MST), and Pacific Standard Time (PST). Alaska and Hawaii have their own zones. For example, when it's 9am in Los Angeles (PST), it's 7am in Honolulu (Hawaii Standard Time), 10am in Denver (MST), 11am in Chicago (CST), noon in New York City (EST), 5pm in London (Greenwich Mean Time), and 2am the next day in Sydney.

Daylight saving time is in effect from 1am on the second Sunday in March to 1am on the first Sunday in November, except in Arizona, Hawaii, the U.S. Virgin Islands, and Puerto Rico. Daylight saving time moves the clock 1 hour ahead of standard time.

TIPPING Tips are a very important part of certain workers' income, and gratuities are the standard way of showing appreciation for services provided. (Tipping is certainly not compulsory if the service is poor!) In hotels, tip **bellhops** at least $1 per bag ($2–$3 if you have a lot of luggage) and tip the **chamber staff** $1 to $2 per day (more if you've left a disaster area for him or her to clean up). Tip the **doorman** or **concierge** only if he or she has provided you with some specific service (for example, calling a cab for you or obtaining difficult-to-get theater tickets). Tip the **valet-parking attendant** $1 every time you get your car.

In Philadelphia restaurants, bars, and nightclubs, tip **service staff** 18% to 20% of the check, tip **bartenders** 15% to 20%, tip **checkroom attendants** $1 per garment, and tip **valet-parking attendants** $1 per vehicle.

As for other service personnel, tip **cabdrivers** 15% to 20% of the fare; tip **skycaps** at airports at least $1 per bag ($2–$3 if you have a lot of luggage); and tip **hairdressers** and **barbers** 20%.

TOILETS You won't find public toilets or "restrooms" on the streets in most U.S. cities but they can be found in hotel lobbies, bars, restaurants, museums, department stores, railway and bus stations, and service stations. Large hotels and fast-food restaurants are often the best bet for clean facilities. Restaurants and bars in resorts or heavily visited areas may reserve their restrooms for patrons.

USEFUL PHONE NUMBERS

U.S. Dept. of State Travel Advisory: ✆ 202/647-5225 (manned 24 hrs.).

U.S. Passport Agency: ✆ 202/647-0518.

U.S. Centers for Disease Control and Prevention International Traveler's Hot Line: ✆ 404/332-4559.

Transit Information: ✆ 215/580-7800.

VISAS For information about U.S. visas go to **http://travel.state.gov** and click on "Visas." Or go to one of the following websites:

Australian citizens can obtain up-to-date visa information from the **U.S. Embassy Canberra,** Moonah Place, Yarralumla, ACT 2600 (✆ **02/6214-5600**), or by checking the U.S. Diplomatic Mission's website at **http://usembassy-australia.state.gov/consular**.

British subjects can obtain up-to-date visa information by calling the **U.S. Embassy Visa Information Line** (✆ **0891/200-290**) or by visiting the "Visas to the U.S." section of the American Embassy London's website at **www.usembassy.org.uk**.

Irish citizens can obtain up-to-date visa information through the **Embassy of the USA Dublin,** 42 Elgin Rd., Dublin 4, Ireland (✆ **353/1-668-8777**), or by checking the "Consular Services" section of the website at **http://dublin.usembassy.gov**.

Citizens of **New Zealand** can obtain up-to-date visa information by contacting the **U.S. Embassy New Zealand,** 29 Fitzherbert Terrace, Thorndon, Wellington (✆ **644/472-2068**), or get the information directly from the website at **http://wellington.usembassy.gov**.

2 TOLL-FREE NUMBERS & WEBSITES

MAJOR U.S. AIRLINES

(*flies internationally as well)

American Airlines*
✆ 800/433-7300 (in the U.S. or Canada)
✆ 020/7365-0777 (in the U.K.)
www.aa.com

Continental Airlines*
✆ 800/523-3273 (in the U.S. or Canada)
✆ 084/5607-6760 (in the U.K.)
www.continental.com

Delta Air Lines*
✆ 800/221-1212 (in the U.S. or Canada)
✆ 084/5600-0950 (in the U.K.)
www.delta.com

Frontier Airlines
✆ 800/432-1359
www.frontierairlines.com

Midwest Airlines
✆ 800/452-2022
www.midwestairlines.com

Northwest Airlines
✆ 800/225-2525 (in the U.S.)
✆ 870/0507-4074 (in the U.K.)
www.nwa.com

United Airlines*
✆ 800/864-8331 (in the U.S. or Canada)
✆ 084/5844-4777 (in the U.K.)
www.united.com

US Airways*
✆ 800/428-4322 (in the U.S. or Canada)
✆ 084/5600-3300 (in the U.K.)
www.usairways.com

USA 3000
✆ 877/872-3000
www.usa3000.com

MAJOR INTERNATIONAL AIRLINES

Air Canada
✆ 888/247-2262 (in the U.S. or Canada)
www.aircanada.com

Air France
✆ 800/375-8723 (the U.S. or Canada)
✆ 087/0142-4343 (in the U.K.)
www.airfrance.com

Air Jamaica
✆ 800/523-5585 (in the U.S. or Canada)
✆ 208/570-7999 (in Jamaica)
www.airjamaica.com

American Airlines
✆ 800/433-7300 (in the U.S. or Canada)
✆ 020/7365-0777 (in the U.K.)
www.aa.com

British Airways
✆ 800/247-9297 (in the U.S. or Canada)
✆ 087/0850-9850 (in the U.K.)
www.ba.com

Continental Airlines
✆ 800/523-3273 (in the U.S. or Canada)
✆ 084/5607-6760 (in the U.K.)
www.continental.com

Delta Air Lines
✆ 800/221-1212 (in the U.S. or Canada)
✆ 084/5600-0950 (in the U.K.)
www.delta.com

Lufthansa
✆ 800/399-5838 (in the U.S.)
✆ 800/563-5954 (in Canada)
✆ 087/0837-7747 (in the U.K.)
www.lufthansa.com

Turkish Airlines
✆ 90/212-444-0-849
www.thy.com

United Airlines*
✆ 800/864-8331 (in the U.S. or Canada)
✆ 084/5844-4777 (in the U.K.)
www.united.com

US Airways*
✆ 800/428-4322 (in the U.S. or Canada)
✆ 084/5600-3300 (in the U.K.)
www.usairways.com

BUDGET AIRLINES

AirTran Airways
✆ 800/247-8726
www.airtran.com

Frontier Airlines
✆ 800/432-1359
www.frontierairlines.com

Southwest Airlines
✆ 800/435-9792 (in the U.S., the U.K., or Canada)
www.southwest.com

CAR-RENTAL AGENCIES

Alamo
✆ 800/GO-ALAMO (462-5266)
www.alamo.com

Avis
✆ 800/331-1212 (in the U.S. or Canada)
✆ 084/4581-8181 (in the U.K.)
www.avis.com

Budget
✆ 800/527-0700 (in the U.S.)
✆ 087/0156-5656 (in the U.K.)
✆ 800/268-8900 (in Canada)
www.budget.com

Dollar
✆ 800/800-4000 (in the U.S.)
✆ 800/848-8268 (in Canada)
✆ 080/8234-7524 (in the U.K.)
www.dollar.com

Enterprise
✆ 800/261-7331 (in the U.S.)
✆ 514/355-4028 (in Canada)
✆ 012/9360-9090 (in the U.K.)
www.enterprise.com

Hertz
✆ 800/645-3131
✆ 800/654-3001 (for international reservations)
www.hertz.com

National
✆ 800/CAR-RENT (227-7368)
www.nationalcar.com

Payless
✆ 800/PAYLESS (729-5377)
www.paylesscarrental.com

Rent-A-Wreck
✆ 800/535-1391
www.rentawreck.com

Thrifty
✆ 800/367-2277
✆ 918/669-2168 (international)
www.thrifty.com

MAJOR HOTEL & MOTEL CHAINS

aloft
✆ 877/GO-ALOFT (462-5638)
www.starwoodhotels.com

Best Western International
✆ 800/780-7234 (in the U.S. or Canada)
✆ 0800/393-130 (in the U.K.)
www.bestwestern.com

Clarion Hotels
✆ 800/CLARION (252-7466) or 877/424-6423 (in the U.S. or Canada)
✆ 0800/444-444 (in the U.K.)
www.clarionhotel.com

Comfort Inns
✆ 800/228-5150
✆ 0800/444-444 (in the U.K.)
www.comfortinn.com

Courtyard by Marriott
✆ 888/236-2427 (in the U.S.)
✆ 0800/221-222 (in the U.K.)
www.marriott.com/courtyard

Crowne Plaza Hotels
✆ 888/303-1746
www.ichotelsgroup.com/crowneplaza

Days Inn
✆ 800/329-7466 (in the U.S.)
✆ 0800/280-400 (in the U.K.)
www.daysinn.com

Doubletree Hotels
✆ 800/222-TREE (8733; in the U.S. or Canada)
✆ 087/0590-9090 (in the U.K.)
www.doubletree.com

Econo Lodges
✆ 800/55-ECONO (552-3666)
www.econolodge.com

Embassy Suites
✆ 800/EMBASSY (362-2779)
www.embassysuites.com

Fairfield Inn by Marriott
✆ 800/228-2800 (in the U.S. or Canada)
✆ 0800/221-222 (in the U.K.)
www.marriott.com/fairfieldinn

Four Seasons
✆ 800/819-5053 (in the U.S. or Canada)
✆ 0800/6488-6488 (in the U.K.)
www.fourseasons.com

Hampton Inn
✆ 800/HAMPTON (426-4766)
www.hamptoninn.com

Hilton Hotels
✆ 800/HILTONS (445-8667; in the U.S. or Canada)
✆ 087/0590-9090 (in the U.K.)
www.hilton.com

Holiday Inn
✆ 800/315-2621 (in the U.S. or Canada)
✆ 0800/405-060 (in the U.K.)
www.holidayinn.com

Howard Johnson
✆ 800/446-4656 (in the U.S. or Canada)
www.hojo.com

Hyatt
✆ 888/591-1234 (in the U.S. or Canada)
✆ 084/5888-1234 (in the U.K.)
www.hyatt.com

InterContinental Hotels & Resorts
✆ 800/424-6835 (in the U.S. or Canada)
✆ 0800/1800-1800 (in the U.K.)
www.ichotelsgroup.com

Loews Hotels
✆ 800/23LOEWS (235-6397)
www.loewshotels.com

Marriott
✆ 877/236-2427 (in the U.S. or Canada)
✆ 0800/221-222 (in the U.K.)
www.marriott.com

Omni Hotels
✆ 888/444-OMNI (6664)
www.omnihotels.com

Radisson Hotels & Resorts
✆ 888/201-1718 (in the U.S. or Canada)
✆ 0800/374-411 (in the U.K.)
www.radisson.com

Ramada Worldwide
✆ 888/2-RAMADA (272-6232; in the U.S. or Canada)
✆ 080/8100-0783 (in the U.K.)
www.ramada.com

Red Carpet Inns
✆ 800/251-1962
www.bookroomsnow.com

Red Roof Inns
✆ 866/686-4335 (in the U.S. or Canada)
✆ 614/601-4075 (international)
www.redroof.com

Renaissance Hotels & Resorts by Marriott
✆ 888/236-2427
www.renaissancehotels.com

Residence Inn by Marriott
✆ 800/331-3131
✆ 800/221-222 (in the U.K.)
www.marriott.com/residenceinn

Rodeway Inns
✆ 877/424-6423
www.rodewayinn.com

Sheraton Hotels & Resorts
✆ 800/325-3535 (in the U.S.)
✆ 800/543-4300 (in Canada)
✆ 0800/3253-5353 (in the U.K.)
www.starwoodhotels.com/sheraton

Super 8 Motels
✆ 800/800-8000
www.super8.com

Travelodge
✆ 800/578-7878
www.travelodge.com

Westin Hotels & Resorts
✆ 800/937-8461 (in the U.S. or Canada)
✆ 0800/3259-5959 (in the U.K.)
www.starwoodhotels.com/westin

Wyndham Hotels & Resorts
✆ 877/999-3223 (in the U.S. or Canada)
✆ 050/6638-4899 (in the U.K.)
www.wyndham.com

INDEX

See also Accommodations and Restaurant indexes, below.

General Index

Accommodations

Restaurants

FROMMER'S® COMPLETE TRAVEL GUIDES

Alaska
Amalfi Coast
American Southwest
Amsterdam
Argentina
Arizona
Atlanta
Australia
Austria
Bahamas
Barcelona
Beijing
Belgium, Holland & Luxembourg
Belize
Bermuda
Boston
Brazil
British Columbia & the Canadian Rockies
Brussels & Bruges
Budapest & the Best of Hungary
Buenos Aires
Calgary
California
Canada
Cancún, Cozumel & the Yucatán
Cape Cod, Nantucket & Martha's Vineyard
Caribbean
Caribbean Ports of Call
Carolinas & Georgia
Chicago
Chile & Easter Island
China
Colorado
Costa Rica
Croatia
Cuba
Denmark
Denver, Boulder & Colorado Springs
Eastern Europe
Ecuador & the Galapagos Islands
Edinburgh & Glasgow
England
Europe
Europe by Rail
Florence, Tuscany & Umbria
Florida
France
Germany
Greece
Greek Islands
Guatemala
Hawaii
Hong Kong
Honolulu, Waikiki & Oahu
India
Ireland
Israel
Italy
Jamaica
Japan
Kauai
Las Vegas
London
Los Angeles
Los Cabos & Baja
Madrid
Maine Coast
Maryland & Delaware
Maui
Mexico
Montana & Wyoming
Montréal & Québec City
Morocco
Moscow & St. Petersburg
Munich & the Bavarian Alps
Nashville & Memphis
New England
Newfoundland & Labrador
New Mexico
New Orleans
New York City
New York State
New Zealand
Northern Italy
Norway
Nova Scotia, New Brunswick & Prince Edward Island
Oregon
Paris
Peru
Philadelphia & the Amish Country
Portugal
Prague & the Best of the Czech Republic
Provence & the Riviera
Puerto Rico
Rome
San Antonio & Austin
San Diego
San Francisco
Santa Fe, Taos & Albuquerque
Scandinavia
Scotland
Seattle
Seville, Granada & the Best of Andalusia
Shanghai
Sicily
Singapore & Malaysia
South Africa
South America
South Florida
South Korea
South Pacific
Southeast Asia
Spain
Sweden
Switzerland
Tahiti & French Polynesia
Texas
Thailand
Tokyo
Toronto
Turkey
USA
Utah
Vancouver & Victoria
Vermont, New Hampshire & Maine
Vienna & the Danube Valley
Vietnam
Virgin Islands
Virginia
Walt Disney World® & Orlando
Washington, D.C.
Washington State

FROMMER'S® DAY BY DAY GUIDES

Amsterdam
Barcelona
Beijing
Boston
Cancun & the Yucatan
Chicago
Florence & Tuscany
Hong Kong
Honolulu & Oahu
London
Maui
Montréal
Napa & Sonoma
New York City
Paris
Provence & the Riviera
Rome
San Francisco
Venice
Washington D.C.

PAULINE FROMMER'S GUIDES: SEE MORE. SPEND LESS.

Alaska
Hawaii
Italy
Las Vegas
London
New York City
Paris
Walt Disney World®
Washington D.C.

Frommer's® Portable Guides

Acapulco, Ixtapa & Zihuatanejo
Amsterdam
Aruba, Bonaire & Curacao
Australia's Great Barrier Reef
Bahamas
Big Island of Hawaii
Boston
California Wine Country
Cancún
Cayman Islands
Charleston
Chicago
Dominican Republic
Florence
Las Vegas
Las Vegas for Non-Gamblers
London
Maui
Nantucket & Martha's Vineyard
New Orleans
New York City
Paris
Portland
Puerto Rico
Puerto Vallarta, Manzanillo & Guadalajara
Rio de Janeiro
San Diego
San Francisco
Savannah
St. Martin, Sint Maarten, Anguila & St. Bart's
Turks & Caicos
Vancouver
Venice
Virgin Islands
Washington, D.C.
Whistler

Frommer's® Cruise Guides

Alaska Cruises & Ports of Call
Cruises & Ports of Call
European Cruises & Ports of Call

Frommer's® National Park Guides

Algonquin Provincial Park
Banff & Jasper
Grand Canyon
National Parks of the American West
Rocky Mountain
Yellowstone & Grand Teton
Yosemite and Sequoia & Kings Canyon
Zion & Bryce Canyon

Frommer's® With Kids Guides

Chicago
Hawaii
Las Vegas
London
National Parks
New York City
San Francisco
Toronto
Walt Disney World® & Orlando
Washington, D.C.

Frommer's® PhraseFinder Dictionary Guides

Chinese
French
German
Italian
Japanese
Spanish

Suzy Gershman's Born to Shop Guides

France
Hong Kong, Shanghai & Beijing
Italy
London
New York
Paris
San Francisco
Where to Buy the Best of Everything.

Frommer's® Best-Loved Driving Tours

Britain
California
France
Germany
Ireland
Italy
New England
Northern Italy
Scotland
Spain
Tuscany & Umbria

The Unofficial Guides®

Adventure Travel in Alaska
Beyond Disney
California with Kids
Central Italy
Chicago
Cruises
Disneyland®
England
Hawaii
Ireland
Las Vegas
London
Maui
Mexico's Best Beach Resorts
Mini Mickey
New Orleans
New York City
Paris
San Francisco
South Florida including Miami & the Keys
Walt Disney World®
Walt Disney World® for Grown-ups
Walt Disney World® with Kids
Washington, D.C.

Special-Interest Titles

Athens Past & Present
Best Places to Raise Your Family
Cities Ranked & Rated
500 Places to Take Your Kids Before They Grow Up
Frommer's Best Day Trips from London
Frommer's Best RV & Tent Campgrounds in the U.S.A.
Frommer's Exploring America by RV
Frommer's NYC Free & Dirt Cheap
Frommer's Road Atlas Europe
Frommer's Road Atlas Ireland
Retirement Places Rated